DIAL YOUR BIRTH NUMBER

A Treatise on Numerology

Also by Dr. M. Katakkar
in UBSPD

- Encyclopaedia of Palm and Palm Reading
- Numerology, Palmistry and Prosperity
- Palmistry, Marriage and Family Welfare

DIAL
YOUR BIRTH NUMBER

A Treatise on Numerology

Dr. M. Katakkar

 UBSPD

UBS Publishers' Distributors Ltd.

New Delhi • Bombay • Bangalore • Madras
Calcutta • Patna • Kanpur • London

UBS Publishers' Distributors Ltd.
5 Ansari Road, New Delhi-110 002
Bombay   Bangalore   Madras
Calcutta   Patna   Kanpur   London

© Dr. M. Katakkar

First Edition	1987
Second Edition	1992
First Reprint	1993
Second Reprint	1993

Cover Design: UBS Art Studio

Printed at Pearl Offset Press (P) Ltd. 5/33 Kirti Nagar Industrial Area, New Delhi-110 015

Dedicated

To

The Cause of Science

Which is in Search of Occult Powers

AN OPINION

Through this book Mr. Katakkar has slashed a documentary challenge in the face of non-believers and so-called irrationalists bragging against Astrology.

Mr. Katakkar, with deep insight, erudition and research has proven beyond doubt in this book, that the influence of cosmic rays radiated from planets do effect and affect the human mind, body and character which when blended homogeneously produce certain specific events in human life.

I, from my personal experience, after reading my birth date and birth month expositions, could not but feel highly astonished at the pin point delineation of my character and high degree of probability of eventualities. The reader for himself is left hereby to judge the reality of my opinion from his birth date and birth month.

The book, no doubt, will prove a valuable treasure for all and every one including believers and non-believers of Astrol- since it will lend them a mirror for their true image which will guide them through odds and evens of their life.

I congratulate Mr. Katakkar for this tremendous task which is an additional plume to his bonnet.

Lastly this treatise will certainly prove an effective silencer for the noisy rattlings of the non-believers of Astrology.

406, Jal Darshan,
B-Wing, 4th Floor,
Ruia Park,
Juhu,
BOMBAY-400 049

Prof. Ghanshyam Joshi
M. A. (Bombay University)
Founder President of Britain's
Cheirological Society's
Research Wing in India.

CONTENTS

JUNE

JULY

AUGUST

DECEMBER

Introduction

Astrology, palmistry, numerology, I Ching, crystal gazing and such other sciences have tried to peep into the future of an individual or a nation. These sciences are known as occult sciences because they are based on experience. Of late, there is a world-wide controversy as to whether these subjects have any scientific platform. The so-called rationalists are forcing the astrologers to prove that astrology is a science. This controversy arose because those who oppose these subjects have not basically studied any of them and the scientists have not gone deep into the occult faculty of man. Though modern science has developed rapidly and man has landed on the Moon, scientists have completely ignored the laws of nature which have an influence on human life.

We cannot dismiss the fact that our ancestors were masters of the above esoteric subjects and we still admire the discoveries made by them. Their main fault was that in transmitting their knowledge to their descendants, they so endeavoured to hide their secrets from the common people that in most cases the key to the problem became lost and the truth that had been discovered became buried in the dust of superstition. Pythagoras, a well-known personality in the field of mathematics, established a study centre at Crotona for the study of occultism where oaths of secrecy were taken. Another cause, and a very important one that has contributed to the non-belief in these subjects is that the students and scholars of astrology, palmistry and numerology have not maintained sufficient statistical records which would support their theories. This has resulted in these subjects falling into the hands of charlatans.

For thousands of years these subjects have been practised in all nations and at all times and even the scientists like Newton and educated people have been taking valuable tips from the scholars of these subjects at critical moments in their lives. Even the topmost political leaders who mould the destiny of their nations take advice from astrologers, palmists and mystics and enquire about their own destiny. It is on record that Julius Ceasar, the Roman dictator was well versed in the study of Palmistry. The great Emperor Napoleon Bonaparte was a believer in the study of palmistry and once said "Perhaps the face can deceive but never the hand." As per the advice of a numerologist, he made a change in the spelling of his name.

In spite of the liberal use of these mystic subjects in everyday life, they have never been acknowledged as scientific till today. They are therefore emperical sciences. Every experience is knowledge and therefore useful in day to day life. Even though these subjects do not meet the requisite tests of science, a day may come when all such esoteric subjects will come in the purview of science. History shows that such subjects have played wonderful roles in life and have given out huge information which is still beyond the comprehension of modern science. It may be pointed out that many of the greatest truths the world has known, though once considered trivialities have become sources of tremendous force, an atom being equal to the whole in the importance of its existence.

It is true that the rules applied to other sciences cannot be applied to these occult sciences. But it is equally true that astrology, palmistry and numerology have their own foundation, a code of principles, methods, rules and results. There is no doubt that prophecies are often found to be falsified by subsequent events. The reason for this must be sought not in the unscientific nature of this study, but in our ignorance of the causes at work. The laws of biology are not always borne out by subsequent events, but no one would, on that ground, deny that biology is a science. The year of change in life can often be predicted a much longer time in advance than the coming of a cyclone. Hence the claim of these occult subjects to be regarded as sciences cannot be denied on the ground that numerologists, astrologers and palmists lack precision and prophetic power.

I have come across people who could cast my horoscope from my hand. I have also been informed by dignitaries in the Central Government of India that such horoscopes were drawn from their palms by people in the North-East parts of India.

IF THE NATAL CHART COULD BE PREPARED FROM THE PALMS ALONE, WHAT MORE PROOF IS REQUIRED TO ESTABLISH THE FACT THAT THE PLANETS RULE THE MAN ?

Still there are very rare scripts available such as the Brighu Sanhita, Surya Nadi and others which are the wonders of the world. These scripts indicate the day when you will go through these scripts, also the surroundings while you read the script They also describe the place of your birth, the names of your mother, grand mother and of other members of your family.

It is necessary to study such scripts and books with an open and rational mind and find out the principles governing the knowledge expounded through these books.

An attempt is made here to prove that there is much sense in what has been expounded by our old masters regarding the occult sciences such as astrology, palmistry, numerology etc.

I AM GRATEFUL TO SCIENTISTS AND THE ORGANISERS FOR "ERADICATION OF SUPERSTITION FRONT" FOR THE CHALLENGE TO THE EXPONENTS OF ASTROLOGY, PALMISTRY AND OTHER STUDIES. THIS BOOK WOULD NOT HAVE COME OUT BUT FOR THEIR CHALLENGE. THIS BOOK ACCEPTS THEIR CHALLENGE AND PROVES THE INFLUENCE OF THE PLANETS ON HUMAN BEINGS. FROM THE BIRTH DATE ALONE, 60% OF YOUR CHARACTER, VOCATION, SICKNESS AND OTHER THINGS ARE EXPLAINED. HOWEVER, BEFORE GOING THROUGH THIS BOOK, IT IS NECESSARY TO UNDERSTAND CERTAIN BASIC PRINCIPLES WHICH ARE THE FOUNDATION OF THIS BOOK. PLEASE TRY TO FOLLOW THE BASIC FACTS EXPLAINED HEREAFTER AND THEN TRY

TO EXAMINE WHETHER WHAT HAS BEEN STATED HEREIN IS ACCORDING TO THESE PRINCIPLES AND HAS ANY BASIS AND SIGNIFICANCE. THIS IS A STUDY LIKE A STUDY OF ANY OTHER SUBJECT.

It is for the younger generation to come forward with adequate data of the influence of planets on human life so that a relation can be established scientifically between the planets and human life. It is necessary for the scientists also to devote their time and attention to discoveries made by our ancient scholars and unveil the occult force behind psychic powers and also behind the unknown laws which govern man's destiny.

I hope this book will be an inspiration to those who are in search of truth.

Every Reader Must Read This First

Astrology is a science wherein the positions of the planets in the solar system at the time of birth are recorded in the form of a horoscope. At the moment a person is born, the planets are moving through certain zodiacal signs and are in particular degrees. Their location can be known depending upon the latitudes and longitudes of the place of birth. This is purely a mathematical working. At a particular moment, several thousands of babies may have been born throughout the globe from East to West but their horoscopes will differ because of the latitudes and longitudes of differents places. Naturally, the influence of the planets of these thousands of babies differs from place to place. Experience proves that these planets govern an individual's mind and body and his character. Behaviour, thinking, likes, dislikes, his health, aptitude for a particular vocation etc. are decided according to the principal planet and the secondary planet ruling the individual and the relation of these planets to other planets in the horoscope. Since the study of astrology is based on a mathematical foundation, we can expect great accuracy in finding out the result.

This is not so in the case of the study of Numerology on

which the present book is based. Numerology is a simple
method of knowing an individual from his birth date alone.
Even though several thousand babies are born on one day from
the East to the West, we notice many common factors in the
mental and physical behaviour of these persons which are
described in the present book. The characteristics explained
herein will be applicable more to those born in the day time. A
real 'truth-seeker' will find this book interesting and will be
surprised as to how a minimum of 60% character reading could
be possible from the birth date alone. I now give below, in
short, the principles of numerology and how the numbers
govern us.

There are 9 numbers and each number has its planet. The
planets exhibit certain characteristics and therefore each number
has its own characteristics. They are as under:

Number	Planet	Basic Characteristics
1.	Sun	Originality, individuality, determination, authority, confidence, show, art, aspiration, research, pride, domination.
2.	Moon	Emotionality, fellowship, uneasiness, whimsicality, introvertedness, impatience
3.	Jupiter	Dignity, prestige, honour, philosophy, ambition, dictatorship, vanity etc.
4.	Uranus	Revolution, activity, endurance, stubbornness, zeal.
5.	Mercury	Shrewdness, co-operation, vigilance, business, calculation, scepticism, unreliability.
6.	Venus	Love, sympathy, art, strong memory, moodiness, timidity.
7.	Neptune	Austerity, tolerance, peace, research, systematic restlessness, whimsicality.
8.	Saturn	Authority, method, systematic, steadiness, practical delay, cynicism, nervousness, laziness.
9.	Mars	Energy, activity, independence, dash, courage, destruction, hot-temper, impatience, quarrelsomeness.

Each month is also dominated by a particular planet depending upon the Sun's entry into the Zodiac. The months and planets are as under.

Month	Planet	Sign of the Zodiac
January	Saturn	Capricorn
February	Saturn	Aquarius
March	Jupiter	Pisces
April	Mars	Aries
May	Venus	Taurus
June	Mercury	Gemini
July	Moon	Cancer
August	Sun	Leo
September	Mercury	Virgo
October	Venus	Libra
November	Mars	Scorpio
December	Jupiter	Sagittarius.

How to Compute your number

We have to consider only the date of the month in a birth date. Supposing a person was born on 15.11.1950, we have to take only the number 15 and add its digits $1 + 5 = 6$. Number 6 is alloted to the planet Venus. Similarly, a person born on the 24th of the month is also governed by number 6 $(2 + 4 = 6)$ and the planet Venus. In all cases, we have to reduce the date of birth to a single digit and find out the planet. A person born on 2,11,20 and 29 of any month is governed by number 2 and the planet Moon. Similarly, a person born on 4,13,22 and 31 of any month is dominated by the number 4 and the planet Uranus.

In the above illustration, the month of birth is November which is governed by the planet Mars. Thus, the individual born on 15th November is dominated by the planet Venus and also the planet Mars. He is therefore a combination of these two planets and the characteristics of the two planets are combined in the individual

In fact, the sun's entry into the first Zodiacal sign Aries starts round about the 21st of March every year and the Sun remains there for about a month i.e. upto 20th April. After the 20th, the sun's influence goes on decreasing and it diminishes upto what is called the period of cusp which is for seven days i.e. upto about the 28th of the month. During these seven days, the influence of the next Zodiac sign, Taurus which is governed by the planet Venus starts. However, in order avoid confusion, I have alloted one complete month to one planet only though its influence is upto the 20th of the month. Actually all dates after 21st of any month are governed by the incoming planet of the next Zodiac sign.

Vocations

As regards vocations there are a thousand different vocations which cannot be mentioned here. The description given here only shows an aptitude for a career. If the person realises his inherent qualities, he will be successful in his life. Therefore, one need not argue that his actual, vocation is different from the one mentioned in his birthdate.

As already stated, one single date is applicable to several thousands of people and therefore the characteristic explained here will be experienced to the extent of about 60 to 70% only. The readers are requested to make their own findings and record the results accordingly. This book does not claim perfection and does not state that whatever is written herein is the only destiny of the individual. There are several other aspects which influence the destiny of man and studying his characteristics only from the birthdate is one of the aspects of such a study.

I am sure the readers and the scientists will try to understand the laws of nature which influence human life and try to find out the hidden and unknown principles governing such laws.

AN IMPORTANT NOTE TO THE READER

In order to get full benefit of the things explained herein and to achieve success in life, the reader may please act upon the following recommendations :-

1. He should do all his important work on his lucky days and also lucky dates. He may try his luck in lottery by purchasing a ticket where the total of all the numbers works out to his lucky number or where the last digit is his lucky number.

2. He can gain confidence if he makes use of his lucky colours for painting his living room or the bed room or uses these colours while selecting his clothes.

3. He can increase the vibrations of his personality by wearing his lucky jewel.

4. He can plan all his important activities during his important years.

CHAPTER I

BORN ON

1st, 10th, 19th and 28th of January

All those born on the 1st, 10th, 19th and 28th of January of any year are governed by number 1 and the planet Sun. The month January is governed by the planet Saturn. Both these planets have strong personalities and sometimes even opposite characteristics producing finally a mixed personality. The character reading applied to number one below is equally applicable to other dates also. In addition, special characteristics of those born on 10th, 19th and 28th are given separately.

Born on 1st January

a) CHARACTER

This number is governed by the planet Sun and shows originality, activity, energy, enthusiasm, art and brilliance. The man is spontaneous, responds to nature and has the capacity to enjoy life. However, he has a sceptical outlook on life and unless he is sure of the result, he is slow in taking a decision. He is usually successful in life due to his active nature and capacity to mix in any society. Though his social circle is large, he has a feeling of loneliness within himself which even his close friends and relatives will never know. He is an artist and has many talents but they are all spontaneous in nature. Though he has the capacity to analyse a thing and the perseverance to follow any subject, he is changeable and finds it difficult to stick to one thing for a long time. He can hardly go deep into any

subject but with his intuition, he has a quick grasp of the subject
and can participate spontaneously in any conversation. He can
influence others with his knowledge and flash. These characteristics make him a hero of the drawing room. He has strong
will power and is independent in thought and action. He
desires leadership, otherwise he loses interest in the work.
His ideas about duty and social behaviour are strange and
though he loves soceity, he sometimes does not feel at ease
with his neighbour unless the neighbour is intelligent and
clever and does not interfere in others' affairs. He is usually
disturbed in his home and family affairs and has to look after
distressed or invalid relatives.

By nature, he is cheerful, happy and bright and his outlook on life is very optimistic. He has a fancy for occultism
and does wonders with his natural gift of intuition. On the
one hand he is practical, but on the other hand, he is idealistic.
Sometimes he is obstinate and selfish. He is fond of inventions
and has creative talents but his changeable nature does not
permit him to achieve any thing in any field.

He is a better judge of human nature than the average
individual. He is born to lead, not to follow   A new idea is a
greater thrill than money in the bank. He will always be young
by reason of another new idea.

In addition to the above, the following are the special
qualities of those born on other dates.

Born on 10th January | you have all the basic characteristics of those born on the 1st of the month, so first go through them and then read your own.

A person born on the 10th of January is very impressive
with a magnetic personality and is respected for his knowledge
and intelligence. He gets financial benefits from relatives
such as father, father-in-law, wife, mother etc. He gets
success after his 46th year. He gets a good position in service
and succeeds in business also. He has broad shoulders and
a manly figure. He loves truthfulness. This number shows
honour and self confidence. The person can get fame or
notoriety depending upon his will-power and character. He
usually has good health and quickly recovers from sickness.

He likes to help others, but hardly gets response from them. This is more true in the case of relatives.

Born on 19th January | you have all the basic characteristics of those born on the 1st of the month, so first go through them and then read your own.

Such a man is very active, energetic and enthusiastic. He has a research aptitude and likes to handle a subject in a systematic and methodical way. He takes quick decisions and always likes to keep himself busy with some concrete project. Sports is his hobby and he is interested in several games such as horse riding, shooting, and other athletic games. He is hasty and impetuous and has force of character. He likes to help others even going out of the way. He can keep secrets of others and others also readily confide in him. This number promises success, honour and happiness. Sometimes it is very difficult for others to understand him. He is always in company but at heart feels lonely. He is obstinate and finds it difficult to extend co-operation. He is prudent and notices even a trivial thing. He is not an excellent speaker but can explain best in writing. He can be a good writer.

Born on 28th January | you have all the basic characteristics of those born on the 1st of the month, so first go through them and then read your own.

This man is very generous and spends on charity for school, institution, hospital etc. He is not as lucky as numbers 1, 10 and 19 and has to undergo difficulties in public and private life. He should select his marriage partner carefully. He has to provide carefully for the future as he is likely to lose through trust in others. He is also likely to make many changes in his career. He hardly reveals his emotions and therefore appears cold. He has unyielding will-power and does not hesitate to carry out his plans.

b) FINANCE

A person born on any of the above dates and in January is a lucky person as far as his financial status is concerned. Even though he is extravagant due to his over-enthusiastic personality, he also earns enough to maintain his ostentatious disposition in life. He may not amass wealth but his personality and behaviour convey to others the impression that he is a rich person. He has temptation for gambling and if not controlled in time, he may lose to a great extent. However the peculiarity is that there is delay in financial stability and it is achieved only at a later age.

c) VOCATION

The main difficulty with a number 1 person is his attitude; he boes not stick to any one profession or job for a long time. Usually, every three to four years, there is a change in career. He is however suitable for advertising concerns, newspaper business, cinema industry and can also be successful in the atrical performance. He can show his art as an interior decorator. He being a good salesman, can choose a vocation which will bring relations with foreign countries, such as an ambassadorship or trade dealing in foreign commodities. He is a leader and can be the head of a department, a managing director etc. He can equally succeed as a surgeon, jeweller, electrician and in research projects.

d) HEALTH

On the whole a number 1 person is a happy-go-lucky fellow and normally of good health. But he is also susceptible to certain health defects and has to be very particular about the following health troubles.

HEART TROUBLE :	It is a structural difficulty and can be observed even in childhood.
WEAK EYE SIGHT :	He suffers from weak eye sight and usually has to wear spectacles.
OVER-EXERTION :	He should always be on guard and see that he does not exert himself too much out of his over enthusiasm. His straining too much is likely to make him susceptible to fevers.
SUNSTROKE	He should take precaution against this danger.

BONE FRACTURE :   He is liable to small accidents resulting in bone fracture.

Since the month January is dominated by the planet Saturn, varicose veins, nervousness, melancholia, irritation, rheumatism and biliousness are also common.

e) MARRIAGE AND FRIENDS

He has a natural attraction towards persons born in the period from 21st March to 20th May, 21st July to 20th September and from 21st November to 20th January. He also has an affinity for those who are governed by numbers 2, 4, 5 and 7. It is therefore advisable that he selects his marriage partner from these periods, or numbers.

Number 1 as a husband

He is generous and desires his wife to shine in society. He wants his family members to dance to his tunes and will not tolerate disrespect. He has a kind and loving disposition and a noble heart. He is considerate and treats his wife and family members with the same courtesy that he accords to strangers. He accepts marriage as a part of the domestic scheme and succeeds in it because of his attitude which contributes a great deal towards harmony at home. His drawback is his impersonality which his wife feels as lack of interest in domestic life.

Number 1 as a wife

She is a fine companion : capable, intelligent, adaptable and talented. Her home is a social centre on account of her social and friendly manners. Her interests are wide and she does not like to watch how her husband spends his spare time. Though basically she is unconventional, she is kind and would rather herself suffer than create a situation which would make others sorrowful. As she is intelligent, she is appreciated as a good wife by an intelligent husband who would use her abilities to his advantage. She is aristocratic by temperament and attracts people to her home and commands great respect. She needs a virile husband who can provide the romantic outlets that her passionate nature requires.

A person born on 1st, 10th, 19th or 28th of January is always predisposed to marriage and he is fond of his helpmate provided his life partner is also of equal enthusiasm and has a love of beauty and of dress, at home and in public. It is however often seen that he hardly gets a companion of his choice, with the result that he is often disappointed in his married life.

FRIENDS : He is always attracted towards those who have originality, creativity, activity and intelligence. His best friends are those who are governed by numbers 1,3,5,7 and 9. He also has a natural affinity towards people born in April, July, October and in his own month, i.e. January.

f) FORTUNATE DAYS :   His lucky days are Sundays,
                       Wednesdays and Thursdays.

g) LUCKY COLOURS :   He should use all shades of gold,
                      yellow, violet and purple.

h) LUCKY JEWELS and STONES : His lucky jewels are Ruby,
                       Emerald and Moon-stone.

i) IMPORTANT YEARS IN LIFE : His important years are 1,
                       10, 19, 28, 37, 46, 55, 64,
                       73 etc.

(j HIS GOOD QUALITIES & DRAWBACKS ARE AS UNDER :

Good Qualities	Drawbacks
Aspiration	Aloofness
Strong will-power	Obstinacy
Attack	Domination
Authority	Impertinence
Confidence	Inflexibility
Determination	Pride
Research	Show
Vigour	Spendthrift
Talents	

CHAPTER 2

BORN ON
2nd, 11th, 20th and 29th of January

All those born on the 2nd, 11th, 20th and 29th of January of any year are governed by number 2 and the planet Moon. The month of January is governed by the planet Saturn. There fore both Moon and Saturn have influence on these individuals. The character reading applied to number two below is equally applicable to other dates also. In addition, special characteristics of those born on 11th, 20th and 29th are given separately.

Born on 2nd of January

a) CHARACTER

The person has high imagination, idealism and dreamy nature. He is slow in taking decisions. Though he is cautious, he is not practical in life. He is analytical and philosophical but he analyses his ideals and dreamy nature and not his reason or logic. He does not like to enjoy the company of others on the mental level but likes to mix with them purely for the sake of society. He is very social and is liked by others. He is warm-hearted and shows little resistance to oppression. He has noble sentiments.

He likes natural and beautiful things in life such as the sea, flowers, natural scenery and the vastness of the sky. He takes pleasure in spending hours in the company of the high tides of the sea or in rivetting his eyes to the galaxy of stars in the sky. He is very unsteady, fickle-minded and a lover of change. He therefore has a fancy for travel, especially long travels which would satisfy his natural urge for things of the imagination

Such travel keeps his imagination engaged and he will go on building castles in the air. He is unassuming but pleasing and has a good taste for dressing. He likes peace and harmony. He has hypnotic power to attract others. He is over-sensitive and gets hurt very easily. Sometimes he feels energetic and enthusiastic and thinks of doing some concrete work but soon loses interest and becomes nervous. His ideas about duty and social behaviour are strange and therefore sometimes he prefers loneliness He is independent in action and does not like others interfering in his affairs. He desires leadership but not of a serious type. If he can develop confidence and perseverance, he can achieve good heights with his high imagination and intuition. He is usually disturbed in his home and family affairs and has to look after distressed or invalid relatives.

Since the person is governed both by Moon and Saturn, he will have a check on his general imagination and idealism and this makes him practical. Wisdom is the main characteristic of Saturn and when added to number 2, the person will use his discretion in his easy going moods. By nature he is shy and when added to the sobriety of Saturn, it will make him more lonely. He will be superstitious, gloomy and sadistic.

The main characteristic of number 2 is that he is always uneasy and emotional.

In addition to the above, these are the special qualities of those born on the other dates.

Born on 11th January you have all the basic characteristics of those born on the 2nd of the month, so first go through them and then read your own.

He is usually successful in life and in love and gets honour, position and authority. He is loyal to his friends and is of a royal disposition. He should guard himself from secret enemies. He has interest in mysticism, philosophy and science. He can expect travel, favours and honours in life. He is very impulsive and gets excited easily. He worries too much over small matters. He has an ability to take quick decisions which endow him with leadership. He is a born advertiser and an inspiration to others.

Born on 20th January you have all the basic characteristics of those born on the 2nd of the month, so first go through them and then read your own.

He has many friends and benefits through wealthy women. He has a flair for writing and can be known as an author or a novelist. His prosperity lies near water, a river or the sea. This number has a peculiar significance. It shows new plans and new resolutions for the betterment of people at large.

Born on 29th January you have all the basic characteristics of those born on the 2nd of the month, so first go through them and then read your own.

This person is moody and changing and therefore uncertain about his action. He is courageous but takes risks in life and does not stick to anything till the end. He is intelligent and also a deep thinker but there is a tendency to carry everything to extremes. He is not very lucky in his married life. His interest is in his business. He is blessed with good fortune. His life is eventful.

b) FINANCE

Since he is a lethargic person and is not capable of doing hard work, he has a moderate financial status. He can however improve his financial condition, provided he is able to create art out of his imagination. He may be a good author or a painter who can create novels and draw unconventional paintings and earn a good living. However, his unstable mind often drags him away from the routine work and this creates an uncertain source of income. Though his financial position is not stable he may get some comfort after his 47th year.

c) VOCATION

The high imaginative power possessed by a number 2 person will help him to be a good composer of music or a writer of fiction or romance. He can as well be a good artist and can create works of lasting value. Immortal paintings, dramas and great poems will be the work of a prominent and influential number 2. He has a great vocabulary and linguistic mastery and can be successful as a teacher or a professor of languages. He can also be a good translator or an editor. The month of January being influenced by the planet Saturn he can also be

successful in occupations connected with occult sciences, chemistry, physics, medicine and even higher mathematics. He
can be successful in industries dealing with coal mines, timber
etc. and in construction companies. He can be a good accountant and also a good administrator. However success is
delayed in his life and he has to strive hard to get the fruits ;
success comes after his 47th year.

d) HEALTH

His main health problem is h's poor blood circulation. It
may result in anaemia and a weak heart His uneasiness creates mental worries and sleeplessness. He is also liable to
diabetes and asthma. Saturn's sicknesses also affect him which
are nervousness, irritation, trouble with legs, teeth and ears,
and paralysis and rheumatism. He is also susceptible to varicose veins.

e) MARRIAGE AND FRIENDS

He has a natural attraction towards persons born in the
period between 20th August and 20th September, 20th October
and 20th November, 20th December and 20th January, 20th
February and 20th March, and 20th April and 20th May. He
also has affinity for those who are governed by numbers 2 and
6. It is therefore advisable for him to select his marriage
partner from these periods or numbers.

Number 2 as husband

There are two types of husbands belonging to this number.
One is dominating and exacting. He is fault-finding and nothing satisfies him. The other type is passive, lazy and indulgent. He will marry for the sake of money so that he may
ultimately get comforts. On the whole, a number 2 husband
has a natural love of and attraction for home and treats his
wife and family members with the same courtesy that he
accords to strangers. He is kind and generous and gives
without thought of return or reward. He accepts marriage as a

part of the domestic scheme and succeeds in it because of his attitude which makes for harmony in the home. His drawback is his impersonality which his wife feels as lack of interest in domestic life.

Number 2 as wife

She is sympathetic, affectionate and devoted. She is satisfied with anything her husband provides her with. However, she is moody, changeable and sensitive. She is a fine companion : capable, intelligent, adaptable and talented. Her home is a social centre on account of her social and friendly manners. Her interests are wide and she does not like to investigate how her husband spends his spare time. She is unconventional and would rather herself suffer than create a situation which would make others unhappy.

Friends

He is always attracted towards those who have originality, creativity, activity and intelligence. His best friends are those who are governed by numbers 2, 4, 6 and 9. He also has a natural affinity towards people born in April, July, October and in his own month, i.e. January.

f) FORTUNATE DAYS : His lucky days are Mondays, Tuesdays and Fridays.

g) LUCKY COLOURS : He should use all shades of white, cream, violet and purple.

h) LUCKY JEWELS AND STONES : His lucky jewels are pearls, diamonds and moonstones.

i) IMPORTANT YEARS IN LIFE : His important years are 2, 11, 20, 29, 38, 47, 56, 65, 74 etc.

j)   HIS GOOD QUALITIES AND DRAWBACKS ARE AS
UNDER :

Good qualities	Drawbacks
Emotionality	Coldness
Fellowship	Envy
Honesty	Haste
Imagination	Introvert
Simplicity	Shyness
	Whimsicality

CHAPTER 3

BORN ON
3rd, 12th, 21st and 30th of January

All those born on the 3rd, 12th, 21st and 30th of January of any year are governed by number 3 and the planet Jupiter. The month of January is governed by the planet Saturn. Both these planets have strong personalities. The characteristics of number 3 given below are equally applicable to other dates also. In addition, special characteristics of those born on the 12th, 21st and 30th are given separately.

Born on 3rd January

a) CHARACTER

This number is governed by the planet Jupiter. It stands for morality, pure love and justice with mercy and is known as most beneficient. The vibrations emitted by this number are essentially harmonious and they lead to sympathy and untiring effort to do good to all, deep piety and true dignity. The abuse of the same vibrations causes the stimulation of Jupiterian virtues leading to hypocrisy, especially in religious matters. The good nature is marred by excess in many directions.

Even though he is religious, he does not throw himself into religion emotionally and the scepticism of Saturn comes in. His virtues of morality, justice and mercy are curbed by caution, analysis and reservation. In moments of trial however his emotions rule him and his scepticism recedes. He has ambition, energy and perseverance. He follows his subject methodically, studiously and seriously. He works independently and does not like any interference. His ideas are original and ambitious. He likes to be left alone when he is busy in translating his thoughts into action. He is usually attracted towards intelligent, clever 'and erudite persons. He does not like to mix with mediocre persons.

He is usually lucky in life. Vibrations radiating through him attract all that is good to him and his affairs prosper as a consequence. The judge who gives sane decisions and merciful sentences, the physician and the church dignitary, the world's teachers and philosophers are all. mostly governed by the number 3.

This is a good number. The person is confident about his ability. He is self-reliant and takes his own decisions. He has a loud voice. He is fond of show and likes to observe form, order and law. He is jovial in spirit and cordial in manner. His passions are healthy, spontaneous and without inhibitions. He is free in his expressions. He is a good conversationalist.

He takes an active interest in sports and outdoor activities from his earliest youth. He has tremendous enthusiasm and is not self-centred. His intellect is of a very high quality. He has a kind of vision that understands the world and loves it for what is and not for what it ought to be. He is a broad minded person, tolerant, humorous and truthful.

He is open-hearted with good understanding and is entirely lacking in malice or petty jealousies. If he is not alert, people take undue advantage of his good nature.

The main characteristics of a number 3 person are, ambition, leadership, dignity, honour, prestige, religion, pride, love of nature, enthusiasm and generosity. He will rise in life by his own efforts but will create jealousy and opposition.

Born on 12th January

you have all the basic characteristics of those born on the 3rd of the month, so first go through them and then read your own.

Authority and honours are the significant acquisition of this person. He has vanity and is proud, ambitious and aspiring. He is fond of pleasures and is attracted to the opposite sex. However sometimes he prefers loneliness. He likes to sacrifice for others but becomes a victim of others' plans or

intrigues. His relations with others are smooth and harmoniou
He is quick to notice trifles. He has lofty ideas.

Born on 21st January you have all the basic characteristics of those born on the 3rd of the month, so first go through them and then read your own.

He is kind and generous and is a loving father. He achieves fame, reputation and honours at a very late age· He is
cheerful and fond of travel. He has a strong sense of self-
respect. Surprisingly, he has a suspicious nature.

Born on 30th January you have all the basic characteristics of those born on the 3rd of the month, so first go through them and then read your own.

He is fortunate, generous and optimistic. He has a noble
and religious mind. He likes to travel and visit places of pilgrimage. He can be successful as a teacher, educationist or in
administration· He appears gentle and sincere but has a hidden
characteristic. He may be active but is restless. When faced
with difficulties, he is strong enough to overcome them.

b) FINANCE

He is a lucky type and somehow manages to earn enough
for his livelihood. He also gets opportunities for higher positions
in life and so earns quite a lot. His ambition, leadership
and enthusiam always push him forward and usually he gets
all comforts in life. The number 3 person is early out of puberty and poverty.

In spite of the financial position described above, the
month of January is dominated by the planet Saturn and has its
own influences, on the financial aspect also. At least in the
early part of the man's life, there are delays, hindrances and
limitations to financial achievements. Money is assured by
carefulness, slow plodding, and perseverance. Acquisition of
wealth is possible more by personal efforts than by dint of
good fortune. This man should never lend money without
security, or otherwise he is sure to lose it.

c) VOCATION

His love for position and command makes him a politician.

I have observed persons of this number occupying very high posts such as those of ministers, ambassadors, judges and secretaries. He is gifted for public life, statesmanship, high offices etc., may be in the army or in the church. He is a good teacher as well as a preacher. Professions such as those of doctors, bankers, advertisers, actors are also suitable for him. His special interest is be in the field of research.

d) HEALTH

Number 3 has a strong influence on the blood and the arterial system. It also governs the sense of smell. This person is liable to suffer from chest and lung disorders, throat afflictions, gout and apoplexy and sudden fevers. He may also suffer from sore throat, diptheria, adenoids, pneumonia, plurisy and tuberculosis. Melancholia, nervousness and irritation are also common.

e) MARRIAGE AND FRIENDS

A number 3 person has a natural attraction towards persons born in the period 20th April to 20th May, 20th June to 20th July, 20th August to 20th September, 20th October to 20th November and 20th December to 20th January. It is therefore advisable that he finds his marriage partner from one of these periods. He also has affinity for those who are governed by numbers 3, 6, and 9.

Number 3 as husband

As a general rule, he attains puberty at an early age and marries early. However as he is ambitious, his ambitious also make him expect too many things from his wife and so he becomes disappointed. He desires to have a wife of whom he can be proud. She should have attraction, personality, a commanding presence, charming manners and intelligence. It is always better for him to choose a number 3 person or a number 6 person as his life partner. He is most loving, thoughtful and considerate. His passions are powerful and demand immediate satisfaction.

Number 3 as wife

She is the best companion to her husband: She is not an intruder but takes an active interest in the business of her husband. She is efficient in house-keeping and has a sympathetic and balanced attitude towards her children. Her passions are healthy and joyous and her approach to physical love is highly refined.

Friends

A No. 3 man is attracted towards those who have a philosophical attitude and those who are learned, intelligent and inventive. His best friends are those who are governed by numbers 3,6,7 and 9. He is atttacted by people born in the months of April, July, October and in his own month, i.e. January.

f) FORTUNATE DAYS : His lucky days are Thursdays and Fridays

g) LUCKY COLOURS : He should use all shades of yellow, violet and purple.

h) LUCKY JEWELS AND STONES : His lucky jewel is Topaz and lucky stones are amethyst, cat's eye or moon stone.

i) IMPORTANT YEARS IN LIFE : His important years are 3, 12,21 30, 39, 48, 57, 66, 75 etc.

j) HIS GOOD QUALITIES AND DRAWBACKS ARE AS UNDER :

Good qualities	Drawbacks
Ambition	Cruelty
Dignity	Dictatorship
Individuality	Hypocrisy
Philosophy	Extravagance
Prestige	Vanity

CHAPTER 4

BORN ON
4th, 13th, 22nd and 31st of January

All those born on the 4th, 13th, 22nd and 31st of January of any year are governed by the number 4 and the planet Uranus. The month of January is governed by the planet Saturn. Therefore both the planets rule these individuals. The characteristics of number 4 given below are equally applicable to other dates also. In addition, special characteristics of those born on 13th, 22nd and 31st are given separately.

Born on 4th January

a) CHARACTER

The number 4 is governed by the planet Uranus and shows energy, force and advancement. It shows revolution and unexpected happenings in life. Usually the changes that take place are for the better. This number represents the higher faculties of the mind. It shows activity and intelligence engaged in the reconstruction or the betterment of human life. The peculiar nature of this person is that he constantly aims at change in life and society and is after the liberation of the mind from the bondage of environment and society. He has an attractive personality. Saturn makes him suspicious and cautious about others' behaviour. His analytical mind usually gives him good judgement of others. It is necessary that his energy and ambition are directed on proper lines, otherwise his revolutionary nature added to the Saturnian ideas about duty and social behaviour will make him a total misfit in society. He is studious, methodical and serious. He is attracted towards intelligent and clever people who have individuality and a creative faculty.

He has an analytical and logical mind but he has a bad habit of forcing his opinions on others. He is usually disturbed in his home and family affairs and has to look after his relatives. He is likely to be misunderstood in his actions and feels lonely in life. He meets with great opposition and has secret enemies. Even then, he has a desire to gain power over others, whether he gains it by his talk, pen or force.

The date four and its subsequent numbers are good for public life but they lean towards unusual actions, originality of thought and a distinct trend towards eccentricity.

Born on 13th January | you have all the basic characteristics of those born on the 4th of the month, so first go through them and then read your own.

Such a man is an intelligent person, of tall stature and good complexion. He is considerate and benevolent. He likes literature and science books. He likes to remain active, though in a quiet way. He occupies positions of high responsibility and gets riches. His success and career start after his 31st year. Though outwardly he looks mild, in fact, he is obstinate. He is faithful and sympathetic but has difficuly in expressing his love. His has all the qualities of number 4 but in an exaggerated form.

Born on 22nd January | you have all the basic characteristics of those born on the 4th of the month, so first go through them and then read your own.

This man also is tall with good eyes. Usually he occupies good positions but without much responsibility. He is rather easy going but unsteady in nature. Sometimes his actions are spasmodic. On the whole he is lucky in his affairs and benefits from the opposite sex. He is happy in his family life but is also fond of a companion. He is faithful and dedicated to others. Sometimes, he feels very lonely. His social field is limited and he has few friends. He does not care for disputes. He has has too much economy of sentiments.

Born on 31st of January you have all the basic characteristics of those born on the 4th of the month, so first go through them and then read your own.

This date shows ambition, pride and austerity. The man is interested in honourable occupations such as working with charitable institutions for the deaf and dumb, the physically handicapped etc. He gets success after his 40th year but he expects quick results and early fame. He is lucky in financial matters. He is realistic and of strong will-power. He has a strong attraction for the opposite sex. He loves travelling.

b) FINANCE

As regards finance and monetary status, he is usually well settled in life though he experiences delays and difficulties in his undertaking. He may not amass wealth but can maintain the show of riches. He is a spendthrift and his home is well decorated. His financial propserity usually starts after the age of 40.

c) VOCATION

He will be successful in trades connected with transport electricity and all sorts of machinery. He will be equally successful as an engineer, a building contractor, scientist and an industrialist. He is also attracted towards mystic subjects such as palmistry and astrology and can do well in these subjects also.

d) HEALTH

His respiratory system is usually weak and he suffers from breathlessness. His knees, shanks and feet are also affected. Sometimes he suffers from urinary infection.

e) MARRIAGE AND FRIENDS

He has a natural attraction towards persons born in the period between 19th February and 20th March and between 21st October and 20th November. He also has an affinity for those who are governed by numbers 1, 2, 7, and 8. It is therefore advisable that he should select his marriage partner from these periods or numbers.

Number 4 as husband

He is shrewd and intelligent and expects his wife to share his views. He is dominating and wants all the affairs of the house to run as per his desire. He is generous and has a kind and loving heart.

Number 4 as wife

She is smart and attractive. She has the art of dressing and has a strong will-power. She aims at several things but hardly succeeds in getting mastery over any one. She loves interior decoration but does not have the capacity to work hard for it and she will get it done trhough others. She is dictatorial and moody and spoils her day due to her own whimsical nature. She is at times restless. It is better for her to find a friend governed by number one or two.

Friends

This man is fond of friends and company but hardly gets a close friend because of his unsteady, changing and moody nature. His close friends come from among those influenced by numbers 1, 2, 7 and 8. He is attracted towards intelligent persons who are studious and of a philosophical mind. He can find his friends among those born in January, April, July and October.

f) FORTUNATE DAYS : His lucky days are Mondays, Fridays and Saturdays.

g) LUCKY COLOURS : His lucky colours are electric blue, grey, violet and white.

h) LUCKY JEWELS AND STONES : His lucky jewels are pearl, garnet, coral.

i) IMPORTANT YEARS IN LIFE: 4, 13, 22, 31, 40, 49, 58, 67,76, etc. are the important years in his life.

**j)   HIS GOOD QUALITIES AND DRAWBACKS ARE AS
        UNDER :**

Good Qualities	Drawbacks
Activity	Changeable
Endurance	Dominating
Energy	Stubborn
Reliability	Vindictive
Method and System	Jealous

CHAPTER 5

BORN ON

5th, 14, and 23rd of January

All those born on the 5th, 14th and 23rd of January of any year are governed by the planet Mercury and the number 5. The month of January is governed by the planet Saturn. Therefore both the planets rule these individuals. The characteristics of number 5 given below are equally applicable to other dates also. In addition, the special characteristics of those born on 14th and 23rd are given separately.

Born on 5th January

a) CHARACTER

This number is governed by the planet Mercury and it shows shrewdness, quickness, scientific pursuits, business ability, industry, intuition and diplomacy. A person governed by this number is active and quick; this applies not only to physical agility but also to mental working. He is very skilful and has intuition. He is proficient in games, where he uses both his hands and his brain. He has the capacity to juoge the ability of his opponents in games and knows very well how to take advantage of the weak points of his opponents. He uses oratory and eloquence in expressing himself. He has the capacity to pursue his objectives and knows very well how to plan for achieving his ends. He is deeply interested in occult subjects and wishes to master all the intricacies of such abtruse subjects. He possesses a pleasant character and dislikes inactivitv. He is sociable and has many acquaintances. He is fond of variety and change and trips and travel. However difficult the situation, he can find a away out.

He is a nervous person. He is therefore restless. He has an intuitive perception and has the capacity to be either good or bad. When he is good, he is a shrewd person and not vicious or criminal. He is fond of family life and loves children. His pleasures are mainly mental and he evaluates everything in terms of business. He is amiable and adaptable.

Born on 14th January | you have all the basic characteristics of those born on the 5th of the month, so first go through them and then read your own.

This person has an attractive personality and is liked by all. His nature is cooperative and he does not like to provoke others. He usually occupies a good position in life and is successful in his business. He is not talkative but slightly reserved. This is an intelligent and shrewd person. In women, it indicates a good marriage but they should take care in child bearing. A number 14 man is inconstent in love and experiences some romantic and impulsive attachment in early years. He is fortunate in money matters. He is fond of gambling and of solving riddles.

The influence of Saturn makes him sceptical and slow in decisions. He is analytical, cautious, studious and methodical. He is usually disturbed in his home and family affairs and has to look after unfortunate or invalid persons.

Born on 23rd January | you have all the basic characteristics of those born on the 5th of the month, so first go through them and then read your own.

Such a man is usually popular with women. His fortune is near water. He is successful in life and enjoys honour and wealth. He may get money through inheritance. He keeps himself busy in his own way He gets help and protection from superiors. He is a lucky person. He is affectionate and loves freedom. He is averse to formalities. He has a spirit of independence and a desire to dominate.

b) FINANCE

Since number 5 is a business number, the person can expect opulence. With his shrewd characteristics, he is capable of developing his industry and carrying out his plans systemati-

cally with the result that he gets good returns for his efforts.
He is lucky in his financial matters. However, whenever the
influence of Saturn comes in, he gets delayed results and difficulties from labour. It will be difficult for him to get the
money he expects and sometimes he may have to lose it. Saturn
is concerned with landed property and the person may get it
through inheritance.

c) VOCATION

He can adapt himself to the role he has to play in the drama
of life. With his adaptability he uses his contact with various
classes of people and becomes successful in business.
Banking is a good business for him. The planet Mercury also
shows ability for medicine or surgery and even medical stores.
His capacity to argue his points can make him a good lawyer.

d) HEALTH

His basic health problem is his biliousness and nervousness.
His biliousness has close relation to his psychological disturbance. His biliousness increases with the increase in tension
and is reduced or disappears when his nervous trouble is under
control. Number 5 rules over nerves, the neck, arms, ears and
the respiratory system. The month of January is governed by the
planet Saturn and shows varicose veins, rheumatism and melancholia.

e) MARRIAGE AND FRIENDS

He has a natural attraction for persons born on the period
between 21st August and 20th October, between 21st
December and 20th February and 20th April and 20th May. He
also has an affinity for those who are governed by numbers 1,7
and 8. It is therefore advisable that he should select his wife
from these periods or numbers.

Number 5 as husband

He is lucky and successful in his married life. His selection
is good and usually he selects a person of his own type. He is

considerate and treats his wife and family with the the same courtesy that he accords to strangers. He is kind and generous and loves his partner. He expects neatness and cleanliness from her and also desires that she should share in his enjoyment of life. He is proud of his wife and likes to see her well-dressed. In turn, he proves himself to be a good husband He loves his children and is fond of his home. Even if he travels long, he is very much attracted to his home and is eager to return early and be with his family. He is liberal in spending on clothing and other needs of his family and furnishes his house with good taste. He accepts marriage as a part of his domestic scheme and succeeds in it because of his attitude which makes for harmony at home. His drawback is his impersonality which his wife feels as lack of interest in domestic life.

Number 5 as wife

She is a fine companion, capable, intelligent, adaptable and talented. Her home is a social centre on account of her social and friendly manners. Her interests are wide and she does not like to spy on her husband in his spare time. Though basically she is unconventional, she is kind and would rather suffer herself than make others sorrowful. As she is intelligent, she would be appreciated as a good wife by an intelligent husband who can use her abilities for his own self. She likes tidiness and though she seldom does her own work, she gets it done through her commanding personality.

Friends

A Number 5 man's best friends are those who are governed by numbers 1, 3, 4, 5, 7 and 8. He is attracted towards those who have originality and intelligence. He can also find friends among those born in January, April, July and October.

f) FORTUNATE DAYS : His lucky days are Wednesdays, Fridays and Saturdays.

g) LUCKY COLOURS : His lucky colours are white, green, purple and violet. He should not use red.

h) LUCKY JEWELS and STONES : Emerald, pearl, garnet and sapphire are his lucky jewels.

i) IMPORTANT YEARS IN LIFE : His important years are 5, 14, 23, 32, 41, 50, 59, 68, 77, etc.

j) HIS GOOD QUALITIES & DRAWBACKS ARE AS UNDER :

Good qualities	Drawbacks
Co-operation	Lack of perseverance
Practical approach	Scepticism
Shrewdness	Unreliability
Vigilance	

CHAPTER 6

BORN ON
6th, 15 and 24th of January

All those born on the 6th, 15th and 24th of January of any year are governed by the planet Venus and the number 6. The month of January is governed by the planet Saturn. Therefore both the planets rule these individuals. The characteristics of number 6 given below are equally applicable to other dates also. In addition, special characteristics of those born on the 15th and the 24th are given separately:

Born on 6th January

a) CHARACTER

This number is governed by the planet Venus which stands for love, sympathy and adoration. A person governed by this number is a born artist: he loves art and beauty in life. He is nervous and sceptical about his love affairs and can take a positive step only if he is sure of the result. He is a pleasant personality, and is always charming Bust he is sometimes very serious and prefers to be lonely. His talk is interesting and lively. In art or inhis work, he is methodical and studious. He is independent in thought and action and does not like anybody's domination. We may sometimes have to keep our ideas of morality and social conduct in suspense to understand and appreciate his feelings and views. His ideas about duty and social behaviour are strange. Number 6 stands for beauty, health, vitality, warmth, attraction and above all love. A Number 6 man is fond of music, dancing and poetry. He prefers to have a life full of ease and luxuries, money and happiness. He likes to spend rather than save. He will have rich clothes, jewellery, perfumes and all sorts of beautiful things.

He is by nature a loving type and he has a feeling of kinship and humanity. He will not desert his friends. He always likes to understand the grievances and difficulties of others considerately. He loves an atmosphere of cheerfulness and his cheerfulness in infectious. His outlook is bright and vivacious. He is emotional but keeps his emotions to himself. His anger does not subside soon. He is responsible and loves his children but gets very little happiness from them. He is a born adviser and needs an audience to whom he can expound his views on matters of importance. He is a good conversationist and enjoys intellectual swordcrossing.

In spite of his joyous and optimistic character, he is usually disturbed in his home and family affairs and has to look after unfortunate or invalid relatives

Born on 15th January

> you have all the basic characteristics of those born on the 6th of the month, so first go through them and then read your own.

This person has good intelligence and a good memory. He is fit for responsible positions such as those of ambassadors, consuls, governors etc. He is very ambitious and boastful but hasty. He is proud by nature. He is interested in occultism of the lower kind. He is also interestad in art and music. He appears to be gentle but has very strong convictions. He has a habit of worrying inwardly and leads a melancholy life. His destiny is such that he has to make sacrifices for others.

Born on 24th January

> you have all the basic characteristics of those born on the 6th of the month, so first go through them and then read your own.

This man is fortunate in getting assistance from people of high rank. He receives help from the opposite sex. He prospers after marriage and marries a rich girl. He succeeds in speculation and enjoys a good monetary position. He defines strictly the line between personal and social matters. He is methodical in his thinking. He possesses a strong ego and sometimes tries to force his opinions on others.

b) FINANCE

He is not attracted by money and accumulation of wealth is not his aim in life. All his interest is directed towards attaining pleasures and gratifying his desires. He therefore spends his earning on anythings that attracts him. He also never repents having spent his money on his art which may not ultimately give him monetary rewards. So he is rarely affluent but he somehow has the knack of making both ends meet and have minimum comforts. He may sometimes also have windfalls.

In addition to his indifference to money, the delay indicated by the planet Saturn is also present. He has therefore to struggle for his livelihood. He relies too much on his friends and relatives and lends them money even going too much out of the way. Even then, he takes matters very lightly.

c) VOCATION

He will shine as an interior decorator, architect, jeweller, musician, hotel manager or confectioner. He can be equally successful as a broker, estate broker or as commission agent. He may have developed the power to write books on history or on philosophy. He may also be engaged in mines of precious stones, especially diamonds.

d) HEALTH

On the whole he has good health. He may suffer from epidemic fever and influenza. In advanced age, he is likely to suffer from nervousness, melancholia, irritation, rheumatism and biliousness.

e) MARRIAGE

He has a natural attraction towards those born in the period from 20th August to 20th September, from 20th December to 20th January and from 20th April to 20th May. He also has an affinity for those who are governed by the numbers 2,4,6 and 9. It is therefore advisable that he should select his marriage partner from these periods or numbers.

Number 6 as husband

He likes marriage and usually marries early in life. He expects his partner to be neat and have charm and grace. His is usually a large family with many children. He loves his children and home. He is very kind, generous and devoted. He is very considerate and treats his wife and family members with the same courtesy that he accords to strangers. He accepts marriage as a part of the domestic scheme and succeeds in it because of his attitude which makes for harmony in the home· Though he creates a lively atmosphere in the house, he finds it difficult to provide all the necessities for the members of his family. Art is everything to him and he remains impractical in not understanding the material values of a successful life· His drawback is his impersonality which his wife feels as lack of interest in domestic life· This may sometimes create unpleasantness and make him unhappy in his married life.

Number 6 as wife

She never resorts to divorce and endures extreme hardship rather than desert her mate. She is a devoted mother and loving. wife, satisfied with her husband's efforts on her behalf. She loves domestic life and is a perfect home-maker. She is also a fine companion, capable, intelligent, adaptable and talented. Her home is a social centre on account of her social and friendly manners. Though basically she is unconventional, she is kind and would rather herself suffer than create a situation which would make others unhappy.

Friends

A number 6 man is interested in those who are original in thought and intelligent. He also likes those who are studious and of a philosophical mind. He has a natural affinity towards those who are born in January, April, July and October. His best friends are those who are governed by the numbers 2, 3, 4, 6 and 9.

f) FORTUNATE DAYS : His lucky days are Mondays, Thursdays and Fridays.

g) LUCKY COLOURS : He should use all shades of grey, violet and purple· He should avoid yellow.

h) LUCKY JEWELS AND STONES : He can use emerald, pearl, diamond, garnet or turquoise.

i) IMPORTANT YEARS IN LIFE : His important years are 6, 15, 24, 33, 42, 51, 60, 69, 78 etc.

j) HIS GOOD QUALITIES AND DRAWBACKS ARE AS UNDER:

Good Qualities	Drawbacks
Harmony	Absence of foresight
Love	Interferencs
Peace	Moodiness
Strong memory	Timidity

CHAPTER 7

BORN ON
7th, 16th, 25th of January

All those born on the 7th, 16th and 25th of January of any year are governed by number 7 and the planet Neptune. The month January is governed by the planet Saturn. Therefore both the planets rule these individuals. The characteristics of number 7 given below are equally applicable to other dates. In addition, the special characteristics of those born on 16th and 25th are given separately.

Born on 7th January

a) CHARACTER

This number is governed by the planet Neptune and has the same qualities as number 2 which is governed by the planet Moon. The person has individuality and is original and independent. He is restless by nature and is fond of change. He likes to visit foreign countries and is interested in far off lands. He has peculiar ideas about religion and dislikes following the beaten track.

This is a spiritual number and Supreme Consciousness is developed in this individual. He is like a free bird and likes to break traditional bondage and restrictions. It is possible that the greatest of the prophets and spiritualists have the planet Neptune dominating them. His behaviour is a mystery to others and he is often absent-minded. He thinks logically and achieves great aims. He is stubborn and disregards the opinions of others. He has good talent to earn money. In general he is somewhat indifferent to materialistic pursuits. He desires the best or none at all. He is sensitive and hides his real feelings by apparent indifference. He dislikes mingling with common people. He prefers to spend his hour with his favourite books. When his opinion is solicited, he speaks with authority.

Being born in the month of January, he has the influence of the planet Saturn to mould his character to a certain extent. He is sceptical about religion and mystic things. He takes slow decisions unless he is sure of the result. He is very cautious and does not like to speculate. His mind is analytical and he thinks deeply. He has energy and ambition and develops perserverance. He is very studious and methodical and takes everything seriously. He is independent in thought and action and does not like to be dominated by others. He is therefore generally misunderstood. He is attracted towards intelligent and clever people but never interferes with their affairs. He is usually worried by his home and family affairs and has to look after distressed or invalid relatives.

Born on 16th January

you have all the basic characteristics of those born on the 7th of the month, so first go through them and then read your own.

He is rather easygoing and does not like to work hard. He is good humoured and generous. He is very sensitive and emotional. He soon gets upset but is soon pleased. He is frequently indisposed. He is fortunate in getting good and successful children. However, there is some sort of sorrow in married life. He appears to be calm but his mind is always in turmoil and he is sometimes short-tempered. He will not disclose his nervousness and is slow in taking decisions. He does not like interference.

Born on 25th January

you have all the basic characteristics of those born on the 7th of the month, so first go through them and then read your own.

He is a jack of all trades but master of none. He is interested in several subjects but does not have the capacity to go into details. His knowledge therefore is very shallow. He likes to travel and has connections with foreign countries. He is honest, faithful and good-natured. But he is fickle-minded and inconsistent. His memory is good and he is a good orator or a teacher.

b) FINANCE

Usually there are a number of changes in the life of a number 7 person and so, it is difficult for him to amass wealth. However this being a mystic number, the person can be well placed in life provided he finds a job of his choice. In that case he can be a wealthy person with all amenities and comforts. January is governed by the planet Saturn, and the Saturnian characteristics of delay and difficulty are present in this number also. This person should be cautious while lending money which will seldom be returned. He achieves monetary stability at a very late stage, but ultimately succeeds in getting all the comforts in life.

c) VOCATION

His love for sea travel and interest in foreign countries make him a successful merchant, exporter or importer. He can also deal in dairy products, fishery, chemical industry and other products such as soap etc. He can also study medicine and surgery.

d) HEALTH

His main trouble is his nervous constitution and all his illness will be due to his nervousness. He is liable to suffer from faulty blood circulation. stomach disorder and fever. He may also suffer from rheumatism and biliousness.

e) MARRIAGE AND FRIENDS

A number 7 person has a natural attraction towards persons born in the period from 20th October to 20th November, from 20th December to 20th January, from 19th February to 20th March, from 20th April to 20th May and from 20th August to 20th September. He also has affinity for those who are governed by numbers 3, 5, and 8. It is therefore advisable that he should select his wife from one of these periods or numbers.

Number 7 as husband

He is very emotional and understands the feelings of his wife. He is very considerate and will never try to impose his ideas on the wife. He is liberal, fond of picnics, travel and cinema theatres. He is a spendthrift and likes to live lavishly. His family is moderate in size and has all comforts in life. He accepts marriage as a part of his domestic scheme and succeeds in it because of his attitude which contributes a great deal to harmony at home. His drawback is his impersonality which his wife feels as lack of interest in domestic life.

Number 7 as wife

She is a fine companion, capable, intelligent, adaptable and talented. Her home is a social centre on account of her social and friendly manners. Her interests are wide and she does not wish to investigate how her husband spends his spare time. Though basically she is unconventional, she is kind and would rather herself suffer than create a situation which would make others unhappy. Though she is social and talented, she is very moody being governed by the planet Neptune, and her behaviour is unpredictable. She is very restless and gets disturbed over small matters. She expects her husband to look after her all the time.

Friends

He is attracted towards those who have originality, creativity and intelligence. His best friends are those who are governed by numbers 1, 3, 5, 7, 8 and 9. He also has a natural affinity towards people born in April, July, October and in his own month, i.e. January.

f) FORTUNATE DAYS : His lucky days are Mondays, Wednesdays and Thursdays. He should take his decisions and act on these days especially when the date is also the 7th or 16 or 25th of the month.

9) LUCKY COLOURS : He should use all shades of green, yellow, violet, grey and purple.

h) LUCKY JEWELS AND STONES : His lucky jewels are topaz and emerald and lucky stones are moon stone and cat's eye.

i) IMPORTANT YEARS IN LIFE : His important years are 7, 16, 25, 34, 43, 52, 61, 70 etc.

j) HIS GOOD QUALITIES AND DRAWBACKS ARE AS UNDER :

Good qualities	Drawbacks
Austerity	Despondency
Reflection	Diffidence
Serenity	Restlessness
Tolerance	Whimsicality

CHAPTER 8

BORN ON
8th, 17th and 26th of January

All those born on the 8th, 17th and 26th of January of any year are governed by number 8 and the planet Saturn. January is also governed by the planet Saturn. Therefore the influence of Saturn is more powerful on these individuals. The character–reading applied to number 8 below is equally applicable to other dates. In addition, special characteristics of those born on the 17th and the 26th are given separately.

Born on 8th January

a) CHARACTER

This number is governed by the planet Saturn and shows an extreme sense of discipline, steadfastness, constancy and dutifulness. The person has a sober and solitude – loving personality. He is a lover of classical music but mostly of a melancholy type. In the arts, he loves landscapes, natural scenery and flowers. Number 8 is considered to be a balance wheel to the character. He can look at the other side of anything. He is a pessimist. He prefers solitude to company. He shuns society rather than courts it. He is cautious about the future and he takes decisions very carefully on matters which pertain to mundane affairs. He is a prudent person, wise and sober, amongst persons of all the numbers. He is never overenthusiastic and is more or less gloomy and melancholy. He is also ambitious and persevering. He is capable of enormous efforts for the attainment of the desired objects.

He is sceptical and analytical. He is creative, productive and dominating. He is likely to be misunderstood. He understands the weak and the oppressed and treats them in a warm-hearted manner. He is a born manager who can keep others busy. He admires fair play and is willing to pay a fair compensation. He has a good memory for names and faces. He does not take quick decisions unless he is sure of the result. His ideas about duty and social behaviour are unconventional and therefore do not fit in easily with his neighbours' ideas. He is attracted towards intelligent and clever people but never interferes in their affairs. He is usually disturbed at home and in his family affairs and has to look after distressed or invalid relatives.

Born on 17th January | you have all the basic characteristics of those born on the 8th of the month, so first go through them and then read your own.

Such a man is a good organiser and a good thinker. He has a creative and constructive mind. He is a lover of peace and is a philanthropist. He is attracted towards occultism and mysticism. He is courageous and proud. He has a strong individuality. He is highly intelligent and clever. As regards emotions, he is calm. At times he is generous to a fault and at times very stingy. He is interested in research and seeks knowledge. He is conservative and dominating.

Born on 26th January | you have all the basic characteristics of those born on the 8th of the month, so first go through them and then read your own.

Such a person wants to enjoy life without doing anything. He is sluggish and lethargic. He revels in wine and women and is fickle-minded. He is not particular about the number of children. He is lucky in money matters and gets easy money. He is smart but lacks positiveness. He likes to put up a good appearance but has a worrying nature. He has problems with his love affairs.

b) **FINANCE**

The peculiarity of number 8 is the delay in life in all respects. naturally in financial matters also there is delay and stability is achieved at a very late age. This person has to work hard and he seldom succeeds in getting opulence. He has therefore to avoid allowing number 8 to play any part in his life and instead he can choose number 1 or 3 for all his important actions and moves in life. However, if his experience shows that 8 is a lucky number for him, he can insist on that number only, and wealth and prosperity will be his. If 8 is found to be a lucky number in one's life, one can try one's luck in lottery and horse racing. But usually this number is connected with delays and hard work and a person he has to be very cautious about his financial matters.

c) VOCATION

Subjects suitable to him are occult sciences, chemistry, physics, medicine and higher mathematics. He can be successful in industries dealing with coal mines, timber etc. and in construction companies. He can be a good accountant and also a good administrator. However, as stated earlier, he has to strive hard in his career and can get the fruits of his hard work only in later years of his life.

d) HEALTH

His main health problems are nervousness, irritation, trouble with legs, teeth, and ears, paralysis and rheumatism. He is a bilious type and often suffers from chronic melancholia. It is very interesting to note that the delaying characteristic in life is also observed in his sickness. The ailments he suffers from also take a long time to cure. A strong 8 personality commonly tends to suffer from varicose veins and haemorrhoids.

e) MARRIAGE AND FRIENDS

He has a natural attraction towards persons born in the period 20th December to 20th January, 20th April to 20th May and 20th August to 20th September. He also has an affinity for those who are governed by numbers 5 and 7. It is therefore advisable that he should select his wife from one of these periods or numbers.

Number 8 as husband

Basically, a number 8 person does not have a desire to get married. He prefers loneliness and likes to be left to himself. He does not have much attraction for the opposite sex. Usually he tries to postpone his marriage with the result that if at all he marries, it is at a very late age. He also finds it difficult to choose a wife. As he prefers seclusion to company, he often makes his married life miserable. He is very orthodox in his views and does not allow his wife to adopt modern ideas in dress. The natural result is disappointment on the part of his wife and hatred for her husband. If, however, he wants a happy married life, he should prefer a person who is also interested in deep and serious studies and likes to devote herself to philosophy and occult subjects. Once he is married, he is considerate and treats his wife and family members with the same courtesy that he accords to strangers. He accepts marriage as a part of his domestic scheme. His drawback is his impersonality which his wife feels as lack of interest in domestic life.

Number 8 as wife

She is of a masculine personality. She is capable and systematic. She enjoys her family life and likes to make sacrifices for her children and for the ambition of her husband. Her fault is that she lacks feminine warmth, sentiment and delicacy. She is a fine companion : capable, intelligent, adaptable and talented. Her home is a social centre on account of her social and friendly manners. Her interests are wide. She does not wish to keep a watch on her husband in his spare time. She is kind and would rather herself suffer than create a situation which would make others unhappy.

Friends

A number 8 man is always attracted towards those who have originality, creativity, activity and intelligence. His best friends are those who are governed by the numbers 3, 4, 5 and 8.

He also has a natural affinity towards people born in April, July, October and in his own month, i.e. January.

f) FORTUNATE DAYS :   His lucky days are Wednesdays, Fridays and Saturdays.

g) LUCKY COLOURS :   He should use dark grey, dark blue, purple and violet.

h) LUCKY JEWELS AND STONES :   He should use sapphire, pearl and garnet. He can also wear cat's eye and amethyst.

i) IMPORTANT YEARS IN LIFE :   His important years are 8, 17, 26, 35, 44, 53, 62, 71 etc.

j) HIS GOOD QUALITIES AND DRAWBACKS ARE AS UNDER:

Good Qualities	Drawbacks
Authority	Cynicism
Method	Delay
Practicality	Vindictiveness
Steadiness	Nervousness
Systematic	

CHAPTER 9

BORN ON
9th, 18th and 27th of January

All those born on 9th, 18th and 27th of January of any year are governed by number 9 and the planet Mars. ⋅ The month January is governed by the planet Saturn. Both these planets are powerful and have certain conflicting characteristics. The character reading given for number 9 below is equally applicable to the other dates. In addition, the special characteristics of those born on the 18th and the 27th are given separately.

Born on 4th January

a) CHARACTER

This number is governed by the planet Mars and shows aggression, resistance, courage, dash and quickness. A Martian is a born fighter. He is aggressive and will not stop till he achieves his end. He has the capacity to fight against all adverse elements and circumstances. He does not know defeat and he will either win or die. A number 9 person is not very tactful or delicate in his talk but his intention is good and his vigorous manner should not be misunderstood as rough behaviour. He should not criticize but should use his words carefully, otherwise they will boomerang. Circumstances over which he has no control will play a great part in all his affairs. He has a love of adventure and excitement, which will lead him to danger in many ways⋅ He is likely to meet with accidents and risk his life under unusual circumstances.

He makes enemies unintentionally and at times suffers because of this.

He is fiery and dashing and does not have sickly sentiments. He has audacity and vigour. He is also fond of games and vigorous exercise. When the date of the month is 9 and the total of the birth date is also 9, the person is governed by a strong number 9 and Mars is very powerful in his life. He has strong sexual passions and is very much attracted to the opposite sex. He is prepared to go through any ordeal to gratify his desire.

He is a brave person to whom conflict does not bring the thought of danger. He is greatly devoted to his friends and will fight for them. He has sympathy and consideration for the weak. He loves children and animals. He takes delight in showing mercy to others. He likes the healing profession. He is backed by self-control moral courage and the quality of forgiveness. His resourcefulness is remarkable and under all circumstances he proves his strength of will and courage. He is quick-tempered. He is very cautious and does not like to speculate. His mind is analytical and philosophical and he thinks deeply. He has energy and ambition and develops perseverance. He is independent in thought and action and does not like to be dominated by others. He is attracted towards intelligent and clever people but never interferes in their affairs. He is usually troubled in his home and family affairs and has to look after relatives in distress or invalids.

Born on 18th January you have all the basic characteristics of those born on the 9th of the month, so first go through them and then read your own.

This person has tenacity and will-power which will overcome any difficulty. He is not as dashing as a number 9 person but he is fearless and courageous. His fine health makes him passionate. He inherits property from his father. He has a disciplined mind and likes to help others. He is painstaking with good judgement and is wise. He loves to exercise total control over others. He does not like to be advised by others.

Born on 27th January | you have all the basic characteristics of those born on the 9th of the month, so first go through them and then read your own.

On the whole he is full of conflicts. He is confident and likes to do something for those whose life is miserable or who are handicapped. He can develop spiritual powers and can practise spiritual healing. On the other hand, he is fond of women and can develop illicit contacts and become involved in scandals. Sometimes he creates unhappiness in his married life. He is very sesitive and moody and his actions and moves are unpredictable. He is self-assured and strong in resolution. He is a seeker of independence and likes to dominate. He hates to work under others. Usually, he is dogmatic.

b) FINANCE

He is lucky in his monetary affairs and earns far more than an average person. He is also very liberal in spending, especially for his sweetheart. He enjoys all the comforts that money can bring. However the delaying tendency shown by the planet Saturn may come in and he may have difficulties in recovering his dues. There will be a clash between the Martian qualities and the Saturnian qualities, and Mars being very erratic and sensitive, the delay factor may affect the nerves of the 9 number person.

c) VOCATION

A Number 9 person is found in all walks of life but he will be more suitable for the army and for professions where there is full scope for his aggression and courage. In the army he will rise to high positions; in politics, he will be eminent and in business he will exhibit his dashing and pushing nature. He can be be a good doctor or a chemist or a businessman dealing in iron and steel. Good and successful engineers are also governed by Mars and number 9. Here we cannot forget the influence of Saturn as shown by the month January, he can be equally successful in mines, quarries and in the construction line.

d) HEALTH

His main health defect arises from heat and he is susceptible to troubles such as piles, fevers, small pox etc. He is also
likely to suffer from kidney trouble or bladder stone. Throat
trouble, bronchitis and laryngitis are also common to him. Being
under the influence of Saturn, he is susceptible to gout and
rheumatic troubles.

e) MARRIAGE AND FRIENDS

He is naturally attracted to persons born in the period between 20th April and 20th May, between 20th July and 20th
September and between 20th November and 20th January. He
also has affinity for those who are governed by the numbers 3
and 6. It is therefore advisable that he should select his wife
from these periods or numbers.

Number 9 as husband

He is vigorous in health and has strong circulation of blood
which makes him more passionate and enthusiastic about
married life. He is fond of a beautiful wife and likes her to be
submissive to his sexual desires. He is fond of his family and
children and likes to have good house. He usually leads a
good married life in spite of his hot-tempered nature and
eccentricities. He has a romantic expectation in his wife. This
mental picture of his wife demands perfection. The most difficult thing in the married life of a number 9 person is the satisfaction of his romantic conception of physical love. He has a
voracious appetite and his wife with devotion can find harmony
with him physically. Usually we find him suspicious about his
wife.

Number 9 as wife

She will make a wonderful wife for an ambitious man. She
is a witty and clever conversationalist with a wonderful social
presence. She will assist her husband in his business. She
may also work by herself and add to the family income. She

will be happy if married to a passionate and possessive man.
But there is some kind of unpleasantness in her married life.

Friends

A number 9 man is always attracted towards those who
have originality, creativity, activity and intelligence. His best
friends are those who are governed by numbers 1,2,4,6,7 and
9. He has also natural affinity towards people born in April,
July, October and in his own month, i.e January.

f) FORTUNATE DAYS : His lucky days are Mondays, Tuesdays
Thursdays and Fridays.

g) LUCKY COLOURS : He should use all shades of red,
white, grey and purple.

g) LUCKY JEWELS AND STONES : His lucky jewels are
topaz, pearl and ruby and
lucky stones are garnet
and moon stone.

i) IMPORTANT YEARS IN LIFE: His important years are 9,
18, 27, 36, 45, 54, 63, 72
etc.

j) HIS GOOD QUALITIES AND DRAWBACKS ARE AS UNDER:

Good qualities	Drawbacks
Activity	Destruction
Courage	Irritability
Dash	Hot temper
Energy	Impertinence
Enthusiasm	Quarrelsomeness

CHAPTER 10

BORN ON
1st, 1Oth, 19th and 28th of February

All those born on 1st, 10th, 19th and 28th of February of any year are governed by number 1 and the planet Sun. February is governed by the planet Saturn. Both these planets have strong personalities. The character reading explained below of number one is equally applicable to other dates also. In addition, special characteristics of those born on 10th, 19th and 28th February are given separately.

Born on 1st February

a) CHARACTER

This number is dominated by the Sun and shows brilliance, authority, confidence, determination, vigour, originality and activity. The number 1 man values honour, prestige and dignity. He is oversensitive and his feelings are easily hurt. He has strong intuition and can read people instinctively. His most outstanding quality is that he has a capacity to keep the secrets of others and relieve their distress and tension. He can give very sound advice and be in a place of trust. He is spontaneous and responds to nature and has the ability to enjoy life. He is usually successful in life because he can mix in any society. Though his social circle is large, he has a feeling of loneliness within himself which even his close friends and relatives will never know. He has many talents. Though he has an analytical mind and perserverance, he is changeable and finds it difficult to stick to one thing for a long time. Generally, he cannot go deep into any subject but with his intuition, he has a quick grasp of the subject and can participate in any discussion. He requires an opportunity to show his qualities but when he gets one, he surprises everyone by his hidden powers and abilities. He uses his energies and abilities for the good of others and usually leaves a name behind by his work for some cause of humanity or by some great invention that has brought unusual benefit to the world at large. He has great power over excitable people or those who are hysterical or insane and he will find himself thrown among such types in life. He has attraction for the mysterious and the unknown and is devoted to the study of occult and esoteric subjects. He is attached to his family and loves his wife. He can influence others with his knowledge and flash. These characteristics make him a hero of the drawing room. He has strong will-power and is independent in thought and action. His ideas about duty and social behaviour are unconventional and though he loves society, he sometimes does not easily get on with the neighbour unless the neighbour is intelligent and clever and does not interfere in other people's affairs.

By nature he is cheerful, happy and bright and his outlook on life is very optimistic. On the one hand he is practical, but on the other hand, he is idealistic. Sometimes he is obstinate and selfish. He is deeply interested in inventions and has creative talents but his changeable nature does not permit him to achieve anything in any field.

He is a better judge of human nature than the average individual. He is born to lead, not to follow. A new idea is a greater thrill than money in the bank. He will always be young by reason of a fresh idea.

Born on 10th February | you have all the basic characteristics of those born on the 1st of the month, so first go through them and then read your own.

A person born on the 10th of February has a good personality. He is respected for his knowledge and intelligence. He is very much attached to his family. He gets monetary benefits from his father, mother or his wife. He gets success after his 37th year and has prosperity after marriage. He gets a good position in service and succeeds in business also. He has broad shoulders and a manly figure. He usually has good health and quickly recovers from any illness. This number shows honour and confidence. He likes to help others but hardly gets a response from them. This is particularly true in the case of relatives.

Born on 19th February | you have all the basic characteristics of those born on the 1st of the month, so first go through them and then read your own.

Such a man is born in a lucky family and with a silver spoon in his mouth. He gets from his childhood, all the comforts which are normally available to an individual at a very late age. He has a good academic career but being very moody, does not like to concentrate on his studies. His interests are varied ; sports, music and reading are his main hobbies. Due to Saturn's influence, he has a philosophical mind. He may expect delays in his educational career. He has an aptitude for research and likes to handle a subject in a systematic and methodical way. He takes quick decisions and always likes to keep himself busy with some concrete project. He likes to help others even going out of his way. This number promises success, honour and happiness. Since the man's birth date is on the border of positive and negative Saturn, people find it difficult to understand him fully. He is obstinate and finds it difficult to extend co-operation. He is not an excellent speaker but can explain best in writing. He can be a good writer.

Born on 28th February | you have all the basic characteristics of those born on the 1st of the month, so first go through them and then read your own.

He is very generous and spends on charity such as schools, institutions, hospitals etc. He experiences difficulties in public and private life. He should be very careful in selecting his wife.

He has to provide carefully for the future as he is likely to lose through trust in others. He is also likely to make many changes in his career. He rarely reveals his emotions and therefore appears cold. He has unyielding will-power and does not hesitate to carry out his plans. The early years of his life will be full and active. Unexpected changes will take place in his family and plans made by them for him are not likely to be carried out. He is versatile and full of original ideas.

b) FINANCE

A person born on any of the above dates in February is a lucky person as far as his financial status is concerned. It is however necessary that he keeps under check his gambling nature and expectation of money in a short time. If he over-comes this habit, he can earn enough to satisfy his ostentatious disposition in life. He may not amass wealth but his persona-lity and behaviour will convey to others the impression that he is a rich person. Persons born on these dates who take up professions like those of doctors and lawyers are not likely to hoard money, but those engaged in banking, industries etc can be successful in their efforts to make money.   A person born on 28th February will be more lucky in his financial affairs. Even then due to the influence of Saturn, luck comes late.

c) VOCATION

Persons born on the 1st, 10th, 19th and 28th of February are self-willed in their career and therefore they do not remain long in the same service or activity. They always need a change and experience it every three to five years. However, such a man can shine in business such as cinema, advertising, interior decoration, music etc. wherein he can show his imagination. He is attracted towards foreign countries and can choose a suitable service or business whereby he can come in contact with agencies abroad, such as import-export business. He has a flair for writing and can be a good author.

d) HEALTH

He has to take care of his digestive system. He is also likely to have poor blood circulation, anaemia and palpitation of the heart. He should drink plenty of water so that he may not suffer from bladder and kidney troubles. His another weakness is his sore throat and trouble with the respiratory tract. He is very much medicine minded and is likely to buy any quack medicine.

e) MARRIAGE AND FRIENDS

Such a man has a natural attraction towards those born in the period 20th January to 20th February, 20th March to 20th June and 20th July to 20th October. He also has an affinity or those who are governed by the numbers 2,4,5 and 7. It is therefore advisable that he selects his bride from one of these periods or numbers. February being governed by Saturn, the person is also attracted towards the numbers 8,17 and 26.

Number 1 as husband

He is a loving, considerate, thoughtful and attentive husband. He loves his home and spends much of his time at home only. He is emotional and of a dreamy nature. His notions are more real to him than the facts of life. He therefore finds it difficult to cope with the realities and difficulties of life. He lacks stability, strength and realism in his career. He is very sensual and can be dangerously perverted by self-indulgence. Sexual satisfaction is very important to him and he seeks it persistently all his life. He wants his family members to dance to his tunes and will not tolerate disrespect. He treats his wife and family members with the same courtesy that he accords to strangers. He accepts marriage as a part of the domestic scheme and succeeds in it because of his attitude which contributes a great deal towards harmony at home. His drawback is his impersonality which his wife feels as lack of interest in domestic life.

Number 1 as wife

She is remarkably adaptable to family life. She likes a luxurious life and desires her house to be restful. She is a devoted, kind and sympathetic type of wife. She is a fine companion, capable, intelligent and talented. Her home is a social centre on account of her social and friendly manners. Her interests are wide and she does not like to watch how her husband spends his spare time. She is interested in dance and music. She is kind and would rather herself suffer than create a situation which would make others unhappy. She is aristocratic by temperament and attracts people to her home and commands great respect. She needs a virile husband who can provide her with the romantic outlets that her passionate nature requires.

A person born on the 1st, 10th, 19th or 28th of February is predisposed to marriage. He is fond of his helpmate provided she is also of equal enthusiasm and has a love of beauty and of dress, at home and in public. However, he hardly gets a companion of his choice, with the result that he is often disappointed in his married life.

Friends

He is always attracted towards those who have fellowship, imagination, honesty, love for travel and simplicity. His best friends are those who are governed by the numbers 1,3,5,7 and 9. He also has a natural affinity towards those born in May, August, November and in his own month, i.e. February.

f) FORTUNATE DAYS : His lucky days are Sundays, Wednesdays, Thursdays and Saturdays.

g) LUCKY COLOURS : He should use all shades of orange, purple, grey and violet.

h) LUCKY JEWELS AND STONES : His lucky jewels are Ruby, Topaz, Diamond and Amethyst

i) IMPORTANT YEARS IN LIFE : His important years are 1, 10, 19, 28, 37, 46, 55, 64, 73 etc.

j) HIS GOOD QUALITIES AND DRAWBACKS ARE AS UNDER:

Good Qualities	Drawbacks
Honour	Obstinacy
Dignity	Domination
Sensitiveness	Impertinence
A Good Advice	Inflexibility
Originality	Showmanship
Aspiration	Spendthrift nature
Authority	Aloofness
Determination	

CHAPTER 11

BORN ON
2nd, 11th, 20th and 29th of February

All those born on the 2nd, 20th and 29th of February are governed by number 2 and the planet Moon. The month February is governed by the planet Saturn. Both these planets have their peculiarities which can be seen in the individuals born on these dates. The characteristics explained below of number 2 are equally applicable to those born on the other dates also. In addition, special characteristics of those born on 11th, 20th and 29th of February are given separately.

Born on 2nd February

a) CHARACTER

This number is governed by the planet Moon. It shows high imagination, idealism and a dreamy nature. The person has fantasies and lacks a practical approach to life. He revels in his own dreams and therefore shuns society. He cannot enjoy the company of others as he finds them too ordinary for his imaginary world. He is somewhat nervous but social and is liked by others. He is warm-hearted and shows little resistance to oppression. He has noble sentiments. His birth in the month of February shows that he values honour, prestige and dignity. He is oversensitive and his feelings are easily hurt. In spite of his large contacts in society, he has a feeling of loneliness in life. He has strong intuition and can read people instinctively. An important thing about him is that he has a capacity to keep the secret of others and relieve their distress. He is capable of giving excellent advice to others and be in a

place of trust. He needs some opportunity to show his qualities. When he gets one, he surprises everyone by the hidden
powers and abilities he possesses. He will use his energies
and abilities for the good of others and usually leaves a name
behind by working for a cause of humanity or by some great
invention that has brought unusual benefit to the world at large.
He will have great powers over excitable people or those who
are hysterical or insane and he will find himself thrown among
such types in his life. He has an attraction for the mysterious
and the unknown and is devoted to the studies of occult and
esoteric subjects. He is attached to his family and loves his wife.

He loves nature and beautiful things in life such as the
sea, flowers, scenery and the vastness of the sky. He takes
pleasure in spending hours in the company of the high tides of
the sea or in rivetting his eyes to the galaxy of stars in the sky.

He is very unsteady, fickle-minded and a lover of change.
He therefore, has a fancy for travel, especially long travel
which satisfy his natural desire for imaginary things. Such
travels engage his imagination and he will go on building
castles in the air. He is unassuming but pleasing and has a
good taste in clothes. He likes peace and harmony. He has a
hypnotic power to attract others.

Persons born between 20th June and 20th July are also
governed by number 2.

ADDITIONAL CHARACTERISTICS OF THOSE BORN ON
THE 11TH, 20TH AND 29 TH OF FEBRUARY

Born on 11th February | you have all the basic characteristics of those born on the 2nd of the month, so first go through them and then read your own.

Such a man is usually successful in life and in love and
gets honour, position and authority. He is loyal to his friends
and is of a royal disposition. He should guard himself against
secret enemies. He has interest in mysticism, philosophy and
science. He can expect travels, favours, and honours in life.
He is very impulsive and gets excited easily. He worries too
much over small matters. He has an ability to take quick decisions and this makes him a leader. He is a born advertiser and
an inspiration to others.

Born on 20th February

you have all the basic characteristics of those born on the 2nd of the month, so first go through them and then read your own.

Such a man has many friends and benefits through wealthy women. He has a flair for writing and can be known as an author or a novelist. His prosperity lies near water, river or the sea. This number has a peculiar significance. It shows new plans and new resolutions for the betterment of people at large. If this number is used in connection with future events, it indicates delays.

Born on 29th February

you have all the basic characteristics of those born on the 2nd of the month, so first go through them and then read your own.

This person is moody and changing and therefore uncertain about his actions. He is courageous and bold but takes risks in life and does not stick to anything to the end. He is intelligent and also a deep thinker but there is a tendency to carry everything to extremes. He is not very lucky in his married life. His interest is in his business. He is blessed with good fortune. His life is eventful.

b) FINANCE

A person governed by this number is a lethargic fellow and he does not like hard work. He also finds it difficult to stand the strain of everyday life. The outcome, therefore, is a modest financial status. He however can improve his financial condition, provided he is able to create art out of his imagination. He may be a good author or a painter who can write novels and draw unusual paintings and earn a good livelihood. However, his unstable mind often drags him away from routine work and this creates an uncertain source of income. This person, therefore, is not stable as far as finance is concerned.

c) VOCATION

The high imaginative power possessed by the number 2 person will help him to be a good composer of music or a writer of stories or romance. He can also be a good artist and can create works of enduring value. Immortal paintings, dramas and poems will be the gifts of a prominent and influential number 2. He has a great vocabulary and linguistic mastery and

can be successful as a teacher or a professor of languages.
He can also be a good translator or an editor. The month of
February is governed by the planet Saturn and therefore
Saturnian characteristics will also be seen in his writing.
Saturn is sceptical, methodical, analytical and philosophical and
therefore these qualities can be seen in his writing or in his
profession.

d) HEALTH

His main health problem is his poor blood circulation. He
is susceptible to illness arising from poor blood circulation,
such as anaemia and weakness of heart.

Since the Moon is the ruling planet of number 2, uneasiness which is a prominent characteristic creates mental
worries and sleeplessness. The person is also susceptible to
diabetes and asthmatic trouble or trouble with the respiratory
track. He is also likely to suffer from Saturnian sickness, such
as, disorder of the bladder and kidneys and sore throat. He
will be inclined to buy any quack medicine.

e) MARRIAGE AND FRIENDS

He has a natural attraction towards those born in the period
between 20th January and 20th March, between 20th May and
20th June and between 20th September and 20th November.
He also has an affinity for those who are governed by numbers
2, 6 and 8. It is therefore advisable that he finds his wife from
one of these periods or numbers.

Number 2 as husband

He has a natural love and attraction for home more than
any other type. There are two types of husbands belonging to
this number. One is dominating and exacting. He is fault-
finding and nothing satisfies him. The other type is passsive,
lazy and indulgent. He will marry for the sake of money so
that he may ultimately get comforts.

He is very sensual and can be dangerously perverted by selfindulgence. Sexual satisfaction is very important to him and he seeks it persistently all his life. He is emotional and of a dreamy nature. His notions are more real to him than the facts of life. He therefore finds it difficult to cope with the realities and difficulties of life. He desires his family members to dance to his tunes and will not tolerate disrespect. He treats his wife and family members with the same courtesy that he accords to strangers. He loves his home and spends much of his time at home. His drawback is his impersonality which his wife feels as lack of interest in domestic life.

Number 2 as wife

She is devoted, affectionate and sympathetic. She is satisfied with anything her husband provides her with. However she is moody, changeable and sensitive. She likes a luxurious life and desires her house to be restful.

Friends

He has a fascination for those who are sober and philosophical. He likes friends with good imagination, who love literary activities and poetry. His best friends are those who are governed by the numbers 2, 4, 6 and 9.

f) FORTUNATE DAYS : His lucky days are Mondays, Tuesdays, Fridays and Saturdays. He should plan all his important actions on these days.

g) LUCKY COLOURS : A Number 2 person should use all shades of white, cream, blue and purple; he should choose clothes of these colours or paint his rooms with these colours.

h) LUCKY JEWELS AND STONES : He may wear pearls, diamonds and topaz.

i) IMPORTANT YEARS IN LIFE :   His important years are
                                2, 11, 20, 29, 38, 47, 56,
                                65, 74 etc.

j) HIS GOOD QUALITIES AND DRAWBACKS ARE AS UNDER:

Good qualities	Drawbacks
Emotionality	Coldness
Fellowship	Envy
Honesty	Haste
Imagination	Introvert
Simplicity	Shyness
Inspiration	Whimsicality

CHAPTER 12

BORN ON
3rd, 12th and 21st of February

All those born on the 3rd, 12th, and 21st February are governed by number 3 and the planet Jupiter. The month February is governed by the planet Saturn. Both these planets have strong personalities. The character reading of number three given below is equally applicable to the other dates also. In addition, special characteristics of those born on 12th and 21st are given separately.

Born on 3rd February

a) CHARACTER

The main characteristics of a number 3 person are ambition, leadership, piety, pride, honour, love of nature, enthusiasm, generosity, respect and reverence.

Number 3 is governed by the planet Jupiter. It stands for morality, pure love and justice with mercy and is known as the greatest benefactor. The vibrations emitted by this number are essentially harmonious and they lead to sympathy and untiring effort to do good to all, piety and true dignity. A number 3 man values honour, prestige and dignity. He is over-sensitive and is easily hurt. In spite of his large contacts in society, he has a feeling of loneliness in life. He requires some opportunity to show his qualities and when he gets one, he surprises everyone by his hidden powers and abilities. He will use his energies and abilities for the good of others and usually leaves behind a name by his work for a noble cause or by some great invention that has brought unusual benefit to the world at large. He has strong intuition and can read people instinctively. He also has the capacity to keep the secrets of others and relieve their distress. He will have great power over excitable people or those who are hysterical or insane and he will find himself thrown among such types in his journey through life.

He is usually lucky in life. Vibrations radiating through him attract all that is good to him and his affairs prosper as a consequence. The judge who gives sane decisions and merciful sentences, the helpful physician and the kindly church dignitary, the world's best teachers and philosophers are all mostly governed by number 3.

This is a good number. A number 3 person is confident about his abilities. He is self-reliant and takes his own decisions. He has the habit of talking loudly. He is fond of show and likes to observe form, order and law. He is jovial in spirit and cordial in manner. His passions are healthy, spontaneous and without inhibitions. He is free in his expression and is a good conversationalist.

He takes a great interest in sports and outdoor activities from his earlier youth. He has tremendous enthusiasm and is not self-centred. His intellect is of a very high quality. He has a mind that understands the world and loves it for what it is and not for what it ought to be. He is a broad-minded person, tolerant, humorous and truthful. He is open-hearted with good understanding and entirely lacking in malice or petty jealousies. If he is not alert, people take advantage of his good nature. He has an attraction for the mysterious and the unknown and is devoted to the study of occult and esoteric subjects. He is attached to his family and loves his wife.

Born on 12th February you have all the basic characteristics of those born on the 3rd of the month, so first go through them and then read your own.

Authority and honour are the significant aspects of this person. He has vanity and is proud, ambitious and aspiring. He is fond of pleasure and is attracted to the opposite sex. However, sometimes he prefers loneliness. He likes to make sacrifices for others but becomes a victim of others' plans or intrigues. His relations with others are smooth and harmonious. He is quick to notice trifles. He has lofty ideals.

Born on 21st February

you have all the basic characteristics of those born on the 3rd of the month, so first go through them and then read your own.

He is kind and generous and is a loving father. He achieves fame, reputation and honours at a very late age. He is cheerful and fond of travels. He has a strong sense of self-respect. Surprisingly, he has a suspicious nature.

b) FINANCE

He is a lucky type and somehow manages to earn enough for his livelihood. He also gets opportunities for high positions in life and thereby earns quite a lot. His ambition, qualities of leadership and enthusiasm always push him forward and usually he gets all the comforts in life. The number 3 person is early out of puberty and poverty.

c) VOCATION

His love for position and command makes him a politician. I have seen certain persons of this number occupying very high posts such as those of ministers, ambassadors, judges and secretaries. Such a man is gifted for public life and for high offices etc., be it in the army or in the church. He is a good teacher as well as a good preacher. Professions such as those of doctors, bankers, advertisers and actors are also suitable for him.

d) HEALTH

Number 3 has considerable influence on the blood and the arterial system. It also governs the sense of smell. This person is liable to suffer from chest and lung disorders, throat afflictions, gout and apoplexy and sudden fevers. He may suffer from diphtheria, adenoids, pleurisy and tuberculosis of the lungs.

e) MARRIAGE AND FRIENDS

He has a natural attraction towards those born in the period

20th January to 20th February, 20th May to 20th July and 20th September to 20th November. He also has an affinity for those governed by the numbers 3, 6 and 9. The month February being governed by Saturn, the person is also attracted towards those who are born on 8, 17 and 26 of any month. It is therefore advisable that he selects his wife from one of these periods or numbers.

Number 3 as husband

As a general rule, he attains puberty at an early age and marries early. However as he is ambitious, his ambition also makes him expect too many things from his wife and so he becomes disappointed. He desires to have a wife of whom he can be proud. She should have an attractive personality, commanding presence, charming manners and intelligence. It is always better for him to choose a number 3 person or a number 6 person as his wife. He is most loving, thoughtful and considerate. His passions are adventurous and demand immediate satisfaction.

Number 3 as wife

She is the best companion to her husband. She is not an intruder but takes active interest in the business of her husband. She is efficient in house-keeping and has a sympathetic and balanced attitude towards children. Her passions are healthy and joyous and her approach to physical love is highly refined. She is remarkably adapted to family life. She likes a luxurious life and desires her house to be a haven. She is a devoted, kind and sympathetic type of wife.

Friends

A number 3 man is naturally attracted towards those who are endowed with the power of imagination, those who love nature and like to travel and also have interest in mysticism. He has an affinity towards those born in May, August, November and in his own month, i.e. February. His best friends are those who are governed by numbers 3, 6, 7 and 9.

f) FORTUNATE DAYS : His lucky days are Tuesdays, Thursdays and Fridays. He should try to plan his important moves on these days.

g) LUCKY COLOURS : He should use all shades of yellow, violet, purple and green as his lucky colours.

h) LUCKY JEWELS AND STONES : His lucky jewels are diamond and topaz and lucky stones are cat's eye and amethyst.

i) IMPORTANT YEARS IN LIFE : His important years are 3, 12, 21, 30, 39, 48, 57, 66, 75, etc.

j) HIS GOOD QUALITIES & DRAWBACKS ARE AS UNDER :

Good qualities	Drawbacks
Ambition	Cruelty
Dignity	Dictatorship
Individuality	Hypocrisy
Philosophy	Spendthrift nature
Prestige	Vanity

CHAPTER 13

BORN ON
the 4th, 13th and 22nd of February

All those born on the 4th, 13th and 22nd of February of any year are governed by number 4 and the planet Uranus. February is dominated by the planet Saturn. Both these planets have their own peculiar and strong characterisics· The reading given below of number 4 is equally applicable to other dates also. Hower, in addition, special characteristics of those born on the 13th and 22nd of February are given separately.

Born on 4th February

a) CHARACTER

This number is governed by the planet Uranus and shows energy, force and advancement. It shows revolution and un-expected happenings in life. Usually the changes that take place are for the better. This number represents the higher faculties of the mind. It shows activity and intelligence enga-ged in the reconstruction or the betterment of human life. The peculiar nature of this person is that he constanly aims at chan-ges in life and society and seeks the liberation of the mind from the bondage of environment and society. He dislikes hypocrisy and loves art and music. He has an attractive personality.

This number is considered as the negative part of number 1. It has same characteristics as those of number 1, but these characteristics are in a dormant state. It means that a number 4 person needs to be pushed forward so that he can show his abilities. He is methodical in his own way. He has a bad habit of forcing his opinions on others· He has a keen, analytical and logical mind.

Because of his peculiar characteristic of opposing the views
of others or starting arguments, he is often misunderstood and
makes a great number of secret enemies who constantly work
against him. He values honour, prestige and dignity. He is
oversensitive and is easily hurt in feelings. In spite of his large
contacts in society, he has a feeling of loneliness in life. He
has strong intuition and can read people intuitively. He can
keep the secrets of others and relieve their distress. He can
give excellent advice to others and be in a place of trust. He
requires some opportunity to show his qualities and when he
gets one, he surprises everyone by the hidden powers and abilities he possesses. He uses his energies and abilities for the
good of others and usually leaves a name behind by his work
for a noble cause or by some great invention that brings unusual benefit to the world at large. He will have great power
over excitable people or those who are hysterical or insane and
he will find himself thrown among such types in his journey
through life. He has an attraction for the mysterious and the
unknown and is devoted to studies of occult and esoteric
subjects. He is attached to his family and loves his wife.

Born on 13th February

you have all the basic characteristics of those born on the 4th of the month, so first go through them and then read your own.

He is an intelligent person, of tall stature and good complexion. He is considerate and benevolent. He likes literary
and scientific books. He likes to remain active though in a
quiet way. He occupies positions of high responsibilities and
gets riches. His success and career start after his 31st year.
Though outwardly he looks mild, inwardly he is obstinate. He
is faithful and sympathetic but has difficulty in expressing his
love. He has all the qualities of number 4 but in an exaggerated form.

Born on 22nd February

you have all the basic characteristics of those born on the 4th of the month, so first go through them and then read your own.

He is also tall and has good eyes. Usually he occupies
good positions but without much responsibility. He is rather
easygoing but unsteady by nature. Sometimes his actions are
spasmodic. On the whole he is lucky in his affairs and bene-

fits from the opposite sex. He is happy in his family life but is also fond of a companion. He is faithful and dedicated to others. Sometimes, he feels very lonely. His social field is limited and he has few friends. He does not care for disputes. He has too much economy of sentiments.

b) FINANCE

As regards finance and monetary status, he is usually well settled in life though he experiences delays and difficulties in his undertakings. He may not amass wealth but can maintain the show of riches. He is a spendthrift. His home is well-decorated. His financial prosperity usually starts after the age of 40

c) VOCATION

He will be successful in trades such as transport, electricity and all sorts of machinery. He will be equally successful as an engineer, building contracter or scientist and industrialist. He is also attracted towards mystic subjects such as palmistry and astrology and can do well in these subjects also.

d) HEALTH

His respiratory system is usually weak and he suffers from breathlessness. His knees, shanks and feet are also affected. Sometimes he suffers from urinary infection. Poor blood circulation, anaemia, palpitation and weakness of the heart and disorder of the bladder and kidneys are the main health defects. He will be inclined to buy any quack medicine.

e) MARRIAGE AND FRIENDS

He has a natural attraction towards those born in the period 20th January to 20th March, 20th May to 20th June and 20th September to 20th October. He also has an affinity for those who are born on the 8th, 17th or 26th of any month. It is therefore advisable that he selects his marriage partner from one of these periods or numbers.

Number 4 as husband

He is shrewd and intelligent and expects his wife to share his views. He is dominating and wants all affairs of the house to run according to his wishes. He is generous and has a kind and loving heart. He loves his home and spends much of his time at home. He is emotional and his notions are more real to him than the facts of life. He therefore finds it difficult to cope with the realities and difficulties of life. He lacks stability, strength and realism in his career. He is sensual and can be dangerously perverted by self-indulgence. Sexual satisfaction is very important to him and he seeks it persistently all his life.

Number 4 as wife

She is remarkably adapted to family life. She likes a luxurious life and desires her house to be a haven. She is a devoted, kind and sympathetic type of wife. She is smart and attractive. She has the art of dressing and has a strong willpower. She aims at several things but hardly succeeds in getting mastery over one. She loves interior decoration but does not have the capacity to work hard at it and she will get it done through others. She is many a time dictatorial and moody and spoils her day because of her own whimsical nature. Though she loves her home, she is not attached to it very much. Many a time she is uneasy and it is better for her to find a friend governed by number one or two.

Friends

A number 4 man is fond of friends and company but hardly gets a close friend because of his unsteady, changing and moody nature. He will get as his close friends persons who are influenced by number 1, 2. 7. 8.

f) FORTUNATE DAYS : Sundays, Mondays and Saturdays are lucky days.

g) LUCKY COLOURS : White, grey and violet are lucky colours.

h) LUCKY JEWELS AND STONES :   Diamond, pearl and topaz
                                        are his lucky jewels.

I) IMPORTANT YEARS IN LIFE :   His important years are, 4,
                                        13, 22, 31, 40, 49, 58, 67,
                                        76 etc.

j) HIS GOOD QUALITIES AND DRAWBACKS ARE AS UNDER:

Good qualities	Drawbacks
Activity	Changeablity
Endurance	Domination
Energy	Stubbornness
Reliability	Vindictiveness
Method and system	Jealousy

CHAPTER 14

BORN ON
5th, 14th, and 23rd of February

All those born on the 5th, 14th and 23rd of February of any year are governed by number 5 and the planet Mercury. The month of February is governed by the planet Saturn. Both planets influence the individual's personality. The character reading given below relating to number 5 is equally applicable to other dates. In addition, the special characteristics of those born on the 14th and 23rd of February are given separately.

Born on 5th February
a) CHARACTER

This number is governed by the planet Mercury and It shows shrewdness, quickness, scientific pursuits, business ability, industry, intuition and diplomacy. A person governed by this number is active and quick; this does not relate to physical agility but only to the mental side. He is very skilful and has intuition. He is equally proficient in games-where he uses his hands as well as his brain. He has the capacity to judge the ability of his opponents in games and knows very well how to take advantage of the weak points of his opponents. He loves oratory and is eloquent in expressing himself. He has the capacity to pursue his objectives and knows very well how to plan for his ends. He is deeply interested in occult subjects and has a desire to master all the intricacies of such abtruse subjects. He possesses a pleasant character and dislikes inactivity. He is sociable and has many acquaintances. He is fond of variety and change and trips and travel. Whatever the situation, he can master it.

He value's honour, prestige and dignity. He can keep the secrets of others and relieve their distress. He can give excellent advice and be in a place of trust.

He is a nervous person. He is therefore restless. He has the potentiality both for goodness and for badness. On the good side, he is a shrewd person and not vicious or criminal. He is fond of family life and loves his children. He is amiable and adaptable but businesslike.

Born on 14th February you have all the basic characteristics of those born on the 5th of the month, so first go through them and then read your own.

Such a person has an attractive personality and is liked by all. His nature is co-operative and he does not like to offend others. He usually occupies a good position in life and is successful in his business. He is not talkative but slightly reserved. This is a number of intelligence and shrewdness. For women, it indicates good marriage but they should take care in child-bearing. A number 14 man is inconsistent in love and experiences some romantic and impulsive attachment in early years. He is fortunate in money matters. He is industrious and positive in speech and action. Usually he is fond of gambling and solving riddles

Born on 23rd February you have all the basic characteristics of those born on the 5th of the month, so first go through them and then read your own.

He is usally popular among women. His fortune is near the water. He is successful in life and enjoys honour and wealth. He may get money through inheritance. He keeps busy in his own way. He gets help and protection from superiors He is a lucky person. He is affectionate and loves freedom. He is averse to formalities. · He has a spirit of independence and a desire to dominate.

b) FINANCE

Since number 5 is a business number, the person can expect opulence. With his shrewdness he is capable of developing his industry and carrying out his plans systematically, with the result that he gets returns for his efforts. On the whole he is lucky as far as his financial position is concerned.

It is to be noted that the planet Saturn, which has influence over the month of February, causes delays in life in all respects and therefore delays the recovery of dues by a number 5 person.

c) VOCATION

He is adaptable to the role he has to play in the drama of life. He comes in contact with various classes of people and becomes successful in any business. Banking is a good vocation for him. The planet Mercury also shows ability for medicine or surgery. His capacity to argue his points can make him a good lawyer.

d) HEALTH

His basic health defect is his biliousness and nervousness. However his biliousness has close relation with his psychological disturbance. Experience shows that his biliousness increases with the increase in tension and is reduced or disappears when his nervous trouble is under control. Number 5 rules over nerves, the neck, arms, the ears and the respiratory system. February is dominated by Saturn and therefore poor blood circulation, anaemia, palpitation and weakness of the heart and disorder of the bladder and kidneys are also common complaints. Being born in February, the man is inclined to buy any quack medicine.

e) MARRIAGE AND FRIENDS

He has a natural attraction towards those born in the period between 20th January and 20th February, 20th May and 20th June and between 20th September and 20th October. He also has an affinity for those who are governed by number 1, 7 and 8. It is therefore advisable that he selects his wife from one of these periods or numbers.

Number 5 as husband

He is lucky and successful in his married life. His selection is good and usually he selects a person of his own type.

He loves his partner. He expects neatness and cleanliness from his partner and also desires that his partner should share in the enjoyment of life. He is proud of his wife and likes to see her well-dressed. In return, he proves himself to be a good husband. He loves his children and is fond of his home. Even if he travels long, he is very much attracted towards his home and is eager to return to his family. He is liberal in spending on clothing and other wants of the members of his family and furnishes his house with good taste. He is very sensual and sexual satisfaction is very important to him and he seeks it persistently all his life.

Number 5 as wife

She likes a luxurious life and desires her house to be a place of rest. She has intetest in her home as well as in outside activities which she manages well. She likes tidiness and though she seldom does her own work, she gets it done through her commanding personality. She is a devoted, kind and sympathetic type of wife.

Friends

The month of birth shows one's social circle. Since this month is February, the man has a fascination towards those who have number 2 and have fellowship, honesty, imagination and simplicity. A number two person likes to travel and enjoy nature's beauty. A Number 5 person prefers the company of such friends. He also has his best friends who are governed by numbers 1, 3, 4, 5, 7 and 8.

f) FORTUNATE DAYS : Wednesdays, Fridays and Saturdays are his lucky days; he should take all his important steps on these days.

g) LUCKY COLOURS : He should use white, green and purple colours in his clothes or in painting the room walls. He should avoid red colour as far as possible.

h) LUCKY JEWELS AND STONES : His lucky jewels are emerald and diamond. He may also use amethyst or topaz.

i) IMPORTANT YEARS IN LIFE : His important years are 5, 14, 23, 32, 41, 50, 59, 68, 77 etc.

j) HIS GOOD QUALITIES AND DRAWBACKS ARE AS UNDER.

Good Qualities	Drawbacks
Co-operation	Lack of perseverance
Practical approach	Scepticism
Shrewdness	Unreliability
Vigilance	

CHAPTER 15

BORN ON
6th, 15th and 24th of February

All those born on the 6th, 15th and 24th of February of any year are governed by the number 6 and the planet Venus. February is governed by the planet Saturn. Both these planets have their peculiarities which can be seen in the individuals born on these dates. The characteristics explained below of number 6 are equally applicable to the other dates. In addition, special characteristics of those born on the 15th and the 24th of February are given separately.

Born on 6th February

a) CHARACTER

This number is governed by the planet Venus which stands for love, sympathy and adoration. A person governed by this number is a born artist and art and beauty in life have an attraction for him. He is a pleasant person to meet. It is always charming to be with him. He is full of enthusiasm, energy and charm. His talk is interesting and lively. We may sometimes be required to put aside our ideas of morality and social conduct in understanding and appreciating his feelings and discussions. Number 6 stands for beauty, health, vitality, warmth, attraction and, above all, love. A person of this number is fond of music, dancing and poetry. He loves to have a life full of ease and luxuries, money and happiness. He prefers spending to saving. He will have rich clothes, jewellery, perfumes and all sorts of beautiful things. Because of his birth in the month of February he values honour, prestige and dignity, He is oversensitive and is easily hurt. In spite of his large contacts in society, he has a feeling of loneliness in life. He has strong intuition and can read people intuitively. An important thing about him is that he can keep the secrets of others and relieve their distress. He is capable of giving excellent advice to others and can be in a place of trust. He needs some opportunity to show his qualities and when he gets one, he surprises everyone by his hidden powers and abilities. He uses his energies and abilities for the good of others and usually leaves a name behind by his service in a great cause or by some great invention that has brought unusual benefit to the world at large. He will have great power over excitable people or those who are hysterical or insane and he will find himself thrown among such types in his journey through life. He has an attraction for the mysterious and the unknown, and is devoted to the study of occult and esoteric subjects. He is attached to his family and loves his wife.

He is necessarily a loving type and has a feeling of kinship and humanity. He will therefore not desert his friends. He wishes to understand the grievances and difficulties of others. He prefers joy to gloom and has the capacity to make others share the moments of enjoyment. His outlook is bright and vivacious.

He is emotional but keeps his emotions to himself. His anger is slow to subside. He is very responsive and loves his children, but receives very little happiness from them. He is a born advisor and needs an audience with whom he can share his views on matters of importance. He is a good conversationalist and enjoys intellectual combats.

Born on 15th February

you have all the basic characteristics of those born on the 6th of the month, so first go through them and then read your own.

This person has intelligence and good memory. He is fit for responsible positions such as those of ambassadors, consuls, governors etc. He is very ambitious and boastful but hasty and proud by nature. He is interested in the lower

type of occultism. He has interest in art and music also.
He appears to be gentle but has very strong convictions.
He has a habit of worrying inwardly and leads a melancholy
life. It is his fate to make sacrifices for others.

Born on 24th February | you have all the basic characteristics of those born on the 6th of the month, so first go through them and then read your own.

He is fortunate in getting assistance from people of high
rank. He benefits through the opposite sex. His prosperity
is after marriage and he marries a rich girl. He succeeds in
speculation and enjoys a good monetary status. He defines
strictly the line between personal and other matters. He is
methodical in his ideas. He possesses a strong ego and some
times tries to force his opinions on others.

b) FINANCE

He is not attracted towards money. Accumulation of wealth
is not his aim in life. He is solely interested in enjoying
pleasures and gratifying his desires. He therefore spends his
earnings on whatever attracts him. He also never repents
having spent his money on his art which may not ultimately
give him monetary rewards. Such a man is rarely opulent
but he somehow has the knack of making both ends meet and
having minimum comforts. He may sometimes be lucky and
have windfalls.

c) VOCATION

He will shine as an interior decorator, architect, jeweller,
musician, hotel manager or a confectioner. He can be equally
successful as a broker, estate broker or as a commission agent.

d) HEALTH

On the whole he is a healthy person. However, he is
susceptible to epidemic fever and influenza. Occasionally,
he is prone to nervousness but not in a chronic way. Since
he is governed by Saturn he is prone to suffer from bladder
and kidney troubles. His another weakness is a sore throat

and difficulty with the respiratory tract. He is very much medicine minded and may buy any quack medicine.

e) MARRIAGE AND FRIENDS

He has a natural attraction towards those born in the period 20th December to 20th February, 20th May to 20th June and 20th August to 20th October. He also has an affinity for those who are governed by numbers 2, 4, 6 and 9. It is therefore advisable that he selects his marriage partner from one of these periods or numbers.

Number 6 as husband

He likes marriage and usually marries early in life. He expects his partner to be neat and have charm and grace. His is usually a large family with many children. He loves his children and home. He is very kind, generous and devoted. Though he creates a lively atmosphere in the house, he somehow finds it difficult to satisfy all the needs of the members of his family. This may sometimes create unpleasantness and make him unhappy. Art is everything to him. He remains impractical and does not understand material values.

Number 6 as wife

She never resorts to divorce and endures extreme hardship rather than desert her mate. She is a devoted mother and loving wife, satisfied with her husband's efforts in her behalf. She loves domestic life and is a perfect housewife.

Friends .

The month of birth shows one's social circle. A man born in February has a fascination for those who have number 2 and have fellowship, honesty, imagination and simplicity. He also likes those who are sober and philosophical. His best friends are those who are governed by numbers 2, 3, 4, 6 and 9.

f) FORTUNATE DAYS : His lucky days are Mondays, Thursdays, Fridays and Saturdays.

g) LUCKY COLOURS : A number 6 person should use all shades of blue, rose, and purple. It is better he avoids yellow colour.

h) LUCKY JEWELS AND STONES : He can use emerald, pearl, diamond and topaz.

i) IMPORTANT YEARS IN LIFE: His important years are 6, 15, 24, 33, 42, 51, 60, 69, 78 etc.

j) HIS GOOD QUALITIES AND DRAWBACKS ARE AS UNDER:

Good qualities	Drawbacks
Harmony	Absence of foresight
Love	Interference
Peace	Moodiness
Strong memory	Timidity

CHAPTER 16

BORN ON
7th, 16th and 25th of February

All those born on the 7th, 16th, and 25th of February of any year are governed by the planet Neptune and number 7. The month February is governed by the planet Saturn. Both these planets have their influence on the individuals born on these dates. The characteristics explained below relating to number 7 are equally applicable to other dates; the special characteristics of those born on 16th and 25th of February are given separately.

Born on 7th February

a) CHARACTER

This number is governed by the planet Neptune and has the same qualities as those of number 2 which is governed by the planet Moon. This person likes to visit foreign countries and becomes interested in far off lands. He has peculiar ideas about religion and dislikes following the beaten track. He has individuality and is original and independent.

He is like a free bird and likes to break the bondage and restrictions of tradition. It is possible that the greatest of the prophets and spiritualists have the planet Neptune dominating them. This man's behaviour is a mystery to others and he is often absentminded. He is stubborn and disregards the opinions of others. This is a spiritual number and Supreme Consciousness is developed in this individual. He thinks logically and achieves great aims. He has a talent for earning money. He desires the best or none at all. He is sensitive

and hides his real feelings by apparent indifference. He prefers
to spend his free hour with his favourite books. He dislikes
mingling with common people. When his opinion is solicited,
he speaks with authority. He knows his ground.

Since he is born in the month of February, he also acquires
the qualities of the planet Saturn. He therefore sometimes
feels lonely in life. He has a strong intuition and can read
people intuitively. He can keep the secrets of others and
relieve their distress. When he is given an opportunity, he
surprises everyone by his hidden powers and abilities. He will
have great power over excitable people and he will find himself
thrown among such types in his life. He is attached to his
family and loves his wife.

Born on 16th February | you have all the basic characteristics of those born on the 7th of the month, so first go through them and then read your own.

He is rather easygoing and does not like to work hard.
He is good-humoured and generous. He is very sensitive and
emotional. He soon gets upset but is soon pleased. He is
frequently indisposed. He is fortunate in having good and
successful children. However, there is some sort of sorrow in
his married life. He appears to be calm but his mind is always
in turmoil and he is sometimes short-tempered. He will not
disclose his nervousness and is slow in taking decisions. He
does not like interference.

Born on 25th February | you have all the basic characteristics of those born on the 7th of the month, so first go through them and then read your own.

He is a jack of all trades but master of none. He is
interested in several subjects but does not have the capacity
to go into details. His knowledge therefore is very shallow.
He likes to travel and has connections with foreign countries.
He is honest, faithful and good-natured. But he is fickle-
minded and inconsistent. His memory is good and he is a
good orator or teacher.

b) FINANCE

Usually, there are a number of changes in the life of a number
7 person and therefore it is difficult for him to amass wealth.

However, this being a mystic number, the person can be well placed in life provided he finds a job of his choice. In that case, he can be a wealthy person with all amenities and comforts.

c) VOCATION

His love of sea travel and interest in foreign countries make him a successful merchant, exporter or importer. He can also deal in dairy products, fishery, chemical industry and other products such as soap etc. He can also study medicine and surgery.

d) HEALTH

His main trouble is his nervous constitution and all his illness will be due to his nervousness. He is liable to suffer from faulty blood circulation, stomach disorder and fever. Being governed by the planet Saturn he is also likely to suffer from a sore throat and difficuilty with the respiratory track. He may also suffer from bladder and kidney troubles.

e) MARRIAGE AND FRIENDS

He has a natural attraction towards those who are born in the period 20th January to 20th March, 20th May to 20th June and 20th September to 20th November. He also has an affinity for those who are governed by numbers 3, 5 and 8. It is therefore advisable that he selects his wife from one of these periods or numbers.

Number 7 as husband

He is very emotional and understands the feelings of his wife. He is very considerate and will never try to impose his ideas on his wife. He is liberal, fond of picnics, travel and cinema theatres. He is a spendthrift and likes to live lavishly. His family is moderate in size and has all comforts.

Number 7 as wife

She is very moody and her behaviour is unpredictable.

She is very uneasy and gets disturbed over small matters. She is good at entertaining friends and she likes to invite people to a party or dinner. She expects her husband to look after her all the time.

FRIENDS

Since the man's birth month is February, he has a fascination for those who have number 2 and have fellowship, honesty, imagination and simplicity. He is also attracted owards numbers 1, 3, 5, 7, 8 and 9.

f) FORTUNATE DAYS

His lucky days are Mondays, Wednesdays and Thursdays. He should take his decisions and actions on these days, especially when the date is also 7th or 16th or 25th of the month.

g) LUCKY COLOURS : He should use all shades of green, yellow and violet.

h) LUCKY JEWELS AND STONES : His lucky jewels are topaz, diamond and cat's eye.

i) IMPORTANT YEARS IN LIFE : His important years are 7, 16, 25, 34, 43, 52, 61, 70, 79 etc.

j) HIS GOOD QUALITIES AND DRAWBACKS ARE AS UNDER:

Good Qualities	Drawbacks
Austerity	Despondency
Peace	Diffidence
Reflection	Restlessness
Serenity	Whimsicality
Tolerance	---

CHAPTER 17

BORN ON
the 8th, 17th, 26th of February

All those born on the 8th, 17th and 26th of February of any year are governed by the planet Saturn and number 8. February is also governed by Saturn. So the persons born on the above dates have powerful charactestics shown by Saturn. The characteristics endowed by number 8 are equally applicable to the other dates also. In addition special characterstics of those born on the 17th and 26th of February are given separately.

Born on 8th February

a) CHARACTER

This number is governed by Saturn and shows an extreme sense of discipline, steadfastness, constancy and dutifulness. He has a sober and solitude-loving personality. He is a lover of classical music but mostly of the melancholy type. In arts he loves landscapes, natural scenery and flowers. Number 8 is considered to be a balance-wheel to the character. The man can look at the other side of the coin. He is a pessimist. He prefers solitude to company. He is cautious about the future and he takes decisions very carefully on matters which pertain to mundane affairs. He is a prudent person, wise and sober. He is never overenthusiastic and is more or less gloomy and melancholy. He is also ambitious and persevering. He is capable of enormous effort for the attainment of what he seeks. He is sceptical and analytical. He is creative, productive and dominating. He is likely to be misunderstood. He usually feels lonely at heart. He understands the weak and oppressed and treats them in a warm-hearted manner. He is a born manager who can keep others busy. He admires fair play and is willing to pay a fair price. He has a good memory for names and faces.

Born on 17th February

you have all the basic characteristics of those born on the 8th of the month, so first go through them and then read your own.

Such a man is a good organiser and a good thinker. He has a creative and constructive mind. He is a lover of peace and a philanthropist. He is attracted towards occultism. He is courageous and proud. He has strong individualism. He is highly inteligent and clever. As regards emotions, he is calm. At times he is generous to a fault and at times very stingy. He is interested in research and loves knowledge. He is conservative and dominating.

Born on 26th February

you have all the basic characteristics of those born on the 8th of the month, so first go through them and then read your own.

This man wants to enjoy life without doing anything. He is sluggish and lethargic. He revels in wine and women and is fickle minded. He is careless about the number of children. He is lucky in money matters and gets easy money. He is smart but lacks positiveness. He likes to put up a good appearance but has a worrying nature. He has problems in his love affairs.

b) FINANCE

The peculiarity of number 8 is the delay in life in all respects. Naturally in financial matters also there is delay and stability is achieved at a very late age. This person has to work hard and he seldom succeeds in getting opulence. He has therefore to avoid number 8 playing a part in his life; instead, he can choose number 1 or 3 for all important actions and moves. However, if his experience shows that 8 is a lucky number for him, he can insist on that number only, and then can gain prosperity. If 8 is found to be a lucky number in one's life, one can try lotteries and luck in horse racing. But usually this number is connected with delays and hard work, and a person has to be very cautious in financial matters.

c) VOCATION

Subjects suitable for him are occult sciences, chemistry, physics, medicine and even higher mathematics. He can be successful in industries dealing with coal mines, timber etc. and in construction companies. He can be a good accountant and also a good administrator. However, as stated earlier, he has to strive hard in his career and he can get the fruits of his hard work only in the later years of his life.

d) HEALTH

His main health problems are nervousness, irritation, trouble with legs, teeth and ears, paralysis and rheumatism. He is of bilious type and often suffers from chronic melancholia. It is very interesting to note that the delaying characteristic of his number is also observed in his illness. The ailments he suffers from also take a long time to cure. Varicose veins and haemorrhoids are a common tendency of a strong 8 personality.

e) MARRIAGE AND FRIENDS

He has a natural attraction for those born in the period 20th January to 20th February, 20th April to 20th June and 20th August to 20th October. He also has an affinity for those who are governed by numbers 5, 7 and 8. It is therefore advisable that he selects his marriage partner from one of these periods or members.

Number 8 as husband

Basically, a number 8 person does not have the desire to get married. He prefers loneliness. He has less attraction for the opposite sex. Usually he tries to postpone his marriage with the result that if at all he marries, it is at a very late age. He also finds it difficult to choose a girl. As he prefers seclusion to a gathering, he often makes his married life miserable. He is very orthodox in his views and does not allow his wife to adopt modern ideas in dress at home or in public places. The natural result is disappointment on the part of his wife and hatred for her husband. If, however, he has a desire to be successful in married life, he should prefer a person who is also interested in deep and serious studies and likes to devote herself to philosophy and occult subjects.

Being born in February, he is a loving, considerate, thoughtful and attentive husband. He loves his home and spends much of his time at home only. He is emotional and of a dreamy nature. His notions are more real to him than the facts of life. He therefore finds it difficult to cope with the realities and difficulties of life. He lacks stability, strength and realism in his career. He is very sensual and can be dangerously perverted by self-indulgence. Sexual satisfaction is very important to him and he seeks it persistently all his life.

Number 8 as wife

She is remarkably adapted to family life. She likes a luxurious life and desires her house to be a haven. She is a devoted, kind and sympathetic wife. She has a masculine personality. She is capable and systematic. She enjoys her family life and likes to make sacrifices for her children and for the ambition of her husband. Her fault is that she lacks feminine warmth, sentiment and delicacy.

Friends

A man of this category is always attracted towards those who have fellowship, imagination, love for travel and simplicity. His best friends are those who are governed by numbers 3, 4, 5, 7 and 8. He has a natural affinity towards those born in May, August and November and in his own month, i e February.

f) FORTUNATE DAYS : His lucky days are Wednesdays, Thursdays and Saturdays and he should plan all his important actions on these days.

g) LUCKY COLOUR : He should use dark grey, dark blue and purple.

h) LUCKY JEWELS AND STONES : His lucky jewels are sapphire amethyst and back diamond.

i) IMPORTANT YEARS IN LIFE : His import years are 8, 17, 26, 35, 44, 53, 62, 71 etc.

j) HIS GOOD QUALITIES AND DRAWBACKS ARE AS UNDER:

Good qualities	Drawbacks
Authoritative	Cynical
Methodical	Delaying
Practical approach	Vindictive
Steady	Nervous
Systematic	Lazy

CHAPTER 18

BORN ON
9th, 18th and 27th of February

All those born on 9th, 18th and 27th of February of any year, are governed by the planet Mars. February is governed by the planet Saturn. Both these planets have strong personalities. The character reading explained below of number 9 is equally applicable to the other dates. In addition, special characteristics of those born on 18th and 27th February are given separately.

Born on 9th February

a) CHARACTER

This number is governed by Mars and shows aggression, resistance, courage, dash and quickness. A Martian is considered as a fighter. He is aggressive in all his acts and will not stop till he achieves his end. He has the capacity to fight even against adverse elements and circumstances. A Martian does not know defeat and if we have an army of Martians, there would not be anything like defeat for them. It would be either victory or death. It is said that the great Emperor Napoleon Bonaparte was a believer in this science and he had a battalion of soldiers who were pure Martians. A number 9 person is not very tactful or delicate in his talk but his intention is good and his vigorous manner should not be taken for rough behaviour. He should not criticize others and he should use his words carefully; otherwise they will boomerang on him.

Being born in the month of February, he values honour,

prestige and dignity. In spite of his large contacts in society, he has a feeling of loneliness in his life. He will use his energies and abilities for the good of others and usually leaves a good name behind.

He is fiery and dashing and does not have sickly senti- ments. He has audacity and vigour from start to finish. He is also fond of games and vigorous exercise. When the date of the month is 9 and the total of all the digits of the birth date is also 9, he is governed by a strong number 9 and his Mars is very powerful. In such a case, he has strong sexual passions and he is attracted towards the opposite sex. He is prepared to go through any ordeal to gratify his desire.

He is a brave person to whom conflict does not bring the thought of danger. He is exceedingly devoted to his friends and will fight for them. He has sympathy and consideration for the weak. He loves children and animals. He takes delight in showing mercy to others. He likes the healing profession. He is backed by self-control, moral courage and the power of forgiveness. His resilience is ' remarkable and under all circumstances he proves his strength of will and exhibits courage. He is short-tempered.

Born on 18th February

> you have all the basic characteristics of those born on the 9th of the month, so first go through them and then read your own.

This person has tenacity and will-power which will over- come any difficulty. He is not as dashing as a number 9, but he is fearless and courageous. His strong health makes him passionate. He inherits property from his father. He has a disciplined mind and likes to help others. He is painstaking with good judgement and is wise. He loves to exercise complete control over others. He does not like to be cautioned by others.

Born on 27th February

> you have all the basic characteristics of those born on the 9th of the month, so first go through them and then read your own.

On the whole his is a conflicting personality. He is confident and likes to do something for those whose life is miserable or the handicapped. He can develop a spiritual personality and can practise spiritual healing. On the other side, he is fond of women and can develop illicit contacts and create scandals. Sometimes he creates unhappiness in his married life. He is very sensitive and moody and his actions and moves are unpredictable. He is self assured and strong in resolution. He is a seeker of independence and domination. He hates to work under others. Usually, he is dogmatic in his thoughts.

b) FINANCE

He is lucky in his monetary affairs and earns far more than an average person. He is also very liberal in spending, especially for his sweetheart. He enjoys all the comforts that money can bring. Being born in February, he is likely to suffer from the influence of Saturn which shows delays and difficulties in monetary affairs· However a Martian, being a fighter, will always overcome difficulties and get the comforts he desires.

c) VOCATION

A number 9 person is found in all walks of life but he will be more suitable for the army and professions where there is full scope for his aggression and courage. In the army he will rise to high positions, in politics he will be eminent and in business he will exhibit his dashing and pushing nature. He can be a good doctor or a chemist or a businessman dealing in iron and steel.

d) HEALTH

His main health defect arises from heat and he is susceptible to troubles such as piles, fevers, small pox etc. He is also likely to suffer from kidney trouble or bladder stone. Throat trouble, bronchitis and laryngitis also pester him.

e) MARRIAGE AND FRIENDS

He has a natural attraction towards persons born in the period between 21st July and 20th August and between 21st November and 20th December. It is therefore advisable that he selects his partner from one of these periods. He also has affinity for those who are governed by numbers 3 and 6.

A Number 9 husband

He is robust in health and has strong circulation of blood which makes him more passionate and enthusiastic about married life. He is rond of a beautiful wife and likes her to be submissive and passive to his sexual desires. He is fond of his family and children and likes to have a good house. He usually leads a good married life in spite of his hot-tempered nature and eccentricities. He has a romantic mental picture of what he wants in his wife. This mental picture demands perfection. The most difficult thing in the married life of a number 9 person is to satisfy his romantic conception of physical love. He has a voracious appetite and his wife with her devotion should harmonize with him physically. Usually, we find him suspicious of his wife.

A Number 9 wife

She will make a wonderful wife for an ambitious man. She is a witty and clever conversationalist with a wonderful social presence. She will assist her husband in his business. She may also start her own activity and add to the family income. She will be happy if married to a passionate and possessive man.

Friends

His best friends are those who are governed by numbers 1, 2, 4, 6, 7 and 9. He also has a natural affinity towards those born in May, August, November and his own month i.e. February. He likes those who have fellowship, imagination, love of travel and simplicity.

f) FORTUNATE DAYS : His lucky days are Mondays, Tuesdays and Thursdays.

g) LUCKY COLOURS : He should use all shades of grey, violet and purple.

h) LUCKY JEWELS AND STONES : His lucky jewels are topaz, diamond and amethyst.

i) IMPORTANT YEARS IN LIFE : His important years are 9, 18, 27, 36, 45, 54, 63, 72 etc.

j) HIS GOOD QUALITIES AND DRAWBACKS ARE AS UNDER:

Good Qualities	Drawbacks
Honour	Obstinacy
Prestige	Domination
Dignity	Impertinence
Sensitivity	Inflexibility
Good Advice	Slowness
Originality	Spendthrift natiure
Aspiration	Aloofness
Authority	
Determination	

CHAPTER 19

BORN ON
1st, 10th, 19th, and 28th of March

All those born on 1st, 10th, 19th and 28th of March are govened by the planet Sun and number 1. March is governed by the planet Jupiter. Both these planets have strong personalities. The character reading given below relatting to number 1 is equally applicable to the other dates. In addition, special characteristics of those born on 10th, 19th and 28th March are given separately.

Born on 1st March

a) CHARACTER

This number is dominated by the Sun and shows brilliance, authority, confidence, determination, vigour, originality and activity. The man is spontaneous, responds to nature and has a capacity to enjoy life. He is an artist and has many talents but they are all spontaneous in nature. He is gifted with intuition and he seldom studies any subject in depth. Even then he can influence others with his knowledge and flash. These characteristics make him a hero of the drawing room. He values honour, prestige and dignity. He is oversensitive and is easily hurt in his feelings. He is changeable and is not constant in his friendship. He is honest and acknowledges his faults. He has a quick grasp of any subject and can participate spontaneously in conversation. He also learns occult sciences and does wonders with his natural gift of intuition. By nature, he is cheerful, happy and bright, and his outlook on life is very optimistic. He is fond of invention and has creative talents. He is a better judge of human nature than the average man. He is born to lead, not to follow. A new idea is a greater thrill than money in the bank. He will always be young by reason of his fresh ideas.

Being born in the month of March, he is governed by Jupiter, which makes him courteous, generous and broad-minded. He is ambitious and feels that he must know his subjects well, but due to the domination of number 1, he finds it difficult to stick to one thing for a long time. He is loyal to his friends and generally succeeds in all positions of responsibility He is strict about law and order. He is very easy going and is surrounded by false friends. He has a dual personality and his action depends upon which personlity is dominant at a particular moment. He has a mystic side as well as a practical side to his nature. He likes to search for the unknown and the esoteric. Although he is gene-rous, he is anxious about money matters and worries about his future monetary position. Artists, musicians and literary people are born in this month.

Born on the 10th of March

you have all the basic characteristics of those born on the 1st of the month, so first go through them and then read your own.

He gets financial benefits from relatives such as his father, father-in-law, wife, mother etc. Usually success comes after his 46th year. He is very impressive and has a magnetic per-sonality. He is respected for his knowledge. He is a spend-thrift and likes to have all comforts in life. He has broad shoulders and a manly figure. He loves truthfulness. This number shows honour and self-confidence. The man usually enjoys good health and quickly recovers from sickness. He likes to help others but hardly gets any response from them. This is more true in the case of relatives. In the end he gets a good position in service and succeeds in business also.

Born on the 19 of March

you have all the basic characteristics of those born on the 1st of the month, so first go through them and then read your own.

He is courageous and has force of character. He likes to help others even going out of the way. He can keep the secrets of others. He is very active, energetic and enthusia-stic. He has an aptitude for research and likes to handle a subject in a systematic and methodical way. He takes quick decisions and likes to keep himself busy with some concrete plan. Sports is his hobby and he is interested in several sports such as horse-riding and shooting, and in athletic games. He is hasty and impetuous in love affairs which end in quarrels. He is obstinate and finds it difficult to extend co-operation. He is prudent and notices even trifles.He is not an excellent speaker but can explain himself best in writing. He can be a good writer.

Born on the 28th of March | you have all the basic characteristics of those born on the 1st of the month, so first go through them and then read your own.

He is very generous and spends on charitable institution such as schools and hospitals. He is not as lucky as numbers 1, 10, and 19 and has to undergo difficulties in public and private life. He should select his marriage partner carefully. He has to provide carefully for the future as he is likely to lose through trust in others. He is also likely to make many changes in his career. He seldom reveals his emotions and therefore appears cold. He has an unyielding will power and does not hesitate to carry out his plans.

b) FINANCE

On the whole, he is a lucky person as far as financial matters are concerned. He may not amass wealth but earns enough to satisfy his ostentatious disposition in life. His personality and behaviour will convey to others the impression that he is a rich person. He is extravagant and has to control his temptation for gambling.

c) VOCATION

The main difficulty with a number 1 person is his inability to stick to any one profession or job for a long time. Usually, every three years there is a change in his career. He is however suitable for advertising concerns, newspaper business and the cinema industry. He can also be successful in theatrical performances. He can show his art as an interior decorator. He being a good salesman can choose a vocation which will imply relations with foreign countries, such as that of an ambassador or a trade dealing in foreign commodities. He is a leader and can be the head of a department, a managing director etc. He can succeed equally well as a surgeon, jeweller, electrician, and in research projects.

d) HEALTH

His illness is mainly psychological and he usually suffers from mental depression, insomnia, nervousness etc. He also suffers from rheumatic trouble, intestinal disturbances and pain in the feet. His over-anxiety often creates faulty digestion and poor blood circulation is the result. On the whole a number 1 person is a happy–go–lucky fellow and normally of good health. But he is also susceptible to certain health defects and has to be very particular about the following health troubles:

Heart trouble :

With a number 1 heart trouble is a structural difficulty. This can be observed even in childhood.

Weak eye-sight :

His another defect is poor eye-sight, sometimes even to the point of blindness.

Over-exertion :

The most common trouble is over-exertion; the man should take care not to exert himself too much because of his over-enthusiasm. Over-straining is likely to make him susceptible to fevers.

Sunstroke :

This is also a common threat to him. In addition to the above, he is likely to suffer from bone fracture.

e) MARRIAGE AND FRIENDS

He has a natural attraction towards those born in the period 20th February to 20th April, 20th June to 20th August and 20th Oct to 20th December· He also has an affinity for those who are governed by numbers 2, 3, 4, 5 and 7. It is therefore advisable that he selects his marriage partner from one of these periods or numbers.

A Number 1 husband

He is highly emotional and sensitive. He enjoys the company of his children and is one with them in many ways. He is a loving, considerate, thoughtful and attentive husband His notions are more real to him than the facts of life. He therefore finds it difficult to cope with the realities and difficulties of life.

He treats his wife and family members with the same courtesy that he accords to strangers. He accepts marriage as a part of domestic scheme and succeeds in it because of his attitude which contributes a great deal towards harmony at home. His drawback is his impersonality which his wife feels as lack of interest in domestic life. He lacks stability, strength and realism in his career. He is very sensual and can be dangerously perverted by self-indulgence. Sexual satisfaction is very important to him and he seeks it persistently all his life. He wants his family members to dance to his tunes and will not tolerate disrespect·

A Number 1 wife

She has a strong sense of comfort and decorates her home in a luxurious way. She is beautiful and talented but spends her time in an idle way. She is a devoted, charming and sympathetic wife. She is remarkably adaptable to family life. Her home is a social centre on account of her social and friendly manners. Her interests are wide and she does not like to watch how her husband spends his spare time. She is interested in dance and music. She is kind and would rather suffer herself than create a situation which would make others unhappy. She is aristocratic by temperament and attracts people to her home and commands great respect. She needs a virile husband who can provide her with the romantic outlets that her passionate nature requires.

Friends

This man is always attracted towards those who are ambitious, generous and broad-minded. He prefers friends who have honour and dignity. His best friends are those who are governed by numbers 1, 3, 5, 7 and 9. He has a natural affinity towards those born in June, September, December and in his own month i.e. March.

f) FORTUNATE DAYS : His lucky days are Mondays, Thursdays and Fridays.

g) LUCKY COLOURS : He should use all shades of yellow, gold and purple.

h) LUCKY JEWELS AND STONES : His lucky jewels are Ruby, Emerald and Topaz.

i) IMPORTANT YEARS IN LIFE : His important years are 1, 10, 19, 28, 37, 46, 55, 64, 73 etc.

j) HIS GOOD QUALITIES AND DRAWBACKS ARE AS UNDER:

Good qualities	Drawbacks
Honour	Obstincy
Prestige	Domination
Dignity	Impertinence
Sensitivity	Inflexibility
God Advice	Slowness
Orginality	Spendthrift Nature
Aspiration	Aloofness
Authority	

CHAPTER 20

BORN ON
2nd, 11th, 20th and 29th March

All those born on the 2nd, 11th, 20th and 29th of March of any year are governed by number 2 and the planet Moon. March is governed by the planet Jupiter. Between these two planets Jupiterian characteristics predominate in the person. The character–reading given below relating to number 2 is equally applicable to the other dates. In addition, special characteristics of those born on the 11th, 20th and 29th March are given separately.

Born on 2nd March

a) CHARACTER

Number 2 shows high imagination, idealism and a dreamy nature. The person has fantasies and lacks a practical approach. He revels in his own dreams and therefore shuns society. He does not like to enjoy the company of others as he finds them too ordinary for his imaginary world. However Jupiter gives him ideas of dignity, prestige and honour. With these qualities, his usual career is such that he has to mix in society and comes in contact with a large number of people. Though the Moon makes him somewhat nervous, Jupiter gives him confidence and he becomes social and is liked by others. He is warm hearted and shows little resistance to oppression. He has noble sentiments.

Being born in March, he is courteous, generous and broad-minded. He is ambitious and feels that he must know his subject well. He has a natural attraction towards the sea, flowers, natural scenery and the vastness of the sky. The

Moon makes him very unsteady, fickle-minded and a lover of change. He has a fancy for travel, especially long travel. He is unassuming and pleasing and has a good taste in clothes. He has a hypnotic power.

Thus we have seen that he has a dual personality and his action depends upon which part of his personality dominates him at a particular moment. He has a mystical side as well as a practical side to his nature. He likes to search for the unknown and the esoteric. Although he is generous, he is anxious about money matters and worries about his financial position in the future. Artists, musicians and literary people are born in this month.

Born on 11th March | you have all the basic characteristics of those born on the 2nd of the month, so first go through them and then read your own.

Such a man is very impulsive and gets exited easily. He worries too much over small matters. He has the ability to take quick decisions and so can be a leader. He is a born adviser and an inspiration to others. He is usually successful in life and in love, and gets honour, position and authority. He is loyal to his friends and is of a royal disposition. He should guard himself against secret enemies. He has interest in mysticism, philosophy and science.

Born on the 20th of March | you have all the basic characteristics of those born on the 2nd of the month, so first go through them and then read your own.

This man has many friends and he benefits through wealthy women. He has a flair for writing and can be known as an author or a novelist. His prosperity lies near water, river or the sea. This number has a peculiar significance. It shows new plans, and new resolutions for the betterment of people at large. If this number is used in connection with future events, it indicates delays.

Born on the 29th of March | you have all the basic characteristics of those born on the 2nd of the month, so first go through them and then read your own.

This person is moody and changing and therefore uncertain about his action. He is courageous but takes risks in life and does not stick to anything to the end. He is intelligent and also a deep thinker but there is a tendency to carry everything to extremes. He is not very lucky in his married life. His interest is in his business. He is blessed with progress. His life is eventful.

b) FINANCE

A person governed by number 2 is a lethargic fellow and is not capable of doing any work. He also does not have the physical capacity to stand the strain of everyday life. The outcome, therefore, is a medicore financial status. However, he can improve his monetary position with his creative art and imagination. His unstable mind often drags him away from routine work and this makes his income uncertain. However being governed by Jupiter he can overcome his drawbacks and can achieve a good financial position. Jupiter always protects one from any hazards and the person overcomes all obstacles and difficulties. Only, a number 2 person has to make the best use of the abilities given by Jupiter, and develop his talents.

c) VOCATION

The high imaginative power possessed by the number 2 person will help him to be a good composer of music or a writer of fiction or romance. He can also be a good artist and can create works of enduring value. Immortal paintings, plays and magnificent poems will be the creation of a powerful number 2 person. He has a great vocabulary and linguistic mastery among all the numbers and can be successful as a teacher or a professor of languages. He can also be a good translator or an editor.

The influence of Jupiter will make him rise to high positions such as those of ministers, ambassadors, judges and secretaries. He is gifted for public life, statesmanship, high offices etc., may be in the army or in the church. He is a good teacher as well as a preacher. Professions such as those of doctors, bankers, advertisers and actors are also suitable for him.

d) HEALTH

His sickness is mainly psychological and he usually suffers from mental depression, insomnia, nervousness etc. His main health weakness is his poor blood circulation. He is susceptible to all illnesses arising out of poor blood circulation such as anaemia and a weak heart.

Since the Moon is the ruling planet of number 2, the uneasiness which is a prominent characteristic, creates mental worries and sleeplessness. He is also susceptible to diabetes and asthmatic trouble.

e) MARRIAGE AND FRIENDS

He has a natural attraction towards those born in the period 20th February to 20th March, 20th June to 20 July and 20th October to 20th November. He also has an affinity for those who are governed by the numbers 2, 3, 6. It is therefore advisable that he selects his wife from one of these periods or numbers.

A Number 2 as husband

He has a greater love and attraction for home than any other type. He enjoys the company of his children and is one with them in many ways. There are two types of husbands belonging to this number. One is dominating and exacting. He is fault-finding and nothing satisfies him. He desires that everything should be given to him without his asking for it. He never thinks that he should contribute something to receive pleasure. The other type is passive, lazy and indulgent. He will marry for the sake of money so that he ultimately gets comforts.

A Number 2 as wife

She is sympathetic, affectionate and devoted. She is satisfied with anything her husband provides her with. However she is moody, changeable and sensitive. She has a great sense of comfort and decorates her home in a luxurious way.

However, she is lazy and spends her time in an idle way. If she is of good and robust health, she makes a devoted, charming and sympathetic wife.

Note

A Number 2 person is cold and does not have the fire of passion. Some times he may select a partner who is either far older or younger than himself.

Friends

He is attracted towards those who are amibitious, generous and broad-minded. He prefers friends who have honour and dignity. His best friends are those who are governed by numbers 2, 3, 4, 6, and 9. He has a natural affinity towards those born in June, September, December and in his own month i.e. March.

f) FORTUNATE DAYS : His lucky days are Mondays, Thursdays and Fridays.

g) LUCKY COLOURS : He should use all shades of white, cream and purple as his lucky colours.

h) LUCKY JEWELS AND STONES : His lucky jewels are pearls and diamonds and lucky stones are moonstone and agate.

I) IMPORTANT YEARS IN LIFE : His important years are 2, 11, 20, 29, 38, 47, 56, 65, 74 etc.

j) HIS GOOD QUALITIES AND DRAWBACKS ARE AS UNDER:

Good qualities	Drawbacks
Emotionality	Coldness
Fellowship	Envy
Honesty	Haste
Imagination	Introvert
Simplicity	Shyness
	Whimsicality

CHAPTER 21

BORN ON
3rd, 12th, 21st and 30th of March

All those born on 3rd, 12th, 21st and 30th of March of any year are governed by the planet Jupiter and number 3. The month of March is also governed by the planet Jupiter. Therefore, the characteristics of Jupiter predominate in the person. The character reading given below relating to number 3 is equally applicable to the other dates. In addition, special characteristics of those born on 12th, 21st and 30th of March are given separately.

Born on 3rd march

a) CHARACTER

This number is governed by the planet Jupiter. It stands for morality, pure love and justice with mercy and is known as the greatest benefactor and uplifter. The vibrations emitted by this number are essentially harmonious and they lead to sympathy and an untiring effort to do good to all, to piety and true dignity. The abuse of the same vibrations causes the stimulation of Jupiterian virtues leading to hypocrisy, especially in religious matters. The good nature is marred by excess in many directions.

This person is usually lucky in life. Vibrations radiating through him attract all that is good to him and his affairs prosper as a consequence. The judge who gives sane decisions and merciful sentences, the physician and the church dignitary, the world's teachers and philosophers are all mostly governed by the number 3.

This is a good number. The person is confident about his ability. He is self-reliant and takes his own decisions. He has the habit of talking loudly. He is fond of show and likes to observe form, order and law. He is jovial in spirit and cordial in manner. His passions are healthy, spontaneous and without inhibitions. He is free in his expression. He is a good conversationalist.

He takes an active interest in sports and outdoor activities from his earliest youth. He has tremendous enthusiasm and is not self-centred. His intellect is of a very high order. He has a vision that understands the world and loves it for what it is and not for what it ought to be. He is open-hearted with good understanding and entirely lacking in malice or petty jealousies. If he is not alert, people take undue advantage of his good nature.

The main characteristics of a number 3 person are ambition, leadership, religion, pride, honour, love of nature, enthusiasm, generosity, respect and reverence.

Born on 12th March

you have all the basic characteristics of those born on the 3rd of the month, so first go through them and then read your own.

Authority and honour are the significant aspects of this person. He likes to make sacrifices for others but becomes a victim of others' plans or intrigues. He has vanity and is proud, ambitious and aspiring. He is fond of pleasures and is attracted to the opposite sex. His relations with others are smooth and harmonious. He is quick to notice trifles. He has lofty ideals.

Born on 21st March

you have all the basic characteristics of those born on the 3rd of the month, so first go through them and then read your own.

This man is kind, generous and a loving father. He achieves fame, reputation and honours at a very late age. He is cheerful and likes to travel. He has a strong sense of self-respect. Surprisingly, he has a suspicious nature.

Born on 30th March

you have all the basic characteristics of those born on the 3rd of the month, so first go through them and then read your own.

This person is fortunate, generous and optimistic. He has a noble and religious mind. He likes to travel and visit places of pilgrimage. He can be successful as a teacher or an educationist or in administration. He appears gentle and sincere, but has a hidden nature. He may be active but is restless. When faced with difficulties, he is strong enogh to overcome them. This date is of thoughtful deduction, introspection, and mental superiority over one's fellows.

b) FINANCE

This person is a lucky type and somehow manages to earn enough for his livelihood. He also gets opportunities for higher positions in life and earns quite a lot. His ambition, leadership and enthusiasm always push him forward and usually he gets all comforts in life. The number 3 person is early out of puberty and poverty.

c) VOCATION

This man's love for position and command makes him a politician. I have observed certain persons of this number occupying very high posts such as those of ministers, ambassadors, judges and secretaries. He is equipped for public life, statesmanship, high offices etc., may be in the army or in the church. He is a good teacher as well as a preacher. Professions such as those of doctors, bankers, advertisers and actors are also suitable for him.

d) HEALTH

Number 3 has chief influence over the blood and the arterial system. It also governs the sense of smell. This person is liable to suffer from chest and lung disorders, throat afflictions, gout and apoplexy and sudden fevers. He may also suffer from sore throat, diptheria, adenoids, pneumonia, pleurisy and tuberculosis of the lungs.

Since he is born in March, his sickness is mainly psychological and he usually suffers from mental depression, insomnia, nervousness etc. He also suffers from rheumatic trouble, instestinal disturbances and pain in the feet. His over-anxiety often creates faulty digestion and poor blood circulation is the result.

e)   MARRIAGE AND FRIENDS

He has a natural attraction towards those born in the period 20th June to 20th July and 20th October to 20th November. He also has an affinity for those who are governed by numbers 3, 6 and 9. It is therefore advisable that he selects his wife from one of these periods or numbers.

Number 3 as a husband

As a general rule, he attains puberty at an early age and marries early. However, as he is ambitious, his ambitions also make him expect too many things from his wife and so he becomes disappointed. He desires to have a wife of whom he can be proud. She should have an attractive personality, a commanding presence, charming manners and intelligence. It is always better for him to choose a number 3 person or a number 6 person as his wife. He is most loving, thoughtful and considerate. His passions are adventurous and demand immediate satisfaction.

Number 3 as a wife

She is the best companion to her husband. She is not an intruder but takes active interest in the business of her husband. She is efficient in house-keeping and has a sympathetic and balanced attitude towards her children. Her passions are healthy and joyous and her approach to physical love is highly refined and inspiring.

Friends

His best friends are those who are governed by numbers 3, 6, 7, 9. He also has a natural affinity towards those born in June, September, December and in his own month i.e. March.

f)   FORTUNATE DAYS :   His lucky days are Tuesdays, Thursdays and Fridays.

g) **LUCKY COLOURS :** He should use all shades of yellow, violet, purple and green as his lucky colours.

h) **LUCKY JEWELS AND STONES :** His lucky jewel is topaz and his lucky stone is amethyst.

i) **IMPORTANT YEARS IN LIFE :** His important years are 3, 12, 21, 30, 39, 48, 57, 66, 75, etc.

j) **HIS GOOD QUALITIES & DRAWBACKS ARE AS UNDER :**

Good qualities	Drawbacks
Ambition	Cruelty
Dignity	Dictatorship
Individuality	Hypocrisy
Philosophy	Extravagance
Prestige	Vanity

CHAPTER 22

BORN ON
4th, 13th, 22nd and 31st of March

All those born on 4th, 13th, 22nd and 31st of March of any year are governed by the number 4 and the planent Uranus. March is governed by Jupiter. Therefore these persons are dominated by the characteristics shown by Jupiter and also Uranus. The character reading explained below with reference to number 4 is equally applicable to the other dates. In addition, the special characteristics of those born on 13th, 22nd and 31st March are given separately.

Born on 4th March

a) CHARACTER

A person born on this date is likely to suffer many sorrows and afflictions in the earlier part of his life. The difficulties are linked with relations, home life and with relatives by marriage. He will be strangely drawn to mystical occult sciences but he will be inclined to keep his interest to himself. This person has energy, force and advancement. His date of birth shows revolution and unexpected happenings. Usually the changes that take place are for the better. This number represents the higher faculties of the mind. It shows activity and intelligence engaged in the reconstruction or the betterment of human life. The peculiar nature of this person is that he constantly aims at changes in life and society and is after the liberation of the mind from the bondage of environment and society. He dislikes hypocrisy and loves art and music. He has an attractive personality.

This number is considered as the negative part of the

number 1. It has the same characteristics as those of number
1, but these characteristics are in a dormant condition. It means
that a number 4 person needs to be pushed forward so that he
can show his abilities. He is methodical in his own way. He
has a bad habit of forcing his opinions on others. He has a
keen, analytical and logical mind.

Because of his peculiar nature of opposing the views of
others or creating controversies, he is often misunderstood and
makes secret enemies who constantly work against him. He
feels lonely in life.

Being born in the month of March, he has a dual personality and his action depends upon which personality dominates
him at a particular moment of his life. He likes to search for
the unknown and the esoteric. Although he is generous, he is
anxious about money matters and worries about his future
monetary position. Artists, musicians and literary people are
born in this month.

Born on 13th March | you have all the basic characteristics of those born on the 4th of the month, so first go through them and then read your own.

This number indicates change of plans and place, and indicates power and dominion. This man is an intelligent person,
of tall stature and good complexion. He is considerate and
benevolent. He likes literature and scientific books. He likes
to remain active though in a quiet way. He occupies positions
of high responsibilities and gets riches. His success and career
start after his 31st year. Though outwardly he looks mild,
inwardly he is obstinate. He is faithful and sympathetic but
has difficulty in expressing his love. He has all the qualities of
number 4 but in an exaggerted form.

Born on 22nd March | you have all the basic characteristics of those born on the 4th of the month, so first go through them and then read your own.

He is also tall with good eyes. Usually he occupies good
positions but without much responsibility. He is rather easy-
going but unsteady in nature. Sometimes his actions are spasmodic. On the whole he is lucky in his affairs and benefits
from the opposite sex. He is happy in his family life but is also
fond of a companion. He is faithful and dedicated to others.

Sometimes, he feels very lonely. His social field is limited and he has few friends. He does not care for disputes. He has too much economy of sentiments.

Born on 31st March

> you have all the basic characteristics of those born on the 4th of the month, so first go through them and then read your own.

This date shows ambition, pride and austerity. The man is interested in honourable occupations such as working with charitable institutions, institutions for the deaf and dumb, the physically handicapped etc. He gets success after his 40th year but he expects quick results and early reputation. He is lucky in financial matters. He is realistic and of strong will power. He has a strong attraction for the opposite sex. He loves to travel.

b) FINANCE

His extreme prudence and distrust of others will safeguard him in financial matters. He is likely to inherit money or property and he should endeavour to guard it carefully rather than attempt to increase it. He is usually well settled in life though he experiences delays and difficulties in his undertakings. He may not amass wealth but can maintain the show of riches. He is a spendthrift and his home is well decorated. His financial prosperity usually starts after the age of 40.

c) VOCATION

He will be successful in trades such as transport, electricity and all sorts of machinery. He will be equally successful as an engineer, building contractor, scientist and industrialist. He is also attracted towards mystic subjects such as palmistry and astrology and can do well in them.

d) HEALTH

His respiratory system is usually weak and he suffers from breathlessness. His knees, shanks and feet are also affected. Sometimes he suffers from urinary infection. Being born in March, he is likely to suffer from mental depression, nervousness and insomnia. His overanxiety often causes faulty digestion and poor blood circulation is the result.

e) MARRIAGE AND FRIENDS

He has a natural attraction towards those born in the period 20th February to 20th March, 20th June to 20th July and 20th October to 20th November. He also has an affinity for those who are governed by numbers 1, 2, 3, 7 and 8. It is therefore advisable that he selects his wife from one of these periods or numbers.

A Number 4 husband

He is shrewd and intelligent and expects his wife to share his views. He desires that everything should be given to him without his asking for it. He is dominating and wants all affairs of the house to run according to his desire. He is generous and kind, and enjoys the company of his children.

A Number 4 wife

She is smart and attractive. She has the art of dressing. She has a strong will-power. She aims at several things but hardly succeeds in getting mastery over one. She loves interior decoration but does not have the capacity to work hard for it and she will get it done through others. She is dictatorial and moody and spoils her day because of her own whimsical nature. She loves her home but is not attached to it very much. She is often uneasy and it is better for her to find a friend governed by number 1 or 2.

Friends

This man is fond of friends and company but hardly gets close friends because of his unsteady, changing and moody nature. He will get friends who are influenced by numbers 1, 2, 3, 7 and 8. He also has a natural attraction towards those born in the months of June, September, December and in his own month i.e. March.

f) FORTUNATE DAYS : His lucky days are Sundays, Mondays
and Saturdays.

g) LUCKY COLOURS : He should use all shades of blue
grey, white and maroon.

h) LUCKY JEWELS AND STONES : His lucky jewels are
diamond, coral and
pearl.

i) IMPORTANT YEARS IN LIFE : His important years are 4,
13, 22, 31, 40, 49, 58, 67,
76 etc.

j) HIS GOOD QUALITIES AND DRAWBACKS ARE ASUNDER:

Good Qualities	Drawbacks
Activity	Changeablity
Endurance	Domination
Energy	Stubbornness
Reliability	Vindictiveness
Method and system	Jealousy

CHAPTER 23

BORN ON
the 5th, 14th and 23rd of March

All those born on the 5th, 14th and 23rd of March of any year are governed by number 5 and the planet Mercury. March is governed by Jupiter. Therefore the person is governed by the characteristics shown by Mercury and Jupiter. The character-reading explained below with reference to number 5 is equally applicable to the other dates also. In addition, the special characteristis of those born on 14th and 23rd March are given separately.

Born on 5th March

a) CHARACTER

This number is governed by the planet Mercury and it shows shrewdness, quickness, scientific pursuits, business ability, industry, intuition and diplomacy. A person governed by this number is active and quick. This is true not only of physical ability only but also of the mental side. He is very skilful and has intuitive faculty. He is equally proficient in games where he uses both his hands and his brain. He has the capacity to judge the ability of his opponents in games and knows very well how to take advantage of the weak points of his opponents. He is fond of oratory and eloquence in expressieg himself. He has the capacity to pursue his objectives and knows very well how to work to achieve his ends. He is deeply interested in occult subjects and has a fancy to master all the intricacies of such abtruse subjects. He possesses a pleasant character. He dislikes activity. He is sociable and has many acquaintances. He is fond of variety and change and trips and travel. However difficult may be the situation, he can find a way out.

He is a nervous person. He is therefore restless. He has an intuitive perception and has the capacity to be either good or bad. On the good side, he is a shrewd person and not vicious or criminal. He is fond of family life and loves children. His pleasures are mainly mental and he evaluates everything in terms of business. He is amiable and adaptable.

Born on 14th March you have all the basic characteristics of those born on the 5th of the month, so first go through them and then read your own.

This person has an attractive personality and is liked by all. His nature is co-operative and he does not like to provoke others. He usually occupies a good position in life and is successful in business. He is not talkative but is slightly reserved. This is an intelligent and shrewd number. In women it indicates good marriage but they should take care in child-bearing. A Number 14 man is inconstant in love and experiences some romantic and impulsive attachment in ealry years, He is fortunate in money matters. He is industrious and positive in speech and action. Usually he is fond of gambling and of sloving riddles.

Born on 23rd March you have all the basic characteristics of those born on the 5th of the month, so first go through them and then read your own.

This man is usually popular among women. His fortune is near water. He is successful in life and enjoys honour and health. He may get money through inheritance. He keeps himself busy in own way. He gets help and protection from superiors. He is a lucky person. He is affectionate. He loves freedom. He is averse to formalities. He has a spirit of independence and a desire to dominate.

b) FINANCE

March is governed by Jupiter. The ambitions of a number 5 person regarding finance are more of a psychological nature. In consequence, many ups and downs of fortune are to be expected. He will be somewhat careless in money matters and not inclined to save much. However, since number 5 is a business number, the person can expect opulence. With his shrewd character he is capable of developing his industry, carrying out his plans systematically with the result that he gets good returns for his efforts. He is lucky in financial matters.

c) VOCATION

This man is adaptable to the role he has to play in the drama of life. With his adaptability he comes in contact with various classes of people and becomes successful in any business. Banking is a good line for him. Mercury also shows ability for medicine or surgery. His capacity to argue his points can make him a good lawyer.

d) HEALTH

This man is likely to suffer from nerves and to become irritable in the face of opposition. This he should endeavour to control as it will be detrimental to his mental pursuits. His basic health defect is biliousness and nervousness. However, his biliousness has close relation with his psychological disturbance. Experience shows that his biliousness increases with the increase in tension and is reduced or disappears when his nervous trouble is under control.

Number 5 rules nerves, the neck, the arms, the ears and the respiratory system.

e) MARRIAGE AND FRIENDS

He has a natural attraction towards persons born in the period between 20th September and 20th November and 20th January and 20th March. He has affinity for those who are governed by numbers 1, 3, 7, 8. It is therefore advisable that he chooses his marriage partner from one of these periods of numbers.

A Number 5 husband

He is lucky and successful in his married life. His selection is good and usually he selects a person of his own type. He loves his partner. He expects neatness and cleanliness from her and also desires that she should share his enjoyment of life He is proud of his wife and likes to see her well-dressed. In return, he proves a good husband. He loves his children and is fond of his home. Even if he travels long, he is very much attracted to his home and is eager to return early and be with his family. He is liberal in spending on clothes and other needs of the members of his family and furnishes his house with good taste.

A Number 5 wife

She has interest at home as well as outside. She has many activities and manages them well. She likes tidiness. Though she seldom does her own work, she gets it done through her commanding personality.

FRIENDS

This man is attracted to those who have honour, prestige and dignity. His best friends are those who are governed by numbers 1,3,4,5,7 and 8. He also has a natural affinity towards those born in June, September, December and in his own month i. e. March.

f) FORTUNATE DAYS : His lucky days are Wednesdays, Thursdays and Fridays.

g) LUCKY COLOURS : His lucky colours are yellow, white and green.

h) LUCKY JEWELS AND STONES : His lucky jewels are emerald, diamond and sapphire.

i) IMPORTANT YEARS IN LIFE : His important years are 5, 14, 23, 32, 41, 50, 59, 68, 77 etc.

j) HIS GOOD QUALITIES AND DRAWBACKS ARE AS UNDER:

Good qualities	Drawbacks
Co-operation	Lack of perseverance
Practical approach	Scepticism
Shrewdness	Unreliability
Vigilance	

CHAPTER 24

BORN ON
6th, 15th and 24th of March

All those born on the 6th, 15th and 24th of March of any year are governed by the number 6 and the planet Venus. March is governed by the planet Jupiter. Therefore, the person is governed by the characteristics shown by Venus and Jupiter. The character-reading explained below relating to number 6 is equally applicable to the other dates also. In addition, the special characteristics of those born on the 15th and 24th of March are given separately.

Born on 6th March

a) CHARACTER

This number is governed by Venus which stands for love, sympathy and adoration. The man is a born artist and he loves art and beauty in life. In his art and his approach to life, we find dignity. He will try to produce art which will give him eternal fame. He has a pleasant personality. It is always charming to be with him. He is full of enthusiasm and energy. His talk is interesting and lively. We may sometimes have to put aside our ideas of morality and social conduct to understand and appreciate his feelings and arguments. Number six stands for beauty, health, vitality, warmth, attraction and, above all, love. This man is strict about law and order. He likes to search for the unknown. He is anxious about money matters and worries about the future. He is loyal to his friends and generally succeeds in positions of responsibility. He loves to have a life full of ease and luxuries, money and happiness. He prefers spending to saving.

He is necessarily a loving type and he has a feeling of kinship and humanity. He will therefore not desert his friends, he is always considerate and wishes to understand the grievances and difficulties of others. He prefers joy to gloom and has the capacity to take others along with him to share his enjoyment. His outlook is bright and vivacious. He is emotional but keeps his emotions to himself. His anger is hard to subside. He is very responsible and loves his children, but receives very little happiness from them. He is a born advisor and needs an audience to whom he can express his views on matters of importance. He is a good conversationalist and enjoys intellectual sword-crossing.

Jupiter is a benefactor and always protects one from difficulties. It is therefore necessary to control the emotional side of Venus and concentrate more on the abilities given by Jupiter. If the man develops a strong side he will have uncommon intellectual gifts, great adaptability to any type of work that interests him and an understanding of things in general; he can be ingenious and inventive and have a quiet way of turning difficulties to his advantage.

However, if he allows the dominance of Venus, he will stick to nothing long and he will be a jack of all trades, but master of none.

Born on 15th March you have all the basic characteristics of those born on the 6th of the month, so first go through them and then read your own.

This person has good intelligence and good memory. He is fit for responsible positions such as those of an ambassador, a consul, a governor etc. He is very ambitious and boastful but hasty and proud by nature. He is interested in the lower type of occultism. He has interest in art and music also. He appears to be gentle but has very strong convictions. He has a habit of worrying inwardly and leads a melancholy life. His destiny is such that he has to make sacrifices for others.

Born on 24 March

He is fortunate in getting assistance from people of high rank. He benefits through the opposite sex. He prospers after he marries a rich girl. He succeeds in speculation and enjoys a good financial position. He strictly defines the line between personal and social matters. He is methodical in his ideas. He possesses a strong ego and sometimes tries to force his opinions on others.

b) FINANCE

As a general rule, he will be lucky in money matters. Money comes to him in unexpected ways. However, because of his spendthrift nature he may suffer in old age unless he makes up his mind to put money aside for a rainy day. There are possibilities of many ups and downs in his financial position. He is not attracted towards money and accumulation of wealth is not his aim in life. All his interest is directed towards attaining pleasures and gratifying his desires. He therefore, spend his earnings on whatever attracts him. He also never repents having spent his money on his art which may not ultimately give him monetary rewards. Therefore, he is seldom affluent but he has the knack of making both ends meet and securing the minimum comforts he wants. He may sometimes be lucky in getting windfalls.

c) VOCATION

Being governed by Jupiter, this man's love of position and command makes him a politician. I have observed certain persons of this number occupying very high posts such as those of ministers, judges and secretaries. He has the gifts for public life, statesmanship, high offices etc., may be in the army or in the church. He is a good teacher as well as a preacher. Professions such as those of doctors, bankers, advertiser and actors are also suitable for him.

Being dominated by Venus, he will shine as an interior decorator, architect, jeweller. musician, hotel manager or a confectioner. He can be equally successful as a broker, estate broker or commission agent.

d) HEALTH

On the whole he has a splendid healthy constitution during his early years, but he runs the risk of ruining health by luxurious living unless he keeps himself well under control. In advanced years he is likely to suffer from heart trouble and high blood pressure. His ambitious nature may bring mental depression, insomnia and nervousness.

e) MARRIAGE AND FRIENDS

He has a natural attraction towards persons born in the period between 20th August and 20th September, and 20th December and 20th January. He has affinity for those who are governed by the numbers 2, 3, 4, 6, and 9. It is therefore advisable that he finds his marriage partner from one of these periods or numbers.

A Number 6 husband

He is attracted to marriage and usually marries early in life. He has charm and grace and he expects his partner to be neat. He desires to have a wife of whom he can be proud. His ambition also makes him expect too many things from his wife and so he becomes disappointed. His passions are adventurous and demand immediate satisfaction. Though he creates a lively atmosphere in the house, he finds it difficult to provide all the needs of the members of his family. This may sometimes create unpleasantness and make him unhappy in his married life. He is impractical and does not understand the material values of a successful life. His is usually a large family with many children.

A Number 6 wife

She is beautiful and talented but spends her time in an idle way. If she has robust health, she makes a devoted,

charming and sympathetic wife. She never resorts to divorce
and endures extreme hardship rather than desert her husband.
She is a devoted mother and loving wife, satisfied with her
husband's efforts in her behalf. She makes a perfect home.

Friends

He is attracted towards those who have ambition and a
religious aptitude. His best friends are those who are governed
by the numbers 2, 3, 4, 6 and 9. He has a natural affinity
towards those born in June, September, December and in his
own month i. e. March.

f) FORTUNATE DAYS : His lucky days are Mondays,
Tuesdays, Thursdays, and Fridays.

g) LUCKY COLOURS : He should use all shades of blue,
rose, violet and pink.

h) LUCKY JEWELS AND STONES : His lucky jewels are
Emerald, Pearl and
Diamond.

i) IMPORTANT YEARS IN LIFE : His important years are
6, 15, 24, 33, 42, 51, 60,
69, 78 etc.

j) HIS GOOD QUALITIES AND DRAWBACKS ARE AS UNDER:

Good Qualities	Drawbacks
Harmony	Absence of foresight
Love	Interference
Peace	Moodiness
Strong memory	Timidity

CHAPTER 25

BORN ON
7th, 16th and 25th of March

All those born on 7th, 16th and 25th of March of any year are governed by the number 7 and Neptune. March is governed by Jupiter. Therefore the person is governed by the characteristics shown by Neptune and Jupiter. The character-reading given below relating to number 7 is equally applicable to the other dates. In addition, special characteristics of those born on 16th and 25th of March are given separately.

Born on 7th March

a) CHARACTER

He has high ideals and great ambitions, but is rather inclined to live an independent, unconventional life. He has a distinct bent for investigation and discoveries. On the one side, he has high ambition and on the other side he is governed by Jupiter, giving him a practical outlook. This makes him full of contradictions. He will be both strong and weak at the same time.

This number is governed by Neptune and has the same qualities as number 2 which is governed by the Moon. This man has individuality and is original and independent. He is restless by nature and is fond of change. He likes to visit foreign countries and becomes interested in far off lands. He has peculiar ideas about religion and dislikes following the beaten track.

This is a spiritual number and Supreme Consciousness is developed in this individual. He is like a free bird and likes to break the traditional bondage and restrictions. It is possible that the greatest of the prophets and spiritualists are dominated by Neptune. This man's behaviour is a mystery to others. He is often absent-minded. He thinks logically and achieves great aims. He is stubborn and disregards the opinions of others. He has a good talent to earn money. In general, he is somewhat indifferent and has few materialistic goals. He desires the best or none at all. He is sensitive and hides his real feelings by apparent indifference. He dislikes mingling with common people. He prefers to spend his hour with his favourite book. When his opinion is solicited, he speaks with authority. He knows his ground.

Born on 16th March <small>you have all the basic characteristics of those born on the 7th of the month, so first go through them and then read your own.</small>

He is rather easy-going and does not like to work hard. He is good-humoured and generous. He is very sensitive and emotional. He easily gets upset and is easily pleased. He is frequently indisposed. He is fortunate in having good and successful children. However, there is some sort of sorrow in his married life. He appears to be calm but his mind is always in turmoil and he is sometimes short-tempered. He will not disclose his nervousness and is slow in taking decisions. He does not like interference.

Born on 25th March <small>you have all the basic characteristics of those born on the 7th of the month, so first go through them and then read your own.</small>

He is a jack of all trades but master of none. He is interested in several subjects but does not have the capacity to go into details. His knowledge, therefore, is very shallow. He likes to travel and has connections with foreign countries. He is honest, faithful and good-natured. But he is fickle-minded and inconsistent. His memory is good and he is a good orator and a good teacher.

b) FINANCE

If the person born in this period of the year has mastered his natural lack of continuity of purpose, there is no position in life he may not attain, for great opportunities will be given to him from time to time. As the result of his own mental efforts, financial matters will be favourable to him. He will create money whatever his line of work may be. He will be inclined at times to be over-generous or to allow others to achieve financial success from his ideas. Accumulation of wealth will never be his object in life.

He will succeed in shipping products from one country to another, in gaining money in lands far from his place of birth, and especially by developing the inspirational side of his nature and by following his intuition.

c) VOCATION

Neptune indicates an attraction towards water and liquids. His love for sea-travel and interest in foreign countries make him a successful merchant, exporter or importer. He can deal in dairy products, fishery and other products such as soap etc. or choose a chemical industry. He can also study medicine and surgery.

d) HEALTH

His over-anxiety often causes faulty digestion, and poor blood circulation is the result. His sickness is mainly psychological and therefore he suffers many a time from mental depression. His main trouble is his nervous constitution.

e) MARRIAGE AND FRIENDS

He has a natural attraction towards those born in the period 20th February to 20th March, 20th June to 20th July and 20th October to 20th November. He also has an affinity for those who are governed by numbers 3, 5, 7 and 8. It is therefore advisable that he should select his marriage partner from one of these periods or numbers.

A Number 7 husband

He is very emotional and understands the feelings of his wife. He is very considerate and will never try to impose his ideas on the wife. He is liberal, fond of picnics, travels and cinema theatres. He is a spendthrift and likes to live lavishly. His family is moderate in size and has all the comforts in life.

A Number 7 wife

She is very moody and her behaviour is unpredictable. She is very uneasy and gets disturbed over small matters. She is good at entertaining friends and she likes to invite people to a party or dinner. She expects her husband to look after her all the time.

Friends

His best friends are those who are governed by numbers 1, 3, 5, 7, 8 and 9. He has also a natural affinity towards those born in June, September, December and in his own month i.e. March.

f) FORTUNATE DAYS : His lucky days are Sundays, Mondays, Wednesdays and Thursdays. He should take his decisions and actions on these days especially when the date is also 7th, 16th or 25th of the month.

g) LUCKY COLOURS : He should use shades of green, yellow and purple.

h) LUCKY JEWELS AND STONES : His lucky jewels are Topaz and Emerald and lucky stones are Moon Stone and Cat's Eye.

i) IMPORTANT YEARS IN LIFE : His important years are 7, 16, 25, 34, 43, 52, 61, 70, 79 etc.

j) HIS GOOD QUALITIES & DRAWBACKS ARE AS UNDER :

Good qualities	Drawbacks
Austerity	Despondency
Peace	Diffidence
Reflection	Restlessness
Serenity	Whimsicality
Tolerance	

CHAPTER 26

BORN ON
8th, 17th and 26th of March

All those born on 8th, 17th, and 26th of March of any year are governed by number 8 and Saturn. The month of March is governed by Jupiter. The character reading given below relating to number 8 is equally applicable to the other dates also. In addition, the special characteristics of those born on 17 and 26th March are given separately.

Born on 8th March

a) CHARACTER

Between the planets Saturn and Jupiter, the influence of Saturn is more evident on this person. The influence of Jupiter only protects the person from going to extremes. Though Jupiter is an ambitious planet, the nervousness of Saturn pulls back the person quite often. Saturn shows an extreme sense of discipline, steadfastness, constancy and dutifulness. The person has a sober and solitude loving personality. He loves classical music but mostly of a melancholy type. In arts he loves landscapes, natural scenery and flowers. Number 8 is considered to be a balance wheel to the character. The man can look at the other side of a subject. He is a pessimist. He prefers solitude to company. He shuns society rather than courts it. He is cautious about the future and he takes decisions very carefully on matters which pertain to mundane affairs. Persons born on these dates often find themselves very much misunderstood and are likely to suffer much slander, calumny and discredit in their lives. Such

things are likely to be caused either from lack of money to
enable the man to carry out his plans and ambitions, or from
ties of relationship or association with others. A man born
on any one of the above dates should brace himself to meet
many secret sorrows and disappoinment which will be con-
tinually cropping up, but by the development of strength of
will and determination and by never giving up his ambition,
he has a chance of surmounting all difficulties finally. He may
expect to have responsibilities placed on his shoulders, and he
will have difficulty in holding situations or positions, not
because of lack of ability on his part, but on account of circumstances likely to crop up to rob him of merit and reward.
He is a prudent person, wise and sober amongst all the
numbers. He is never over-enthusiastic and is more or less
gloomy and melancholy. He is also ambitious and persevering. He is capable of enormous efforts towards the attainment of his objects. He is sceptical and analytical. He is
creative; productive and dominating. He usually feels lonely
at heart. He understands the weak and the oppressed and
treats them in a warm-hearted manner. He is a born manager
who can keep others busy. He admires fair play and is willing to
pay a fair compensation. He has a good memory for names
and faces.

Born on 17th March you have all the basic characteristics of those born on the 8th of the month, so first go through them and then read your own.

Such a man is a good organizer and a good thinker. He
has a creative and constructive mind. He is a lover of peace
and a philanthropist. He is attracted to occultism and
mysticism. He is courageous and proud. He has strong
individualism. He is highly intelligent and clever. As regards
emotions, he is calm. At times he is generous to a fault and
at times very stingy. He is interested in research and loves
knowledge. He is conservative and dominating.

Born on 26th March you have all the basic characteristics of those born on the 8th of the month, so first go through them and then read your own.

This man wants to enjoy life without doing anything. He
is sluggish and lethargic. He revels in wine and women and

is fickle-minded. He is careless about the number of children.
He is lucky in money matters and gets easy money. He is
smart but lacks positiveness. He likes to put up a good
appearance but has a worrying nature. He has problems in
his love affairs.

b) FINANCE

The peculiarity of number 8 is the delay in life in all
respects. Naturally in financial matters also there is delay and
stability is achieved at a very late age. This person has to
work hard and he seldom succeeds in getting opulence. He
has therefore to avoid number 8 playing a part in his life.
Instead he can choose nnmber 1 or 3 for his important actions
and moves. However, if his experience shows that 8 is a
lucky number for him, he can insist on that number only, in
which case wealth and prosperity come to him. If 8 is found
to be a lucky number in one s life, one can try lottery and luck
in horse racing. But usually this number is connected with
delays and hard work and a person has to be very cautious
about his financial matters.

c) VOCATION

Subjects suitable for this person are occult sciences,
chemistry, physics, medicine and even higher mathematics. He
can be succesful in industries related to coal mines, timber etc,
and in construction companies. He can be a good accountant
and also a good administrator. However, as stated earlier, he
he has to strive hard in his career and can get fruits of his hard
work only in the later years of his life.

d) HEALTH

His main health defects are nervousness, irritation, trouble
with legs, teeth and ears, paralysis and rheumatism. He is a
bilious type and often suffers from chronic melancholia. It is
very interesting to note that the delaying characteristic in life
is also observed in his sickness. His ailments also take a

long time to cure. A number 8 man with a strong personality often suffers from varicose veins and haemorrhoids.

e) MARRIAGE AND FRIENDS

This man has a natural attraction towards those born in the period 20th April to 20th May and 20th August to 20th September. He also has an affinity for those who are governed by the numbers 5 and 7. It is therefore advisable that he selects his wife from one of these periods or numbers.

A Number 8 husband

Jupiter is the only planet protecting his married life. Basically, he prefers loneliness. He has little attraction for the opposite sex. Usually he tries to postpone his marriage with the result that if at all he marries, it is at a very late age. He also finds it difficut to choose a wife. As he prefers seclusion to gatherings, he often makes his married life miserable. He is very orthodox in his views and does not allow his wife to adopt modern ideas in dress either at home or in public places. The natural result is disappointment for his wife and hatred for her husband. If, however, he has a desire to be successful in married life, he should prefer a person who is also interested in deep and serious studies and likes to devote herself to philosophy and occult subjects.

A Number 8 wife

She has a masculine personality. She is capable and systematic. She enjoys her family life and likes to make sacrifices for her children and for the ambition of her husband. Her fault is that she lacks femininewarmth, sentiment and delicacy.

Friends

This man's best friends are those who are governed by numbers 3, 4, 5, 7 and 8. He also has a natural affinity towards those born in June, September, December and his own month i.e. March.

f) FORTUNATE DAYS :   His   lucky   days are   Wednesdays, Thursdays and Saturdays.

g) LUCKY COLOURS :   He should use   all   shades of   grey, dark blue,   purple and black.

h) LUCKY JEWELS AND STONES :   His   lucky   jewels   are sapphire, black pearl and black diamond.   His lucky stones are cat's eye and amethyst.

i) IMPORTANT   YEARS IN LIFE :   His important years are 8, 17, 26, 35, 44, 53, 62, 71 etc.

j) HIS GOOD QUALITIES AND DRAWBACKS ARE AS UNDER:

Good qualities	Drawbacks
Authority	Cynicism
Method	Delay
Practical approach	Vindictiveness
Steadiness	Nervousness
System	Laziness

CHAPTER 27

BORN ON
9th, 18th and 27th March

All those born on 9th, 18th and 27th March of any year are governed by the number 9 and the planet Mars. March is governed by Jupiter. The character reading explained below with reference to number 9 is equally applicable to other dates also. In addition, the special characteristics of those born on the 18 and the 27th March are given separately.

Born on 9th March

a) CHARACTER

This number is governed by Mars and shows aggression, resistance, courage, dash and quickness. A Martian is considered as a fighter. He is aggressive in all his acts and will not stop till he achieves his ends. He has the capacity to fight against all adverse elements and circumstances. A Martian does not know defeat and he will have either victory or death. It is said that the great Emperor Napoleon Bonaparte was a believer in this science and he had a battalion of soldiers who were all Martians. A number 9 person is not very tactful or delicate in his talk but his intention is good and his vigorous manner should not be misunderstood as rough behaviour. He should not criticise others but should use his words carefully, otherwise they will boomerang on him. The influence of Mars will make him at times rash and impulsive in thought and action. He will have a more or less erratic nature. He will be restless, making changes in his occupation or career. He will be inclined to rush into new schemes without due thought.

He should learn to control his temper, especially over little things and try to be tolerant with those around him. He is fiery and dashing and does not have sickly sentiments. He has audacity and vigour from start to finish. He is also fond of games and vigorous exercise. When the date of the month is 9 and the total of all the digits in the date of birth is also 9, the man is governed by a strong number 9 and Mars is very powerful in his life. In such a case, he has strong sexual passions and he is attracted towards the opposite sex. He is prepared to go through any ordeal to gratify his desire.

He is a brave person to whom conflict does not bring the thought of danger. He is exceedingly devoted to his friends and will fight for them. He has sympathy and consideration for the weak. He loves children and animals. He takes delight in showing mercy to others. He likes the healing profession. He is backed by self-control, moral courage and the power of forgiveness. His psychological attitude is remarkable and under all circumstances he proves his strength of will and exhibits courage. He is short-tempered.

Being born in the month of March, he is courteous and broad-minded. He has intuition. He is loyal to his friends and generally succeeds in all positions of responsibility. He is strict about law and order. He will suffer a good deal from hidden enemies, from slander and false reports, and whether he deserves it or not, he will be likley to be harshly and unjustly treated if he is drawn into litigation in any form whatsoever. In business schemes he will have to be most careful about partners and associates, because he is likely to get the blame if anything should go wrong.

Born on 18th March you have all the basic characteristics of those born on the 9th of the month, so first go through them and then read your own.

This person has tenacity and will-power which will overcome any difficulty. He is not as dashing as a number 9 man, but he is fearless and courageous. His strong health makes him passionate. He inherits property from his father. He has a disciplined mind and likes to help others. He is painstaking with good judgement and is wise. He loves to exercise complete control over others. He does not like to be cautioned by others.

Born on 27th March | you have all the basic characteristics of those born on the 9th of the month, so first go through them and then read your own.

On the whole this man has a personality of conflicts. He is confident and likes to do something for those whose life is miserable or who are handicapped. He can develop a spritual personality and can practise spritual healing. On the other side he is fond of women and may develop illicit contacts and create a scandal. Sometimes he creates unhappiness in his married life. He is very sensitive and moody and his actions and moves are unpredictable. He is self-assured and strong in resolution. He is a seeker of independence and domination. He hates to work under others. Usually, he is dogmatic in his views.

b) FINANCE

He is lucky in monetary affairs and earns far more than an average person. He is also very liberal while spending, especially for his sweetheart. He enjoys all the comforts that money can bring.

c) VOCATION

A Number 9 person has a magnetic personality and he will meet with success in any public career such as that of a writer, speaker or preacher, or as a leader in any big movement. A number 9 person is found in all walks of life but he will be more suitable for the army and professions where there is full scope for his aggression and courage. In the army he will rise to high positions, in politics he will be eminent and in business he will exhibit his dashing and pushing nature. He can be a good doctor, or a chemist or a businessman dealing in iron and steel.

d) HEALTH

A person born on the 9th, 18th or 27th of March wil escape all serious illness in his early years, but in his forties considerable changes are likely to take place in his constitution. If he studies himself carefully during this period, especially in matters of diet, he may be able to build himself up for another period. If not, he will be liable to experience many serious ailments, such as trouble with the liver, kidneys, piles, throat trouble, bronchitis, laryngitis and fevers. He will have much experience of the surgeon's knife.

e) MARRIAGE AND FRIENDS

He has a natural attraction towards persons born in the period between 20th February and 20th March, 20th June and 20th August and 20th October and 20th December. He also has an affinity for those who are governed by numbers 3, 6 and 9. It is therefore advisable that he should select his marriage partner from one of these periods or numbers.

A Number 9 husband

He is vigorous in health and has strong circulation of blood which makes him quite passionate and enthusiastic about married life. He is fond of a beautiful wife and likes her to be submissive to his sexual desires. He is fond of family and children and likes to have a good house. He usually leads a good married life in spite of his hot-tempered nature and eccentricities. He has a romantic mental picture of what he wants in his wife. This mental picture demands perfection. The most difficult thing in the married life of a number 9 person is to satisfy his romantic conception of physical love. He has a voracious appetite and his wife with her devotion should harmonise with him physically. Usually, he is suspicious of his wife.

A Number 9 wife

She will make a wonderful wife for an ambitious man. She is a witty and clever conversationalist with a wonderful social presence. She will assist her husband in his business. She may also start her own activity and add to the family income. She will be happy if married to a passionate and possessive man.

Friends

This man will make friends easily with those in high positions but will be prone to make many bitter enemies. His best friends are those who are governed by numbers 1,2,4,6,7 and 9. He has a natural affinity towards those born in June, September, December and in his own month i.e. March.

f) FORTUNATE DAYS :   His lucky days are Mondays, Tuesdays, Thursdays and Fridays.

g) LUCKY COLOURS : He should use all shades of red, white and yellow.

h) LUCKY JEWELS AND STONES ;   His   lucky jewels are topaz, pearl, ruby and lucky stones are blood-stones and garnet.

i) IMPORTANT YEARS IN LIFE :   His important years are 9,18 27, 36, 45, 54, 63, 72 etc

j) HIS GOOD QUALITIES AND DRAWBACKS ARE AS UNDER:

Good qualities	Drawbacks
Active	Destrucive
Courageous	Erratic
Dashing	Hot-tempered
Energtic	Impatient
Enthusiastic	Quarrelsome

CHAPTER 28

BORN ON
1st, 10th, 19th and 28th of April

All those born on 1st, 10th, 19th, and 28th of April of any year are governed by number 1 and the planet Sun. April is governed by Mars. Both these planets have strong personalities. The character reading explained below relating to number 1 is equally applicable to other dates also. In addition, the special characteristics of those born on 10th, 19th and 28th April are given separately.

Born on 1st April

a) CHARACTER

Being born in the month of April a person is dominating, energetic, active, hot-tempered, enthusiastic and a fighter. He has the capacity to organise an industry or business. He is an independent worker and can do his job when left to himself, He does not like any interference in his work, but if subjected to interference, he will step out and let the other fellow take his place. If he keeps cool, he can go to any heights and achieve great success in life, but his arrogance and obstinacy are the factors which often create enemies and thus spoil his career. He is endowed with a strong will-power and determination and always has new and original schemes. However, he is too hasty in his decisions and actions. Sometimes he goes to extremes and creates enemies because of his frank and outspoken nature. He is usually lucky in life and amasses money. He is gifted with intuition and can know what is likely to happen in the future. He is a warrior and will fight through all obstacles experiencing many dangers and changes in life.

Since he is governed by number 1, he is influenced by the Sun and acquires qualities associated with the Sun. He therefore has originality, activity, energy, enthusiasm, art and brilliance. A person governed by this number is spontaneous, responds to nature and has the capacity to enjoy life. He is usually successful in life due to his active nature and capacity to mix in any society. He is an artist and has many talents but they are all spontaneous. He has good taste and chooses always the beautiful. He is gifted with intuition and rarely studies any subject in depth. Yet he can influence others with his knowledge and flash. These characteristics make him a hero of the drawing room. He is changeable and is not constant in his friendship. He is honest and acknowledges his faults. He has a quick grasp of any subject and can participate spontaneously in conversation. He has a religious attitude but not in a fanatical or superstitious way. He also learns occult sciences and does wonders with his natural gift of intuition. By nature, he is cheerful, happy and bright and his outlook on life is very optimistic. Sometimes he is obstinate and selfish. He loves inventions and has creative talent. He is a better judge of human nature than the average individual. He is born to lead, not to follow. A new idea is a greater thrill to him than money in the bank. He will always be young by reason of fresh ideas.

Born on 10th April | you have all the basic characteristics of those born on the 1st of the month, so first go through them and then read your own. |

This man is very impressive with a magenetic personality and is respected for his knowledge and intelligence. He gets financial benefits from relatives such as his father, father-in-law, wife, mother etc. He gets success after his 46th year. He gets a good position in service and succeeds in business also. He has broad shoulders and a manly figure. He loves truthfulness. This number shows honour and self-confidence. The person can get fame or notoriety depending upon his will-power and character. He usually has good health and recovers quicky from sickness. He likes to help others, but seldom gets a response from them. This is more true in the case of relatives.

He will have an intense desire for outdoor life and a love of sport in all its forms. He should however be extremely careful in the matter of carrying guns. He will also run considerable risk from fire, explosions, motor car accidents etc.

Born on 19th April

> you have all the basic characteristics of those born on the 1st of the month, so first go through them and then read your own.

This man is very active, energetic and enthusiastic. He has research aptitude and likes to handle a subject in a systematic and methodical way. He takes quick decisions and always likes to keep himself busy with some concrete project. Sports is his hobby and he is interested in several games such as horse riding, shooting, and other athletic games. He is hasty and impetuous in love affairs which end in quarrels. He is courageous and has force of character. He likes to help others even going out of the way. He can keep the secrets of others. This number promises success, honour and happiness. It is very difficult for others to understand him. He is always in company but at heart feels lonely. He is obstinate and finds it difficult to extend co-operation. He is prudent and notices even trivial things. He is not an excellent speaker but can explain himself best in writing. He can be a good writer.

Born on 28th April

> you have all the basic characteristics of those born on the 1st of the month, so first go through them and then read your own.

This person is very generous and spends on charitable work to help schools, hospitals etc. He is not as lucky as those born on 1, 10 or 19 and has to undergo difficulties in public and private life. He should select his marriage partner carefully. He has to provide carefully for the future as he is likely to lose through trust in others. He is also likely to make many changes in his career. He hardly reveals his emotions and therefore appears cold. He has an unyielding will power and does not hesitate to carry out his plans.

b) FINANCE

The Number 1 man will have many ups and downs in money matters, but chiefly owing to his own rashness and in attempting enterprises beyond his power of execution. Owing to his magnetic nature he will have great influence over others, especially on the opposite sex. He will always have the ability to make money but he is likely to make many bitter enemies in the course of his career.

Even though he is extravagant due to his over enthusiastic personality, he also earns enough to support his ostentatious way of life. He may not amass wealth but his personality and behaviour will convey to others the impression that he is a rich person. He has temptation for gambling and if not controlled in time, he may lose to a great extent.

c) VOCATION

The main difficulty with a number 1 person is that he does not stick to any one profession or job for a long time. Usually, every three years there is a change in career. He is however the right man for advertising concerns, newspaper business and the cinema industry and he can also be successful in theatrical performances. He can show his art as an interior decorator. Being a good salesman, he can choose a vocation which will mean contacts with foreign countries, such as that of a political ambassador, or a trade dealing in foreign commodites. He is a born leader and can be the head of departments, a managing director etc. He can equally succeed as a surgeon, a jeweller or an electrician.

d) HEALTH

On the whole a number 1 person is a happy-go-lucky fellow and normally enjoys good health. He has great vitality and a splendid constitution. However, he is generally troubled by overexertion, he should always be on his guard against exerting himself too much. Overstraining is likely to bring fevers.

His greatest danger will be from high blood pressure, heart disease or apoplexy. He should try to keep to a simple diet and above all things avoid the use of alcohol and strong stimulants of any kind.

e) MARRIAGE AND FRIENDS

He has a natural attraction towards persons born in the period between 20th July and 20th August, 20th November and 20th December and 20th March and 20th April. He also has affinity for those who are governed by numbers 2, 4, 5, 7 and 9. It is therefore advisable that he selects his marriage partner from these periods or numbers.

A Number 1 husband

He is generous and desires his wife to shine in society. He is dictatorial and hot tempered and wants his family members to dance to his tunes and will not tolerate disrespect. In spite of his eccentricities, he leads a good married life. He has a romantic mental picture of what he wants in his wife. This mental picture demands perfection. On account of his vigorous health he desires his wife to be submissive to his sexual demands. Usually he is suspicious of his wife.

A Number 1 person is always predisposed to marriage and he is fond of his helpmate provided his wife also has equal enthusiasm. He has a love of beauty and of dress, at home and in public. However, he hardly gets a companion of his choice, with the result that he is often disappointed in his married life.

A Number 1 wife

She will be a wonderful wife for an ambitious man. She will assist her husband in his business. She needs a virile husband who is passionate and possessive and provides her with the romantic outlets her nature requires.

Friends

His best friends are those who are governed by numbers 1, 3, 5, 7 and 9. He has also a natural affinity towards persons born in July, October, January and in his own month i.e. April.

f) FORTUNATE DAYS : His lucky days are Sundays, Mondays and Thursdays. and lucky numbers are 1 and 9.

g) LUCKY COLOURS : He should use all shades of gold and yellow and also of orange and purple as his lucky colours.

h) LUCKY JEWELS AND STONES : His lucky jewels are Ruby and Emerald and lucky stones are Moon-stone and pale green stone.

i) IMPORTANT YEARS IN LIFE : His important years are 1, 10, 19, 28, 37, 46, 55, 64, 73 etc.

j) HIS GOOD QUALITIES AND DRAWBACKS ARE AS UNDER :

Good Qualities	Drawbacks
Strong will power	Obstinacy
Aspiration	Aloofness
Initiative	Domination
Authority	Impertinence
Confidence	Inflexibility
Determination	Pride
Research aptitude	Showmanship
Vigour	Extravagance
Talents	

CHAPTER 29

BORN ON
2nd, 11th, 20th and 29th April

All those born on the 2nd, 11th, 20th and 29th of April of any year are governed by number 2 and the planet Moon. April is governed by Mars. The character reading which relates to number 2 is equally applicable to the other dates. In addition, the special characteristics of those born on 11th, 20th and 29th April are given separately.

Born on 2nd April

a) CHARACTER

The combination of the Moon and Mars gives him a character full of contradictions, one with great individuality, will power and determination, but largely swayed by imagination and romantic qualities. He is original and unconventional in ideas. He resents being tied down in any way and is inclined to rebel against restrictions and conventionalites. He is likely to experience a great amount of trouble in his domestic life unless he overcomes the romantic desires of his nature. He is an enthusiast in everything he attempts but rather inclined to carry his opinions too far.

He loves natural and beautiful things in life such as the sea, flowers, scenery and the vastness of the sky. He takes pleasure in spending hours in the company of the high tides of the sea or in rivetting his eyes to the galaxy of stars in the sky.

He is very unsteady, fickle-minded and a lover of change. He therefore has a fancy for travel, especially long travel which would satisfy his natural urge for imaginary things. Such travels feed his imagination and he goes on building castles in

the air.   He is unassuming but pleasing and has a good taste
in clothes.   He likes peace and harmony.   He has hypnotic
power.

Born on 11th April   you have all the basic characteristics of those born on the 2nd
of the month, so first go through them and then read your own.

Such a man is usually successful in life and in love ; he gets
honour, position aud authority.   He is loyal to his friends and
is of a royal disposition.   He should guard himself from
secret enemies.   He has interest in mysticism, philosophy and
science.   He can expect travels, favours, and honours in life.
He is very impulsive and gets excited easily.   He worries too
much over small matters.   He has the ability to take quick
decisions and this ability endows him with leadership.   He is a
born advertiser and an inspiration to others.

Born on 20th April   you have all the basic characteristics of those born on the 2nd
of the month, so first go through them and then read your own.

He has many friends, and he benefits through wealthy
women.   He has a flair for writing and can be known as an
author or a novelist.   His prosperity lies near water, a river or
the sea.   This number has a peculiar significance.   It shows
new plans and resolutions for the betterment of people at large.
If this number is used in connection with future events, it indicates delays.

This number has a peculiar interpretation :   the awakening
of new purpose, new ambitions, the call to action, but for some
great purpose, cause or duty.

According to the Tarot system this number is called "the
Awakening", also "the judgement".   It is symbolised by the
figure of a winged angel sounding a trumpet, while from below
a man, a woman and a child are seen rising from a tomb with
their hands clasped in prayer.   The delays and hindrances to
his plans can only be conquered through the development of
the spiritual side of his nature.

Born on 29th April   you have all the basic characteristics of those born on the 2nd
of the month, so first go through them and then read your own.

This person is moody and changing and therefore uncertain
about his action.   He is courageous and bold but takes risks in

life and does not stick to anything to the end. He is intelligent and also a deep thinker but there is a tendency to carry everything to extremes. He is not very lucky in his married life. His interest is in his business. He is blessed with good fortune. His life is eventful.

He undergoes uncertainties, experiences treachery and deception from unreliable friends, and grief from members of the opposite sex.

b) FINANCE

In financial matters he gains authority and weight and is successful in carrying out his own plans if not hampered by partners. However, he does not have the physical ability to stand the strain of everday life. The outcome therefore is mediocre financial status. He can improve his financial condition provided he is able to create art out of his imagination. He may be a good author or a painter who can create novels and weird paintings and earn a good livelihood. However, his unstable mind often drags him away from routine work and this makes his income uncertain. This person therefore is not stable as far as finance is concerned.

c) VOCATION

The powerful imagination of a number 2 person will help him to be a good composer of music or a writer of fiction or romance. He can be a good artist and create works of enduring value. Immortal paintings dramas and poems are the works of a prominent and influential number 2. He has a great vocabulary and linguistic capacity and can be successful as a teacher or a professor of languages. He can also be a good translator or an editor. The Moon has control over liquids and this person can deal in chemicals, medicines, irrigation etc.

d) HEALTH

He is liable to suffer from fevers and disorders of blood causing boils and eruptions on the head, face and body. He will be subject to many experiences of the surgeon's knife and will have intestine trouble. He has to guard against trouble with teeth, gums, nose, throat and ears.

Since the Moon is the ruling planet of number 2, the uneasiness which is a prominent characteristic, creates mental worries and sleeplessness. He is also susceptible to diabetes and asthmatic trouble.

e)   MARRIAGE AND FRIENDS

This man has a natural attraction towards persons born in the period from 20th February to 20th April, 20th July to 20th August, and 20th October to 20th December. He also has affinity for those who are governed by numbers 2 and 6. .it is therefore advisable that he selects his wife from one of these periods or numbers.

A Number 2 husband

Marriage is not likely to turn out well unless he controls his emotions and compels himself to settle down to a conventional life. He has a greater love and attraction for home than any other type.   There are two types of husbands belonging to this number.   One is dominating and exacting.   He is fault_ finding and nothing satisfies him. The other type is passive, lazy and indulgent.   He will marry for the sake of money so that he may ultimately get comforts.

Being born in the month of April, he is governed by the planet Mars and therefore he is romantic and wants his wife to be beautiful, good, and clever. He has a voracious appetite for sex and his wife has to understand how to satisfy his romantic conception of physical love. He is very dashing and courageous and looks after his wife and children well.

A Number 2 wife

She is proud of her appearance and of her family and makes others jealous of her by her behaviour. She needs a passionate and possessive husband who will allow her to spend lavishly. Her outlook towards her children is generous but not sympathetic. She is irritable and impatient and not willing to see their problems from their point of view.

Friends

His best friends are those who are governed by numbers 2,4,6 and 9. He also has a natural affinity towards people born in July, October, January and in his own month i.e. April.

f) FORTUNATE DAYS AND NUMBERS :

His lucky days are Mondays, Thursdays and Fridays and his lucky numbers 2 and 9. He should therefore take all important steps on one of these days and also dates if possible. He should try his luck in lottery by purchasing a ticket where the total of all the numbers is 2 or 9, or where the last number is 2 or 9.

g) LUCKY COLOURS : A number 2 person should use all shades of white, crimson or blue as his lucky colours.

h) LUCKY JEWELS AND STONES : His lucky jewels are pearls, diamonds and corals. He may also use Moonstone and Agate.

i) IMPORTANT YEARS IN LIFE : His important years are 2, 11, 20, 29, 38, 47, 56, 65, 74 etc.

j) HIS GOOD QUALITIES AND DRAWBACKS ARE AS UNDER:

Good qualities	Drawbacks
Emotionality	Coldness
Fellowship	Envy
Honesty	Haste
Imagination	Introvert
Simplicity	Shyness
	Whimsicality

CHAPTER 30

BORN ON
3rd, 12th, 21st and 30th of April

All those born on the 3rd, 12th, 21st and 30th April of any year are governed by number 3 and the planet Jupiter. April is governed by Mars. The character-reading given below for number 3 is equally applicable to the other dates also. In addition, the special characteristics of those born on 12th, 21st and 30th April are given separately.

Born on 3rd April

a) CHARACTER

The combination of Jupiter and Mars makes the person more than usually ambitious and determined to rise in life and to succeed. He will be successful in all positions of authority over others, very definite in opinions but rather dictatorial in his views. He is exceptionally independant in character and resents being placed under an obligation. Usually he leads a charming life escaping accidents and dangers that would destroy others. He is both progressive and aggressive.

A person born in April is dominating, energetic, active, hot tempered, enthusiastic and a fighter. He has a capacity to organise an industry or business. He is an independent worker and can do his job when left to himself. He does not like any interference in his work, but if subjected to interference, he will step out and let the other fellow take his place. If he keeps his head cool, he can go to any heights and achieve great success in life, but his arrogance and obstinacy are the factors which often create enemies and thus spoil his career.

Number 3 is governed by Jupiter. It stands for morality, pure love and justice with mercy, and is known as the greatest benefactor. The vibrations emitted by this number are essentially harmonious and they lead to sympathy and untiring effort to do good to all; the man is devoutly religious and of true dignity. The abuse of the same vibrations causes the stimulation of Jupiterian virtues leading to hypocrisy, especially in religious matters. The good nature is marred by excess in many directions.

This is a good number. The person is confident about his ability. He is self-reliant and takes his own decisions. He has the habit of talking loudly. He is fond of show and likes to observe form, order and law. He is jovial in spirit and cordial in manner. His passions are healthy, spontaneous and without inhibitions. He is free in his expression. He is a good conversationalist. He takes an active interest in sports and outdoor activities from his earliest youth. He has tremendous enthusiasm and is not self-centered. He is a broad-minded person, tolerant, humorous and truthful. He is open-hearted with a good understanding and is entirely lacking in malice or petty jealousies.

Born on 12th April | you have all the basic characteristics of those born on the 3rd of the month, so first go through them and then read your own.

Authority and honours come to this person. He has vanity and is proud, ambitious and aspiring. He is fond of pleasures and is attracted to the opposite sex. However, sometimes he prefers loneliness. He is quick to notice trifles.

Born on 21st April | you have all the basic characteristics of those born on the 3rd of the month, so first go through them and then read your own.

This number is symbolised by the picture of 'the Universe' and is called 'the Crown of the Magi'. It is a number of advancement, honours, elevation in life and general success. It means victory after a long fight. The man achieves fame, reputation and honours at a very late age. He is cheerful and fond of travels. He has a strong sense of self respect. Surprisingly, he has a suspicious nature.

Born on 30th April | you have all the basic characteristics of those born on the 3rd of the month, so first go through them and then read your own.

This man is fortunate, generous and optimistic. He has a noble and religious mind. He likes to travel and visit places of piligrimage. He can be successful as a teacher, educationist or in administration. He appears gentle and sincere but has a hidden characteristic. He may be active but is restless. When faced with difficulties, he is strong enough to overcome them.

b) FINANCE

This man is a lucky type ana somehow manages to earn enough for his livelihood. He also gets opportunities for high positions in life and thereby earns quite a lot. His ambition, leadership and enthusiasm always push him forward and usually he gets all comforts in life. The number 3 person is early out of puberty and poverty.

c) VOCATION

This man's love for position and command makes him a politician. I have observed certain persons of this number occupying very high posts such as those of ministers, ambassadors, judges and secretaries. The man is gifted for public life, statesmanship, high offices etc, it may be in the army or in the church. He is a good teacher as well as a preacher. Professions such as those of doctors, bankers, advertisers, and actors are also suitable for him.

d) HEALTH

Being a lover of outdoor games, and sports of every kind, he is expected to have a robust and vigorous constitution. He however suffers from indigestion and stomach trouble, largely brought on by indiscretion in diet and perhaps by the many banquets he will be obliged to attend. After middle life he is likely to put on weight and develop heart trouble.

Number 3 mainly influences the blood and the arterial system. It also governs the sense of smell. This person is liable to suffer from chest and lung disorders, throat afflictions, gout and apoplexy and sudden fevers. He may also suffer from sore throat, diptheria, adenoids, pneumonia, pluerisy and tuberculosis of the lungs.

e) MARRIAGE AND FRIENDS

He has a natural attraction towards persons born in the period between 20th June and 20th August and 20th October and 20th December. He has affinity also for those who are governed by numbers 3, 6, 9. It is therefore advisable that he selects his wife from one of these periods or numbers.

A Number 3 husband

He is romantic and wants his wife to be beautiful, good and clever. As he is ambitious, his ambitions also make him expect too many things from his wife and thus he becomes disappointed. It is always better for him to choose a number 3 person or a number 6 person as his wife. He has a voracious appetite for sex and his wife has to understand how to satisfy his romantic conception of physical love. He is very dashing and courageous and looks after his wife and children well. He is most loving, thoughtful and considerate. As a general rule, he attains puberty at an early age and marries early.

A Number 3 wife

She is the best companion to her husband. She is very energetic and enthusiastic and likes to help her husband either in his work or business or would like to start her own activities. She is proud of her appearance and of her family and makes others jealous of her by her behaviour. She needs a passionate and possessive husband who will allow her to spend lavishly. Her attitude towards children is generous but not sympathetic. She is a good conversationalist and witty. She is not an intruder in her husband's activities.

Friends

His best friends are those who are governed by numbers 1, 3, 5, 6, 7, 8 and 9. He also has a natural affinity towards

people born in July, October, January and in his own
month i.e. April

f) FORTUNATE DAYS AND NUMRERS :

His lucky days are Tuesdays,
Thursdays and Fridays and his lucky
numbers are 3, 6, 9. He should therefore take important steps on one of
these days and also dates if possible.
He should try his luck in lottery by
purchasing a ticket where the total
of all the numbers is 3, 6, 9, or where
the last digit is 3, 6 or 9.

g) LUCKY COLOURS : He should use all shades of crimson,
yellow and violet.

h) LUCKY JEWELS AND STONES : His lucky jewels are
Topaz, Pearl, and
Cat's Eye..

i) IMPORTANT YEARS IN LIFE : His important years are 3, 12,
21, 30, 39, 48, 57, 66, 75 etc.

j) HIS GOOD QUALITIES & DRAWBACKS ARE AS UNDER :

Good qualities	Drawbacks
Ambition	Destructiveness
Activity	Dictatorship
Courage	Hot-tempered
Dignity	Hypocrisy
Philosophy	Quarrelsomeness
Prestige	Vanity

CHAPTER 31

BORN ON
4th, 13th and 22nd of April

All those born on the 4th, 13th and 22nd April of any year are governed by the number 4 and the planet Uranus. April is governed by Mars. Both these planets have strong personalities which rule the individuals governed by this number. The character reading explained with reference to number 4 is equally applicable to the other dates also. In addition, the special characteristics of those born on 13th and 22nd April are given separately.

Born on 4th April
a) CHARACTER

The person has a strong but rather peculiar combination, so that he meets with strange contradictions in life He will have periods of success as well as of failure. The unexpected will happen more often than the expected. He will be a child of circumstances where Fate will play an important part He is likely to make changes in his career and plans and feel restless and unsettled in life. The number 4 is governed by the planet Uranus and shows energy, force and advancement. It shows revolutions and unexpected happenings. Usually the changes that take place are for the better. This number represents the higher faculties of the mind. It shows activity and intelligence engaged in the reconstruction or betterment of human life. He seeks the liberation of mind from the bondage of environment and society. He dislikes hypocrisy and loves art and music.

He has an attractive personality. He needs to be pushed for—
ward, so that he can show his abilities.

Because of his peculiar nature of opposing the views of
others or to start an argument, he is often misunderstood and
makes a great number of secret enemies who consistently work
against him. He does not like any interference in his work, but
if subjected to interference he will step out and let the other
fellow take his place. If he keeps his head cool, he can achieve great success in life, but his arrogance and obstinacy are
the factors which often spoil his career. He is a warrior and
will fight all obstacles experiencing many dangers and changes
in life.

Born on 13th April
you have all the basic characteristics of those born on the 4th
of the month, so first go through them and then read your own.

This man is an intelligent person, of tall stature and good
complexion. He is considerate and benevolent. He likes
literature and scientific books. He likes to be active though in
a quiet way. He occupies positions of high responsibilities
and gets riches. His success and career starts after his 31st
year. Though outwardly he looks mild, inwardly, he is obstinate. He is faithful and sympathetic but has difficulty in expressing his love. He has all the qualities of number 4 but in an
exaggerated form. Usually there are a number of changes in
his plans and place. It. is said in ancient writings, "He who
understands the number 13 will be given power and dominion."

Born on 22nd April
you have all the basic characteristics of those born on the 4th
of the month, so first go through them and then read your own.

He is a good man, but affected by the folly of others. The
person is dominated by false judgement owing to the influence
of others. He is also tall, with good eyes. Usually he occupies good positions but without much responsibility. He is
rather easy going and is unsteady by nature. Sometimes his
actions are spasmodic. On the whole he is lucky in his affairs
and benefits from the opposite sex. He is happy in his family
life but is also fond of a companion. He is faithful and dedicated to others. Sometimes, he feels very lonely. His social

field is limited and he has few friends. He does not care for disputes. He has too much economy of sentiments.

b) FINANCE

As regards finance and monetary status, he is usually well-settled in life though he experiences delays and difficulties in his undertakings. He may not amass wealth but can maintain the show of riches. Being overanxious about the future, he is prudent and cautious and tries to make good provision for the future. His financial prosperity usually starts after the age of 40.

c) VOCATION

He will be inventive and likes machinery, electrical devices, radio, television, and transport. He will be equally successful as an engineer, a building contractor, scientist and industrialist. If he is a businessman, he is likely to retire early in life from active work.

d) HEALTH

He is likely to suffer from mysterious illnesses which are difficult to diagnose. His respiratory system is usually weak and he suffers from breathlessness. His knees, shanks and feet are also affected. Sometimes he suffers from urinary infection.

e) MARRIAGE AND FRIENDS

He has a natural attraction towards persons born in the period from 20th February to 20th April and 20th October to 20th December. He also has an affinity for those who are governed by numbers 1,2,7,8 and 9. It is therefore advisable that he selects his wife from one of these periods or numbers.

A Number 4 husband

He is shrewd and intelligent and expects his wife to share his views. He is dominating and wants all affairs of the house to run as per his desire. He is generous and has a kind and loving heart.

He has robust health and has strong circulation of blood which makes him passionate and enthusiastic about married life. He is fond of a beautiful wife and likes her to be submissive and passive to his sexual desires. He is fond of his family and children and likes to have a good house. He usually leads a good married life in spite of his hot-tempered nature and eccentricities. He has a romantic mental picture of what he wants in his wife. This mental picture demands perfection. The most difficult thing in the married life of a number 4 person is for his wife to satisfy his romantic conception of physical love. He has a voracious appetite and his wife with her devotion can harmonise with him physically. Usually, we find him suspicious of his wife.

A number 4 wife

She is smart and attractive. She has the art of dressing and has a strong will-power. She aims at several things but hardly succeeds in getting mastery over one. She loves interior decoration but does not have the capacity to work hard for it and she will get it done through others. She is often dictatorial and moody and spoils her day due to her own whimsical nature. She loves her home but is not attached to it very much. She is often uneasy and it is better for her to find a friend governed by number one or two.

Friends

This man is fond of friends and company but rarely gets close friends because of his unsteady, changing and moody nature. His best friends are those who are governed by numbers 1, 2, 4, 5, 7, 8, 9. He also has a natural affinity towards persons born in July, October, January and in his own month i. e. April,

f) FORTUNATE DAYS AND NUMBERS : His lucky days are Sundays, Mondays, Fridays   a n d Saurdtays.   His lucky numbers are 4 and 9. He should therefore take important steps on one of these days and also dates if possible. He should try his luck in lottery by purchasing a ticket where the total of all the numbers is 4 or 9, or where the final digit is 4 or 9.

g) LUCKY COLOURS : His lucky colours are electric blue, pink, white and maroon.

h) LUCKY JEWELS AND STONES : His lucky jewels are Diamond, Coral and Pearl.

i) IMPORTANT YEARS IN LIFE : His important years are 4, 13, 22, 31, 40, 49, 58 67, 76 etc.

j) HIS GOOD QUALITIES AND DRAWBACKS ARE AS UNDER:

Good Qualities	Drawbacks
Activity	Changeablity
Endurance	Domination
Energy	Stubbornness
Reliability	Vindictiveness
Method and system	Jealousy

CHAPTER 32

BORN ON

5th, 14th and 23rd of April

All those born on the 5th, 14th and 23rd of April of any year are governed by number 5 and the planet Mercury. The month April is governed by Mars. The character-reading relating to number 5 below is equally applicable to the other dates also. In addition, the special characteristics of those born on 14th and 23rd April are given separately.

Born on 5th April

a) CHARACTER

This person is governed by the planet Mercury and also by the planet Mars. This combination can be either very good or very bad, depending upon the way he develops his will power and character. It can also be very lucky or the very reverse. He will be versatile, clever and intelligent but his mind should be properly directed. If the mind is under control, there is nothing he can not master or accomplish. He is inclined to quickness of thought, speech and action. He likes new ideas and is inclined to rebel against conservative and conventional behaviour. He can have great influence over others because of his gift of speech or his pen. Mercury indicates scientific pursuits, business ability, industry, intuition and diplomacy. This man is equally proficient in games where he uses both his hands and his brain. He has the capacity to judge the ablitiy of his opponents in games and knows very well how to take advantage of the weak points of his opponents. He is fond of oratory and eloquence in expressing himself.

He has the capacity to pursue his objectives and knows very well how to plan to achieve his ends.

He is a nervous person. He is, therefore, restless. He is fond of family life and loves his children. His pleasures are mainly mental and he evaluates every thing in terms of business.

Born on 14th April

> you have all the basic characteristics of those born on the 5th of the month, so first go through them and then read your own.

This person has an attractive personality and is liked by all. His nature is co-operative and he does not like to provoke others. He usually occupies a good position in life and is successful in his business. He is not talkative but is slightly reserved. This is an intelligent and shrewd number. In women, it indicates favourable marriage but they should take care in child-bearing. A Number 14 man is inconsistent in love and experiences some romantic and impulsive attachment in early years. He is fortunate in money matters. He is industrious and positive in speech and action. Usually he is fond of gambling and of solving ridles.

Born on 23rd April

> you have all the basic characteristics of those born on the 5th of the month, so first go through them and then read your own.

This man is usually popular with women. His fortune is near water. He is successful in life and enjoys honour and wealth. He may inherit money. He keeps himself busy in his own way. He gets help and protection from superiors. He is a lucky person. He is affectionate. He loves freedom. He is averse to formalities. He has a spirit of independence and a desire to dominate.

b) FINANCE

With regard to money matters, too, he will have either good days or the reverse. If he uses his natural gifts, he will find that money comes to him easily but if he is inclined to vices, he will spend his money on drinks and loose living and will gamble away his good opportunities. If he develops his good side, he can develop his plans systematically and will be amply rewarded.

c) VOCATION

He is adaptable to the the role he has to play in the drama of life. With his adaptabillty he comes in contact with various classes of people and is successful in business. Banking is a good line for him. Mercury also shows ability for medicine or surgery. His capacity to argue his points can make him a good lawyer.

d) HEALTH

His nervous system is over-strung by reason of his active brain. He runs the risk of exhaustion. His basic health defect is biliousness and nervousness. However, his biliousness is closely related to his psychological disturbance. His biliousness increases with the increase in tension and is reduced or disappears when his nervous trouble is under control. Number 5 rules over nerves, the neck, the ears, the arms and the respiratory system.

e) MARRIAGE AND FRIENDS

He has a natural attraction towards persons born in the period between 20th January and 20th February, 20th March and 20th April and 20th September and 20th October. He also has affinity for those who are governed by numbers 1, 7. 8 and 9. It is therefore advisable that he selects his wife from one of these periods or numbers.

A Number 5 husband

He is romantic and wants his wife to be beautiful, good and clever. He has a voracious appetite for sex and his wife has to understand how to satisfy his romantic conception of physical love. He is very dashing and courageous and looks after his wife and children well. He is lucky and successful in his married life. His selection is good and usually he selects a person of his own type. He loves his partner. He expects neatness and cleanliness from his partner and also desires that she should share in the enjoyment of life. He is proud of his wife and likes to see her well-dressed. In return, he proves a good husband. He loves his children and is fond of his home. Even if he travels long, he is very much attracted towards his home and is eager to return early and join his family. He is liberal in spending on clothes and the other needs of the members of his family and furnishes his house with good taste.

A Number 5 wife

She has interest at home as well as outside. She has many activities and manages them well. She likes tidiness and though she seldom does her own work, she gets it done through her commanding personality. Her attitude towards her children is generous but not sympathetic. She is irritable and impatient and not willing to see their point of view.

Friends

His best friends are those who are governed by the numbers 1, 3, 4, 5, 7, and 8. He also has a natural affinity towards those born in July, October, January and in his own month i. e April,

f) FORTUNATE DAYS AND NUMBERS :

His lucky days are Wednesdays, Fridays and Saturdays and his lucky numbers are 5 and 8. He should therefore take all important steps on one of those days and also dates if possible. He should try his luck in lottery by purchasing a ticket where the total of all the digits is 5 or 8, or where the last number is 5 or 8.

g) LUCKY COLOURS :   He should use all shades of white and green.

h) LUCKY JEWELS AND STONES :   His lucky jewels are Pearl, Emerald, and Diamond. He may use Sapphire also.

i) IMPORTANT YEARS IN LIFE : His important years are 5, 14, 23, 32, 41, 50, 59, 68, 77 etc.

j) HIS GOOD QUALITIES AND DRAWBACKS ARE AS UNDER:

Good qualities	Drawbacks
Initiative	Hot temper
Energy	Impatience
Enthusiasm	Quarrelsomeness
Co-operation	Lack of perseverance
Practical approach	Scepticism
Shrewdness	Unreliability
Vigilance	

CHAPTER 33

BORN ON
6th, 15th and 24th of April

All those born on the 6th, 15th and 24th of April of any year are governed by number 6 and the planet Venus. The month of April is governed by the planet Mars. The character reading relating to number 6 below is equally applicable to the other dates also. In addition, the special characteristics of those born on 15th and 24th April are given separately.

Born on 6th March

a) CHARACTER

This is a favourable combination giving a generous nature backed by the energy and enthusiasm of the planet Mars. This man is affectionate, demonstrative, warm-hearted and passionate and greatly attracted towards the opposite sex. He is a pleasant personality to meet. It is always charming to be with him. His talk is interesting and lively. We may sometimes have to put aside our ideas of morality and social conduct in understanding and appreciating his feelings and views. Number 6 stands for beauty, health, vitality, warmth, attraction and above all love. A person of this number is fond of music, dancing and poetry. He loves to have a life full of ease and luxuries, money and happiness. He prefers spending to saving. He will have rich clothes, jewellery, perfume and all sorts of beautiful things.

He is necessarily a loving type and he has a feeling of kinship and humanity. He will therefore not desert his friends and he always tries to understand considerately the grievances and difficulties of others. He prefers joy to gloom and can

make others share his moments of enjoyment. His outlook is
bright and vivacious. He is emotional but keeps his emotions
to himself. His anger does not easily subside. He is very responsible and loves his children, but receives very little happiness from them. He is a born adviser and needs some audience
to whom he can express his views on matters of importance.
He is a good conversationalist and enjoys intellectual combats.

Born on 15th April you have all the basic characteristics of those born on the 6th
of the month, so first go through them and then read your own.

The birthdate 15th has occult significance, magic and
mystery. It however does not represent the higher side of
occultism. It means that the person born on this date will make
use of every art to carry out his purpose. This date of birth is
peculiarly associated with a good talker, often with eloquence.
He is very intelligent and has a good memory. He is fit for
responsible positions such those of ambassadors, consuls,
governors etc. He is very ambitious and boastful but hasty and
proud by nature. He also has interest in art and music. He
appears to be gentle but has very strong convictions. He has a
habit of worrying inwardly and leads a melancholy life. His
destiny is such that he has to make sacrifices for others.

Born on 24th April you have all the basic characteristics of those born on the 6th
of the month, so first go through them and then read your own.

He is fortunate in getting assistance from people of high
rank. He benefits through the opposite sex. He marries a rich
girl and prospers after marriage. He succeeds in speculation
and is financiall well-off. He strictly defines the line between
personal and social matters. He is methodical in his ideas. He
possesses a strong ego and sometimes tries to force his opinions on others.

c) FINANCE

He is not attracted by money and accumulation of wealth
is not his aim in life. All his interest is directed towards attaining pleasures and gratifying his desires. He therefore spends
his earnings on whatever attracts him. He also never repents
having spent his money on his art which may not ultimately

bring him monetary rewards. This man is seldom affluent but he somehow has the knack of making both ends meet having the minimum comforts he wants. He may sometimes have windfalls. In money matters he may be lucky during the early years of his life, but because of his own extravagance and improvidence, he will be in danger of poverty in his last years.

c) VOCATION

He will shine as an interior decorator, architect, jeweller, musician, hotel manager or confectioner. He can be equally successful as a broker, estate broker or commission agent.

d) HEALTH

On the whole he has a good constitution and quickly recovers from any illness. However, he is liable to suffer from a delicate throat and from trouble connected with the nose and ears and from severe headaches. He is also susceptible to epidemic fever and influenza. He is prone to nervousness but not chronically.

e) MARRIAGE AND FRIENDS

He has a natural attraction towards persons born in the periods from 20th July to 20th September and 20th November to 20th January. He has an affinity also fro those who are governed by the numbers 2,4,6, and 9.It is therefore advisable that he should select his wife from one of these periods or numbers.

A Number 6 husband

He likes marriage and usually marries early in life. He expects his partner to be neat and have charm and grace. His is usually a large family with many children. He loves his children and home. He is very kind, generous and devoted. Though he creates a lively atmosphere in the house, he somehow finds it difficult to satisfy all the necessities of the members of his family. This may sometimes create unplesantness and make him unhappy in his married life. Art is everything to him and he remains impractical in not understanding the material values of a successful life.

Occasionally an early marriage is not conducive to harmony. A second marriage later in life may be more favourable.

A Number 6 wife

She is proud of her appearance and her family and makes others jealous by her behaviour. She needs a healthy husband who would allow her to spend lavishly. She is impatient and does not attend to the problems of her children. She is devoted to her husband and will never resort to divorce ; she endures extreme hardship rather than desert him.

Friends

He will make many friends and be extremely popular but is inclined to waste too much time and money in the entertainment of those he meets. His best friends are those who are governed by numbers 2,3,4,6, and 9. He also has a natural affinity towards people born in July, October, January and in his own month i.e. April.

f) FORTUNATE DAYS
   AND NUMBERS : His lucky days are Mondays, Tuesdays, Thursdays and Fridays and his lucky numbers are 2 and 6. He should therefore take all his important steps on one of these days and also dates, if possible. He should try his luck in lottery by purchasing a ticket where the total of all the digits is 2 or 6 or where the last number is 2 or 6.

g) LUCKY COLOURS : He should use all shades of blue, rose and pink.

h) LUCKY JEWELS AND STONES : He can use Turquoise, Emerald, Pearl and Diamond.

i) IMPORTANT YEARS IN LIFE : His important years are 6,
                                15, 24, 33, 42, , 51, 60, 69,
                                78, etc·

j) HIS GOOD QUALITIES AND DRAWBACKS ARE AS UNDER:

Good Qualities	Drawbacks
Harmony	Erratic nature
Courge	Impatience
Love	Quarrelsomeness
Strong memory	Absence of foresight
Peace	Destructiveness
Dash	Hot temper

CHAPTER 34

BORN ON
7th, 16th and 25th of April

All those born on the 7th, 16th and 25th of April of any year are governed by the number 7 and the planet Neptune. April is governed by the planet Mars. The character reading relating to number 7 below is equally applicable to the other dates. In addition, the special characteristics of those born on 16th and 25th of April are given separately.

Born on 7th April

a) CHARACTER

He has individuality and is original and independent. He is restless by nature and is fond of change. He likes to visit foreign countries and becomes interested in far off lands. He has peculiar ideas about religion and dislikes following the beaten track.

This is a spiritual number and Supreme Consciousness is developed in this individual. He is like a free bird and likes to break the traditional bondage and restrictions. He is likely to be considered eccentric by those who do not understand him but he will pursue his way in spite of opposition. The planet Neptune governs sentiments and emotions and it is not regarded as having material aspects. He therefore finds it hard to settle down to a regular conventional life. His behaviour is a mystery to others. He is often absent-minded. He thinks logically and achieves great aims. He is stubborn and disregards the opinions of others. He has good talent for earning money. In general, he is somewhat indifferent and cares little for materialistic goals. He will have the best or none at all. He is sensitive and hides his real feelings by apparent indifference. He dislikes mingling with common people. He prefers to spend his free hour with his favourite book. When his opinion is solicited, he speaks with authority. He knows his ground.

Born on 16th April | you have all the basic characteristics of those born on the 7th of the month, so first go through them and then read your own.

He is dominating, energetic, active, hot-tempered and enthusiastic, and a fighter. He has the capacity to organise an industry or business. He is an independent worker and can do his job when left to himself. He does not like any interference in his work, but if subjected to interference, he will step out and let the other fellow take his place. He is rather easy-going and does not like to work hard. He is good-humoured and generous. He is very sensitive and emotional. He gets upset soon but is soon pleased. He is frequently indisposed. He is fortunate in getting good and successful children. However there is some sort of sorrow in his married life. He appears to be calm but his mind is always in turmoil. He is sometimes short-tempered. He does not disclose his nervousness and is slow in taking decisions.

Born on 25th April | you have all the basic characteristics of those born on the 7th of the month, so first-go through them and then read your own.

He is a jack of all trades but master of none. He is interested in several subjects but cannot go into details. His knowledge therefore is very shallow. He likes to travel and has connections with foreign countries. He is honest, faithful and good-natured. But he is fickle-minded and inconsistent. His memory is good and he is a good orator and a good teacher.

b) FINANCE

Usually, there are a number of changes in the life of a number 7 person and so, it is difficult for him to amass wealth. However, this being a mystic number, the person can be well placed in life provided he finds a job of his choice. In that case he can be a wealthy person with all amenities and comforts.

c) VOCATION

His love of sea travel and interest in foreign countries make him a successful merchant, exporter or importer. He can also deal in dairy products, fishery and other products such as soap etc. or run a chemical industry. He can also study medicine and surgery.

d) HEALTH

Though he has a strong constitution and energy, he is susceptible to mild fevers and inflammation. In his emotional exccitement he is likely to take alcohol which he should avoid; he needs control and not stimulation. Since he is governed by Mars, his head and face are more affected than any other part of the body. He is also liable to suffer from liver, bladder and stomach troubles.

In health matters he is liable to rapid changes in physical condition. He will be subject to colds, chills, and fevers and will be run down easily when his nerves are taxed

e) MARRIAGE AND FRIENDS

He has a natural attraction towards persons born in the period from 20th February to 20th April and 20th October to 20th December. He also has affinity for those who are governed by the numbers 3, 5, 8 and 9. It is therefore advisable that he should select his wife from one of these periods or numbers.

A Number 7 husband

He is very dashing and courageous and looks after his wife and children well. He is dominating but does not impose his ideas on his wife. He is very considerate but emotional. He understands his wife very well. He is liberal, and fond of picnics, travels and the cinema. He is a spendthrift and likes to live lavishly. His family is moderate in size and has all comforts in life. He usually leads a good married life in spite of his hot–tempered nature and eccentricities. He has a romantic mental picture of what he wants in his wife. This mental picture demands perfection. The most difficult thing for his wife is to satisfy his romantic conception of physical love. He has a voracious appetite and his wife with her devotion should achieve physical harmony with him. Usually, we find him suspicious of his wife.

A Number 7 wife

She is very moody and her behaviour is unpredictable. She is very uneasy and gets disturbed over small matters. She is good at entertaining friends and she likes to invite people to a party or dinner. She expects her husband to look after her all the time· She will be a wonderful wife if married to a passionate, possessive and ambitious man.

Friends

His best friends are those who are governed by the numbers 1, 3, 4, 5, 7, 8 and 9. He also has a natural affinity towards people born in July, October and January and in his own month i.e. April.

f) FORTUNATE DAYS AND MEMBERS : His lucky days are Sundays, Mondays, Wednesdays and Thursdays, and his lucky numbers are 2 and 7. He should therefore take all important steps on one of these days and also dates if possible. He should try his luck in lottery by purchasing a ticket where the total of all the digits is 2 or 7, or where the last digit is 2 or 7.

g) LUCKY COLOURS : He should use all shades of white, cream and green.

h) LUCKY JEWELS AND STONES : His lucky jewels are Topaz, Emarald and Pearl.

i) IMPORTANT YEARS IN LIFE : His important years are 7, 16. 25, 34, 43, 52, 61, 70, 79 etc,

j) HIS GOOD QUALITIES & DRAWBACKS ARE AS UNDER:

Good qualities	Drawbacks
Austerity	Despondency
Peace	Diffidence
Reflection	Restlessness
Serenity	Whimsicality
Tolerance	Hot temper
Courage	Impatience
Enthusiasm	

CHAPTER 35

BORN ON
8th, 17th and 26th of April

All those born on the 8th, 17th and 26th April of any year are governed by the number 8 and the planet Saturn. April is governed by the planet Mars. The character reading relating to number 8 is equally applicable to the other dates. In addition, the special characteristics of those born on 17th and 26th of April are given separately.

Born on 8th April

a) CHARACTER

The combination of the planets Saturn and Mars is not a very favourable one unless the person exercises great caution and prudence in all his actions. He is likely to meet with great difficulties and obstacles during the first half of his life. He will be held back by ties of home and relations and is likely to have many people to support or care for.

The dominance of Saturn shows extreme sense of discipline, steadfastness, constancy and sense of duty. The person has a sober personality and is a solitary man. He is a lover of classical music but mostly of the melancholy type. In arts he loves landscapes, natural scenery and flowers. Number 8 is considered to be a balance-wheel to the character. The man tends to look at the other side of life. He is a pessimist. He prefers solitude to company. He is cautious about the future and he takes decisions very carefully on matters which pertain to mundane affairs. He is a prudent person, wise and sober. He is never over-enthusiastic and is more or less gloomy and melancholy. He is also ambitious and persevering. He is capable of enormous efforts for the attainment of desired objects. He is sceptical and analytical. He is creative, productive and dominating. He is likely to be misunderstood. He usually feels lonely at heart. He understands the weak and the oppressed and treats them in a warm-hearted manner. He is a born manager who can keep others busy. He admires fair play and is willing to pay a fair compensation. He has a good memory for names and faces.

Born on 17th April you have all the basic characteristics of those born on the 8th of the month, so first go through them and then read your own.

Number 17 is a highly spiritual number and is represented in symbolism by the 8-pointed Star of Venus : a symbol of Peace and Love. It means a person has risen superior in spirit to the trials and difficulties of his life. Number 17 is considered a number of immortality and the person's name lives after him. He is a good organiser and a good thinker. He has a creative and constructive mind. He is a lover of peace and a philanthropist. He is attracted to occultism and mysticism. He is courageous and proud. He has strong individualism. He is highly intelligent and clever. He is calm. At times he is generous to a fault and at times very stingy. He is interested in research and seeks knowledge. He is conservative and dominating.

Born on 26th April you have all the basic characteristics of those born on the 8th of the month, so first go through them and then read your own.

This man wants to enjoy life without doing anyting. He is sluggish and lethargic. He revels in wine and women and is fickle-minded. He is careless about the number of children. He is lucky in money matters and gets easy money. He is smart but lacks positiveness. He likes to put up a good appearance but has a worrying nature. He has problems in his love affairs.

b) FINANCE

The peculiarity of number 8 is the delay in life in all respects. Naturally in financial matters also there is delay and stability is achieved only at a very late age. This person has to work hard and he is seldom affluent. He has therefore to avoid number 8 playing a part in his life and instead he can choose number 1 or 3 for all his important actions and moves in life. However, if his experience shows that 8 is a lucky number in his life, he can try lottery and luck in horse racing. But usually this number is connected with delays and hard work and a person has to be very cautious about financial matters.

c) VOCATION

Subjects suitable for him are occult sciences, chemistry, physics, medicine and higher mathematics. He can be successful in industries dealing with coal mines, timber etc, and in construction companies. He can be a good accountant and also a good administrator. However, as stated earlier, he has to strive hard in his career and can get the fruits of his hard work only in the later years of his life.

d) HEALTH

He is likely to have some very peculiar experience such as wrong diagnosis of his ailments and may have medicines prescribed for him. He should therefore studiously avoid drugs of all kinds. He should be careful about his diet and keep his intestines in good condition or he will be liable to auto-poisoning, boils, skin complaints, constipation etc. His main health defects are nervousness, irritation, trouble with legs, teeth, and ears, paralysis and rheumatism. He is a bilious type and often suffers from chronic melancholia. It is very interesting to note that the delaying characteristic in his life manifests in his sickness. The ailments he suffers from also take a long time to cure. Varicose veins and haemorrhoids are common tendency of a strong 8 personality.

e) MARRIAGE AND FRIENDS

He has a natural attraction towards persons born in the period between 20th March and 20th May and 20th July and

20th September. He also has an affinity for those who are governed by numbers 5 and 7. It is therefore advisable for him to select his wife from one of these periods or numbers.

A Number 8 husband

Basically, a number 8 person does not desire marriage. However as he is born in the month of April his life is dominated by Mars which shows vigour and passions. Thus there is a combination of Saturn and Mars in his married life. On the one side, he shows Martian qualities and on the other side, he shows Saturnian qualities. Of the two he is mostly governed by the planet Saturn. Usually he tries to postpone his marriage with the result that if at all he marries, it is at a very late age. He also finds it difficult to make a choice of his wife. As he prefers seclusion to gathering, he often makes his married life miserable. He is very orthodox in his views and does not allow his wife to adopt modern ideas in dress at home or in public places. The natural result is disappointment on the part of his wife and hatred for her husband. If however he has a desire to be successful in married life, he should prefer a person who is also interested in deep and serious studies and likes to devote herself to philosophy and occult subjects.

A Number 8 wife

She is of a masculine personality. She is capable and systematic. She enjoys her family life and likes to make sacrifices for her children and for the ambition of her husband. Her fault is that s ' lacks womanly warmth, sentiment and delicacy.

Friends

This man's best friends are those who are governed by numbers 3, 4, 5, 7 and 8. He also has a natural affinity towards people born in July, October, January and in his own month i.e. April.

f) FORTUNATE DAYS AND NUMBERS : His lucky days are Wednesdays, Thursdays and Saturdays and lucky numbers are 5 and 8. He should therefore take all important steps on one of these days and also dates if possible. He should try his luck in lottery by purchasing a ticket where the total of all the digits is 5 or 8, or where the last number is 5 or 8.

g) LUCKY COLOURS : He should use dark grey, dark blue, purple and black.

h) LUCKY JEWELS AND STONES : His lucky jewels are Sapphire, Black Pearl, Black Diamond. His lucky stones are cat's eye and Amethyst.

i) IMPORTANT YEARS IN LIFE : His important years are 8, 17, 26, 35, 44, 53, 62, 71 etc.

j) HIS GOOD QUALITIES AND DRAWBACKS ARE AS UNDER :

Good qualities	Drawbacks
Authority	Cynicism
Method	Delay
Practical approach	Vindictiveness
Steady nature	Nervousness
Systematic	Laziness.

CHAPTER 36

BORN ON
9th, 18th and 27th of April

All those born on the 9th, 18th and 27th of April of any year are governed by the number 9 and the planet Mars : April is also governed by Mars. The character reading relating to number 9 below is equally applicable to, the other dates also. In addition, the special characteristics of those born on 18th and 27nd April are given separately.

Born on 9th April

a) CHARACTER

He is extremely independent in thought and action. He has a strong dislike of all restrictions and limitations. He is much inclined to express his views and opinions too frankly, regardless of the feelings of others. As he is dominated too much by Mars, he has aggression, resistance, courage dash and quickness. A Martian is considered as a fighter. He is aggressive in all his acts and will not stop till he achieves his end. He has the capacity to fight even against all adverse elements and circumstances. A Martian does not know defeat and if we have an army of Martians, there would not be anything like defeat for them. It would be either victory or death. It is said that the great Emperor Nepoleon Bonaparte was a believer in this science and he had a battalion of soldiers who were pure Martians. A Number 9 person is not very tactful or delicate in his talk but his intention is good and his vigorous manner should not be mistaken for rough behaviour. He should

not criticise others but should use his words carefully, otherwise they will boomerang.

He is firm and dashing and does not have sickly sentiments. He has audacity and vigour from start to finish. He
is also fond of games and vigorous exercise. When the date
of the month is 9 and the total of all digits of the date birth
is also 9, he is governed by a strong number 9 and his Mars is
very powerful. In such a case, he has strong sexual passions
and he is attracted towards the opposite sex. He is prepared
to go through any ordeal to gratify his desire.

He is a brave person to whom conflict does not bring the
thought of danger. He is exceedingly devoted to his friends
and will fight for them. He has sympathy and consideration
for the weak. He loves children and animals. He takes delight
in showing mercy to others. He likes the healing profession.
He is backed by self-control, moral courage and the power of
forgiveness. Under all circumstances he proves his strength
of will and exhibits courage. He is short-tempered.

Born on 18th April you have all the basic characteristics of those born on the 9th of the month, so first go through them and then read your own.

This person has tenacity and will-power which will overcome any difficulty. He is not as dashing as a number 9
person but he is fearless and courageous. His strong health
makes him passionate. He inherits property from his father.
He has a disciplined mind and likes to help others. He is
painstaking with good judgement and is wise. He loves to
exercise total control over others. He does not like to be
cautioned by others.

Born on 27th April you have all the basic characteristics of those born on the 9th of the month, so first go through them and then read your own.

On the whole this man is a conflicting personality. He is
confident and likes to do something for those whose life is
miserable or who are handicapped. He can develop a
spiritual personality and can practise spiritual healing. On the
other side he is fond of women and can develop illicit contacts and create scandals. Sometimes he creates unhappiness
in his married life. He is very sensitive and his actions and
moves are unpredictable. He is self-assured and strong in

resolution. He is a seeker of independence and likes to dominate. He hates to work under others. Usually, he is dogmatic.

b) FINANCE

He is lucky in his monetary affairs and earns far more than an average person. He is also very liberal while spending, especially for his sweetheart. He enjoys all the comforts that money can bring.

c) VOCATION

A Number 9 person is found in all walks of life but he will be more suitable for the army and for professions where there is full scope for his aggression and courage. In the army he will rise to high positions, in politics he will be eminent and in business he exhibits his dashing and pushing nature. He can be a good doctor, or a chemist or a business-man dealing in iron and steel.

d) HEALTH

His main health defect arises from heat and he is suscep- tible to troubles such as piles, fevers etc. He is also likely to suffer from trouble of bladder stone. Throat trouble, bronchites, laryngitis are also common to him.

e) MARRIAGE AND FRIENDS

He has natural attraction towards persons born in the period from 20th July to 20th August and 20th November to 20th December. He also has affinity for those who are governed by numbers 3, 6 and 9. It is therefore advisable that he should select his wife from one of these periods or numbers.

A Number 9 husband

He is vigorous in health and has strong circulation of blood which makes him very passionate and enthusiastic about married life. He is fond of a beautiful wife and likes her to be submissive and passive to his sexual desires. He is fond of family and children and likes to have a good home. He usually leads a good married life in spite of his hot-tempered nature and eccentricities. He has a romantic mental picture of what he wants in his wife. This mental picture demands perfection. The most difficult thing in the married life of a number 9 person is to satisfy his romantic conception of physical love. He has a voracious appetite and his wife with her devotion can achieve physical harmony with him. Usually, we find him suspicious of his wife.

A number 9 wife

She will make a wonderful wife for an ambitious man. She is a witty and clever conversationalist with a wonderful social presence. She will assist her husband in his business. She may also start her own activity and add to the family income. She will be happy if married to a passionate and possessive man.

Friends

His best friends are those who are governed by numbers 1, 2, 4, 6, 7 and 9. He also has a natural affinity towards people born in July, October, and January and in his own month i. e. April.

f) FORTUNATE DAYS
   AND NUMBERS : His lucky days are Mondays, Thursdays and Fridays and lucky numbers are 3, 6, 9. He should take all important steps on one of these days and also dates if possible. He should try his luck in lottery by purchasing a ticket where the total of all the digits is 3, 6, or 9, or where the last number is 3, 6, or 9.

g) LUCKY COLOURS : He should use all shades of yellow, red and white.

h) LUCKY JEWELS AND STONES : He lucky jewels are Topaz, Pearl and Ruby and lucky stones are blood-stones and Garnet.

i) IMPORTANT YEARS IN LIFE : His important years are 9, 18, 27, 36, 45, 54, 63, 72 etc.

j) HIS GOOD QUALITIES AND DRAWBACKS ARE AS UNDER:

Good Qualities	Drawbacks
Activity	Destructive tendency
Courage	Erratic nature
Dash	Hot temper
Energy	Impatience
Enthusiasm.	Quarrelsomeness.

CHAPTER 37

BORN ON
1st, 10th, 19th and 28th of May

All those born on 1st, 10th, 19th and 28th of May of any year are governed by number 1 and the planet Sun ; May is governed by the planet Venus. The character reading relating to number 1 given below is equally applicable to the other dates. In addition, the special characteristics of those born on 10th, 19th and 28th May are given separately.

Born on 1st May

a) CHARACTER

The man has great power of endurance, both physically and mentally and can stand great strain. He is very social and loves society, theatres, cinema houses, picnics, travel etc. Others take him to be richer than he really is. He is a good host and has a taste for good food. He has originality, activity, enthusiasm, art and brilliance. He is spontaneous and responds to nature. He is usually successful in life due to his active nature and the capacity to mix in any society. He is gifted with intuition and seldom studies any subject deeply. Even then he can influence others with his knowledge and flash. He has interest in occult sciences and does wonders with his natural gift of intuition. By nature he is cheerful, happy and bright and his outlook on life is very optimistic. He has a strong will power and is independent in thought and action. On one hand, he is practical, but on the other hand, he is idealistic. Sometimes he is obstinate and selfish. He is fond of inventions and has creative talents. He is a better judge of human nature than the average individual. He is born to lead, not to follow. A new idea gives him a greater thrill than money the bank. He will always be young by reason of a fresh idea.

Born on 10th May   you have all the basic characteristics of those born on the 1st of the month, so first go through them and then read your own.

He is very impressive with a magnetic personality and is respected for his knowledge and intelligence. He gets financial benefits from relatives such as his father, father-in-law, wife, mother, etc. He gets success after his 46th year. He gets a good position in service and succeeds in business also. He has broad shoulders and a manly figure. He loves truthfulness. This number shows honour and self-confidence. The person gets fame or notoriety depending upon his will-power and character. Usually he has good health and quickly recovers from sickness. He likes to help others, but rarely gets a response from them. This is particularly true in the case of relatives.

Born on 19th May   you have all the basic characteristics of those born on the 1st of the month, so first go through them and then read your own.

He is very active, energetic and enthusiastic. He has research aptitude and likes to handle a subject in a systematic and methodical way. He takes quick decisions and always likes to keep himself busy with some concrete project. He loves sports and is interested in several games such as horse riding, shooting, and other athletic games. He is hasty and impetuous in love affairs which end in quarrels. He is courageous and has force of character. He likes to help others even going out of the way. He can keep the secrets of others and people can confide in him. This number promises success, honour and happiness. It is very difficult for others to understand him. He is always in company but at heart feels lonely. He is obstinate and finds it difficult to extend co-operation. He is prudent. He notices even a trivial thing. He is not an excellent speaker but can explain himself best in writing. He can be a good writer

Born on 28th May | you have all the basic characteristics of those born on the 1st of the month, so first go through them and then read your own.

He is very generous and spends on charitable institutions such as schools, hospitals, etc. He is not as lucky as numbers 1, 10 and 19 and has to undergo difficulties in public and private life. He should choose his marriage partner carefully. He has to provide carefully for the future as he is likely to lose through trust in others. He is also likely to make many changes in his career. He hardly reveals his emotions and therefore appears cold. He has an unyielding will-power and does not hesitate to carry out his plans.

b) FINANCE

He is lucky in money matters, but inclined to indulge in luxury and an extravagant style of living. He is prone to take great risks in speculation or in attempting to do business on too large a scale. But speaking generally he may expect to be successful.

c) VOCATION

He has a large vision about whatever work he may be engaged in, but cannot easily stand interference of any kind. He will meet with success in any career that would bring him before the public and also in offices or in executive work of any kind. However, the main difficulty with a number 1 person is that he cannot stick to any one profession or job for a long time. Usually, every three years there is a change in his career. He is, however, suitable for advertising concerns, newspaper business and the cinema industry. He can also be successful in theatrical performances. He can show his art as an interior decorator. Being a good salesman, he can choose a vocation which will have relations with foreign countries, such as that of a political ambassador or a trade dealing in foreign commodities. He is a leader and can be the head of departments, a managing director etc. He can succeed also as a surgeon, jeweller and electrician, and in research projects.

He is also an excellent public servant, official or head of government departments. He succeeds in the army and navy.

d) HEALTH

Venus gives abundance of vitality which should be guided into the proper channels. The chief danger to health comes through inertia and self-indulgence. The man is likely to expend too much energy in carrying out his plans and not having enough rest and sleep. The chief source of trouble will be neglected colds settling on the lungs and chest· Being governed by the Sun, he is susceptible to heart trouble, weak eyesight, over-exertion and sunstroke.

e) MARRIAGE AND FRIENDS

He has a natural attraction towards persons born in the period between 20th July and 20th September, 20th November and 20th January and 20th March and 20th May. He also has affinity for those who are governed by numbers 2, 4, 5 and 7. It is therefore advisable that he selects his marriage partner from one of these periods or numbers.

A Number 1 husband

As a husband, he is very generous, devoted and faithful. He always looks after his famly in spite of any outside intefest. He tries his best to provide good education and clothes to his children. He generally marries a person above him economically. He is attracted to beauty and usually he gets a good looking wife. He finds his married life attractive.

A Number 1 person is predisposed to marriage and he is fond of his helpmate provided she also has equal enthusiasm and has a love of beauty and of dress, at home and in public. It is, however, often seen that he does not get a companion of his choice, with the result that he is often disappointed in his married life.

A Number 1 wife

She is aristocratic by temperament and attracts people to

her home and commands great respect. She needs a virile
husband who can provide her with the romantic outlets that her
passionate nature requires. She is a devoted and affectionate
wife and dependent on her husband. She has the capacity to
endure hardships and to adapt herself to circumstances. She is
calm and reserved but at the same time social and everybody's
friend. She makes herself dependent although she can look
after herself if necessary. She is an easy going type and enjoys
picnics, theatres and the company of friends.

Friends

He is usually attracted towards those who have a scienific
mind, intelligence and shrewdness. He likes those who have
the capacity to discuss subjects which give food for thought.
His best friends are those who are governed by numbers 1,3,4,
5, 7 and 9. He has a natural affinity towards people born in
August, November, February and in his own month i.e. May.

f) FORTUNATE DAYS
   AND NUMBERS : His lucky days are Sundays, Mondays,
   Thursdays and Fridays and lucky
   numbers are 1 and 6. He should
   therefore take important steps on one
   of these days and also dates if possible. He should try his luck in lottery
   by purchasing a ticket where the total
   of all the digits is 1 and 6, or where
   the last digit is 1 or 6.

g) LUCKY COLOURS : He should use all shades of gold,
   orange and blue.

h) LUCKY JEWELS AND STONES : His lucky jewels are
   Ruby, Emerald and
   Pearl,

i) IMPORTANT YEARS IN LIFE: His important years are 1, 10,
   19, 28, 37, 46, 55, 64, 73 etc.

j) HIS GOOD QUALITIES & DRAWBACKS ARE AS UNDER :

Good qualities	Drawbacks
Strong memory	Interference
Harmony	Absence of foresight
Research	Pride
Vigour	Impertinence
Confidence	Domination
Determination	Spendthrift nature
Authority	Aloofness
Aspiration	Inflexibility

CHAPTER 38

BORN ON
2nd, 11th, 2Oth and 29th of May

All those born on the 2nd, 11th, 20th and 29th of May of any year are governed by number 2 and the planet Moon. May is governed by the planet Venus. The character reading with regard to number 2 given below is equally applicable to the other dates. In addition, the special characteristics of those born on 11th, 20th and 29th May are given separately.

Born on 2nd May

a) CHARACTER

In such a person the gentler qualities manifest clearly. The Moon will have a special influence on him, as it is in its exaltation. He will be imaginative, romantic and artistic with a decided leaning towards idealism, mystical studies, occultism and spirualism. He will have many changes in the places of his residence and be rather restless. His sympathies will be easily aroused for the suffering of others and many demands are likely to be made on his time. He has an affable disposition, is very attractive to strangers and is very adaptable to new surroundings. He will have a number of friends and as a general rule, he will be lucky, espically in his relations with the opposite sex. He will have remarkable intuition and accurate dreams.

He loves beautiful things in life such as the sea and flowers, and the vastness of the sky. He takes pleasure in spending hours in the company of the high tides of the sea or in rivetting his eyes to the galaxies in the sky.

He is very unsteady aud fickle-minded. He therefore has a fancy for travel, especially long travels which satisfy his natural urge for imaginary things. Such travels stimulate his imagination and he will go on building castles in the air. He is unassuming and pleasing and has a good taste in clothes. He likes peace and harmony. He has hypnotic power.

He is very emotional and sentimental and has great power of endurance. In love he is generous and will make any sacrifices. Others take him to be richer than he is.

Born on 11th May

you have all the basic characteristics of those born the 2nd of the month, so first go through them and then read your own.

This person is usually successful in life and in love, and gets honour, position and authority. He is honest with his friends and is of a royal disposition. He should guard himself from secret enemies. He has interest in mysticism, philosophy and science. He can expect travel favours and honours in life. He is very impulsive and gets excited easily. He worries too much over small matters. He has the ability to take quick decisions which endow him with leadership. He is a born advisor and an inspiration to others.

Born on 20th May

you have all the basic characteristics of those born on the 2nd of the month, so first go through them and then read your own.

This man has many friends and benefits through wealthy women. He has a flair for writing and can be known as an author or a novelist. His prosperity lies near water, a river or the sea. This number has a peculiar significance. It shows new plans and new resolutions for the betterment of people at large.

Born on 29th May

you have all the basic characteristics of those born on the 2nd of the month, so first go through them and then read your own.

This person is moody and changing and therefore uncertain about his action. He is courageous but takes risks in life and does not stick to anything to the end. He is intelligent and also a deep thinker but there is a tendency to carry everything to extremes. He is not very lucky in his married life. His interest is in his business. He is blessed with good fortune. His life is eventful.

b) FINANCE

Financial conditions will be fluctuating. He will have good luck followed by reverses and nothing seems to go right. It is better he avoids speculation and gambles of all kinds. He can make money in any career that brings him before the public. On the whole a person governed by number 2 is a lethargic man and does not like to work hard. He can improve his financial position provided he is able to create art out of his imagination. In spite of the setbacks in financial matters he is lucky and gains through association, partnership or through marriage.

c) VOCATION

He can be a good public servant or the head of a depart—ment by virtue of his faithfulness and loyal friendship. He can be a good author or a painter. He can also create works of enduring value. He has a copious vocabulary and linguistic capacities and can be successful as a teacher or a professor of languages. He can also be a good translator or an editor.

d) HEALTH

He will have to be particularly careful of chills, influenza, and colds lying too long on the bronchial tubes, lungs and throat. From middle life the nasal passages are likely to become affected and unless care is taken, he will at times suffer from growths in the nose, also from sinus trouble, mastoids and some defect in hearing.

Since the Moon is the ruling planet of number 2, the uneasiness which is a prominent characteristic, creates mental worries and sleeplessness. He is also susceptible to diabetes and asthmatic troubles.

e) MARRIAGE AND FRIENDS

He has a natural attraction towards persons born in the period between 20th February and 20th March, 20th April and 20th May and 20th October and 20th November. He also has affinity for those who are governed by numbers 2 and 6. It is therefore advisable that he selects his wife from one of these periods or numbers.

A Number 2 husband

He always looks after his home in spite of any outside interest. He tries his best to provide good education and clothes to his children. He generally marries a person richer than himself. He finds his married life interesting. There are 2 types of husbands belonging to this number. One is dominating and exacting. He is fault-finding and nothing satisfies him. The other type is passive, lazy and indulgent. He will marry for the sake of money so that he may ultimately get comforts.

A Number 2 wife

She is sympathetic, affectionate and devoted. She is satisfied with anything her husband provides. She has the capacity to endure hardships and to adapt herself to circumstances. She is calm and reserved but at the same time social and is everybody's friend.

Friends

This man's best friends are those who are governed by numbers 2,4,6 and 9. He also has a natural affinity towards those who are born in the months of August, November and February and in his own month i.e. May. He also likes those who have a scientific mind and a research aptitude. He likes to discuss subjects which give food for thought.

f) FORTUNATE DAYS
   AND NUMBERS : His lucky days are Mondays, Tuesdays and Fridays and his lucky numbers are 2 and 6. He should therefore take all important steps on one of these days and also dates if possible. He should try

his luck in lottery by purchasing a ticket where the total of all the digits is 2 or 6 or where the last figure is 2 or 6.

g) LUCKY COLOURS : He should use all shades of white cream or blue as his lucky colours.

h) LUCKY JEWELS AND STONES : His lucky jewels are Emerald, Pearl and Diamond.

i) IMPORTANT YEARS IN LIFE : His important years are, 2, 11, 20, 29, 38, 47, 56, 65, 74 etc

j) HIS GOOD QUALITIES AND DRAWBACKS ARE AS UNDER :

Good qualities	Drawbacks
Strong Memory	Moodiness
Harmony	Coldness
Emotionality	Envy
Honesty	Haste
Imagination	Introvert
Simplicity	Shyness
Fellowship	Whimsicality

CHAPTER 39

BORN ON
3rd, 12th, 21st and 30th May

All those born on the 3rd, 12th, 21st and 30th of May of any year are governed by number 3 and the planet Jupiter. May is governed by the planet Venus. The character reading relating to number 3 given below is equally applicable to the other dates. In addition, the special characteristics of those born on 12th, 21st and 30th May are given separately.

Born on 3rd May

a) CHARACTER

The combination of Jupiter and Venus is a good one and makes the person successful in life provided he does not allow the Venus or love side of his nature to become too strong. He should give full scope to the ambitious side of his nature and always try to associate with persons above him in social or business life. He has independent views about religion and will shape a philosophy of his own. He is positive and determined in his ideas and rather obstinate in carrying out his plans.

He is usually lucky in life. Vibrations radiating through him attract all that is good to him and his affairs prosper as a consequence. The judge who gives sane decision and merciful sentences, the physician and the church dignitary, the world's teachers and philosophers are all mostly governed by number 3.

This is a good number. The person is confident of his ability. He is self-reliant and takes his own decisions. He has the habit of talking loudly. He is fond of show and likes to observe form, order and law. He is jovial in spirit and cordial in manner. His passions are healthy, spontaneous and without inhibitions. He is free in his expressions. He is a good coeversationalist.

This man is governed by Jupiter, which stands for morality, pure love and justice with mercy and is known as the greatest benefactor and the uplifter. The vibrations emitted by this number are essentially harmonious and they lead to sympathy and an untiring effort to do good to all. The man is devoutly religious and has true dignity. The abuse of the same vibrations causes the stimulation of Jupiterian virtues leading to hypocrisy, especially in religious matters. The good nature is marred by excess in many directions.

From his earliest youth, this man takes an active interest in sports and outdoor activities. He has tremendous enthusiasm and is not self-centred. His intellect is of a very high order. He has a vision that understands the world and he loves it for what it is and not for what it ought to be. He is a broad-minded person, tolerant, humorous and truthful. He is open-hearted with good understanding and is entirely lacking in malice or petty jealousies. If he is not alert, people take undue advantage of his good nature.

Born on 12th May

you have all the basic characteristics of those born on the 3rd of the month, so first go through them and then read your own.

Authority and honours are the significant aspects of this person. He has vanity and is proud, ambitious and aspiring. He is fond of pleasures and is attracted to the opposite sex. However sometimes he prefers loneliness. He likes to make sacrifices for others but becomes a victim of other people's plans or intrigues. His relations with people are smooth and harmonious. He is quick to notice trifles. He has lofty ideals.

Born on 21st May

you have all the basic characteristics of those born on the 3rd of the month, so first go through them and then read your own.

This man is kind, generous and a loving father. He achieves fame and honours very late in life. He is cheerful and fond of travels. He has a strong sense of self-respect. Surprisingly, he has a suspicious nature.

Born on 30th May | you have all the basic characteristics of those born on the 3rd of the month, so first go through them and then read your own.

This person is fortunate, generous and optimstic. He has a noble and religious mind. He likes to travel and visit places of pilgrimage. He can be successful as a teacher or as an educationist or in administration. He appears gentle and sincere, but has a hidden characteristic. He may be active but is restless. When faced with difficulties he is strong enough to overcome them.

b) FINANCE

In matters of finance he need not worry. Great opportunities will come to him. He can create much out of nothing. His only danger is that he may undermine his resources by going in for large schemes of a speculative nature. His ambition, leadership and enthusiasm always push him forward and usually he gets all the comforts in life. He also gets opportunities for higher positions and thereby earns quite a lot. The number 3 person is early out of puberty and poverty.

c) VOCATION

His love of position and command makes him a politician. He can occupy very high posts such as those of ministers, ambassadors, judges and secretaries. He is gifted for public life and high offices etc.,may be in the army or in the church.He is a good teacher as well as a preacher. Professions such as those of doctors, bankers, advertisers and actors are also suitable for him.

d) HEALTH

Number 3 has a strong influence on the blood and the arterial system. It also governs the sense of smell. This person is liable to suffer from chest and lung disorders, throat afflictions, gout and apoplexy and sudden fevers. He may also suffer from sore throat, diphtheria, adenoids, pneumonia, plurisy and tuberculosis of the lungs.

e) MARRIAGE AND FRIENDS :

He has a natural attraction towards persons born in the period from 20th April to 20th May, 20th June to 20th July and 20th October to 20th November. He also has affinity for those who are governed by numbers 3,6 and 9. It is therefore advisable that he selects his wife from one of these periods or numbers.

A Number 3 husband

As a general rule, he attains puberty at an early age and marries early. He generally marries a person above his economic status. He has an attraction towards beauty and usually he gets a good-looking wife.   However his ambitious nature makes him expect too many things from his wife and thus he becomes disappointed. It is always better for him to choose a number 3 person or a number 6 person as his wife. He is most loving, thoughtful and considerate. He is very generous, devoted and fatihful.

A Number 3 wife

She is the best companion to her husband. She is not an intruder but takes an active interest in the business of her husband. She is a devoted and affectionate wife and depends on her husband. She is calm and reserved but at the same time very social. She is efficient in house-keeping and has a sympathetic and balanced attiutde towards her children.She is of an easy-going type and enjoys theatres and the company of friends.

Friends

This man's best friends are those who are governed by numbers 1, 3, 5, 6, 7, 8, 9. He also has a natural affinity towards those born in August, November and February and in his own month i.e. May.

f) FORTUNATE DAYS

AND NUMBERS : His lucky days are Tuesdays, Thursdays

and Fridays and his lucky numbers area
3 and 6. He should therefore take all
important steps on one of these days
and also dates if possible. He should
try his luck in lottery by purchasing a
ticket where the total of all the figures
is 3 or 6, or where the last digit is
or 6.

g) LUCKY COLOURS : He should use all shades of yellow,
violet, purple and green as his lucky
colours.

h) LUCKY JEWELS AND STONES : His lucky jewels are
Topaz, Amethyst and
Cat's Eyes.

i) IMPORTANT YEARS IN LIFE : His important years are
3, 12, 21, 30, 39, 48, 57,
66, 75 etc.

j) HIS GOOD QUALITIES AND DRAWBACKS ARE AS UNDER:

Good qualities	Drawbacks
Ambition	Cruelty
Dignity	Dictatorship
Individuality	Hypocrisy
Philosophy	Spendthrift
Prestige	Vanity

CHAPTER 40

BORN ON
4th, 13th, 22nd and 31st of May

All those born on the 4th, 13th, 22nd and 31st of May are governed by number 4 and the planet Uranus. May is governed by the planet Venus. The character reading relating to number 4 below is equally applicable to the other dates. In addition, the special characteristics of those born on the 13th, 22nd and 31st May are given separately.

Born on 4th May

a) CHARACTER

A combination of the planets Uranus and Venus is a peculiar one and it promises a life which is distinctive and unusual. It is the unusual and unexpected that is likely to happen in the life of this individual. He is likely to choose a path out of the ordinary. This combination is favourable to philosophers, writers, composers etc. It may not be a purely lucky date from the wordly stand point, and in financial matters the person is likely to have many changes. He does not easily tind acceptance and in a general way he will arouse opposition in his work and ideas. He will, however, surmount obstacles and rise to any occasion. Uranus shows energy, force and advancement. It shows a revolution and unexpected happenings in life. Usually the changes that take place are for the better. This number represents the higher faculties of the mind. It shows activity and intelligence engaged in the reconstruction or the betterment of human life. The peculiar nature of this person is that he constantly aims at changes in life and society, and seeks the liberation of the mind from the bondage of environment and society. He dislikes hypocrisy and loves art and music. He has an attractive personality

Because it is his peculiar nature to oppose the views of others or to create arguments, he is often misunderstood and makes a large number of secret enemies who constantly work against him. He feels lonely in life.

Born on 13th May | you have all the basic characteristics of those born on the 4th of the month, so first go through them and then read your own. |

He is an intelligent person, of tall stature and good complexion. He is considerate and benevolent. He likes literature and scientific books. He likes to remain active though in a peaceful way. He occupies positions of high responsibilities and gets riches. His success and career start after his 31st year. Though outwardly he looks mild, inwardly, he is obstinate. He is faithful and sympathetic but has difficulty in expressing his love. He has all the qualities of number 4 but in an exaggerated form.

Born on 22th May | you have all the basic characteristics of those born on the 4th of the month, so first go through them and then read your own. |

He is also tall, with good eyes. Usually he occupies good positions but without much responsibility. He is rather easy-going and unsteady by nature. Sometimes his actions are spasmodic. On the whole he is lucky in his affairs and benefits from the opposite sex. He is happy in his family life but is also fond of a companion. He is faithful and dedicated to others. Sometimes he feels very lonely. His social field is limited and he has few friends. He does not care for disputes. He has too much economy of sentiments.

Born on 31th May | you have all the basic characteristics of those born on the 4th of the month, so first go through them and then read your own. |

This date shows ambition, pride and austerity. He is interested in honourable occupations such as working with charitable institutions and institutions for the deaf and dumb and the physically handicapped etc. He gets success after his 40th year but he expects quick results and early reputation. He is lucky in financial matters. He is realistic and of strong

will-power. He has a strong attraction for the opposite sex.
He loves travelling.

b) FINANCE

As regards finance and monetary status, he is usually well
settled in life though he experiences delays and difficulties in
his undertaking.   In financial affairs he is likely to have many
changes, but always of a sudden and unexpected kind;   on the
whole he cannot be said to be a lucky person in money
matters.   He may not amass wealth but can maintain the show
of riches.   He is likely to make money by unusual methods.
He can be an inventor or an unconventional writer, painter or
musician.   He is a spendthrift and his home is well decorated.
His financial prosperity usually starts after the age of 40.

c) VOCATION

He will be successful in trades such as transport, electrical
goods and all sorts of machinery. He will be equally
successful as an engineer, a building contractor, a scientist and
an industrialist. Being born in the month of May he will
succeed as an author or a composer of music.   Since he is of
an original turn of mind, new ideas and methods will always
appeal to him and he can achieve fame as a painter or a musician.

d) HEALTH

His respiratory system is usually weak and he suffers from
breathlessness.   His sickness is also sudden and unexpected.
His ailments are difficult to diagnose and he may have sudden
pains and cramps in the stomach and lesions in the internal
organs. He is subject to chills and colds without warning, and
inflammation of the lungs.   His knees, shanks and feet are
also affected.   Sometimes he suffers from urinary infection.

e) MARRIAGE AND FRIENDS

He has a natural attraction towards persons born in the

period from 20th February to 20th March and 20th October to 20th November. He also has affinity for those who are governed by numbers 1, 2, 7 and 8. It is therefore advisable that he should select his wife from one of these periods or numbers.

A Number 4 husband

As a husband, he is very generous, devoted and faithful. He looks after his home in spite of any outside interest. He tries his best to provide good education and clothes to his children. He often marries a person richer than he. He has an attraction towards beauty and usually he gets a good-looking wife. His married life is attractive to him and it is 'never' tiresome.

A Number 4 wife

She is a devoted and affectionate wife and depends on her husband. She has the capacity to endure hardships and adapt herself to circumstances. She is smart and attractive. She has the art of dressing and has a strong will-power. She aims at several things but rarely succeeds in getting mastery over one. She loves interior decoration but does not have the capacity to work hard for it and she will get it done through others. She is often dictatorial and moody and spoils her day because of her own whimsical nature. She loves her home but is not attached to it very much. She is often uneasy and it is better for her to find a friend governed by number one or two.

Friends

This man's best friends are those who are governed by numbers 1, 2, 4, 5, 7, 8, 9. He has also a natural affinity towards people born in August, November, February and in his own month i.e. May.

f) FORTUNATE DAYS
AND NUMBERS : His lucky days are Mondays, Fridays and Saturdays and his lucky numbers are 4 and 7. He should therefore

take all his important steps on one of these days and also these dates, if possible. He should try his luck in lottery by purchasing a ticket where the total of all the numbers is 4 or 7, or where the last digit is 4 or 7.

g) LUCKY COLOURS : He should use all shades of electric blue, electric grey, yellow and orange.

h) LUCKY JEWELS AND STONES : His lucky jewels are Emerald, Topaz and Diamond.

i) IMPORTANT YEARS IN LIFE : His important years are 4, 13, 22, 31, 40, 49, 58, 67, 76 etc.

j) HIS GOOD QUALITIES & DRAWBACKS ARE AS UNDER:

Good qualities	Drawbacks
Activity	Changeable
Endurance	Dominating
Energy	Stubborn
Reliability	Vindictive
Method and system	Jealous

CHAPTER 41

BORN ON
5th, 14th and 23rd of May

All those born on the 5th, 14th and 23rd May of any year are governed by the number 5 and the planet Mercury. May is governed by the planet Venus. The character reading relating to number 5 given below is equally applicable to the other dates. In addition, the special characteristics of those born on 14th and 23rd May are given separately.

Born on 5th May
a) CHARACTER

He is independent in spirit but extremely capable of adapting himself to persons and conditions, without allowing them to influence him in any way. He has great versatility in work and can succeed in almost any line, provided he is interested to make the effort. He will not be easily tied down to any one thing or to any one person and in consequence may expect to have many changes in his life or career. He will be much influenced by the opposite sex and yet strangely independent of them. He may have many love affairs but will be rather changeable in his affections.

Being governed by Mercury, he is shrewd and quick, and interested in scientific pursuits He has business ability. He is very skilful. He has intuition. He likes oratory and is eloquent in expressing himself. He has the capacity to pursue his objectives and knows very well how to plan to achieve his ends.

Born on 14th May

> you have all the basic characteristics of those born on the 5th of the month, so first go through them and then read your own.

This person has an attractive personality and is liked by all. His nature is cooperative and he does not like to displease others. He usually occupies good positions in life and is successful in his business. He is not talkative but is slightly reserved. This is an intelligent and shrewd number. In women, it indicates good marriage but they should be careful in child bearing. A number 14 man is inconsistent in love and experiences some romantic and impulsive attachments in early years. He is fortunate in money matters. He is industrious and positive in speech and action. Usually he is fond of gambling and of solving riddles.

Born on 23rd May

> you have all the basic characteristics of those born on the 5th of the month, so first go through them and then read your own.

He is usually liked by women. His fortune is near the water. He is successful in life and enjoys honour and wealth. He may get money through inheritance. He keeps busy in his own way. He gets help from superiors and gets protection from them. He is a lucky person. He is affectionate and loves freedom. He is averse to formalities. He has a spirit of independence and a desire to dominate.

b) FINANCE

Since 5 is a business number, the person can expect opulence. With his shrewdness, he is capable of developing his industry and carrying out his plans systematically, with the result that he gets good returns for his efforts. He is lucky in his finances.

c) VOCATION

He can adapt himself to the role he has to play in the drama of life. He comes in contact with various classes of people and succeeds in every business. Banking is a good line for him. Mercury also indicates an aptitude for medicine or surgery. His capacity to argue his points can make him a good lawyer.

d) HEALTH

His basic health defects are biliousness and nervousness·
However his biliousness has close relation with his psychological disturbance. It increases with the increase in tension and
decreases or disappears when his nervous trouble is under
control. Number 5 rules over nerves, neck, arms, ears and the
respiratory system·

e) MARRIAGE AND FRIENDS

He has a natural attraction towards persons born in the
period between 20th January and 20th February, 20th April and
20th May and 20th September and 20th October. He also has
affinity for those who are governed by numbers 1, 7 and 8. It
is therefore advisable that he should select his wife from one
of these periods or numbers.

A Number 5 husband

This man generelly marries a person richer than himself.
He has an attraction towards beauty and usually he gets a good-
looking wife. He finds his married life attractive. He is lucky
and successful in his married life. His selection is good and
usually he selects a person of his own type. He loves his
partner. He expects neatness and cleanliness in her and also
desires that she should share in the enjoyment of life. He is
proud of his wife and likes to see her well-dressed. In return,
he proves a good husband. He loves his children and is fond
of his home. Even if he travels long, he is very much attracted
to his home and is eager to return early and join his family. He
is liberal in spending on clothing and the other needs of the
members of his family and furnishes his house with good taste.

A Number 5 wife

She has interest at home as well as outside. She has
many activities and manages them well. She likes tidiness and
though she seldom does her own work, she gets it done
because of her commanding personality.

Friends

This man's best friends are those who are governed by numbers 1, 3, 4, 5, 7 and 8. He also has a natural affinity towards people born in August, November, February and in his own month i. e May.

f) FORTUNATE DAYS
   AND NUMBERS : His lucky days are Wednesdays, Fridays and Saturdays, and his lucky numbers are 3 and 5. He should therefore take all important steps on one of these days and also dates if possible. He should try his luck in lottery by purchasing a ticket where the total of all the digits is 3 or 5. or where the last digit is 3 or 5,

g) LUCKY COLOURS : He should use all shades of white, green and blue.

h) LUCKY JEWELS AND STONES : His lucky jewels are Emerald, Diamond. and Pearl.

i) IMPORTANT YEARS IN LIFE : His important years are 5, 14, 23, 32, 41, 50, 59, 68, 77 etc.

j) HIS GOOD QUALITIES AND DRAWBACKS ARE AS UNDER

Good qualities	Drawbacks
Harmony	Moodiness
Emotionality	Timidity
Fellowship	Coldness
Honesty	Envy
Imagination	Introvert
Simplicity	Haste
	Shyness
	Whimsicality

CHAPTER 42

BORN ON
the 6th, 15th and 24th of May

All those born on the 6th, 15th and 24th of May of any year are governed by number 6 and the planet Venus. The month of May is also governed by Venus. Therefore the persons born on these dates have influence of Venus twice over. The character reading relating to number 6 given below is equally applicable to the other dates. In addition, the special characteristics of those born on 15th and 24th May are given separately.

Born on 6th May

a) CHARACTER

Being dominated by the power of Venus twice over the love aspect of his nature or love of humanity will be very important. Impelled by this characteristic he will do any kind of work, make any sacrifice or bend his back to any hardship. He has intense feelings and emotions, and a devotional nature swayed by enthusiasm for whatever his purpose may be whether it leads him through war or revolution. A person governed by 'is number is a born artist and art and beauty in life have an ai ction for him. He is a pleasant personality to meet. In his c npany one feels enthusiasm, energy and charm. His talk is interesting and lively. We may sometimes be required to keep aside our ideas of morality and social conduct in understanding and appreciating his feelings and views. Number 6 stands for beauty, health, vitality. warmth, attraction and above all' love. A person of this number is fond of music, dancing and poetry. He loves to have a life full of ease and luxuries, money and happiness. He prefers spending to saving. He will have rich clothes, jewellery, perfumes and all sorts of beautiful things.

He is necessarily a loving type and he has feeling of kinship and humanity. He will therefore not desert his friends. He always likes to understand the grievances and difficulties of others. He prefers joy to gloom and has the capacity to carry others along with him to participate in the moments of enjoyment. His outlook is bright and vivacious. He is emotional but keeps his emotions to himself. His anger is hard to subside. He is very responsible and loves his children but receives very little happiness from them. He is a born advisor and needs some audience to whom he can express his views on matters of importance. He is a good conversationalist and enjoys intellectual combats.

There is a danger in his affections. If he does not keep his nature well under control, he is likely to suffer from jealousy. He can either love or hate with the greatest intensity. He can either be an angel or a devil. He should therefore be cautions.

Born on 15th May | you have all the basic characteristics of those born on the 6th of the month, so first go through them and then read your own.

Keeping well in hand the fires of emotions and enthusiasm burning in his heart, he should devote himself to some high ideal leaving behind him "Footprints on the sands of time." This person has good intelligence and good memory. He is fit for responsible positions such as those of ambassadors, consuls, governors etc. He is very ambitious and boastful but hasty and proud by nature. He is interested in the lower type of occultism. He also has interest in art and music. He appears to be gentle but has very strong convictions. He has a habit of worrying inwardly and leading a melancholy life. His destiny is such that he has to make sacrifices for others.

Born on 24th May | you have all the basic characteristics of those born on the 6th of the month, so first go through them and then read your own.

He is fortunate in getting assistance from people of high

rank. He benefits through the opposite sex. He marries a rich girl and succeeds in speculation and enjoys a good monetary status. He strictly defines the line between personal and social matters. He is methodical in his ideas. He possesses a strong ego and sometimes tries to force his opnions on others. Music and all forms of art appeal to him. He loves to give pleasure to his friends and he is particularly successful in social life in organising fetes, entertainments and amusements of all kinds.

b) FINANCE

He is not attracted towards money and accumulation of wealth is not his aim in life. All his interest is directed towards attaining pleasures and gratifying his desires. He, therefore, spends his earnings on whatever attracts him. He also never repents having spent his money on art which may not ultimately give him monetary rewards. Therefore he is rarely opulent but he has the knack of somehow making both ends meet and having the minimum comforts he wants. He may sometimes be lucky and have windfalls.

c) VOCATION

He will shine as an interior decorator, architect, jeweller, musician, hotel manager or a confectioner. He can equally be successuful as a broker, an estate broker or as a commission agent.

d) HEALTH

On the whole he is a healthy person. However, he is susceptible to epidemic fever and influenza. He is occassionally prone to nervousness but not in a chronic way.

e) MARRIAGE AND FRIENDS

He has a natural attraction towards persons born in the period between 20th August and 20th September and 20th December and 20th January. He also has affinity for those who are governed by the numbers 2, 4, 6 and 9. It is therefore advisable that he selects his wife from one of these periods or numbers.

A Number 6 husband

He likes marriage and usually marries early in life. He expects his partner to be neat and have charm and grace. His is usually a large family with many children. He loves his children and home. He is very kind, generous and devoted. Though he creates a lively atmosphere in the house, he somehow finds it difficult to satisfy all the needs of the members of his family. This may sometimes create unpleasantness and make him unhappy in his married life. Art is everything to him and he remains impractical, not understanding the material values of a successful life.

A Number 6 wife

She never resorts to a divorce and endures extreme hardship rather than desert her husband. She is a devoted mother and loving wife, satisfied with her husband's efforts in her behalf. She loves domestic life and is a perfect house-wife.

Friends

This man's best friends are those who are governed by numbers 2, 3, 4, 6 and 9. He also has a natural affinity towards people born in August, November, February and in his own month i. e. May.

f) FORTUNATE DAYS
   AND NUMBERS: His lucky days are Mondays, Tuesdays, Thursdays and Fridays and lucky numbers are 3, 6 and 9. He should therefore take all important steps on one of these days and also these dates if possible. He should try his luck in lottery by purchasing a ticket where the total of all the digits is 3, 6 or 9 or where the last digit is 3, 6 or 9.

g) LUCKY COLOURS : He should use all shades of blue, rose and pink.

h) LUCKY JEWELS AND STONES : He can use Turquoise, Emerald, Pearl and Diamond.

i) IMPORTANT YEARS IN LIFE : His important years are 6, 15, 24, 33, 42, , 51, 60, 69, 78 etc.

j) HIS GOOD QUALITIES AND DRAWBACKS ARE AS UNDER:

Good Qualities	Drawbacks
Harmony	Absence of foresight
Love	Interference
Peace	Moodiness
Strong memory	Timidity.

CHAPTER 43

BORN ON
7th, 16th and 25th of May

All those born on the 7th, 16th and 25th May of any year are governed by the number 7 and the planet Neptune. May is governed by the planet Venus. The character reading relating to number 7 given below is equally applicable to the other dates. In addition, the special characteristics of those born on 16th and 25th of May are given separately.

Born on 7th May

a) CHARACTER

A person born on this date has the same qualities as those of number 2 which is governed by the planet Moon. He has individuality and is original and independent. He is restless by nature and is fond of change. He likes to visit foreign countries and becomes interested in far off lands. He has peculiar ideas about religion and dislikes following the beaten track. On the whole he is gentle and has a broad vision. The combination of the planets Neptune and Venus makes him inclined towards the love of odd and curious things and a deep regard for mysticism. He is likely to take interest in secret societies or political organisations dealing with large masses of people. He has a gift of expression in writing and eloquence which will give him position and weight in varied circles. He does not care much for the ordinary pleasures of life and may be considered odd or eccentric in his behaviour.

This date has a spiritual significance and Supreme Consciousness is developed in this individual. He is like a free bird and likes to break the traditional bonds and restrictions. His behaviour is a mystery to others. He is often absent–minded. He thinks logically and achieves great aims. He has a good talent for earning money. In general, he is somewhat indifferent to materialistic desires. He wants the best or none at all. He is sensitive and hides his real feelings by apparent indifference. He dislikes mingling with common people. He prefers to spend his hour with his favourite book. When his opinion is solicited, he speaks with authority. He knows his ground.

Born on 16th May | you have all the basic characteristics of those born on the 7th of the month, so first go through them and then read your own.

He is rather easy-going and does not like to work hard. He is good humoured and generous. He is very sensitive and emotional. He soon gets upset but is soon pleased. He is often indisposed. He is fortunate in getting good and successful children. However there is some sort of sorrow in his married life. He appears to be calm but his mind is always in turmoil. He is sometimes short-tempered. He will not disclose his nervousness and is slow in taking decisions. He does not like interference.

Born on 25th May | you have all the basic characteristics of those born on the 7th of the month, so first go through them and then read your own.

He is a jack of all trades but master of none. He is interested in several subjects but does not have the capacity to go into details. His knowledge, therefore, is very shallow. He likes to travel and has connections with foreign countries. He is honest, faithful and good natured. But he is fickle-minded and inconsistent. His memory is good and he is a good orator and a good teacher. There is some sort of sorrow in his married life. He is likely to have a second marriage.

b) FINANCE

Usually, there are many changes in the life of this person and so, it is difficult for him to amass wealth. However, this being a mystic number, the person can be well placed in life provided he finds a job of his choice. In that case he can be a wealthy person with all amenities and comforts. If he has sufficient money at his disposal, he is likely to use it in aid of clinics, hospitals or institutions and for the benefit of others.

c) VOCATION

His love for sea travel and interest in foreign countries make him a successful merchant, exporter or importer. He can deal successfully in dairy products, fishery, and other products such as soap etc, and manage a chemical industry. He can also study medicine and surgery. He has ideas for inventions of an unusual order and he can do well with his new ideas. He can also go in for wireless, television and radio work. He is endowed with unusual brain power and can be successful as a writer, poet, painter, musician or inventor.

d) HEALTH

His main trouble is his nervous constitution and all his illness will be due to his nervousness. He is liable to suffer from faulty blood circulation, stomach disorder and fever. As a rule he is not strong or robust and gets tired easily in any continuous efforts. He is liable to suffer from functional weakness of the intestines. He should be very careful in matters of diet. He is not likely to have as much physical stamina as he has nerve force, perseverance and endurance. He is subject to periods of mental depression and it is better he avoids drugs and stimulants in his desire to escape from his gloomy moods.

e) MARRIAGE AND FRIENDS

He has a natural attraction towards persons born in the period between 20th February and 20th March, 20th April and 20th May and 20th October and 20th November. He also has affinity for those who are governed by numbers 3, 5, and 8.

It is therefore advisable that he selects his wife from one of these periods or numbers.

A Number 7 husband

He is very emotional and understands the feelings of his wife. He is very considerate and will never try to impose his ideas on his wife. He is liberal, fond of picnics, travels and cinema theatres. He is a spendthrift and likes to live lavishly. His family is moderate in size and has all the comforts in life.

A Number 7 wife

She is very moody and her behaviour is unpredictable. She gets disturbed over small matters. She is good at entertaining friends and she likes to invite people to parties or dinners. She expects her husband to look after her all the time.

Friends

This man's best friends are those who are governed by numbers 1, 3, 4, 5, 7, 8 and 9. He also has a natural affinity towards people born in August, November, February and in his own month, i.e. May.

f) FORTUNATE DAYS AND NUMBERS : His lucky days are Sundays, Mondays, Wednesdays and Thursdays and his lucky numbers are 2,6 and 7. He should therefore take all important steps on one of these days and also dates if possible. He should try his luck in lottery by purchasing a ticket where the total of all the digits is 2,6 or 7 or where the last figure is 2,6 or 7.

g) LUCKY COLOURS : He should use all shades of white, cream, green and blue.

h) LUCKY JEWELS & STONES :   His lucky jewels are Emerald
                                                   Pearl,   Cat's   Eye   and
                                                   Turquoise.

i) IMPORTANT YEARS IN LIFE :   His important years are 7, 16,
                                                   25, 34, 43, 52, 61, 70, 79 etc.

j) HIS GOOD QUALITIES & DRAWBACKS ARE AS UNDER :

Good Qualities	Drawbacks
Austerity	Despondency
Peace	Diffidence
Reflection	Restlessness
Serenity	Whimsicality
Tolerance	

CHAPTER 44

BORN ON
8th, 17th and 26th of May

All those born on the 8th, 17th and 26th of May of any year are governed by the number 8 and the planet Saturn. May is governed by the planet Venus. The character reading relating to number 8 given below is equally applicable to the other dates. In addition, the special characteristics of those born on 17th and 26th of May are given separately.

Born on 8th May

a) CHARACTER

This number is governed by Saturn and shows an extreme sense of discipline, steadfastness, constancy and dutifulness. The person has a sober and retiring personality. He is a lover of classical music but mostly of a melancholy type. In arts he loves landscapes, natural scenery and flowers. Number 8 is considered to be a balance wheel to the character. The man is a pessimist. He prefers solitude to company. He shuns society rather than courts it. He is cautious about the future and he takes decisions very carefully on matters which pertain to mundane affairs. He is a prudent person, wise and sober. He is never over-enthusiastic and is more or less gloomy and melancholy. He is also ambitious and persevering. He is capable of enormous efforts for the attainment of his object. He is sceptical and analytical. He is creative, productive and dominating. He is likely to be misunderstood. He usually feels lonely at heart. He understands the weak and the oppressed and treats them in a warm hearted manner. He is a born manager who can keep others busy. He admires fair play and is willing to pay a fair compensation. He has a good memory for names and faces.

The combination of Saturn and Venus gives the man an unusual life and career, either fortunate and powerful or the very reverse. He is a "Child of Fate" and cirumstances, surroundings and conditions play the most important part. He craves for love and affection from others and yet feels very isolated in life. He is not demonstrative in his emotions and finds great difficulty in expressing his feelings. He will sacrifice greatly for others, especially for his own relations. He is likely to have much sorrow and loss caused by relatives. He finds difficulties in carrying out his individual abmition. He may rise to high positions but at the same time have to bear heavy responsibilities.

Born on 17th May | you have all the basic characteristics of those born on the 8th of the month, so first go through them and then read your own.

This man is a good organizer and a good thinker. He has a creative and constructive mind. He is a lover of peace and a philanthropist. He is attracted towards occultism and mysticism. He is courageous and proud. He has a strong individuality. He is highly intelligent and clever. As regards emotions, he is calm. At times he is generous to a fault and at times very stingy. He is interested in research and loves knowledge. He is conservative and dominating.

Born on 26th May | you have all the basic characteristics of those born on the 8th of the month, so first go through them and then read your own.

This man wants to enjoy life without doing anything. He is sluggish and lethargic. He revels in wine and women and is fickle-minded. He is careless about the number of children. He is lucky in money matters and gets easy money. He is smart but lacks positiveness. He likes to put up a good appearance but has a worrying nature. He has problems in his love affairs.

b) FINANCE

The peculiarity of number 8 is the delay in life in all

respects. Naturally in financial matters also there is delay and stability is achieved at a very late age. This person has to work hard and he seldom succeeds in getting opulence. He has therefore to avoid number 8 playing a part in his life and instead he can choose number 1 or 3 for all his important actions and moves in life. However, if his experience shows that 8 is a lucky number for him. he can insist on that number only in which case wealth and prosperity come to him. If it is found to be lucky number in one's life one can try lottery and luck in horse racing. But usually this number is connected with delays and hard work and a person has to be very cautious in financial matters.

c) VOCATION

Subjects suitable for him are the occult sciences, chemistry, physics, medicine and also higher mathematics. He can be successful in industries connected with coal mines, timber etc. and in construction companies. He can be a good accountant and also a good administrator. However, as stated earlier, he has to strive hard in his career and he can get the fruits of his hard work only in the later years of his life.

d) HEALTH

His main health defects are nervousness, irritation, trouble with legs, teeth and ears, paralysis and rheumatism. He is a bilious type and often suffers from chronic melancholia. It is very interesting to note that the delaying characteristic in his life applies to his sickness. The ailments he suffers from also take a long time to cure. A strong 8 personality tends to suffer from varicose veins and haemorrhods.

e) MARRIAGE AND FRIENDS

He has a natural attraction towards persons born in the period between 20th April and 20th May, 20th August and 20th September and 20th December and 20th January. He also has affinity for those who are governed by numbers 5 and 7. It is therefore advisable that he selects his marriage partner from one of these periods or numbers.

A Number 8 husband

Basically a number 8 person does not have a desire to get married. He prefers loneliness and likes to be left to himself. He does not have much attraction for the opposite sex. However being influenced by Venus he cannot escape completely the attraction of the company of the opposite sex. Sometimes he is influenced by Saturn and sometimes Venus. Usually he tries to postpone his marriage with the result that if at all he marries, it is at a very late age. He also finds it difficult to choose his wife. As he prefers seclusion to a gathering he often makes his married life miserable. He is very orthodox in his views and does not allow his wife to adopt modern ideas in dress at home or in public places. The natural result is disappointment for his wife and hatred of her husband. If however he has a desire to be successful in married life, he should prefer a person who is also interested in deep and serious studies and likes to devote herself to philosophy and occult subjects.

A Number 8 wife

She has a masculine personality. She is capable and systematic. She enjoys her family life and likes to make sacrifices for her children and for the ambition of her husband. Her fault is that she lacks feminine warmth, sentiment and delicacy. She has the capacity to endure hardships and to adapt herself to circumstances. She makes herself dependent on her husband although she can help herself if necessary.

Friends

This man's best friends are those who are governed by numbers 3,4,5, 7 and 8. He also has a natural affinity towards people born in August, November, and February and in his own month i.e. May.

f) FORTUNATE DAYS AND NUMBERS :

His lucky days are Wednesdays, Thursdays, Fridays and Saturdays and his lucky numbers are 2, 5, and 6. He should therefore take all important steps on one of these days and also these dates if possible. He should try his luck in lottery by purchasing a ticket where the total of all the digits is 2, 5 or 7 or where the last digit is 2, 5 or 7.

g) LUCKY COLOURS : He should use dark grey. dark blue, purple and black.

h) LUCKY JEWELS AND STONES : His lucky jewels are Sapphire, Black pearls, and Black Diamond. His lucky stones are Cat's Eye and Amethyst.

i) IMPORTANT YEARS IN LIFE : His important years are 8, 17, 26, 35, 44, 53, 62, 71 etc.

j) HIS GOOD QUALITIES AND DRAWBACKS ARE AS UNDER:

Good qualities	Drawbacks
Authority	Cynicism
method	Delay
practicality	Vindictiveness
Steadiness	Nervousness
System	Laziness.

CHAPTER 45

BORN ON
9th, 18th and 27th of May

All those born on the 9th, 18th and 27th of May of any year are governed by number 9 and the planet Mars. May is governed by Venus. The character reading relating to number 9 given below is equally applicable to the other dates. In addition, the special characteristics of those born on 18th and 27th May are given separately.

Born on 9th May

a) CHARACTER

A powerful combination of Mars and Venus means an eventful life but one largely based on adventure, danger, love and romance. At the back of events, the man will have courage, headstrong will-power and determination of purpose, whether it be for good or evil. The person has talent for organisation, a desire for large ambitious schemes and the ability to amass wealth and power. However, he is inclined to spend heavily in all his undertakings. He makes powerful enemies and provokes opposition. His life is likely to be threatened by danger and violence. He will be forced into legal proceedings and often be faced with heavy financial losses. In practice if he controls himself, he may be able to make excellent capital of his great qualities but there will always be a danger of his allowing his Martian qualities and hasty temper to get the better of his judgement and provoke opposition.

Mars shows aggression, resistance, courage, dash and quickness. A Martian in considered as a fighter. He is always aggressive and will not stop till he achieves his end. He has the capacity to fight against all adverse elements and circumstances. A Martian does not know defeat and if we have an army of Martians, there would not be anything like defeat for them. It would be either victory or death. It is said that the great Emperor Napoleon Bonaparte was a believer in this science and he had a battalion of soldiers who were pure Martians. A Number 9 person is not very tactful or delicate in his talk but his intentions and good and his vigorous manner should not be misunderstood as rough behaviour. He should not criticise others and should choose his words carefully, otherwise they will act as a boomerang.

He is fiery and dashing and does not have sickly sentiments. He has audacity and vigour from start to finish. He is also fond of games and vigorous exercise. When the date of the month is 9 and the total of all the digits of the date of birth is also 9, the man is governed by a strong number 9 and his Mars is very powerful. In such a case, he has strong sexual passions and he is attracted towards the opposite sex. He is prepared to go through any ordeal to gratify his desire.

He is a brave person to whom conflict does not bring the thought of danger. He is exceedingly devoted to his friends and will fight for them. He has sympathy and consideration for the weak. He loves children and animals. He takes delight in showing mercy to others. He likes the healing profession. He is backed by self-control, moral courage and the power of forgiveness His psychological aptitude is remarkable and under all circumstances he proves his strength of will and exhibits courage. He is short–tempered.

Born on 18th May | you have all the basic characteristics of those born on the 9th of the month, so first go through them and then read your own.

This person has tenacity and will-power which will overcome any difficulty. He is not as dashing as the number 9 man, but he is fearless and courageous. His strong health makes him passionate. He inherits property from his father. He has a disciplined mind and likes to help others. He is painstaking, with good judgement, and is wise. He loves to exercise perfect control over others. He does not like to be cautioned by others.

Born on 27th May | you have all the basic characteristics of those born on the 9th of the month, so first go through them and then read your own.

On the whole this man has a conflicting personality. He is confident and likes to do something for those whose life is miserable or who are handicapped. He can develop a spirit-ual personality and can practise spiritual healing. On the other side, he is fond of women and may develop illicit contacts and create scandal. Sometimes he creates unhappiness in his married life. He is very sensitive and moody, and his actions and moves are unpredictable. He is self-assured and strong in resolution. He is a seeker of independence and domination. He hates to work under others. Usually, he is dogmatic in his thoughts.

b) FINANCE

He is lucky in his monetary affairs and earns far more than the average man. He is also very liberal while spending, especially for his sweetheart. He enjoys all the comforts that money can bring.

c) VOCATION

A Number 9 person is found in all walks of life but he will be more suited to the army and to professions where there is full scope for his aggression and courage. In the army he will rise to high positions, in politics he will be eminent and in business he will exhibit his dashing and pushing nature. He can be a good doctor chemist or a businessman dealing in iron and steel.

d) HEALTH

His main health defect arises from heat and he is susce-ptible to troubles such as piles, fevers, smallpox etc. He is also likely to suffer from kidney trouble or bladder stone. Throat trouble, bronchitis and laryngitis also frequently trouble him.

e) MARRIAGE AND FRIENDS :

He has a natural attraction towards persons born in the period between 20th July and 20th September and 20th November and 20th January.He also has affinity for those who are governed by numbers 3,6 and 9. It is therefore advisable that he selects his wife from one of these periods or numbers.

A Number 9 husband

He has robust health and strong circulation of blood which makes him very passionate and enthusiastic about married life. He is fond of a beautiful wife and likes her to be submissive and passive to his sexual desires. He is fond of his family and children and likes to have a good house. He usually leads a good married life inspite of his hot-tempered nature and eccentricities. He has a romantic mental picture of what he wants in his wife. This mental picture demands perfection. The most difficult thing in the married life of a number 9 person is to satisfy his romantic conception of physical love. He has a voracious appetite and his wife with her devotion can harmonise with him physically. Usually, we find him suspicious of his wife.

A Number 9 wife

She will make a wonderful wife for an ambitious man. She is a witty and clever conversationalist with a wonderful social presence. She will assist her husband in his business. She may also start her own activity and add to the family income. She will be happy if married to a passionate and possessive man.

Friends

His best friends are those who are governed by numbers 1, 2, 3, 4, 6, 7 and 9. He also has a natural affinity towards people born in August, November, February and in his own month i.e. May.

f) FORTUNATE DAYS
    AND NUMBERS : This man's lucky days are Mondays,
                   Tuesdays, Thursdays and Fridays and
                   his lucky numbers are 3,6 and 9. He
                   should therefore take all important
                   steps on one of these days and also
                   dates if possible. He should try his luck
                   in lottery by purchasing a ticket where
                   the total of all the numbers is 3,6 and 9
                   or where the last digits is 3,6 or 9.

g) LUCKY COLOURS : He should use all shades of red,
                    white and yellow.

h) LUCKY JEWELS AND STONES : His lucky jewels are
                   Topaz, Pearl and Ruby
                   and lucky stones are
                   blood-stone   and
                   Garnet.

i) IMPORTANT YEARS IN LIFE : His important years are
                   9, 18, 27, 36, 45, 54, 63,
                   72 etc.

j) HIS GOOD QUALITIES AND DRAWBACKS ARE AS UNDER:

Good qualities	Drawbacks
Activity	Destructiveness
Courage	Erratic nature
Dash	Hot temper
Energy	Impatience
Enthusiasm	Quarrelsomeness

CHAPTER 46

BORN ON
1st, 1Oth, 19th and 28th of June

All those born on the 1st, 10th, 19th and 28th of June of any year are governed by the number 1 and, the Sun June is governed by Mercury. The character reading relating to number 1 given below is equally applicable to the other dates. In addition, the special characteristics of those born on 10th, 19th and 28th of June are given separately.

Born on 1st June

a) CHARACTER

He is exceptionally kind-hearted and sympathetic, easily influenced by sympathy and praise, but often to his detriment. He is very sensitive, idealistic and is endowed with imagination. He is likely to have two occupations at the same time, but he must work in his own way as he cannot tolerate any interference. His has dual nature and it is difficult for others to understand him. He is usually restless, and desires travel or change. In spite of this he will take great interest in new problems of science. He is good reasoner and investigator. He desires to have a happy home life and makes every effort for it but has many serious difficulties. He has an active mind, always ready for any emergency

Being governed by the Sun he has originality, activity, energy, enthusiasm, art and brilliance. A person governed by this number is spontaneous, responds to nature and has the capacity to enjoy life. He is usually successful in life due to his active nature and the capacity to mix in any society. He is gifted with intuition ; he seldom goes deep into a subject. He is changeable and is not constant in friendship   He is honest and acknowledges his faults.   He has a quick grasp of any subject and can participate spontaneously in conversation.   By nature, he is cheerful and happy and his outlook on life is very optimistic.   He is a better judge of human nature than the average individual   He is born to lead, not to follow.   A new idea is to him a greater thrill than money in the bank. He will always be young by reason of a fresh idea.

Born on 10th June

you have all the basic characteristics of those born on the 1st of the month, so first go through them and then read your own.

Being born in the month of June, he ia governed by the Rasi (Zodiacal sign) Gemini which is symbolised as Twins. The main characteristic of the person is dualism and he plays a double role in life. Sometimes he looks hot headed and sometimes he appears very cool. He may like a particular thing but at the same time he may criticize it. He is ambitious but hardly knows what he wants to achieve. His behaviour is very uncertain and one cannot expect him to be constant in his ideas or plans.

He is very impressive with a magnetic personality and is respected for his knowlege and intelligence. He gets financial benefits from relatives such as his father, father-in-law, wife, mother etc. He gets success after his 46th year. He gets a good position in service and succeeds in business also. He has broad shoulders and a manly figure. He loves truthfulness. This number shows honour and self-confidence. The person can get fame or notoriety depending upon his will-power and character. He usually has good health and quickly recovers from sickness. He likes to help others, but gets no response from them. This is more true in the case of relatives.

Born on 19th June

you have all the basic characteristics of those born on the 1st of the month, so first go through them and then read your own.

This man is very active, energetic and enthusiastic. He has research aptitude and likes to handle a subject in a systematic aud methodical way. He takes quick decisions and always likesto keep himself busy with some concrete project. Sports is his hobby and he is interested in several games such as horse-riding, shooting and other athletic games. He is hasty and impetuous in love affairs which end in quarrels. He is courageous and has force of character. He likes to help others even going out of the way. He can keep the secrets of others. This number promises success, honour and happiness. It is very difficult for others to understand him. He is always in company but at heart feels lonely. He is obstinate and finds it difficult to extend co-operation. He is prudent and notices even a trivial thing. He is not an excellent speaker but can explain himself best in writing. He can be a good writer.

Born on 28th June

> you have all the basic characteristics of those born on the 1st of the month, so first go through them and then read your own.

He is very generous and spends on charitable institutions. He is not as lucky as numbers 1, 10 and 19 and has to undergo difficulties in public and private life. He should select his wife carefully. He has to provide carefully for the future as he is likely to lose through trust in others. He is also likely to make many changes in his career. He hardly reveals his emotions and therefore appears cold   He has unyielding will power and does not hesitate to carry out his plans.

b)   FINANCE

He gains success in finance by his own intelligence. He has an intuitive understanding of the course of stocks and shares in business. He is strongly inclined to speculation and can be successful only if he relies on his intuition. He is a lucky person as far as finance is concerned. Even though he is extravagant due to his overenthusiasm, he also earns sufficient to maintain his ostentatious disposition in life. He may not amass wealth but his personality and behaviour will make others believe that he is a rich person. He has a temptation for gambling and if it is not controlled in time, he may lose considerably.

c)   VOCATION

He can adapt himself to the role he has to play in his life. He comes in contact with various classes of people and is successful in all his business. June is governed by Mercury and shows business ability. This man can be equally successful in banking, medicine or surgery. However, being governed by number 1, his main difficulty is in sticking to any one job or profession for a long time. Usually, every three to four years there is change in career. He is a good salesman and can choose vocations which will imply relations with foreign countries, such as the post of a political ambassador or a trade dealing in foreign commodities. He is a leader and can be the head of a department, a managing director etc. He has an aptitude also for research.

d) HEALTH

There are no special diseases he is liable to suffer from except attacks of indigestion, mainly brought on by excessive mental exertion and living on his nerves. He is likely to suffer from nervous trouble unless he gets good sleep and change of atmosphere. The main cause of his sicknes is overexertion.

e) MARRIAGE AND FRIENDS

He has a natural attraction towards persons born in the period 20th July to 20th August, 20th November to 20th December, and 20th March to 20th April. He has also affinity for those who are goverend by the numbers 2,4,5 and 7. It is therefore advisable that he selects his wife from one of these periods or numbers.

A Number 1 husband

As a husband, he is good. He is intelligent, talented and social. He should get a wife who will understand his mental interests and who is not tied to household affairs. Though he has a lot of interest in women, he is not flirtatious.

A Number 1 wife

She is an intelligent companion to her husband. She is always busy and likes to take active part in social life. She is not mentally engrossed much in her home affairs,but she likes to make use of her energy and activity. She is, of course, of the practical type and expects returns for her services. She adheres to discipline, is tidy and commands obedience. Though she has conversational abilities and a romantic personality, she never sacrifices her home and husband for her romantic life. She makes a good wife to a doctor, lawyer, industrialist or any man who spends most of his time amongst clients and in society.

Friends

This man's best friends are those who are governed by numbers 1, 3, 4, 5, 7 and 9. He also has natural affinity towards people born in September, December and March and in his own month i.e. June.

f) **FORTUNATE DAYS AND NUMBERS :** His lucky days are Mondays, Tuesdays and Thursdays and his lucky numbers are 1,4, and 5. He should therefore take all important decisions on one of these days and also dates if possible. He should try his luck in lottery by purchasing a ticket where the total of all the digits is 1,4 or 5 or where the last digit is 1,4 or 5.

g) **LUCKY COLOURS :** He should use all shades of gold, yellow and green.

h) **LUCKY JEWELS AND STONES :** His lucky jewels are Emerald and Pearl.

i) **IMPORTANT YEARS IN LIFE :** His important years are 1, 10, 19, 28, 37, 46, 55, 64, 73 etc.

i) HIS GOOD QUALITIES AND DRAWBACKS ARE AS UNDER:

Good qualities	Drawbacks
Strong will power	Obstinacy
Aspiration	Aloofness
Dash	Domination
Authority	Impertinence
Confidence	Inflexbility
Determination	Pride
Research	Showmanship
Vigour	Extravagance
Talents	—

CHAPTER 47

BORN ON
2nd, 11th, 20th and 29th of June

All those born on the 2nd, 11th, 20th and 29th of June of any year are governed by the Moon and the number 2. June is governed by Mercury. The character reading relating to number 2 given below is equally applicable to other dates. In addition, the special characteristics of those born on 11th, 20th and 29th June are given separately.

Born on 2nd June

a) CHARACTER

He is gentle and has a strong imagination. He is very responsive to new thought and new ideas. His views are broad and sympathetic. His distinct quality is his aversion to fighting, quarrelling or war in any form. He is good at diplomacy and settling troubles by negotiations, but often meets with difficult situations. He has a great attraction for books, literature and history. He travels a great deal and makes many changes of place and residence. He is warm-hearted and intensely human. He has a very receptive mind and keen intellect. Routine work does not suit him. He cannot enjoy the company of others as he finds them too ordinary for his imaginary world.

Born on 11th June

you have all the basic characteristics of those born on the 2nd of the month, so first go through them and then read your own.

He is usually successful in life and in love and gets honour, position and authority. He is honest with his friends and is of a royal disposition. He should guard himself from secret enemies. He has interest in mysticism, philosophy and science.

He can expect travels, favours and honours in life.   He is very
impulsive and gets excited easily.   He worries too much over
small matters. He has the ability to take quick decisions and
this makes him a leader. He is a born advisor and an inspiration
to others.

Born on 20th June
you have all the basic characteristics of those born on the 2nd of the month, so first go through them and then read your own.

He has many friends and benefits through wealthy women.
He has a flair for writing and can be known as an author or a
novelist.   His prosperity lies near water, a river or the sea.
This number has a peculiar significance. It shows new plans
and new resolutions for the betterment of people at large.

Born on 29th June
you have all the basic characteristics of those born on the 2nd of the month, so first go through them and then read your own.

This person is moody and changing and therefore uncertain
about his actions. He is courageous and bold but takes risks in
life and does not stick to anything to the end. He is intelligent
and also a deep thinker but there is a tendency to carry everything to extremes. He is not very lucky in his married life.
His interest is in his business. He is blessed with good fortune.
His life is eventful.

b) FINANCE

He is governed by the Moon and Mercury which have
their own peculiar approach towards finance. The Moon shows
lethargy whereas Mercury indicates business approach.
Being governed by the Moon, the person is not capable of
doing any hard work. He also does not have the physical
capacity to stand the strain of everyday life. The result, therefore, is a mediocre financial position. He can improve his
monetary position provided he understands and absorbs the
business qualities of Mercury. He can be a good businessman
and earns his livelihood. The difficulty is his unstable mind
which often drags him away from routine work.

c) VOCATION

His love of books, literature and history will make him a

good librarian. He can also be a good diplomat. He has a large vocabulary and linguistic capacities among all the numbers and can be successful as a teacher or a professor of languages. He can also be a good translator or an editor.

d) HEALTH

His main health weakness is poor blood circulation. He is susceptible to all sickness such as anaemia and weak heart arising out of poor blood circulation.

Since the Moon is the ruling planet of number 2, the uneasiness which is a prominent characteristic, creates mental worries and sleeplessness. He is also susceptible to diabetes and asthmatic troubles.

e) MARRIAGE AND FRIENDS

He has a natural attraction towards persons born in the period from 20th September to 20th November and 20th Januay to 20th March. He also has an affinity for those who are governed by the numbers 2, 5 and 6. It is therefore advisable that he select his wife from one of these periods or numbers.

A Number 2 husband

There are two types of husbands belonging to this date ; one is dominating and exacting, the other is passive, lazy and indulgent. This other type marries for the sake of money so that he may ultimately get comforts. Usually he is a good husband and selects a person of his own type. He expects neatness and cleanliness from his wife and likes to see her well dressed. He is fond of home and children. Even if he travels long, he is strongly attracted to his home and is eager to return early and be with his family. He is liberal in spending and furnishes his house with good taste.

A number 2 wife

She has interest at home as well as outside. She seldom does her own work and gets it done through her commanding personality. She is sympathetic, affectionate and devoted. She

is satisfied with anything her husband provides her with.
However, she is moody, changeable and sensitive.

Friends

This man is attracted to those who are intelligent, artistic
and sincere. His best friends are those who are governed by
numbers 2, 4, 6 and 9. He has a natural affinity also towards
people born in September, December, March and in his own
month i.e. June.

f) FORTUNATE DAYS
   AND NUMBERS : His lucky days are Mondays, Thursdays
   and Fridays and his lucky numbers are
   2 and 7. He should, therefore, take
   all important steps on one of these
   days and also dates if possible. He
   should try his luck in lottery by purchasing a ticket where the total of all
   the digits is 2 or 7, or where the last
   digit is 2 or 7.

g) LUCKY COLOURS : He should use all shades of white,
   cream, blue and purple

h) LUCKY JEWELS AND STONES : His lucky jewels are Pearls
   and Diamonds and lucky
   stones are Moonstone and
   Agate.

i) IMPORTANT YEARS IN LIFE : His important years are 2, 11,
   20, 29, 38, 47, 56, 65, 74 etc.

j) HIS GOOD QUALITIES & DRAWBACKS ARE AS UNDER:

Good qualities	Drawbacks
Emotionality	Coldness
Fellowship	Envy
Honesty	Haste
Imagination	Introvert
Simplicity	Shyness
	Whimsicality

CHAPTER 48

BORN ON

3rd, 12th, 21st and 30th June

All those born on the 3rd, 12th, 21st and 30th of June of any year are governed by number 3 and the planet Jupiter. June is governed by Mercury. The character reading relating to number 3 given below is equally applicable to the other dates. In addition, the special characteristics of those born on 12th, 21st and 30th June are given separately.

Born on 3rd June

a) CHARACTER

Ambition is the dominant characteristic of this person. He may reach great heights but will never be satisfied but will continue his pursuits till the end. He has good organising ability and will do well as the head of a large business or in positions of authority under governments, municipal bodies etc. He will make friends wherever he goes and will dominate others quickly and easily. He is versatile and has the ability to hold an audience or talk on any subject. He loves quickness and speed in all his activities.

Jupiter stands for morality, pure love and justice with mercy and is known as the greatest benefactor and the uplifter. The vibrations emitted by this number are essentially harmonious and they lead to sympathy and untiring effort to do good to all; the person is devout and religious and has true dignity. The abuse of the same vibrations causes the stimulation of Jupiterian virtues leading to hypocrisy, especially in religious matters. The good nature is marred by excess in many directions.

This man is usually lucky in life. Vibrations radiating

through him attract all that is good to him and his affairs prosper as a consequence. The judge who gives sane decisions and merciful sentences, the physician and the church dignitary, the world's teachers and philosophers are all mostly governed by the number 3

This is a good number. The person is confident of his ability. He is self-reliant and takes his own decisions. He has a habit of talking loudly. He is fond of show and likes to obeserve form, order and law. He is jovial in spirit and cordial in manner. His passions are healthy, spontaneous and without inhibitions. He is free in his expression. He is a good conversationalist.

Born on 12th June

> you have all the basic characteristics of those born on the 3rd of the month, so first go through them and then read your own.

Authority and honours are the significant aspects of this person's life. He has vanity and is proud, ambitious and aspiring. He is fond of pleasures and is attracted to the opposite sex. However, sometimes he prefers loneliness. He likes to make sacrifices for others but becomes the victim of other people's plans or intrigues. His relations with others are smooth and harmonious. He is quick to notice trifles. He has lofty ideals.

Born on 21st June

> you have all the basic characteristics of those born on the 3rd of the month, so first go through them and then read your own.

He is kind and generous and is a loving father. He achieves fame, reputation and honours at a very late age. He is cheerful and fond of travels. He has a strong feeling of self-respect. Surprisingly, he has a suspicious nature.

Born on 30th June

> you have all the basic characteristics of those born on the 3rd of the month, so first go through them and then read your own.

He is fortunate, generous and optimistic. He has a noble and religious mind. He likes to travel and visit places of pilgrimage. He can be successful as a teacher or educationist or in administration. He appears gentle and sincere, but has a hidden characteristic. He may be active but is restless. When faced with difficulties, he is strong enough to overcome them.

b) FINANCE

He is a lucky type and somehow manages to earn enough for his livelihood. He also gets opportunities for higher positions in life and thereby earns quite a lot. His ambition, leadership and enthusiasm always push him forward and usually he gets all the comforts in life. The number 3 person is early out of puberty and poverty.

c) VOCATION

His love of position and command makes him a politician. He is gitfed for public life, statesmanship and high offices in the army or in the church. He is a good teacher and a good a preacher Professions such as those of doctors, bankers, advertisers and actors are also suitable for him. He will also succeed in all matters concerning air travel, wireless, television or research. He will also be fortunate in literary and scientific work.

d) HEALTH

Number 3 has chief influence over the blood and the arterial system. It also governs the sense of smell. This person is liable to suffer from chest and lung disorders throat afflictions, gout aud apoplexy and sudden fevers. He may also suffer from sore throat, diptheria, adenoids, pneumonia, pleurisy and tuberculosis of the lungs. He will be inclined to have periodical breakdowns from overwork or exhaustion of the nervous system. He will fall ill quickly but will also recover rapidly. He should take exceptional care of his eyes and in case he wears glassess he should get them changed often so as not to strain his eyesight.

e) MARRIAGE AND FRIENDS

This person has a natural attraction towards persons born in the period between 20th May and 20th July and 20th September and 20th November. He also has affinity for those who are governed by numbers 3,5, and 6. It is therefore

advisable that he selects his wife from one of these periods or
numbers.

A Number 3 husband

As a general rule, he attains puberty at an early age and
marries early. However, as he is ambitious, his ambitions also
make him expect too much from his wife and thus he becomes
disappointed. He desires to have a wife of whom he can be
proud. She should have an attractive personality, a commanding presence, charming manners and intelligence. It is always
better for him to choose a number 3 person or a number 6
person as his wife   He is most loving, thoughtful and considerate. His passions are adventurous and demand immediate
satisfaction.

A Number 3 wife

She is an intelligent companion to her husband. She is
always busy and likes to take an active part in social life. She
is not so much mentally engrossed in her home affairs, but she
likes to make use of her energy and activity. She is a practical
type and expects returns for her services.   She adores discipline and tidiness and commands obedience. Though she has
conversational abilities and a romantic personality, she never
sacrifices her home and husband for a romantic life. She makes
a good wife to a doctor or lawyer or industrialist or any man who
spends most of his time with his clients and social contacts.
She is the best companion to her husband. She is not an
intruder but takes an active interest in the business of her
husband. She is efficient in house-keeping and has a sympathetic and balanced attitude towards her children.   Her passions
are healthy and joyous and her approach to physical love is
highly refined and inspiring.

Friends

This man's best friends are those who are governed by
numbers 1, 3, 5, 6, 7, 8, 9.   He also has a natural affinity

towards people born in September, December, March and in his own month i.e. June.

f) FORTUNATE DAYS AND NUMBERS : His lucky days are Tuesdays, Thursdays and Fridays and his lucky numbers are 3,5 and 6. He should therefore take all important steps on one of these days and also dates if possible. He should try his luck in lottery by purchasing a ticket where the total of all the digits is 3,5 or 6 or where the last digit is 3,5 or 6.

g) LUCCKY COLOURS : He should use all shades of yellow, violet, purple and green.

h) LUCKY JEWELS AND STONES : His lucky jewels are Topaz and Emerald and lucky stones are Amethyst and Cat's Eye.

i) IMPORTANT YEARS IN LIFE : His important years are 3, 12, 21, 30, 39, 48, 57, 66, 75 etc.

j) HIS GOOD QUALITIES AND DRAWBACKS ARE AS UNDER:

Good Qualities	Drawbacks
Ambition	Cruelty
Dignity	Dictatorship
Individuality	Hypocrisy
Philosophy	Extravagance
Prestige	Vanity
Shrewdness	
Vigilance	

CHAPTER 49

BORN ON
4th, 13th, and 22nd of June

All those born on the 4th, 13th, and 22nd of June of any year are governed by number 4 and the planet Uranus. June is governed by Mercury. The character reading given below relating to number 4 is equally applicable to the other dates. In addition, the special characteristics of those born on 13th and 22nd June are given separately.

Born on 4th June

a) CHARACTER

The influence of Uranus and Mercury being a combination which bestows special qualities, this man's life is expected to run on most unusual lines. He is highly individual in character. He likes peculiar people and things and it will be the sudden and the unexpected that plays the greatest role in his life. He displays great originality in all his undertakings. He is inventive and attracted to new ideas, reforms in social life and out of the way studies. He has peculiar ideas about religion, government problems and social questions. He may be attracted to some branch of mysticism and may expound it to the public through his writings and lectures. He is likely to have a considerable amount of annoyance and trouble from relations on account of his independent character.

Uranus shows energy, force and advancement. It shows revolution and unexpected happenings in life. Usually the changes that take place are for the better. This number represents the higher faculties of the mind. It shows activity

17

and intelligence engaged in the reconstruction or the betterment of human life. The peculiar nature of this person is that he constantly aims at change in life and society and is after the liberation of mind from the restrictions of environment and society. He dislikes hypocrisy and loves art and music. He has an attractive personality.

Born on 13th June
> you have all the basic characteristics of those born on the 4th of the month, so first go through them and then read your own.

He is an intelligent person, of tall stature and good complexion. He is considerate and benevolent. He likes literature and scientific books. He likes to remain active though in a peaceful way. He occupies positions of high responsibilities and gets riches. His career and success start after his 31st year. Though outwardly he looks mild, inwardly, he is obstinate. He is faithful and sympathetic but has difficulty in expressing his love. He has all the qualities of number 4 but in an exaggerated form.

Born on 22nd June
> you have all the basic characteristics of those born on the 4th of the month, so first go through them and then read your own.

This man also is tall and has good eyes. Usually he occupies good positions but without much responsibility. He is rather easy-going but unsteady by nature. Sometimes his actions are spasmodic. On the whole he is lucky in his affairs and benefits from the opposite sex. He is happy in his family life but is also fond of a companion. He is faithful and dedicated to others. Sometimes he feels very lonely. His social field is limited and he has few friends. He does not care for disputes. He has too much economy of sentiments.

b) FINANCE

In matters of finance this man's condition is rather uncertain. He may get money by fits and starts but he is not likely to keep it. He has a desire to indulge in speculation. In spite of this he is usually well settled in life though he experiences delays and difficulties in his undertakings. He may not amass wealth but can maintain the show of wealth.

He is a spendthrift and his home is well decorated. His financial prosperity usually starts after the age of 40.

c) VOCATION

He will be successful in trades connected with transport, electricity and all sorts of machinery. He will be equally successful as an engineer, building contractor, a scientist and an industrialist. He is also attracted towards mystic subjects such as palmistry and astrology and can do well in these subjects also.

d) HEALTH

The peculiar influence of Uranus shows itself in matters of health also. Though the man is not robust, his ailments are of a mysterious kind. He is not easily influenced by doctors and changes them frequently. He is very sensitive to drugs which will affect his constitution. He will make experiments on his health, especially for mental troubles. His respiratory system is usually weak and he suffers from breathlessness. His knees, shanks and feet are also affected. Sometimes he suffers from urinary infection.

e) MARRIAGE AND FRIENDS

This man has a natural attraction towards persons born in the period between 20th January and 20th March and 20th September and 20th November. He has affinity also for those who are governed by numbers 1,2,7 and 8. It is therefore advisable that he selects his wife from one of these periods or numbers.

A Number 4 husband

As a husband he is good. He is intelligent, talented and social. He expects his wife to share his views. He is dominating and wants all affairs of the house to run according to his wishes. He is generous and has a kind and loving heart.

A Number 4 wife

She is smart and attractive· She has the art of dressing and has a strong will-power. She aims at several things but seldom succeeds in getting mastery over one. She loves interior decoration but does not have the capacity to work hard for it and she will get it done through others. She is often dictatorial and moody and spoils her day due to her own whimsical nature. She loves her home but is not attached to it very much. She is at times uneasy and it is better for her to find a friend governed by number one or two.

Friends

This man's best friends are those who are governed by numbers 1,2.4,5,7,8 and 9. He is fond of friends and company but hardly gets a close friend because of his unsteady, changing and moody nature. He has a natural affinity towards people born in September, December, March and in his own month i.e. June.

f) FORTUNATE DAYS
AND NUMBERS : His lucky days are Sundays, Mondays, and Fridays and his lucky numbers are 1,2 and 4. He should therefore take all important steps on one of these days and also dates if possible. He should try his luck in lottery by purchasing a ticket where the total of all the digits is 1,2 or 4 or where the last digit is 1,2 or 4.

g) LUCKY COLOURS : He should use all shades of purple, blue and white.

h) LUCKY JEWELS AND STONES : His lucky jewels are Diamond, Emerald, and Pearl.

i) IMPORTANT YEARS IN LIFE : His important years are 4, 13, 22, 31, 40, 49, 58, 67, 76 etc.

j) HIS GOOD QUALITIES AND DRAWBACKS ARE AS UNDER:

Good qualities	Drawbacks
Activity	Changeability
Endurance	Domination
Energy	Stubbornness
Reliability	Vindictive
Method and system	Jealousy

CHAPTER 50

BORN ON
5th, 14th and 23rd of June

All those born on the 5th, 14th and 23rd of June of any year are governed by number 5 and the planet Mercury. June is governed by Mercury. Therefore the person is doubly swayed by Mercury. The character reading relating to number given 5 below, is equally applicable to other dates. In addition, special characteristics of those born on 14th and 23rd June are given separately.

Born on 5th June

a) CHARACTER

This number is governed by Mercury and it shows shrewdness, quicksess, scientific pursuits, business ability, industry, intuition and diplomacy. A person governed by this number is active and quick, this applies not only to physical agility but also to the mental side. He is very skilful and has intuition. He is equally proficient in games where he uses both his hands and his brain. He has the capacity to judge the ability of his opponents in games and knows very well how to take advantage of the weak points of his opponents. He likes oratory and eloquence in expressing himself. He has the capacity to pursue his objectives and knows very well how to plan for success. He is deeply interested in occult subjects and wishes to master all the intricacies of such abstruse subjects. He possesses a pleasant character and dislikes inactivity. He is sociable and has many aquaintances. He is fond of variety and change and trips. Whatever may be the situation, he has the power to get out of it.

He is a nervous person· He is, therefore, restless. He has an intuitive perception and has the capacity to be either good or bad. On the good side, he is a shrewd person and not vicious or criminal. He is fond of family life and loves children. His pleasures are mainly mental and he evaluates everything in terms of business. He is amiable and adaptable.

Born on 14th June

| you have all the basic characteristics of those born on the 5th of the month, so first go through them and then read your own. |

This person has an attractive personality and is liked by all. His nature is co-operative and he does not like to instigate others. He usually occupies good positions in life and is successful in his business. He is not talkative but is slightly reserved. This is an intelligent and shrewd number. In women, it indicates good marriage but they should take care in child bearing. A Number 14 man is inconstant in love and experiences some romantic and impulsive attachment in early years. He is fortunate in money matters. He is industrious and positive in speech and action. Usually he is fond of gambling and of solving riddles.

Born on 23rd June

| you have all the basic characteristics of those born on the 5th of the month, so first go through them and then read your own. |

He is usually popular with women. His fortune is near the water. He is successful in life and enjoys honour and wealth. He may get money through inheritance. He keeps himself busy in his own way. He gets help from superiors and gets protection from them. He is a lucky person. He is affectionate and loves freedom. He is averse to formalities. He has a spirit of independence and a desire to dominate.

b) FINANCE

Since number 5 is a business number, the person can expect opulence. With his shrewdness, he is capable of developing his industry and carrying out his plans systematically, and so his efforts are rewarded. He is lucky as far as his financial position is concerned.

c) VOCATION

He can adapt to the role he has to play in the drama of life. He comes in contact with various classes of people and with his adaptability becomes successful in any business. Banking is a good line for him. Mercury also shows aptitude for medicine or surgery. His capacity to argue his points can make him a good lawyer.

d) HEALTH

His basic health defect is his biliousness and nervousness. However, his biliousness has close relation with psychological disturbances. His biliousness increases with the increase in tension and is reduced or disappears when his nervous trouble is under control

Number 5 rules over nerves, the neck, the arms, the ears and the respiratory system.

e) MARRIAGE AND FRIENDS :

This man has a natural attraction towards persons born in the period between 20th September and 20th October and 20th January and 20th February. He also has an affinity for those who are governed by numbers 1, 7 and 8. It is, therefore, advisable that he should select his wife from one of these periods or numbers.

A Number 5 husband

He is lucky and successful in his married life. His selection is good and usually he selects a person of his own type. He loves his partner. He expects neatness and cleanliness from her and also desires that she should share his pleasures. He is proud of his wife and likes to see her well-dressed. In return, he proves himself a good husband. He loves his children and is fond of his home. Even if he travels long, he is much attracted towards home and is eager to return early to his family. He is liberal in spending on clothing and other needs of the members of his family and furnishes his house with good taste.

A Number 5 wife

She has interest at home as well as outside. She has many activities and manages them well. She likes tidiness and though she seldom does her own work, she gets it done because of her commanding personality.

Friends

This man's best friends are those who are governed by numbers 1,3,4,5,7 and 8. He has has also a natural affinity towards people born in September, December, March and in his own month i.e. June.

f) FORTUNATE DAYS AND NUMBERS : His luckyu days are Wednesdays Fridays and Saturdays and his lucky numbers are 3,5 and 7. He should therefore take all important steps on one of these days and also dates if possible. He should try his luck in lottery by purchasing a ticket where the last figure is 3,5 or 7.

g) LUCKY COLOURS : He should use green and white.

h) LUCKY JEWELS AND STONES : His lucky jewels are Emerald and Diamond. He may use Sapphire also.

i) IMPORTANT YEARS IN LIFE : His important years are 5, 14, 23, 32, 41, 50, 59, 68, 77 etc.

j) HIS GOOD QUALITIES AND DRAWBACKS ARE AS UNDER:

Good qualities	Drawbacks
Co-operation	Lack of perseverance
Practicality	Scepticism
Shrewdness	Unreliability
Vigilance	—

CHAPTER 51

BORN ON
6th, 15th and 24th June

All those born on the 6th, 15th and 24th of June any year are governed by the number 6 and Venus. June is governed by Mercury. The character reading relating to number 6 given below is equally applicable to the other dates. In addition, the special characteristics of those born on 15th and 24th of June are given separately.

Born on 6th June

a) CHARACTER

The combination of Venus and Mercury is a very fortunate one as far as public relations are concerned. The person is likely to get money from more than one source and will get many great opportunities in his life. He has strong magnetism and is very attractive to the opposite sex. He has many unusual love affairs and romances, and goes through and eventfull life. He dislikes any form of restraint and has a great desire for independence. His ambition is to rise above his friends.

This number is governed by Venus which stands for love, sympathy and adoration. A person governed by this number is a born artist and is attracted to art and beauty in life. He is a pleasant personality to meet. It is always charming to be with him. His company creates enthusiasm, energy and charm. His talk is interesting and lively. We may sometimes be required to keep aside our ideas of morality and social conduct in understanding and appreciating his feelings and views. Number 6 stands for beauty, health, vitality, warmth, attraction and above all, love. A person of this number is fond of music, dancing and poetry. He loves a life full of ease and luxuries, money and happiness. He prefers spending to saving. He will have rich clothes, jewellery, perfumes and all sorts of beautiful things.

He is necessarily a loving type and he has a feeling of kinship and humanity. He will therefore not desert his friends. He seeks to understand the grievances and difficulties of others and is considerate. He prefers joy to gloom and can make others share his pleasure. His outlook is bright and vivacious. He is emotional but keeps his emotions to himself. His anger does not easily subside. He is very responsible and loves his children, but receives very little happiness from them. He is a born advisor and needs an audience to whome he can expound his views on matters of importance. He is a good conversationalist and enjoys intellectual combats.

Since he is born in the month of June, he is governed by Mercury. The zodiacal sign for this month is Gemini which is symbolised as twins. Therefore this person is mainly dual and plays a double role in life. It is very difficult to understand him. Sometimes he looks hot-headed and sometimes he appears very cold. He may like a particular thing but at the same time he may criticize it. He is sharp, brilliant and quick and can win over his rivals. He is ambitious but hardly knows what he wants to achieve. His company is enjoyable, but only when he is in the right mood, otherwise his behaviour is very uncertain. One cannot expect him to be constant in his ideas or plans. He is usually restless and wants what he does not have. He can be an actor or a lawyer or take up any other occupation where he is required to change his role quite often. However he will hardly admit his dual personality unless he is in a self-analytical mood. Due to his changing moods, he cannot cope with a project demanding much time. He is therefore not reliable in his plans which he often postpones until forced by circumstances to carry them out. He is very sensitive and finds it difficult to bear worry or disturbance and experiences mental exhaustion and nervous-

.ness. Even though there are many ups and downs in his life, he is not much affected by them.

Born on 15th June
> you have all the basic characteristics of those born on the 6th of the month, so first go through them and then read your own.

This person is very intelligent and has a good memory. He is fit for responsible positions such as those of an ambassador, a consul, a governor etc. His dual personality will make him a politician, he will be a friend of all. He is very ambitious and boastful but hasty and proud by nature. Though he appears to be gentle he has very strong convictions. He worries inwardly and leads a melancholy life. His destiny is such that he has to make sacrifices for others.

Born on 24th June
> you have all the basic characteristics of those born on the 6th of the month, so first go through them and then read your own.

He is fortunate in getting assistance from people of high rank. He benefits through the opposite sex. He marries a rich girl. His prosperity is usually after marriage. He strictly defines the line between personal and social matters. He possesses a strong ego and sometimes tries to force his opinions on others.

b) FINANCE

In a way he is a lucky person in financial matters. He is lucky in getting presents and property and some times benefits through legacies. In spite of his getting unexpected money he does not seek to accumulate wealth. He likes to spend his earnings on pleasures and gratifying his desires.

c) VOCATION

He will shine as an interior decorator, architect, jeweller, musician, hotel manager or a confectioner. He can be equally successful as a broker, an estate broker. or as a commission agent.

d) HEALTH

On the whole he is a healthy person, and bad health is

not associated with him. However he is susceptible to epidemic fever and influenza. Occasionally, he is prone to nervousness but not in a chronic way. He is also liable to suffer from overstrung nerves together with spasmodic attacks of asthma.

e) MARRIAGE AND FRIENDS

He has a natural attraction towards persons born in the period between 20th August and 20th September and 20th December and 20th January. He also has affinity for those who are governed by numbers 2, 4, 6 and 9. It is therefore advisable that he selects his marriage partner from one of these periods or numbers.

A Number 6 husband

He likes marriage and usually marries early. He is intelligent, talented and social. He should get a wife who will understand his mental interests and who is not tied to household affairs. He expects her to be neat and have charm and grace. He loves his children and home. Though he creates a lively atmosphere in the house, he somehow finds it difficult to meet all the needs of the members of his family. This may sometimes create unpleasantness in married life. Though he has a lot of interest in women, he is not flirtatious.

A Number 6 wife

She is an intelligent companion to her husband. She keeps herself very busy and takes active part in social life. She is a practical type and makes use of her energy. She makes a good wife to a doctor, a lawyer, an industrialist or any one who spends most of his time with his clients and social contacts. She never resorts to a divorce and endures extreme hardship rather than desert her husband. She is a devoted mother and loving wife, satisfied with her husband's efforts in her behalf. She loves domestic life and is a perfect housewife.

Friends

This man's best friends are those who are governed by

numbers 2, 3, 4, 6 and 9.   He also has a natural affinity towards people born in September, December, March and in his own month i. e. June.

f) FORTUNATE DAYS AND NUMBERS: His lucky days are Mondays, Tuesdays, Thursdays and Fridays and his lucky numbers are 2, 3 and 6. He should therefore take all important steps on one of these days and also dates if possible.   He should try his luck in lottery by purchasing a ticket where the total of all the digits is to 2, 3 or 6 or where the last digit is 2, 3 or 6.

g) LUCKY COLOURS : He should use blue violet and rose.

h) LUCKY JEWELS AND STONES : His lucky jewels are Emerald, Pearl and Diamond.

i) IMPORTANT YEARS IN LIFE : His important years are 6, 15, 24, 33, 42, 51, 60, 69, 78 etc.

j) HIS GOOD QUALITIES AND DRAWBACKS ARE AS UNDER:

Good Qualities	Drawbacks
Harmony	Absence of foresight
Love	Interference
Peace	Moodiness
Strong memory	Timidity

CHAPTER 52

BORN ON
7th, 16th and 25th June

All those born on the 7th, 16th and 25th of June of any year are governed by number 7 and the planet Neptune. June is governed by Mercury. The character relating to number 7 given below is equally applicable to the other dates. In addition, the special characteristics of those born on 16th and 25th June are given separately.

Born on 7th June

a) CHARACTER

The influence of Mercury shows a dual character and the person plays a double role in life. He is sharp, brilliant and quick and can win over his rivals. He is ambitious but hardly knows what he wants to achieve. He has individuality and is original and independent. He is restless by nature and is fond of change. He has an attraction for foreign countries and becomes interested in far off lands. He has peculiar ideas about religion and dislikes following the beaten track. He is like a free bird and likes to break traditional bondage and restrictions. His behaviour is a mystery to others. He is often absent-minded. His company is enjoyable but only when he is in the right, otherwise his behaviour is very uncertain. He can shine as an actor or a lawyer or in any other occupation where he is required to change his role quite often. Due to his changing moods he can hardly succeed in a project where much time is required for thought and decisions. Even though there are many ups and downs in his life, he is not much affected by them. He is stubborn and disregards the opinions of others. He desires the best or none at all. He is sensitive and hides his real feelings by apparent indifference. He dislikes mingling with common people. He prefers to spend time with his favourite book. When his opinion is solicited, he speaks with authority.

Born on 16th June | you have all the basic characteristics of those born on the 7th of the month, so first go through them and then read your own.

He is rather easy going and does not like to work hard. He is good-humoured and generous. He is very sensitive and emotional. He soon gets upset and is soon pleased. He is frequently indisposed. He is fortunate in getting good and successful children. However, there is some sort of sorrow in his married life. He appears to be calm but his mind is always in turmoil and he is sometimes short-tempered. He will not disclose his nervousness and is slow in taking decisions. He does not like interference.

Born on 25th June | you have all the basic characteristics of those born on the 7th of the month, so first go through them and then read your own.

At heart he will be gifted with unusual idealism, great delicacy of feeling, refinement of thought and visions of things about to happen. His ambitions are not high, but they are strong. He can talk well and write successfully about new ideas or medicine. He is likely to be much disturbed by close relations. Marriage is not likely to bring him happiness and he is likely to be much misunderstood. He is a jack of all trades but master of none. He is interested in several subjects but does not have the capacity to go into details. His knowledge therefore is very shallow. He likes to travel and has connections with foreign countries. He is honest, faithful and good-natured. But he is fickle-minded and inconsistent. His memory is good and he is a good orator and teacher.

b) FINANCE

He will have peculiar experiences in money matters. He will be cheated and will find it difficult to keep anything in his hands. Finance will be very uncertain. There will be a number of changes in his life and therefore he cannot be wealthy. However, number 7 being a mystic number the person can be well-placed in life provided he finds a job of his choice.

c) VOCATION

His love for sea-travel and interest in foreign countries make him a successful merchant or exporter.. He can also deal in fishery, and products such as soap etc. He can succeed in a chemical industry. He can also study medicine and surgery.

d) HEALTH

His main trouble is his nervous constitution and all his illness will be due to his nervousness. He is liable to suffer from faulty blood circulation, stomach disorder and fever. The stomach and digestive organs are easily upset by worry or unhappy surroundings. He is affected by cold and delicacy of the lungs.

e) MARRIAGE AND FRIENDS

He has a natural attraction towards persons born in the period between 20th January and 20th March and 20th October and 20th November. He also has affinity for those who are governed by numbers 3, 5 and 8. It is therefore advisable that he should select his wife from one of these periods or numbers.

A Number 7 husband

He is intelligent, talented and social. He should get a wife who will understand his mental interests and who is not tied down to household affairs. He is very emotional and understands the feelings of his wife. He is very considerate and will never try to impose his ideas on his wife. He is liberal and likes picnics, travel and cinema theatres. He is a spendthrift and likes to live lavishly. His family is moderate in size and has all comforts in life.

18

A Number 7 wife

She is always busy and likes to take an active part in social life. She is of a practical type and expects returns for her service. She adores discipline and tidiness and commands obedience. However she is very moody and her behaviour is unpredictable. She gets disturbed over small matters. She is good at entertaining friends and she likes to invite people to parties. She wants her husband to look after her all the time.

Friends

This man's friends are those who are governed by numbers 1, 3, 4, 5, 7, 8 and 9. He also has a natural affinity towards people born in September, December and March and in his own month i. e. June· He likes those who are shrewd and intelligent and have business aptitude.

f) FORTUNATE DAYS
   AND NUMBERS : His lucky days are Mondays, Wednes-days and Thursdays and his lucky numbers are 2, 7, and 5. He should therefore take all important steps on one of these days and also dates if possible.He should try his luck in lottery by purchasing a ticket where the total of all the digits is 2, 5 and 7 or where the last digit is 2, 5 or 7.

g) LUCKY COLOURS : His should use shades of yellow and green.

h) LUCKY JEWELS AND STONES : His lucky jewels are Topaz, Emerald, Sapphire, Moonstone and Cat's Eye.

i) IMPORTANT YEARS IN LIFE : His important years are 7, 16, 25 34, 43, 52, 61 70, 79 etc.

j) HIS GOOD QUALITIES & DRAWBACKS ARE AS UNDER :

Good Qualities	Drawbacks
Co-operation	Scepticism
Shrewdness	Unreliability
Peace	Restlessness
Tolerance	Diffidence
Vigilance	Whimsicality

CHAPTER 53

BORN ON
8th, 17th and 26th of June

All those born on the 8th, 17th and 26th of June of any year are governed by the number 8 and the planet Saturn. June is governed by Mercury. The character reading relating to number 8 given below is equally applicable to the other dates. In addition, the special characteristics of those born on 17th and 26th of June are given separately.

Born on 8th June

a) CHARACTER

All his work will be marked by strong individuality. He is very much a "Child of Fate". He is influenced by circumstances and conditions over which he has little or no control. He will be drawn into unfortunate legal matters and will have to exercise great care and caution. He will defend himself against scandal. He has very few friends on whom he can depend in times of crisis. The planet Saturn shows an extreme sense of discipline, constancy and dutifulness. He is a lover of classical music but of a melancholy type. Number 8 is considered to be a balance wheel to the character. This man can look at the other side of the coin. He is a prudent person, wise and sober among all the numbers. He is never overenthusiastic and is more or less gloomy. He is capable of enormous efforts for the attainment of his object. He is sceptical and analytical. Even though there are many ups and downs in his life, he is not much affected by them.

Born on 17th June   you have all the basic characteristics of those born on the 8th of the month, so first go through them and then read your own.

He is a good organiser and a good thinker. He has a creative and constructive mind. He is a lover of peace and a philanthropist. He is attracted towards occultism and mysticism. He is courageous and proud. He has strong individuality. He is highly intelligent and clever. As regards emotions, he is calm. At times he is generous to a fault and at times very stingy. He is interested in reasearch and loves knowledge. He is conservative and dominating.

Born on 26th June   you have all the basic characteristics of those born on the 8th of the month, so first go through them and then read your own.

He wants to enjoy life without doing anything. He is sluggish and lethargic. He revels in wine and women and is fickleminded. He is careless about the number of children. He is lucky in money matters and gets easy money. He is smart but lacks positiveness. He likes to put up a good appearance but has a worrying nature. He has problems in his love affairs.

b) FINANCE

He is prudent and cautious as regards money. He likes serious methods in business and builds up his finances slowly and painstakingly. He is reserved and secretive, trusting very few people. In spite of all his precaution, he undergoes losses and is robbed by his servants. He has to work hard to get rich. It is better he avoids number 8 playing a part in his life; instead he should choose number 1 or 3 for all important actions and moves in life.

c) VOCATION

If he is in business, it is better to avoid partnerships and work alone and independently. He can be successful in subjects like chemistry, physics, medicine and even higher mathematics. He can also do well in coal mines, the timber industry etc, and in construction companies. He can be a good accountant and also a good administrator. However, as stated earlier, he has to strive hard in his career and he can get the fruits of his hard work only in the later years of his life.

d) HEALTH

His main health problems are nervousness, irritation, trouble with legs, teeth and ears, paralysis and rheumatism. He is of a bilious type and suffers often from chronic melancholia it is interesting to note that the delaying characteristic in life is also observed in his sickness. The ailments he suffers from take a long time to cure. Varicose veins and hemorrhoids generally trouble a strong 8 personality.

e) MARRIAGE AND FRIENDS

He has a natural attraction towards persons born in the period between 20th April and 20th June and 20th August and 20th October. He has affinity also for those who are goverend by the numbers 5 and 7. It is therefore advisable that he should select his wife from one of these periods or numbers

A Number 8 husband

Usually he has less attraction for the opposite sex and tries to postpone his marriage with the result that he marries at a very late age. He also finds it difficult to choose his wife. As he prefers seclusion to gathering, he often makes his married life miserable. He is very orthodox in his views and the result is dis-appointment on the part of his wife. If he wants a happy married life he should select a partner who is interested in serious studies.

A Number 8 wife

She has a masculine personality. She is capable and systematic. She enjoys her family life and likes to make sacrifices for her children and for the ambition of her husband. Her fault is that she lacks feminine warmth, sentiment and delicacy. She adores discipline and tidiness, and commands obedience. Though she has conversational abilities and a romantic personality, she never sacrifices her home and her husband for her romantic life. She makes a good wife to a doctor, lawyer, industrialist or anyone who spends most of his time with his clients and social contacts.

Friends

This man's best friends are those who are governed by numbers 3, 4, 5, 7 and 8. He has natural affinity also towards people born in September, December and March and in his own month i.e. June. He also likes those who are shrewd and intelligent and have business aptitude.

f) FORTUNATE DAYS AND NUMBERS : His lucky days are Wednesdays, Thursdays and Fridays and his lucky numbers are 2,7 and 8. He should therefore take all important steps on one of these days and also dates if possible. He should try his luck in lottery by purchasing a ticket where the total of all the digits is 2,7 or 8, or where the final digit is 2, 7 or 8.

g) LUCKY COLOURS : He should use dark grey, dark blue, purple and green.

h) LUCKY JEWELS AND STONES : His lucky jewels are Sapphire, Black Pearl, Emerald. His lucky stones are Cat's Eye and Amethyst.

i) IMPORTANT YEARS IN LIFE : His important years are 8, 17, 26, 35, 44, 53, ,62 71, 80 etc.

j) HIS GOOD QUALITIES AND DRAWBACKS ARE AS UNDER:

Good qualities	Drawbacks
Authority	Cynicism
Methodical	Delay
Practicality	Vindictiveness
Steadiness	Nervousness
System	Laziness

CHAPTER 54

BORN ON
9th, 18th and 27th of June

All those born on the 9th, 18th and 27th of June of any year are governed by the number 9 and the planet Mars. June is governed by Mercury. The character reading relating to number 9 given below is equally applicable to the other dates.   In addition, the special characteristics of those born on 10th, 18th and 27th of June are given separately.

Born on 9th June

a) CHARACTER

He is frank and outspoken and inclined to make enemies by hitting straight from the shoulder. He is inventive, mechanical and ingenious with a love of chemistry, science and mathematics. He is highly charged like a dynamo and makes sparks fly all around him. He causes much opposition due to his being too plain-spoken and satirical. He is likely to have estrangements with his relations and trouble with brothers, sisters and members of his family.

Number 9 is governed by Mars and shows aggression, resistance, courage, dash and quickness. He is considered as a fighter. He is aggressive in all his acts and will not stop till he achieves his end. He is fiery and dashing and does not have sickly sentiments. He is also fond of games and vigorous exercise. He has strong sexual passions and is attracted towards the opposite sex. He is prepared to go through any ordeal to gratify his desires.

He has sympathy and consideration for the weak and takes delight in showing mercy to others. He is backed by self-control, moral courage and the power of forgiveness. His psychological aptitude is remarkable and under all circumstances he proves his strength of will and exhibits courage. He is short-tempered and should not criticize others. It is better he uses his words carefully, otherwise they will act as a boomerang.

Born on 18th June | you have all the basic characteristics of those born on the 9th of the month, so first go through them and then read your own.

This person has tenacity and will-power which will over—come any difficulty. He is not as dashing as one born on the 9th, but he is fearless and courageous. His strong health makes him passionate. He inherits property from his father. He is painstaking with good judgement and is wise. He loves to exercise complete control over others. He does not like to be cautioned by others.

Born on 27th June | you have all the basic characteristics of those born on the 9th of the month, so first go through them and then read your own.

On the whole this man is a conflicting personality. He is confident and likes to do something for those whose life is miserable or who are handicapped. He can practise spiritual healing. On the other hand he is fond of women and may develop illicit contacts and create a scandal. Sometimes he creates unhappiness in his married life. He is very sensitive and moody and his actions and moves are unpredictable. He is self-assured and strong in resolution. He is a seeker of inde—pendence and wishes to dominate. He hates to work under others. Usually, he is dogmatic in his thoughts.

b) FINANCE

He has clever and original ideas as to how things should be done, but as he is not likely to get on easily with partners he is likely to see many of his good plans come to nothing. Being very impulsive, he is inclined to rush into schemes without much consideration. However, on the whole, he is lucky in his monetary affairs and earns far more than an average person. He is also very liberal while spending, especially for his sweetheart. He enjoys all the comforts that money can bring.

c) VOCATION

This man is found in all walks of life but he fits best into the army and into professions where there is full scope for his aggression and courage. In the army he will rise to high positions, in politics he will be eminent and in business he will exhibit his dashing and pushing nature. He has also aptitude for medicine or surgery. His capacity to argue his points can make him a good lawyer.

d) HEALTH

His main health problem arises from heat and he is susceptible to troubles such as piles, fevers, small pox etc. He is also likely to suffer from kidney trouble or bladder stone. Throat trouble, bronchitis and laryngitis also frequently trouble him.

He is liable to suffer more through accidents than through ill-health, and to sustain injuries to the hips, shoulders, arms and hands. He is also susceptible to accidents caused by electricity, and danger from matters relating to and from the air, and some danger from water, if born on 27th June.

e) MARRIAGE AND FRIENDS

He has a natural attraction towards persons born in the period between 20th July and 20th September and 20th November and 20th January. He also has affinity for those who are governed by the numbers 3 and 6. It is therefore advisable that he should select his wife from one of these periods or numbers.

A Number 9 husband

He is vigorous in health and has strong circulation of blood which makes him very passionate and enthusiastic about married life. He is fond of a beautiful wife and likes her to be submissive and passive to his sexual desires. He is fond of his family and children and likes to have a good house. He usually leads a good married life in spite of his hot-tempered nature and eccentricities. He has a romantic mental picture of what he wants in his wife. This mental picture demands perfection. The most difficult thing in the married life of a number 9 person is to satisfy his romantic conception of physical love. He has a voracious appetite and his wife with her devotion should harmonise with him physically. Usually, we find him suspicious of his wife.

A number 9 wife

She will make a wonderful wife for an ambitious man. She is a witty and clever conversationalist with a wonderful social presence. She will assist her husband in his business. She may also start her own activity and add to the family income. She will be happy if married to a passionate and possessive man.

Friends

His best friends are those who are governed by numbers 1, 2, 3, 4, 6, 7 and 9. He also has a natural affinity towards people born in September, December, March and in his own month i.e. June. He also likes those who are shrewd, intelligent and clever.

f) FORTUNATE DAYS AND NUMBERS : His lucky days are Mondays, Tuesdays, Thursdays and Fridays and his lucky numbers are 1,3 and 6. He should therefore take all important steps on one of these days and also dates if possible. He should try his luck in lottery by purchasing a ticket where the total of all the digits is 1, 3 and 6 or where the last digits is 1, 3 or 6.

g) LUCKY COLOURS : He should use all shades of red, white and yellow.

h) LUCKY JEWELS AND STONES : His lucky jewels are Topaz, Pearl and Ruby and lucky stones are blood-stone and Garnet.

i) IMPORTANT YEARS IN LIFE : His important years are 9, 18, 27, 36, 45, 54, 63, 72 etc.

j) HIS GOOD QUALITIES AND DRAWBACKS ARE AS UNDER:

Good qualities	Drawbacks
Activity	Destructive tendency
Courage	Erratic nature
Dash	Hot temper
Energy	Impatience
Enthusiasm	Quarrelsomeness

CHAPTER 55

BORN ON
1st, 10th, 19th and 28th of July

All those born on the 1st, 10th, 19th and 28th of July of any year are governed by the number 1 and the Sun. July is governed by the planet Neptune. The character reading relating to number 1 given below is equally applicable to the other dates. In addition, the special characteristics of those born on 10th, 19th and 28th July are given separately.

Born on 1st July

a) CHARACTER

This date gives good promise of advancement in life. The person will have many changes in his career or position. He will have many strange adventures and experiences and will be greatly influenced by his surroundings. He is patriotic and is attracted to his home and family. By nature he is quiet and reserved and has a sensitive disposition and yet in apparent contradiction, he gets a great deal of publicity whether he seeks it or not. He is prudent and conscientious, with a strong desire to accumulate money, more as a protection than out of the love of wealth. At heart he is deeply religious, more inclined to some simple form of faith but not show.

This number is governed by the Sun and shows originality, activity, energy, enthusiasm, art and brilliance. A person governed by this number is spontaneous, responds to nature and has the capacity to enjoy life. He is usually successful in life due to his active nature and capacity to mix in any society. He is an artist and has many talents but they are all spontaneous in nature. He has good taste in everything and always chooses the beautiful. He is gifted with intuition and seldom studies any subject deeply. Even then he can influence others with his knowledge and flash. These characteristics make him a hero of the drawing room. He is changeable and is not constant in friendship. He is honest and acknowledges his faults. He has a quick grasp of any subject and can participate spontaneously in conversation. He has a religious attitude but is not fanatical or superstitious. He also learns occult sciences and does wonders with his gift of intuition. By nature, he is cheerful, happy and bright and his outlook on life is very optimistic. He has a strong will-power and is independent in thought and action. On the one hand, he is practical, but on the other hand he is idealistic. Sometimes he is obstinate and selfish. He is fond of inventions and has creative talents. He is a better judge of human nature than the average man. He is born to lead not to follow. A new idea is a greater thrill than money in the bank. He will always be young by reason of a fresh idea.

Born on 10th July

you have all the basic characteristics of those born on the 1st of the month, so first go through them and then read your own.

Number 10 is symbolised as the "Wheel of Fortune". It is a number of honour, of faith and self-confidence, of rise and fall. This is a fortunate number in the sense that one's plans are likely to be carried out. The person born on 10th July is very impressive with a magnetic personality and is respected for his knowledge and intelligence. He gets financial benefits from relatives like his father, father-in-law, wife, mother etc. He gets success after his 46th year. He gets a good position in service and succeeds in business also. He has broad shoulders and a manly figure. He loves truthfulness. This number shows honour and self-confidence. The person can get fame or notoriety depending upon his will-power and character. He usually has good health and quickly recovers from sickness. He likes to help others, but rarely gets a response from them. This is more true in the case of relatives.

Born on 19th July

The birth date 19th July promises happiness, success, esteem and honour and success in one's plans. The person is secretive, having a distinct hidden side. This man has a tendency to be gloomy and grave. He has also powerful enemies. He is frequently hasty in actions, quarrels and strife in home life.

He is very active, energetic and ethusiastic. He has research aptitude and likes to handle a subject in a systematic and methodical way. He takes quick decisions and always likes to keep himself busy with some concrete project. Sports is his hobby ; he is interested in several sports such as horse riding, shooting and other athletic games. He is hasty and impetuous in love affairs which end in quarrels. He is courageous and has force of character. He likes to help others even by going out of the way. He can keep the secrets of others and people can confide in him. It is very difficult for others to understand him. He is always in company but at heart feels lonely. He is obstinate and finds it difficult to extend co-operation. He is prudent and notices even trifles. He is not en excellent speaker but can explain himself best in writing. He can be a good writer.

Born on 28th July

He is very generous and spends on charitable institutions such as schools and hospitals. He is not as lucky as numbers 1,10,19 and has to undergo difficulties in public and private life. He should select his wife carefully. He has to provide carefully for the future as he is likely to lose through trust in others. He is also likely to make many changes in his career. He rarely reveals his emotions and therefore appears cold. He has an unyielding will-power and does not hesitate to carry out his plans.

He is practical. The begining of his life is not so happy. He is a self-made man and beats his enemies. There are many ups and downs in his life and many changes in occupation. His relations with his mother or with his mother-in-law are rarely happy.   She is either a burden to him or dominating and stern in her attitude.

b) FINANCE

There are two types of persons born on the 1st, 19th and 28th of July who are distinctly different from each other in their attitude towards the financial side of life. One is the proverbial rolling stone that gathers no moss, the restless individual that cannot remain long at any one thing or any one place, a person with the fever of wanderlust in his or her blood, that must travel and change and seek adventure at any cost. One can easily recognize this type by a restless look in the eyes, continual movements of the hands and feet and the inability to sit for sometime. This type of man or woman seldom makes good.

The other type is the very reverse-quiet, reserved, with great love of home and family, a traveller also, at times, but with some definite object or purpose, a conscientious person, one who says little but accomplishes much. These two opposite types are born in larger numbers in this period of the year than under any other Sign of the Zodiac. To the restless type, finance will always be difficult, to the other it will be a problem to be solved by patience and conscientious work.

c) VOCATION

The main difficulty with the number 1 person is his inability to stick to any one profession or job for a long time. Usually, every three years there is a change in career. He is however suitable for advertising conerns, the newspaper business and the cinema industry and can also be successful in theatrical performances. He can show his art as an interior decorator. Being a good salesman, he can choose a vocation with relations with foreign countries, such as the post of a political ambassador or a trade dealing in foreign commodities. He is a leader and can be the head of departments, a managing director etc. He can succeed equally well as a surgeon, a eweller and an electrican and in research projects.

19

d) HEALTH

Though he has great vitality, he does not look physically strong. He is likely to suffer from trouble of digestive organs and the intestinal tract. He is usually his own doctor and by careful diet he keeps his ailments in check and surprises his friends by his vitality and length of life. The most common trouble to be found with this number is overexertion. He should always be on his guard and see that he does not exert himself too much in his overenthusiasm. Excessive strain is likely to bring on fevers. He is also likely to suffer from eye trouble and heart trouble.

e) MARRIAGE AND FRIENDS

He has a natural attraction towards persons born in the period between 20th June and 20th August, 20th October and 20th December and 20th February and 20th April. He also has a natural affinity for those who are governed by numbers 1,2,4,5 and 7. It is, therefore, advisable that he should select his wife from one of these periods or numbers.

A Number 1 husband

He is generous and desires his wife to shine in society. He is good-natured and devoted to his family and children. He likes to spend most of his time at home. Though he has a kind and loving disposition he wants his family to dance to his tunes and will not tolerate disrespect.

A Number 1 wife

She is devoted, sympathetic, adaptable and satisfied with her own work. Occasionally she is moody, whimsical and changing. This creates trouble for her as well as for others. She is aristocratic by temperament and attracts people to her home and commands great respect. She needs a virile husband who can provide her with the romantic outlets that her passionate nature requires.

Friends

His best friends are those who are governed by numbers 1,3,4,5,7 and 9. He has a natural affinity also towards people born in October, January, April and in his own month i.e. July. He likes those who have imagination, literary bias and love of travel.

f) FORTUNATE DAYS AND NUMBERS : His lucky days are Sundays, Mondays, Wednesdays and Thursdays and his lucky numbers are 1,4 and 7. He should therefore take important steps on one of these days and also dates if possible. He should try his luck in lottery by purchasing a ticket where the total of all the digits is 1,4 or 7 or where the last digit is 1,4 or 7.

g) LUCKY COLOURS : He should use all shades of yellow, gold and orange.

h) LUCKY JEWELS AND STONES : His lucky jewels are Ruby, Emerald and Moonstone.

i) IMPORTANT YEARS IN LIFE : The important years in his life are 1, 10, 19, 28, 37, 46, 55, 64, 73 etc.

j) HIS GOOD QUALITIES AND DRAWBACKS ARE AS UNDER:

Good Qualities	Drawbacks
Strong will-power	Obstinacy
Aspiration	Aloofness
Enterprise	Domination
Authority	Impertinence
Confidence	Inflexibility
Determination	Pride
Research	Showmanship
Vigour	Spendthrift nature

CHAPTER 56

BORN ON

2nd, 11th, 20th and 29th July

All those born on the 2nd, 11th, 20th and 29th of July of any year are governed by number 2 and the Moon. July is governed by the planet Neptune. The character reading relating to number 2 given below is equally applicable to the other dates. In addition, the special characteristics of those born on 11th, 20th and 29th July are given separately.

Born on 2nd July

a) CHARACTER

He has great dreams of what he wants to accomplish and the chances are that he will carry them out. He is enthusiastic about every aspect of his work and sometimes extremely dictatorial in laying down the law for others to follow. He will create dramatic situations in which he will play the leading role and come into the limelight of publicity. He dislikes a monotonous life. He has fantasies and lacks the practical approach to life. He revels in his own dreams and therefore shuns society. He does not like the company of others as he finds them too ordinary for his imaginary world. He is somewhat nervous, but social and is liked by others. He is warm-hearted and shows little resistance to oppression. He has noble sentiments.

He loves natural and beautiful things in life such as the sea, flowers, and the vastness of the sky. He takes pleasure in spending hours in the company of high tides or with his eyes rivetted to the galaxy of stars.

He is very unsteady, fickle-minded and a lover of change. He therefore has a fancy for travel, especially long travels which engage his imagination and he will go on building castles in the air. He is unassuming, but pleasing and has a good taste in clothes. He likes peace and harmony. He has a hypnotic power to attract others.

Born on 11th July

you have all the basic characteristics of those born on the 2nd of the month, so first go through them and then read your own.

He is usually successful in life and in love and gets honour, position and authority. He is honest with his friends and is of a royal disposition. He should guard himself from secret enemies. He has interest in mysticism, philosophy and science. He can expect travels, favours and honours in life. He is very impulsive and gets excited easily. He worries too much over small matters. He has the ability to take quick decisions which endow him with leadership. He is a born adviser and inspiration to others.

Born on 20th July

you have all the basic characteristics of those born on the 2nd of the month, so first go through them and then read your own.

He has many friends and benefits through wealthy women. He has a flair for writing and can be known as an author or a novelist. His prosperity lies near water, a river or the sea. This number has a peculiar significance. It shows new resolutions for the betterment of people at large.

Born on 29th July

you have all the basic characteristics of those born on the 2nd of the month, so first go through them and then read your own.

This person is moody and changing and therefore uncertain about his action. He is courageous and takes risks in life and does not stick to anything till the end. He is intelligent and also a deep thinker but there is a tendency to carry everything to extremes. He is not very lucky in his married life. His interest is in his business. He is blessed with good fortune. His life is eventful.

b) FINANCE

In matters of finance this man's position is very uncertain. The person is likely to have a desire to jump at any chance to make money. In the end this is likely to be a vicious circle which becomes worse as he gets older. It is necessary that he should exercise extreme caution in financial matters. It is better he avoids speculation and all forms of gambles. He should try to build up his reserves no matter how slowly. He should avoid all schemes to get rich quickly. A person governed by number 2 does not have the physical capacity to stand the strain of every day iife. He can improve his financial status provided he is able to create art out of his imagination. He can be a good author or a painter and earn a good livelihood.

c) VOCATION

His planetary position is suitable for shipping, exports and imports, and transportation. As he has a rich vocabulary and linguistic capacities, he can be successful as a teacher or a professor of languages.

d) HEALTH

His main health weakness is his poor blood circulation. He is susceptible to all sickness arising out of poor blood circulation such as anaemia and a weak heart. Since the Moon is the ruling planet of number 2, the uneasiness which is a prominent characteristic, creates mental worries and sleeplessness. He is also susceptible to diabetes and asthmatic troubles.

e) MARRIAGE AND FRIENDS

He has a natural attraction towards persons born in the period from 20th June to 20th July, 20th October to 20th November and 20th February to 20th March. He also has an affinity for those who are governed by numbers 2 and 6. It is advisable that he should select his wife from one of these periods or numbers.

A Number 2 husband

He is on the whole of a good nature. He is devoted to his family and children. He likes to spend most of his time at home. However, there are two types of the July husband. One is dominating and the other is easy-going.   The first type likes others to dance to his tunes. He is very exacting and tries to find fault with everything. He is critical about everything and that creates tension in the family members.   Nothing satisfies him. He is constantly interfering in the family routine. He is very sensual and seeks constant erotic stimulation.

The other type of the July husband is passive, lazy and self-indulgent and marries for money and comfort. Since he is submissive he often gets what he wants in life.

A Number 2 wife

She is devoted, sympathetic, adaptable and satisfied with her work, position and status. She is a good mother and loves her children and family. Her presence is sanctifying and she is loved and respected by others. She has intutition and some-times can guide her husband in his business with wonderful accuracy. However, a July wife may have another side; she may be very moody, whimsical and changing. This creates trouble for her as well as for others. In that case she is very possessive and demanding.

Friends

This man's best friends are those who are governed by numbers 2,4 6 and 9. He also has a natural affinity towards people born in October, January and April and in his own month i.e. July. He likes those who have fellowship, honesty and simplicity.

f) FORTUNATE DAYS
AND NUMBERS : His lucky days are Mondays, Thursdays and Fridays and lucky numbers are 2,6 and 7. He should, therefore, take all important steps on one of these days and also dates if possible. He should try his luck in lottery by pur-chasing a ticket where the total of all

the digits is 2,6 or 7, or where the last digit is 2,6 or 7.

g) LUCKY COLOURS : He should use all shades of white, cream and blue as his lucky colours.

h) LUCKY JEWELS AND STONES : His lucky jewels are Pearls and Diamonds and lucky stones are Moonstone and Agate.

i) IMPORTANT YEARS IN LIFE : His important years are 2, 11, 20, 29, 38, 47, 56, 65, 74 etc.

j) HIS GOOD QUALITIES & DRAWBACKS ARE AS UNDER:

Good qualities	Drawbacks
Emotionality	Coldness
Fellowship	Envy
Honesty	Haste
Imagination	Introvert
Simplicity	Shyness
—	Whimsicality

CHAPTER 57

BORN ON
3rd, 12th, 21st and 3Oth of July

All those born on the 3rd, 12th, 21st and 30th of July of any year are governed by number 3 and the planet Jupiter. July is governed by the planet Neptune. The character reading of number 3 given below is equally applicable to the other dates. In addition, the special characteristics of those born on 12th, 21st and 30th July are given separately.

Born on 3rd July

a) CHARACTER

He has a decided love for home and country and at the same time has a desire to extend his knowledge by travel and study of other lands. He views life from a high and intellectual stand point. He does well in positions of authority and public, municipal or governmental work of any kind, or as the head of large enterprises. He is very independent in spirit and fearless and courageous in his views and opinions. He is popular with his superiors as well as inferiors.

Jupiter stands for morality, pure love and justice. He is sympathetic by nature and is untiring in his effort to do good to all. He is devoutly religious and a man of true dignity. The judge who gives sane decisions and merciful sentences, the physician and the church dignitary, the world's preachers and philosophers are all mostly governed by number 3.

The person is confident of his ability. He is self-reliant and takes his own decisions. He has a habit of talking loudly. He is fond of show and likes to observe form, order and law.

He is jovial in spirit and cordial in manner. His passions are healthy, spontaneous and without inhibitions. He is free in his expression. He is a good conversationalist.

He takes an active interest in sports and outdoor activities from early youth. He has tremendous enthusiasm and is not self-centred. His intellect is of a very nigh quality. He has a kind of vision that understands the world and loves it for what it is and not for what it ought to be. He is a broad-minded person, tolerant, humorous and truthful. He is open-hearted with good understanding and entirely lacking in malice or petty jealousies. If he is not alert, people take undue advantage of his good nature. The main characteristics of a number 3 person are ambition, leadership, love of religion, pride, sense of honour, love of nature, enthusiasm, generosity, and commanding respect.

Born on 12 th July | you have all the basic characteristics of those born on the 3rd of the month, so first go through them and then read your own.

Authority and honours are the significant aspects of this person's life. He has vanity and is proud, ambitious and aspiring. He is fond of pleasures and is attracted to the opposite sex. However, sometimes he prefers loneliness. He likes to make sacrifices for others but becomes the victim of others, plans or intrigues. His relations with others are smooth and harmonious. He is quick to notice trifles. He has lofty ideals.

Born on 21st July | you have all the basic characteristics of those born on the 3rd of the month, so first go through them and then read your own.

He is kind and generous and is a loving father. He achieves fame, reputation and honours at a very late age. He is cheerful and fond of travel. He has a strong sense of self-respect. Surprisingly, he has a suspicious nature.

Born on 30th July | you have all the basic characteristics of those born on the 3rd of the month, so first go through them and then read your own.

He is fortunate, generous and optimistic. He has a noble and religious mind. He likes to travel and visit places of pilgrimage. He can be successful as or teacher or educationist or in administration. He appears gentle and sincere but has a hidden quality. He may be active but is restless. When faced with difficulties, he is strong enough to overcome them.

b) FINANCE

He is a lucky type and somehow manages to earn enough for his livelihood. He also gets opportunities for higher positions in life and thereby earns quite a lot. His ambition, leadership and enthusiasm always push him forward. Usually he gets all comforts in life. The number 3 person is early out of puberty and poverty.

c) VOCATION

His love of position and command makes him a politician. He is gifted for public life, statesmanship and high offices, may be in the army or in the church. He is good as a teacher as well as a preacher. Professions such as those of doctors, bankers, advertisers and actors are also suitable for him.

d) HEALTH

Number 3 has chief influence over the blood and the arterial system. It also governs the sense of smell. This person is liable to suffer from chest and lung disorders, throat afflictions, gout and apoplexy and sudden fevers. He may also suffer from sore throat, diptheria, adenoids, pneumonia, pleurisy and tuberculosis of the lungs.

e) MARRIAGE AND FRIENDS

He has a natural attraction towards persons born in the period from 20th February to 20th March, 20th June to 20th July and 20th October to 20th November. He also has an affinity for those who are governed by numbers 3, 6 and 9. It is therefore advisable for him to select his wife from one of these periods or numbers.

A Number 3 husband

He is good-natured and is devoted to his family and children. He likes to spend most of his time at home. However, as he is ambitious, he expects too many things from his wife and is likely to be disappointed. He wants a wife of whom he can be proud. She should have an attractive personality, a commanding presence, charming manners and intelligence. It is always better for him to choose a number 3 person or a number 6 person as his wife. He is most loving, thoughful and considerate. His passions are adventurous and demand immediate satisfaction.

A Number 3 wife

She is a good mother and loves her children and family. She has intuitive faculties and sometimes guides her husband in his business with wonderful accuracy. She is a good companion to her husband. She is not an intruder but takes active interest in the business of her husband. However, a July wife is likely to be moody, whimsical and changing. This creates trouble for her as well as for others. In that case she is very possessive and demanding.

Friends

His best friends are those who are governed by the numbers 1, 3, 5, 6, 7, 8 and 9. He also has a natural affinity towards people born in October, January and April and in his own month i. e, July.

f) FORTUNATE DAYS
   AND NUMBERS : His lucky days are Tuesdays, Thursdays and his lucky numbers are 1, 3, 5. He should therefore take all important steps on one of these days and also dates if possible. He should try his luck in lottery by purchasing a ticket where the total of all the digits is 1,3 or 5 or where the last digit is 1,3 or 5.

h) LUCKY COLOURS : He should use all shades of yellow, violet, purple and green as his lucky colours.

h) LUCKY JEWELS AND STONES : His lucky jewel is Topaz and lucky stones are Amethpst and Cat's eye.

i) IMPORTANT YEARS IN LIFE : His important years are 3, 12, 21, 30, 39, 48, 57, 66, 75 etc.

j) HIS GOOD QUALITIES AND DRAWBACKS ARE AS UNDER:

Good qualities	Drawbacks
Ambition	Cruelty
Dignity	Dictatorship
Individuality	Hypocrisy
Philosophical nature	Spendthrift nature
Prestige	Vanity

CHAPTER 58

BORN ON
4th, 13th, 22nd and 31st July

All those born on the 4th, 13th, 22nd and 31st of July .of any year are governed by the number 4 and the planet Uranus. July is governed by the Moon. The character reading of number 4 given below is equally applicable to the other dates. In addition, the special charactersttcs of those born on 13th, 22nd and 31st July are given separately.

Born on 4th July

a) CHARACTER

The combination of the planets Uranus and the Moon make an unusual personality, but not one to cope with eventualities. He is highly oriinal in thought and ideas, sentiments or emotional nature. He is likely to have consi- sensitive and touchy in everything that concerns his feelings, sentiment or emotional nature. He is likely to have consi- derable trouble and estrangement through relations and in domestic matters. He may go through law-suits and experience great injustice at various times in his life. He should be very careful regarding partnerships and in the selection of his spouse.

Uranus shows revolution and unexpected happenings in life. Usually the changes that take place are for the better. This number represents the higher faculties of the mind. It shows activity and intelligence engaged in the reconstruction or the betterment of human iife. The peculiar nature of this person is that he constantly aims at changes in life and society and seeks the liberation of the mind from bondage to environment and society. He dislikes hypocrisy and loves art and music. He has an attractive personality.

Born on 13th July

> you have all the basic characteristics of those born on the 4th of the month, so first go through them and then read your own.

He has all the qualities of a number 4 person but in an exaggerated form. He is faithful and sympathetic but has difficulty in expressing his love. His success and career usually start after his 31st year. He occupies positions of high responsibilities and gets riches. He likes to remain active though in a quiet way. He is interested in literary and scientific books. Though outwardly he looks mild, inwardly he is obstinate.

Born on 22nd July

> you have all the basic characteristics of those born on the 4th of the month, so first go through them and then read your own.

On the whole he is lucky in his affairs and benefits from the opposite sex. He is happy in his family life but is also fond of a companion. He is rather easy-going but unsteady in nature. His actions are spasmodic. He occupies good positions but without much responsibility. His social field is limited and he has few friends. He does not care for disputes. He has too much economy of sentiment.

Born on 31st July

> you have all the basic characteristics of those born on the 4th of the month, so first go through them and then read your own.

This date shows ambition, pride and austerity. He is interested in honourable occupations such as working with charitable institutions for the deaf and dumb and the physically handicapped etc. He gets success after his 40th year. He expects quick results and early reputation. He is lucky in financial matters. He is realistic and has a strong will-power. He has a strong attraction for the opposite sex. He loves travelling.

b) FINANCE

As regards finance and monetary status, he is usually well settled in life though he experiences delays and difficulties in his undertakings. He may not amass wealth but can maintain the show of riches. He is a spendthrift and his home is well decorated. His financial prosperity usually starts after the age of 40.

c) VOCATION

He will be successful in trades such as transport, electricity and all sorts of machinery. He will be equally successful as an engineer, a building contractor, a scientist and an industrialist. He is attracted towards mystic subjects such as palmistry and astrology and can do well in these subjects also.

d) HEALTH

In health matters he will have many unusual experiences and it will be difficult to get doctors to understand him. His friends and relatives will not believe the symptoms he describes. In order to maintain good health he has to be very particular about his diet. Due to his disturbed stomach, he suffers from gastric trouble, rheumatism, gout and sometimes trouble of the respiratory tract. He is also likely to suffer from urinary trouble.

e) MARRIAGE AND FRIENDS

He has a natural attraction towards persons born in the period from 20th February to 20th March, 20th June to 20th July and 20th October to 20th November. He also has affinity for those who are governed by numbers 1,2,7 and 8. It is therefore advisable that he should select his wife from one of these periods or numbers.

A Number 4 husband

He is shrewd and intelligent and expects his wife to share his views. He is dominating and fault-finding and wants all affairs of the house to run according to his wishes. He is critical of every thing and thus creates tension in his family. Nothing satisfies him. He is very sensual and seeks constant erotic stimulation.

A Number 4 wife

She is smart and attractive. She loves interior decoration but gets it done through others. She is dictatorial and moody and spoils her day due to her own whimsical nature. She loves her home but is not attached to it very much. She aims at several things but seldom succeeds in getting mastery over one.

Friends

His best friends are those who are governed by numbers 1, 2, 4, 5, 7, 8 and 9. He also has a natural affinity towards people born in October, January, April and in his own month i.e. July. He is attracted towards those who have orginality, imagination and philosophy.

f) FORTUNATE DAYS
AND NUMBERS : His lucky days are Sundays, Mondays and Wednesdays and lucky numbers are 2, 4 and 7. He should therefore take all important decisions on one of these days and dates if possible. He should try his luck in lottery by purchasing a ticket where the total of all the digits is 2,4 or 7, or where the last digit is 2, 4 or 7.

g) LUCKY COLOURS : He should use all shades of blue, gray, maroon and white.

h) LUCKY JEWELS AND STONES : His lucky jewels are Diamond, Coral and Pearl.

i) IMPORTANT YEARS IN LIFE : His important years are 4, 13, 22, 31, 40, 49, 58, 67, 76 etc.

20

j) HIS GOOD QUALITIES AND DRAWBACKS ARE AS UNDER:

Good qualities	Drawbacks
Activity	Co-operation
Endurance	Practicality
Energy	Shrewdness
Reliability	Vigilance
Method and system	Jealous

CHAPTER 59

BORN ON
5th, 14th and 23rd of July

All those born on the 5th, 14th and 23rd of July of any year are governed by number 5 and the planet Mercury. July is governed by the Moon. The character reading relating to number 5 given below, is equally applicable to the other dates. In addition, the special characteristics of those born on 14th and 23rd July are given separately.

Born on 5th July

a) CHARACTER

The person is extremely sensitive and impressionable with regard to both people and surroundings. He will be readily responsive to all acts of kindness and praise, and encouragement willbe to his nature as water is to flowers. In his early years he will have difficulty in acquiring self-confidence. He has an intense desire for intellectual things and a great ambition to dominate others. His greatest fault is that he may go too far in forcing his plans to an issue, making enemies and inviting great opposition. In advanced years he may develop a strong will and self-confidence. With these two powerful weapons he can easily succeed in the battle of life, on accout of his unsual intellect.

Being governed by Mercury he has shrewdness, quickness, interest in scientific pursuits, business ability, industry, intuition and diplomacy. A person governed by this number is active and quick; this does not apply to physical agility only but to the mind as well. He has the capacity to judge the ability of his opponents in games and knows very well how to take advantage of their weak points. He is fond of oratory and eloquence in expressing himself. He has the capacity to pursue his objectives and knows very well how to plan to achieve his ends. He is deeply interested in occult subjects and has a fancy to master all their intricacies. He possesses a pleasant character and dislikes inactivity. He is sociable and has many acquaintances. He is fond of variety and change, and trips and travels. However difficult the situation, he can get out of it.

He is a nervous person. He is therefore, restless. He has an intuitive perception and has the capacity to be either good or bad. On the good side, he is a shrewd person and not vicious or criminal. He is fond of family life and loves children. His pleasures are mainly mental and he revaluates everything in terms of business. He is amiable and adaptable.

Born 14th July

> you have all the basic characteristics of those born on the 5th of the month, so first go through them and then read your own.

He has a good memory and love for his own people. He is industrious in his undertaking but is inclined to speculate and seeks quick money. He has the capacity to appeal to people to donate generously to funds in aid of hospitals and such institutions. His peculiarity is his contradictory behaviour. He is moody, timid and uncertain. A person born on 14th July has an attractive personality and is liked by all. His nature is co-operative and he does not like to provoke others He usually occupies a good position in life and is successful in his business. He is not talkative but is slightly reserved. This is a number of intelligence and shrewdness. For women, it indicates a goodmarriage but they should take care in child-bearing. A number 14 man is inconsistent in love and experiences some romantic and impulsive attachment in early years. He is fortunate in money matters. He is positive in his speech and action. Usually he is fond of gambling and solving riddles.

Born on 23rd July

> you have all the basic characteristics of those born on the 5th of the month, so first go through them and then read your own.

He is usually popular with women. His fortune is near the

water. He is successful in life and enjoys honour and wealth. He may get money through inheritance. He keeps himself busy in his own way. He gets help and protection from superiors. He is a lucky person. He is affectionate and loves freedom. He is averse to formalities. He has a spirit of independence and a desire to dominate.

b) FINANCE

Since number 5 is business number, the person can expect opulence. With his shrewdness he is capable of developing his industry and carrying out his plans systematically with the result that his efforts are well rewarded. He is lucky in his financial position.

c) VOCATION

He can adapt himself to the role he has to play in the drama of life. With his adaptability he comes into contact with various classes of people and is successful in any business. Banking is a good line for him. Mercury also shows aptitude for medicine or surgery. His capacity to argue his points can make him a good lawyer.

d) HEALTH

His basic health defect is his biliousness and nervousness. However his biliousness has close relation with psychological disturbance. His biliousness increases with increased tension and is reduced or disappears when his nervous trouble is under control.

Number 5 rules over nerves, the neck, the arms, the ears and the respiratory system. In order to maintain good health, this man has to be very particular about his diet. Due to his disturbed stomach, he suffers from gastric troubles, rheumatism, gout and sometimes trouble of the respiratory tract.

e) MARRIAGE AND FRIENDS :

He has a natural attraction towards persons born in the period from 20th September to 20th November, and 20th

January to 20th March.   He also has affinity for those who
are governed by numbers 1,5,7 and 8. It is, therefore, advisable
that he should select his wife from one of these periods or
numbers.

A Number 5 husband

He is devoted to his family and children. He likes to spend
most of his time at home. He expects neatness and cleanliness
from his wife and also desires that she should share in the
enjoyment of life. He is proud of her and likes to see her
well dressed. Even if he travels long, he is very much attracted
to his home and is eager to return. He is liberal in spending
on clothes and other wants of the members of his family and
furnishes his house with good taste.

A Number 5 wife

She has interest at home as well as outside. She has
many activities and manages them well. She likes tidiness
and though she seldom does her own work, she gets it done
through her commanding personality. She has intuitive faculties and sometimes can guide her husband in his business with
wonderful accuracy.   However, being born in July, she is
very moody, whimsical and changing. This creates trouble for
her as well as for others. In that case she is very possesive
and demanding.

Friends

His best friends are those who are governed by
numbers 1, 4,5,7 and 8. He has a natural affinity also
towards people born in October, January, April and in his
own month i.e. July. He likes those who have discretion,
honesty and simplicity.

f) FORTUNATE DAYS
       AND NUMBERS : His lucky days are Wednesdays,
                     Thursdays and Fridays and his lucky
                     numbers, are 3,5 and 7. He should

therefore take all important steps on
one of these days and also dates if
possible. He should try his luck in
lottery by purchasing a ticket where
the total of all the digits is 3,5 or 7,
or where the last digit is 3, 5 or 7.

g) LUCKY COLOURS : He should use white and shades of
green.

h) LUCKY JEWELS AND STONES : His lucky jewels are
Emerald, Diamond and
Pearl.

i) IMPORTANT YEARS IN LIFE : His important years are 5,
14, 23, 32, 41, 50, 59, 68,
77 etc.

j) HIS GOOD QUALITIES AND DRAWBACKS ARE AS UNDER:

Good qualities	Drawbacks
Co-operative	Lack of perseverance
Practical	Scepticism
Shrewd	Unreliability
Vigilant	

CHAPTER 60

BORN ON
6th, 15th and 24th July

All those born on the 6th, 15th and 24th of July of any year are governed by number 6 and the planet Venus. July is governed by the Moon. The character reading related to number 6 given below is equally applicable to the other dates. In addition, the special characteristics of those born on 15th and 24th July are given separately.

Born on 6th July

a) CHARACTER

The person will have an interesting and unusual life, one in which love, romance and powerful ambition will play an important part. He is kind-hearted, generous, impressionable and extremely magnetic. He has considerable interest in mystical things but he will keep this under control and not allow any idle superstition to gain a hold on him. Still he is a believer in fate. He has affection and respect for his mother's relatives. It is always charming to be with him. His company is full of enthusiasm, energy and charm. His talk is interesting and lively. We may sometimes be required to put aside our ideas of morality and social conduct in understanding and appreciating his feelings and views. Number 6 stands for beauty, health, vitality, warmth, attraction and above all, love. A person of this number is fond of music, dancing and poetry. He loves a life of ease and luxuries, money and happiness. He prefers spending to saving. He will have rich clothes, jewellery, perfumes and all sorts of beautiful things.

He is necessarily a loving type and he has a feeling of kinship and humanity. He will, therefore, not desert his friends. He always likes to understand the grievances and difficulties of others, and is considerate. He prefers joy to gloom and has the capacity to make others share his joy. His outlook is bright and vivacious. He is emotional but keeps his emotions to himself. His anger is hard to subside. He is very responsible and loves his children, but receives very little happiness from them. He is a born advisor and needs an audience to whom he can express his views on matters of importance. He is a good conversationalist and enjoys crossing swords intellectually.

Born on 15th July you have all the basic characteristics of those born on the 6th of the month, so first go through them and then read your own.

Number 15 is associated with good talkers, often with eloquence, gifts of music and art and a dramatic personality, combined with a certain voluptuous temperament and strong personal magnetism. For obtaining money, gifts and favours from others, it is a forunate number. This person has high intelligence and a good memory. He is fit for responsible positions such as those of ambassadors, consuls, governors etc. He is very ambitious and boastful but is hasty and proud. He is interested in the lower type of occultism. He is interested also in art and music. He appears to be gentle but has very strong convictions. He has a habit of worrying inwardly and leads a melancholy life. He has to make sacrifices for others.

Born on 24th July you have all the basic characteristics of those born on the 6th of the month, so first go through them and then read your own.

This man is fortunate in getting assistance from people of high rank. He benefits through the opposite sex. He marries a rich girl and prospers. He succeeds in speculation and enjoys a good monetary status. He defines strictly the line between personal and social matters. He is methodical in his ideas. He possesses a strong ego and sometimes tries to force his opinions on others.

b) FINANCE

In financial matters he is likely to be more fortunate than otherwise. He gains money by marriage and by legacies. He spends his earnings on whatever attracts him. He also never repents spending his money on his art which may not ultimately give him monetary rewards. So he is rarely wealthy but he somehow has the knack of making both ends meet and having the minimum comforts. He may sometimes have windfalls.

c) VOCATION

He will shine as an interior decorator, architect, jeweller, musician, hotel manager or a confectioner. He can be equally successful as a broker, an estate broker or as a commission agent. He can also be a good artist and create works of lasting value. He has a rich vocabulary and linguistic capacities and can be successful as a teacher or a professor of languages. He can also be a good translator or editor.

d) HEALTH

His main health weakness is his poor blood circulation. He is susceptible to sickness arising out of poor blood circulation such as anaemia and a weak heart. Since the moon is the ruling planet of July, the uneasiness which is its prominent characteristic creates mental worries and sleeplessness. He is also susceptible to diabetes and asthma.

e) MARRIAGE AND FRIENDS

He has a natural attraction towards persons born in the period from 20th August to 20th September, 20th December to 20th January and 20th February to 20th March. He has affinity for those who are governed by numbers 2,4,6 and 9. It is therefore advisable that he should select his wife from one of these periods or numbers.

A Number 6 husband

He is very exacting and tries to find fault with everything. He is very critical about details and creates a tension in his family. Nothing satisfies him. However, he likes married life and usually marries early. He loves his children and home. He is kind, generous and devoted. Though he creates a lively atmosphere in the house, he somehow finds it difficult to meet all the needs of his family. This may sometimes create unpleasantness and make him unhappy in his married life.

A Number 6 wife

She never resorts to divorce and endures extreme hardship rather than desert her husband. She is a devoted mother and a loving wife, satisfied with her husband's efforts in her behalf. She loves domestic life and makes a perfect home.

Friends

His best friends are those governed by numbers 2,3,4,6 and 9. He has a natural affinity also towards people born in October, January, April and in his own month i.e. July.

f) FORTUNATE DAYS
   AND NUMBERS : His lucky days are Mondays,Tuesdays, Thursdays and Fridays and his lucky numbers are 2, 4, 6 and 9. He should therefore take all important decisions on one of these days and also dates if possible. He should try his luck in lottery by purchasing a ticket where the total of all the digits is 2,4,6 or 9, or where the last digit number is 2,4,6 or 9.

g) LUCKY COLOURS : He should use blue, rose and pink.

h) LUCKY JEWELS AND STONES : He can use Turquioise, Emerald, Pearl and Diamond.

i) IMPORNANT YEARS IN LIFE : His important years are 6, 15, 24, 33, 42, 51, 60, 69 78 etc.

j) HIS GOOD QUALITIES AND DRAWBACKS ARE AS UNDER:

Good qualities	Drawbacks
Harmony	Absence of foresight
Love	Interference
Peace	Moodiness
Strong memory	Timidity

CHAPTER 61

BORN ON
7th, 16th and 25th July

All those born on the 7th, 16th and 25th of July of any year are governed by the number 7 and the planet Neptune. July is governed by the Moon. The character reading relating to number 7 given below is equally applicable to the other dates. In addition, special characteristics of those born on 16th and 25th are given separately.

Born on 7th July

a) CHARACTER

If he develops strength of character and will power, the combination of Neptune and the Moon will bring him great advantage over others because of his intellectual attainments. He is likely to choose mental pursuits of an unusual kind. He is emotional, artistic and imaginative with psychic gifts of a very high order. He has very highly refined tastes and ideals and will aspire to great things. The planetary combination produces a philosophical and deeply religious nature.

He has individuality and is original and independent. He is restless by nature · and is fond of change. He likes to visit foreign countries and becomes interested in far off lands. He has peculiar ideas about religion and dislikes following the beaten track. His behaviour is a mystery to others. He is often absent-minded. He thinks out logically and achieves great aims. He is stubborn and ingnores the opinions of others. He has a good talent to earn money. In general, he is somewhat indifferent to materialistic desires. He desires the best or none at all. He is sensitive and hides his real feel-

ings by apparent indifference. He dislikes mingling with
common people. He prefers spending his hour with his favour-
rite book. When his opinion is solicited, he speaks with authority. He knows his ground.

Born on 7th July | you have all the basic characteristics of those born on the 7th of the month, so first go through them and then read your own.

He is rather easy-going and does not like to work hard.
He is good-humoured and generous. He is very sensitive and
emotional. He soon gets upset but is soon pleased. He is
frequently indisposed. He is fortunate in having good and
successful children. However there is some sort of sorrow in
his married life. He appears to be calm but his mind is always
in turmoil. He is sometimes short-tempered. He will not
disclose his nervousness and is slow in taking decisions. He
does not like interference.

Born on 25th July | you have all the basic characteristics of those born on the 7th of the month, so first go through them and then read your own.

He is a Jack of all trades but master of none. He is
interested in several subjects but does not have the capacity to
go into details. His knowledge therefore is very shallow. He
likes to travel and has connections with foreign countries. He
is honest, faithful and good-natured. But he is fickle-minded
and inconsistent. His memory is good; he is a good orator and
a good teacher.

b) FINANCE

Usually, there are many changes in the life of this
person and so it is difficult for him to amass wealth. However
this being a mystic number, the person can be well placed in
life provided he finds a job of his choice. In that case he can
be a wealthy person with all amenities and comforts.

c) VOCATION

His love for sea travel and interest in foreign countries can
make him a successful merchant, exporter or importer. He can
also deal in dairy products and other products such as soap

etc, or choose fishery and the chemical industry. He can also study medicine and surgery.

d) HEALTH

His health is mainly governed by his state of mind. Though he is not a robust person physically, he can show great power of endurance if his mind is set on some definite objects. Physically he is likely to have peculiar illnesses out of the ordinary run such as tumours, and underfunctioning of the internal organs. If he keeps his mind in a happy, cheerful condition, his sickness will be considerably under control. He has also a nervous constitution and suffers from faulty blood circulation.

e) MARRIAGE AND FRIENDS

He has a natural attraction towards persons born in the period from 20th June to 20th July, 20th October to 20th November, 20th February to 20th March. He also has affinity for those who are governed by numbers 3, 5 and 8. It is therefore advisable that he should select his wife from one of these periods or numbers.

A Number 7 husband

He is very emotional and understands the feelings of his wife. He is very considerate and will never try to impose his views on his wife. He is liberal, fond of picnics, travels and cinema theatres. He is a spendthrift and likes to live lavishly. His family is moderate in size and has all the comforts in life. However, there is another type of husband. He is dominating and likes others to dance to his tunes. He is very exacting and tries to find fault with everything. He is critical about everything and that creates tension for the family members. Nothing statisfies him. He is constantly demanding and interfering in the family routine. He is very sensual and seeks constant erotic stimulation.

A Number 7 wife

She is devoted, sympathetic, adaptable and satisfied with her work, position and status. She is a good mother and loves her children and family. Her presence is sanctifying. She is loved and respected by others. She has intuitive faculties and sometimes can guide her husband in his business with wonderful accuracy. However, a July wife may be different also when she is very moody, whimsical and changing. This creates trouble for her as well as for others. In that case she is very possessive and demanding.

Friends

His best friends are those who are governed by numbers 1, 3, 4, 5, 7 8 and 9. He has natural affinity also towards people born in October, January, April and in his own month i.e. July.

f) FORTUNATE DAYS
   AND NUMBERS : His lucky days are Sundays, Mondays, Wednesdays, and Thursdays. His lucky numbers are 2 and 7. He should therefore take all important steps on one of these days and also dates if possible. He should try his luck in lottery by purchasing a ticket where the total of all the digits is 2 or 7, or where the last digit is 2 or 7.

g) LUCKY COLORS : He should use all shades of green and yellow.

h) LUCKY JEWELS & STONES : His lucky jewels are Topaz and Emerald and lucky stones are Moonstone and Cat's Eye.

i) IMPORTANT YEARS IN LIFE : His important years are 7, 16, 25, 34, 43, 52, 61, 70, 79 etc.

j) HIS GOOD QUALITIES AND DRAWBACKS ARE AS UNDER:

Good qualities	Drawbacks
Austerity	Despondency
Peace	Diffidence
Reflection	Restlessnes
Serenity	Whimsicality
Tolerance	

CHAPTER 62

BORN ON
8th, 17th and 26th of July

All those born on the 8th, 17th and 26th of July of any year are governed by the number 8 and the planet Saturn. July is governed by the Moon. The character reading relating to number 8 given below is equally applicable to the other dates. In addition, the special characteristics of those born on 17th and 26th July are given separately.

Born on 8th July

a) CHARACTER

He is a person of strong will and is very decided in his opinions. Till about middle life he is likely to have restrictions and responsibilities which check him. He is like a prisoner in a cage that can look through the bars at the world beyond and yet is unable to change his condition. He is like a "Child of Fate" subject to circumstances beyond his control. He is extremely serious and earnest in his emotions but not demonstrative or able to express his nature. He has to make sacrifices for others in his early years and in matters of love or affection he has to face very hard trials and heavy responsibilities. He is likely to experience either of the following things. He may be one of those persons forced by surroundings or family obligations into some routine career where he may remain for the greater part of his life, working for others; or he may belong to the more fortunate class who get the opportunity quite early, to steadily accumulate money and become a kind of fatalistic power in the world of men. The peculiarity of persons born on 8th, 17th and 26th of July is that they have either a deeply religious nature or the very reverse.

This number is governed by Saturn and shows extreme sense of discipline steadfastness, constancy and dutifulness. The person has a sober and solitude-loving personality. He is a lover of classical music but mostly of a melancholy type. In arts he loves landscapes, natural scenery and flowers. Number 8 is considered to be a balance wheel to the character. The man has a natural ability of looking at the other side of the coin. He is a pessimist. He prefers solitude to company. He shuns society rather than courts it. He is cautious about the future. He takes decisions very carefully on matters which pertain to mundane affairs. He is a prudent person, wise and sober among all the numbers. He is never overenthusiastic and is more or less gloomy and melancholy. He is also amibitious and persevering. He is capable of enormous efforts towards the attainment of his objects. He is sceptical and analytical. He is creative, productive and dominating. He is likely to be misunderstood. He usually feels lonely at heart. He understands the weak and the oppressed and treats them in a warm-hearted manner. He is a born manager who can keep others busy. He admires fair play and is willing to pay a fair compensation. He has a good memory for names and faces.

Born on 17th July | you have all the basic characteristics of those born on the 8th of the month, so first go through them and then read your own.

He is a good organizer and a good thinker. He has a creative and constructive mind. He is a lover of peace and a philanthropist. He is attracted towards occultism and mysticism. He is courageous and proud. He has strong individuality. He is highly intelligent and clever. As regards emotions, he is calm. At times he is generous to a fault and at times very stingy. He is interested in research and loves knowledge. He is conservative and dominating.

Born on 26th July | you have all the basic characteristics of those born on the 8th of the month, so first go through them and then read your own.

He wants to enjoy life without doing anything. He is

sluggish and lethargic. He revels in wine and women and is fickle-minded. He is careless about the number of children. He is lucky in money matters and gets easy money. He is smart but lacks positiveness. He likes to put up a good appearance but has a worrying nature. He has problems in his love affairs.

b) FINANCE

The peculiarity of number 8 is delay in life in all respects. Naturally in financial matters also there is delay and stability is achieved at a very late age. This person has to work hard and he rarely succeeds in getting opulence. He has therefore to avoid number 8 playing a part in his life and instead he can choose number 1 or 3 for all his important actions and moves. However, if his experience shows that 8 is a lucky number for him, he can insist on that number only in which case wealth and prosperity come easily. If 8 is found to be a lucky number in one's life, one can try lottery and luck in horse racing. But usually this number is connected with delays and hard work and the person has to be very cautious in financial matters.

c) VOCATION

Subjects suitable for him are occult sciences, chemistry, physics, medicine and higher mathematics. He can be successful in industries dealing with coal mines, timber etc., and in construction companies. He can be a good accountant and also a good administrator. However, as stated earlier, he has to strive hard in his career and can get the fruits of his hard work only in the later years of his life.

d) HEALTH

His main health defects are nervousness, irritation, trouble with legs, teeth, ears, paralysis and rheumatism. He is a bilious type and often suffers from chronic melancholia. It is very interesting to note that the delay characterising his life is observed in his sickness also. His ailments also take a long time to cure. Varicose veins and haemorrhoids commonly afflict a strong 8 personality.

e) MARRIAGE AND FRIENDS

He has a natural attraction towards persons born in the period from 20th April to 20th May and 20th September to 20th November. He also has affinity for those who are governed by numbers 5 and 7 It is therefore advisable that he should select his wife from one of these periods or numbers.

A Number 8 husband

On the whole he is of a good nature. He is devoted to his family and children and likes to spend most of his time at home. As a general rule a person governed by number 8 prefers loneliness. He is very orthodox in his view and does not allow his wife to adopt modern ideas in dress at home or outside. Naturally his wife is disappointed and hates him. If, however, he desires a successful married life, he should prefer a person who is also interested in deep and serious studies and likes to devote herself to philosophy and occult subjects.

A Number 8 wife

She is of a masculine personality. She is capable and systematic. She enjoys her family life and likes to make sacrifices for her children and for the ambition of her husband. Her fault is that she lacks feminine warmth, sentiment and delicacy. Being born in July she is very moody, whimsical and changing. This creates trouble for her as well as for others. In that case she is very possessive and demanding.

Friends

His best friends are those who are governed by numbers 3,4,5,7 and 8. He has a natural affinity also towards people born in October, January, April and in his own month i.e. July.

f) FORTUNATE DAYS

AND NUMBERS : His lucky days are Wednesdays,

Thursdays and Saturdays and his lucky numbers are 1 and 3. He should therefore take all important steps on one of these days and also dates if possible. He should try his luck in lottery by purchasing a ticket where the total of all the digits is 1 or 3 or where the last digit is 1 or 3.

g) LUCKY COLOURS : He should use dark grey, dark blue purple and black.

h) LUCKY JEWELS AND STONES : His lucky jewels are Sapphire, Black Pearl and Black Diamond. His lucky stones are Cat's Eye and Amethyst.

i) IMPORTANT YEARS IN LIFE : His important years are 8, 17, 26, 35, 44, 53, 62, 71 etc.

j) HIS GOOD QUALITIES AND DRAWBACKS ARE AS UNDER:

Good qualities	Drawbacks
Authority	Cynicism
Methodical	Delay
Practical approach	Vindictiveness
Steady	Nervousness
Systematic	Laziness

CHAPTER 63

BORN ON
9th, 18th and 27th of July

All those born on the 9th, 18th and 27th of July of any year are governed by the number 9 and the planet Mars. July is governed by the Moon. The character reading relating to number 9 below is equally applicable to the other dates. In addition, special characteristics of those born on 18th and 27th of July are given separately.

Born on 9th July

a) CHARACTER

As Mars is considered to be in its "Fall" in July, the man is likely to be full of contradictions and requires the development of a strong will-power and character shown by number 9 to achieve his ambition. He will be forceful and enterprising in all his undertakings with a kind of pioneering spirit and love of adventure. He may have many changes of residence and not easily settle down at any one place for a long time. He can expect considerable frictions with relations and it is advisable that he should not marry early. He is inclined to rebel against restraint and will have to develop tact and prudence in dealing with others. He may experience a peculiarly eventful life as far as danger and accidents are concerned, especially from such causes as fire, firearms, cyclones, earthquakes and from the watery elements. He may go through many law suits in the course of his life; as a rule he will lose in litigation and also through lawyers.

He is fiery and dashing and does not have sickly

sentiments. He has audacity and vigour from start to finish.
He is also fond of games and vigorous exercise. When the
date of the month is 9 and the total of all the digits in the birth
date is also 9, he is governed by a strong number 9 and his
Mars is very powerful. In such a case he has strong sexual
passions and he is attracted towards the opposite sex. He is
prepared to go through any ordeal to gratify his desire.

He is a brave person to whom conflict does not bring the
thought of danger. He is exceedingly devoted to his friends
and will fight for them. He has sympathy and consideration
for the weak. He loves children and animals. He takes delight
in showing mercy to others. He likes the healing profession.
He is backed by self-control, moral courage and the power of
forgiveness. His psychological aptitude is remarkable and
under all circumstances he proves his strength of will and
exhibits courage. He is short-tempered.

Born on 18th July

you have all the basic characteristics of those born on the 9th
of the month, so first go through them and then read your own.

This person has tenacity and will-power which will overcome any difficulty. He is not that dashing as a number 9,
but he is fearless and courageous. His strong health makes
him passionate. He inherits property from his father. He
has a disciplined mind and likes to help others. He is painstaking, has good judgement and is wise. He loves to exercise
perfect control over others. He does not like to be cautioned
by others.

Born on 27th July

you have all the basic characteristics of those born on the 9th
of the month, so first go through them and then read your own.

On the whole he is a conflicting personality. He is
confident and likes to do something for those whose life is
miserable or who are handicapped. He can develop a spiritual
personality and can practise spiritual healing. On the other
side, he is fond of women and may develop illicit contacts and
cause a scandal. Sometimes he creates unhappiness in his
married life. He is very sensitive and moody and his actions
and moves are unpredictable. He is self-assured and strong in
resolution. He is a seeker of independence and tends to

dominate. He hates to work under others. Usually, he is dogmatic.

b) FINANCE

In matters of finance he is either a success or a great failure. There is no likehood of any happy middlepoint. Still he has enterprising ideas and plans for making big money. Normally, he is very liberal in spending but even then enjoys all the comforts that money can bring.

c) VOCATION

A Number 9 person is found in all walks of life but he will be more suitable to the army and to professions where there is full scope for his aggression and courage. In the army he will rise to high positions, in politics he will be eminent and in business he will exhibit his dashing and pushing nature. He can be a good doctor, or a chemist or a businessman dealing in iron and steel.

d) HEALTH

He is likely to undergo dangers from accidents, especially affecting the legs and feet. He may experience such dangers during travel. He may experience trouble of the eyes. His other health defects such as piles, fevers etc., may arise from heat. Throat trouble, bronchitis and laryngitis also frequently trouble him.

e) MARRIAGE AND FRIENDS

He has a natural attraction towards persons born in the period from 20th June to 20th August and 20th October to 20th December. He has affinity also for those who are governed by numbers 3 and 6. It is therefore advisable that he should select his wife from one of these periods or numbers.

A Number 9 husband

He is vigorous in health and has strong circulation of blood which makes him very passionate and enthusiastic about

married life. He is fond of a beautiful wife and likes her to be
submissive and passive to his sexual desires. He is fond of
family and children and likes to have a good house. He usually
leads a good married life in spite of his hot-tempered nature
and eccentricities. He has a romantic mental picture of what
he wants in his wife. This mental picture demands perfection.
The most difficult thing in the married life of a number 9 person
is to satisfy his romantic conception of physical love. He has
a voracious appetite and his wife with her devotion should
harmonise with him physically. Usually, we find him
suspicious of his wife.

A Number 9 wife

She will make a wonderful wife for an ambitious man. She
is a witty and clever conversationalist with a wonderful social
presence. She will assist her husband in his business. She
may also start her own activity and add to the family income.
She will be happy if married to a passionate and possessive
man.

Friends

This man's best friends are those who are governed by
numbers 1, 2, 3, 4, 6, 7 and 9. He has a natural affinity also
towards people born in October, January, April and in his own
month i.e. July.

f) FORTUNATE DAYS
    AND NUMBERS : His lucky days are Mondays,
    Tuesdays, Thursdays and Fridays and
    lucky numbers are 3,6 and 9. He
    should therefore try his luck in lottery
    by purchasing a ticket where the total
    of all the digits is 3,6 or 9, or where
    the last digit is 3,6 or 9.

g) LUCKY COLOURS : He should use all shades of red,
    yellow and white.

h) LUCKY JEWELS AND STONES : His lucky jewels are Topaz, Pearl and Ruby and lucky stones are Blood-stone and Garnet.

i) IMPORTANT YEARS IN LIFE : His important years are 9, 18, 27, 36, 45, 54, 63, 72 etc.

j) HIS GOOD QUALITIES AND DRAWBACKS ARE AS UNDER:

Good qualities	Drawbacks
Activity	Destructive tendency
Courage	Erratic nature
Dash	Hot temper
Energy	Impatience
Enthusiasm	Quarrelsomeness

CHAPTER 64

BORN ON

1st, 10th, 19th and 28th of August

All those born on the 1st, 10th, 19th and 28th of August of any year are governed by number 1 and the Sun. August is governed by the Sun. The character reading relating to number 1 given below is equally applicable to the other dates. In addition, the special characteristics of those born on 10th, 19th and 28th August are given separately.

Born on 1st August

a) CHARACTER

Persons born in this period have high ambition; their aim is to get above the common herd. No matter how low or humble the sphere of life into which they are born, and whatever the career they choose they generally rise by their will, determination and ability, to high positions of authority. They are keenly attracted to other strong personalities; in fact, they are ready to forgive any fault in a man so long as he has individuality and purpose. People born on this day are large-hearted and generous. They have an extremely independent spirit, and detest control and dictation. They have much tenacity of purpose and will power, and if they decide on some plan, purpose or position, they usually reach their goal in spite of every difficulty or obstacle. Such persons must, however, be always actively employed. If forced by circumstances out of the heat and stress of the battle of life, they become morbid and despondent.

As a rule, they are extremely patient and long suffering, but if once aroused, like the lion they know no fear and will not even acknowledge defeat if it should come. They make enemies by their frankness of speech and their hatred of anything underhand or anything savouring of subterfuge. They will defend a friend in the face of all attacks; it is only treachery, disloyalty or deceit that can ever break or crush their proud spirit. Being essentially large-hearted, honest and truthful themselves, they expect great things from those around them, and frequently get terribly disappointed and deceived. They radiate warmth, affection, kindness and a strong personal magnetism which make them exceedingly popular. Highly susceptible to the environment, they exhibit a strong tendency to take on the habits and conditions of others. Their exaggerated faith in human nature is their stumbling block in love and friendship, leading to many tragedies, heartaches and estrangements. They possess splendid organizing ability and great ambition, but are rather too apt to accept responsibilities and take too much on their shoulders. They must also guard against carrying the 'regal attitude' to excess, or else they will become somewhat domineering. Always striving to raise themselves above the common herd, they are naturally attracted to strong personalities and those in high positions. They are intensely proud, determined, frank and straightforward, though somewhat impetuous and quicktempered. Their will power is exceptionally strong and they display tenacity and great persistence if they have chosen the right line of work. At times they have a tendency to despondency and dissatisfaction for not having reached the high position to which they aspire. As they represent what may be termed the heart force of humanity, the keynote to their character in all its phases is magnanimity; consequently they blame no one but themselves for any shortcomings they may have.

They are endowed with unusual intuition, independence of views and originality. They have strong likes and dislikes. They are inclined to violent attachments and will make an early union or marriage. They wish to receive honours and approbation and are likely to be drawn into some form of political life.

The main characteristics of these persons are originality, activity, energy, enthusiasm, art and brilliance.

Born on 10th August   you have all the basic characteristics of those born on the 1st of the month, so first go through them and then read your own.

This man is very impressive, has a magnetic personality and is respected for his knowledge and intelligence. He gets financial benefits from relatives like his father, father-in-law, wife, mother etc. He gets success after his 46th year. He gets a good position in service and succeeds in business also. He has broad shoulders and a manly figure. He loves truthfulness. This number shows honour and self-confidence. The person can get fame or notoriety depending upon his will-power and character. Usually he has good health and recovers quickly from sickness. He likes to help others, but hardly gets a response from them. This is more true in the case of relatives.

Born on 19th August   you have all the basic characteristics of those born on the 1st of the month, so first go through them and then read your own.

This man is very active, energetic and enthusiastic. He has a research aptitude and likes to handle a subject in a systematic way. He takes quick decisions and always likes to be busy with some concrete project. Sports is his hobby and he is interested in horse riding, shooting and other athletic games. He is hasty and impetuous in love affairs which end in quarrels. He is courageous and has force of character. He likes to help others even going out of the way. He can keep the secrets of others and people can confide in him. This number promises success, honour and happiness. It is very difficult for others to understand him. He is always in company but at heart feels lonely. He is obstinate and finds it difficult to extend co-operation. He is prudent and notices even a trivial thing. He is not an excellnt speaker but can explain himself best in writing. He can be a good writer.

Born on 28th August   you have all the basic characteristics of those born on the 1st of the month, so first go through them and then read your own.

This man is very generous and spends on charitable

institutions such as schools and hospitals. He is not as lucky as numbers 1, 10 and 19 and has to undergo difficulties in public and private life. He should select his wife carefully. He has to provide carefully for the future as he is likely to lose through trust in others. He is also likely to make many changes in his career. He hardly reveals his emotions and therefore appears cold. He has an unyielding will power and does not hesitate to carry out his plans.

b) FINANCE

A number 9 person is found in all walks of life but he will financial status is concerned. Even though he is extravagant because of over-enthusiasm, he also earns enough to maintain his ostentatious disposition in life. He may not amass wealth but his personality and behaviour will make others believe that he is a rich person. He is tempted to gamble and if not controlled in time, he may lose to a great extent. His career is divided into two halves. Upto about 37 years he has to work hard to overcome difficulties; from 37 he experiences success and prosperity.

c) VOCATION

He often benefits through speculation and through judicious investments connected with gold mining, brass work and import and export etc. He succeeds in occupations connected with government and municipal bodies. The main difficulty with a number 1 person is his inability to stick to any one profession or job for a long time. Usually, every three years there is a change in his career. He is, however, suitable for advertising concerns, the newspaper business and the cinema industry, he can also be successful in theatrical performances. He can show his art as an interior decorator. Being a good salesman, he can choose a vocation which will be related to foreign countries, such as the post of an ambassador or a trade connected with foreign commodities. He is a leader and can be head of departments or a managing director etc. He can

succeed equally well as a surgeon, jeweller, an electrician
and in research projects.

d) HEALTH

In his childhood and early years he is likely to have many
minor illnesses, especially fevers, rheumatism, inflammation of
the blood, carbuncles, boils etc. But from about the 28th year
there is promise of his growing out of such things and becoming
healthy and vigorous. He is also likely to suffer from irregular
heart-beats which tend to affect the circulation of blood.
Grief or prolonged worry impairs his health more quickly than
anything else.

e) MARRIAGE AND FRIENDS

He has a natural attraction towards persons born in the
period from 20th July to 20th August, 20th November to 20th
December and 20th March to 20th April. He also has affinity
for those who are governed by numbers 2,4,5 and 7. It is
therefore advisable that he should select his wife from one of
these periods or numbers.

A Number 1 husband

He is generous and desires his wife to shine in society.
He has a kind and loving disposition and a great heart. He is
proud of his family and gives them the best of everything. His
love is deep and romantic. He expects his family members to
dance to his tunes and will not tolerate disrespect. His opinions
are fixed and he has fixed ideas as to what he should get from
his wife and children. He may have a romantic affair outside
but will not tolerate such behaviour on the part of his wife. In
this way he is very suspicious of her.

A Number 1 wife

She is a lovable person and by her grace, dignity and
sociable nature she attracts many people. She can manage her
house very efficiently and she is just the sort of wife for an

energetic and enthusiastic husband. She is patient and sacrificing. She pays every attention to the welfare of her husband and her children. Only she knows what sacrifices she makes for them, but others seldom understand her devotion. She is very passionate and needs a virile and masculine husband to satisfy her romantic nature.

Friends

His best friends are those who are governed by numbers 1,3,4,5,7 and 9. He has a natural affinity also towards people born in October, November, February, May, and in his own month i.e. August.

f) FORTUNATE DAYS AND NUMBERS : His lucky days are Sundays, Mondays and Thursdays and his lucky numbers are 1, 5 and 7. He should therefore take all important steps on one of these days and also dates if possible. He should try his luck in lottery by purchasing a ticket where the total of all the digits is 1, 5 or 7 or where the last figure is 1, 5 or 7.

g) LUCKY COLOURS : He should use all shades of gold, yellow, orange and purple.

h) LUCKY JEWELS AND STONES : His lucky jewels are Ruby, Topaz and Amber.

i) IMPORTANT YEARS IN LIFE : His important years are 1, 10, 19, 28, 37, 46, 55, 64, 73 etc.

j) HIS GOOD QUALITIES AND DRAWBACKS ARE AS UNDER:

Good Qualities	Drawbacks
Strong will–power	Obstinacy
Aspiration	Aloofness
Attack	Domination
Authority	Impertinence
Confidence	Inflexibility
Determination	Pride
Research aptitude	Showmanship
Vigour	Extravagance
Talents	—

CHAPTER 65

BORN ON
2nd, 11th, 20th and 29th August

All those born on 2nd, 11th, 20th and 29th of August of any year are governed by the number 2 and the Moon. August is governed by the Sun. The character reading relating to number 2 given below is equally applicable to the other dates. In addition, the special characteristics of those born on 11th 20th and 29th August are given separately.

Born on 2nd August

a) CHARACTER

The combination of the Moon and the Sun is a favourable one. It will raise the person mentally and socially, winning people's trust and confidence, and will bring many opportunities of advancement in his career. He will be popular with the opposite sex, with idealistic love affairs and romances bringing strange and unusual episodes into his life. He is likely to exhibit considerable talent for art, literature, music or drama. In any zone of life that he chooses, he will take a prominent position, and will show great tact, diplomacy and good management. He will be exceptionally loyal to his friends and to those who love him. He is not likely to make any serious enemies, even though people may disagree with his views. He is very unsteady and fickle-minded and loves change. Therefore he has a fancy for travel, especially long travels which satisfy his natural urge for new things. Such travels keep his imagination engaged and he goes on building castles in the air. He is unassuming but pleasing and has a good taste in clothes. He likes peace and harmony. He has a hypnotic power.

Born on 11th August

> you have all the basic characteristics of those born on the 2nd of the month, so first go through them and then read your own.

This man is usually successful in life and in love, and gets honour, position and authority. He is loyal to his friends and is of a royal disposition. He should guard himself from secret enemies. He has interest in mysticism, philosophy and science. He can expect travel, favours and honours in life. He is very impulsive and gets excited easily. He worries too much over small matters. He has an ability to take quick decisions which endow him with leadership. He is a born advisor and an inspiration to others.

Born on 20th August

> you have all the basic characteristics of those born on the 2nd of the month, so first go through them and then read your own.

This man has many friends and benefits through wealthy women. He has a flair for writing and can be known as an author or a novelist. His prosperity lies near water, river or the sea. This number has a peculiar significance. It shows new plans, new resolutions for the betterment of people at large.

Born on 29th August

> you have all the basic characteristics of those born on the 2nd of the month, so first go through them and then read your own.

This person is moody and changing and, therefore, uncertain about his actions. He is courageous but takes risks in life and does not stick to anything to the end. He is intelligent and also a deep thinker but there is a tendency to carry everything to extremes. He is not very lucky in his married life. His interest is in his business. He is blessed with good fortune. His life is eventful.

b) FINANCE

In all matters regarding financial questions he will be rather fortunate and yet have little regard for the value of money. Money will come to him in strange ways, by gifts, legacies and wills, but he will be likely to impoverish himself at times by his generosity. He is more likely to make money by his mental talents, such as his eloquence or talent in art, music or writing or by some profession rather than in business.

c) VOCATION

The high imaginative power possessed by the number 2 person will help him to be a good composer of music or a writer of fiction or romance. He can also be a good artist and can create works of enduring value. Immortal paintings and dramas and great poems will be the creation of a prominent and influential number 2 men. Of all the numbers he has great vocabulary and linguistic capacities and can be successful as a teacher or a professor of languages. He can also be a good translator or an editor.

d) HEALTH

His main health weakness is his poor blood circulation. He is susceptible to all sicknesses arising out of this such as anaemia, and a weak heart.

Since the Moon is the ruling planet of number 2, the uneasiness which is a prominent characteristic, creates mental worries and sleeplessness. He is also susceptible to diabetes and asthmatic trouble.

e) MARRIAGE AND FRIENDS

He has a natural attraction towards persons born in the period from 20th October to 20th December and 20th February to 20th April. He also has affinity for those who are governed by numbers 2 and 6. It is therefore advisable that he should select his wife from one of these periods or numbers.

A Number 2 husband

He has a greater natural love and attraction for home than any other type. There are two types of husbands belonging to this number. One is dominating and exacting. He is fault-finding and nothing satisfies him. The other type is passive lazy and indulgent. He will marry for the sake of money so that he may ultimately get comforts. His opinions are fixed and he has fixed ideas as to what he should get from his wife and children. He may have a romantic affair outside but will not tolerate such behaviour on the part of his wife. In that way he is very suspicious of her.

A Number 2 wife

She is sympathetic, affectionate and devoted. She is satisfied with anything her husband provides her with. However, she is moody, changeable and sensitive. She pays every attention to the welfare of her husband and children. Only she knows what sacrifices she has made for them; others rarely understand her devotion. She is very passionate and needs a virile husband to satisfy her romantic nature.

Friends

His best friends are those who are governed by numbers 2, 4, 6 and 9. He has a natural affinity also towards people born in November, February and May and in his own month i.e. August.

f) FORTUNATE DAYS
   AND NUMBERS : His lucky days are Mondays, Tuesdays and Fridays and lucky numbers are 2 and 6. He should therefore take all important steps on one of these days and also dates if possible. He should try his luck in lottery by purchasing a ticket where the total of all the digits is 2 or 6, or where the last number is 2 or 6.

g) LUCKY COLOURS : He should use white and all shades of cream or blue as his lucky colours.

h) LUCKY JEWELS AND STONES : His lucky jewels are Pearl and Diamond and lucky stones are Moonstone and Agate.

i) IMPORTANT YEARS IN LIFE : His important years are 2, 11, 20, 29, 38, 47, 56, 65, 74 etc.

j) HIS GOOD QUALITIES & DRAWBACKS ARE AS UNDER:

Good Qualities	Drawbacks
Emotionality	Coldness
Fellowship	Envy
Honesty	Haste
Imagination	Introvert
Simplicity	Shyness
	Whimsicality

CHAPTER 66

BORN ON
3rd, 12th, 21st and 30th of August

All those born on the 3rd, 12th, 21st and 30th of August of any year are governed by number 3 and the planet Jupiter. August is governed by the Sun. The character reading relating to number 3 given below is equally applicable to the other dates. In addition, the special characterstics of those born on 12th, 21st and 30th August are given separately.

Born on 3rd August

a) CHARACTER

At the back of his nature this man has strong ambition that will never allow him to be satisfied with ordinary success. Sooner or later he will develop a keen desire to fill positions of prominence and responsibility. He is a hard worker in all his undertakings. He has great idealism and will make many friends. In love matters he will meet with many disappointments and heart-breaks. He shows an outstanding ability in positions of authority over others. He gets praise and encouregement from others, which act as a kind of stimulant to impel him to rise to great heights. He has a keen sense of home life, a great love of children and a desire to train and bring them up. He has lofty and noble aspirations. He will always rise in life to hold high positions, the only danger is that his ambition has no limit.

This is a good number. The person is confident of his ability. He is self-reliant and takes his own decisions. He has a habit of talking loudly. He is fond of show and likes to observe form, order and the law. He is jovial in spirit and cordial in manner. His passions are healthy, spontaneous and without inhibitions. He is free in his expressions. He is a good conversationalist.

He takes an active interest in sports and outdoor activities from his earliest youth. He has tremendous enthusiasm and is not self-centred. His intellect is of a very high quality. He has a kind of vision that understands the world and loves it for what it is and not for what it ought to be. He is open-hearted with a good understanding and is entirely lacking in malice or petty jealousies. If he is not alert, people take undue advantage of his good nature.

The main characteristics of a number 3 person are ambition, leadership, love of religion, pride, honour, love of nature, enthusiasm, generosity, respect and reverence.

Born on 12th August
you have all the basic characteristics of those born on the 3rd of the month, so first go through them and then read your own.

Authority and honours are the significant aspects of this person's life. He has vanity and is proud, ambitious and aspiring. He is fond of pleasures and is attracted to the opposite sex. However, sometimes he prefers loneliness. He likes to make sacrifices for others but becomes a victim of other people's plans or intrigues. His relations with others are smooth and harmonious. He is quick to notice trifles. He has lofty ideals.

Born on 21st August
you have all the basic characteristics of those born on the 3rd of the month, so first go through them and then read your own.

This man is kind and generous and is a loving father. He achieves fame, reputation and honours at a very late age. He is cheerful and fond of travels. He has a strong feeling of self-respect. Surprisingly, he has a suspicious nature.

Born on 30th August
you have all the basic characteristics of those born on the 3rd of the month, so first go through them and then read your own.

This man is fortunate, generous and optimistic. He has a noble and religious mind. He likes to travel and visit places of pilgrimage. He can be successful as a teacher or educationist or in administration. He appears gentle and sincere, but has a hidden characteristic. He may be active but is restless. When faced with difficulties, he is strong enough to overcome them.

b) FINANCE

He will be successful in his investments if he follows his intuition, and does not allow himself to be carried away by flattery. As a general rule, he may expect by his own good judgement to steadily increase his wealth and financial position. He has an almost uncanny vision of the trend of events likely to affect commerce, industry and business. He is not a hoarder of money but will spend lavishly for his huge schemes. His ambition, leadership and enthusiasm always push him forward and usually he gets all the comforts in life. The number 3 person is early out of puberty and poverty.

c) VOCATION

The combination of the planets Jupiter and the Sun promises success in all forms of government employment or in political or municipal work of any kind. This man will also be successful in any career that brings him before the public. He is a good teacher as well as a good preacher. Professions such as those of doctors, bankers, advertisers and actors are also suitable for him.

d) HEALTH

On the whole he can expect good health all through his life. However, it is possible that due to his important positions, he may attend banquets and dinners where he may be indiscreet and eats heavy and rich food. This will naturally spoil his health. He is also likely to suffer from high blood pressure and heart trouble due to overwork.

e) MARRIAGE AND FRIENDS

He has a natural attraction towards persons born in the period from 20th June to 20th August and 20th October to 20th December. He also has affinity for those who are governed by numbers 3, 6 and 9. It is therefore advisable that he should select his wife from one of these periods or numbers.

A Number 3 husband

He is generous and desires his wife to shine in society. He has a kind and loving disposition and a great heart. He is proud of his family and gives them the best of everything. His love is deep and romantic. He expects his family members to dance to his tunes and will not tolerate disrespect.

A Number 3 wife

She is the best companion to her husband. She is not an intruder but takes active interest in the business of her husband. She is efficient in house-keeping and has a sympathetic and balanced attitude towards her children. Her passions are healthy and joyous; her approach to physical love is highly refined and inspiring. She is a lovable person and by her grace, dignity and social nature she attracts many people. She can manage her house very efficiently and she is the right wife for an energetic and enthusiastic husband. She is patient and sacrificing.

Friends

His best friends are those who are governed by numbers 3 6 and 9. He also has a natural affinity towards people born in November, February and May and in his own month, i.e. August.

f) FORTUNATE DAYS
   AND NUMBERS : His lucky days are Tuesdays, Thursdays and Fridays and lucky numbers are 3, 5 and 6. He should therefore take all important steps on one of these days and also dates if possible. He should try his luck in lottery by purchasing a ticket where the total of all

the digits is 3, 5 or 6 or where the last
digit is 3, 5 or 6.

g) LUCKY COLOURS : He should use all shades of yellow,
violet, purple and green.

h) LUCKY JEWELS AND STONES : His lucky jewel is
topaz and lucky stones
are amethyst and cat's
eye.

IMPORTANT YEARS IN LIFE : His important years are 3, 12,
21, 30, 39, 48, 57, 66, 75
etc.

j) HIS GOOD QUALITIES AND DRAWBACKS ARE AS UNDER:

Good qualities	Drawbacks
Ambition	Cruelty
Dignity	Dictatorship
Individuality	Hypocrisy
Philosophy	Extravagance
Prestige	Vanity

CHAPTER 67

BORN ON
4th, 13th, 22nd and 31st August

All those born on the 4th, 13th, 22nd and 31st of August of any year are governed by the number 4 and the planet Uranus. August is governed by the Sun. The character reading relating to number 4 given below is equally applicable to the other dates. In addition, the special characteristics of those born on 13th, 22nd and 31st of August are given separately.

Born on 4th August

a) CHARACTER

This person has a very decided love of independence, both in thought and in action. He is inclined to be unconventional in every way. He is likely to be considered more or less eccentric and will not easily fit in with the plans of others. His close relations will be the most difficult to get on with. He will resent restraint and criticism and if he is in a position to do so he will break away from home ties and travel extensively. He will have to develop great patience, especially in dealing with any intimate relationships. If he has the means to strike out a path for himself and does so he will probably make a distinct success in some unusual kind of work or career. He will have unconventional views as regards both religion and life in general and will be inclined to make many enemies by the extreme frankness of his expression. He will have many unusual adventures in the course of his life, together with experiences in his affections with many disappointments and sorrows in love, and also in domestic life.

This number is governed by the planet Uranus and shows

energy, force and advancement. It shows revolution and unexpected happenings in life. Usually the changes that take
place are for the better. This number represents the higher
faculties of the mind. It shows activity and intelligence engaged in the reconstruction or the betterment of human life. The
peculiar nature of this person is that he constantly aims at
changes in life and society and seeks the liberation of the mind
from bondage to environment and society. He dislikes
hypocrisy. He loves art and music. He has an attractive
personality. He is methodical in his own way. He has a bad
habit of forcing his opinions on others. He has a keen, analytical and logical mind. Because of his peculiar nature of
opposing the views of others or starting arguments, he is often
misunderstood and makes a great number of secret enemies
who constantly work against him. He feels lonely in life.

Born on 13th August | you have all the basic characteristics of those born on the 4th of the month, so first go through them and then read your own.

This man is an intelligent person, of tall stature and a good
complexion. He is considerate and benevolent. He likes
literature and scientific books. He likes to remain active though
in a quiet way. He occupies positions of high responsibilities
and gets riches. His career and success start after his 31st
year. Though outwardly he looks mild, inwardly, he is
obstinate. He is faithful and sympathetic but has difficulty in
expressing his love He has all the qualities of number 4 but
in an exaggerated form.

Born on 22nd August | you have all the basic characteristics of those born on the 4th of the month, so first go through them and then read your own.

This man is also tall, and has good eyes. Usually he
occupies good positions but without much responsibility.
He is rather easy-going and unsteady in nature. Sometimes
his actions are spasmodic. On the whole he is lucky in his
affairs and benefits from the opposite sex. He is happy in his
family life but is also fond of a companion. He is faithful and
dedicated to others. Sometimes he feels very lonely. His
social field is limited and he has few friends. He does not care
for disputes. He has too much economy of sentiments.

Born on 31st August   you have all the basic characteristics of those born on the 4th of the month, so first go through them and then read your own.

This date shows ambition, pride and austerity. This man is interested in honourable occupations such as working for charitable institutions and institutions for the deaf and dumb and the physically handicapped etc. He gets success after his 40th year but he expects quick results and early reputation. He is lucky in financial matters. He is realistic and of strong will power He has a strong attraction for the opposite sex. He loves travelling.

b) FINANCE

In matters of finance he will be difficult to understand. He will apparently care little about money, and yet attract it to him for the power it can give. In business matters he will either trust implicitly, or be suspicious of the persons he is associated with. He will do better working alone. He can see both the sides of every question and argue out either side with equal force and conviction. As regards finance and monetary matters, he is usually well settled in life, though he experiences delays and difficulties in his undertakings. He may not amass wealth but can maintain the show of riches. He is a spendthrift and his home is well decorated. His financial prosperity usually starts after the age of 40.

c) VOCATION

He can make a success as a banker. He will be likely sooner or later to work on some new idea that will bring him large returns. He will also be successful in trades such as transport, electricity and all sorts of machinery. He will be equally successful as an engineer, a building contractor, a scientist and an industrialist. He is also attracted towards mystic subjects such as palmistry and astrology and can do well in these subjects also.

d) HEALTH

He will have a good constitution, but will be largely dependent on whether his surroundings are congenial or other-

wise. Good health or the reverse will be enormously influenced by his state of mind. If unhappy he will be inclined to
brood, become melancholy and shrink, as it were, too much
within himself. His system tends towards auto-poisoning,
obstructions and mysterious ailments difficult to diagnose. The
bones of the body will be more or less brittle, and he will have
to be particularly careful against sudden falls and injuries to
the feet and legs; some weakness or injury to the spine may
also be expected. There are two classes of persons especially
among those born under the Uranian numbers and dates in
August. One type is inclined to put on weight rapidly towards
middle life. If such a man belongs to this class he should guard
himself against heart disease or coma affecting the brain. If on
the contrary he belongs to the type that begins to lose weight
readily towards middle life, the man should take precautions
against all forms of nerve diseases that may otherwise threaten
paralysis in later years. Sometimes the man suffers from
urinary infection.

e) MARRIAGE AND FRIENDS

He has a natural attraction towards persons born in the
period from 20th February to 20th April and 20th October to
20th December. He also has affinity for those who are governed
by numbers 1, 2, 7 and 8. It is therefore advisable that he
should select his wife from one of these periods or numbers.

A Number 4 husband

He is generous and desires his wife to shine in society.
He has a kind and loving disposition and a great heart. He is
proud of his family and gives them the best of everything. His
love is deep and romantic. He expects his family members to
dance to his tunes and will not tolerate disrespect His opinions
are fixed; he has fixed ideas about what he should get from his
wife and children. He may have a romantic affair outside but
will not tolerate such behaviour on the part of his wife. In that
way he is very suspicious of her.

.A Number 4 wife

She is smart and attractive. She has the art of dressing and has a strong will-power. She aims at several things but hardly succeeds in getting mastery over one. She loves interior decoration but does not have the capacity to work hard and so she will get it done through others. She is often dictatorial and moody and spoils her day due to her own whimsical nature. She loves her home but is not attached to it very much. She is at times uneasy. It is better for her to find a friend governed by number one or two.

Friends

This man's best friends are those who are governed by numbers 1, 2, 4, 5, 7, 8 and 9. He also has a natural affinity towards people born in November, February and May and in his own month i.e. August. He is fond of friends and company but hardly gets a close friend because of his unsteady, changing and moody nature.

f) FORTUNATE DAYS AND NUMBERS : His lucky days are Sundays, Mondays and Saturdays. His lucky numbers are 2, 4 and 7. He should therefore take all important steps on one of these days and also dates if possible. He should try his luck in lottery by purchasing a ticket where the total of all the digits is 2, 4 or 7, or where the last digit is 2, 4 or 7.

g) LUCKY COLOURS : He should use all shades of electric blue, electric grey, maroon and white

h) LUCKY JEWELS AND STONES : His lucky jewels are Diamond, Coral and Pearl.

i) IMPORTANT YEARS IN LIFE : His important years are 4, 13, 22, 31, 40, 49, 58, 67, 76 etc.

23

j) HIS GOOD QUALITIES AND DRAWBACKS ARE AS UNDER:

Good qualities	Drawbacks
Activity	Changeablity
Endurance	Domination
Energy	Stubbornness
Reliability	Vindictiveness
Method and system	Jealousy

CHAPTER 68

BORN ON
5th, 14th and 23rd of August

All those born on the 5th 14th and 23rd of August of any year are governed by number 5 and the planet Mercury. August is governed by the Sun. The character reading relating to number 5 given below is equally applicable to the other dates. In addition, special characteristics of those born on 14th and 23rd August are given separately.

Born on 5th August

a) CHARACTER

Influence of the planet Mercury bestows shrewdness, quickness, scientific pursuits, business ability, industry, intuition and diplomacy. A person governed by this number is active and quick this applies not only to physical agility onlybut also to the mind. He is very skilful and has intuitive faculty. He is equally proficient in games where he uses his hands as well as his brain. He has the capacity to judge the ability of his opponents in games and knows very well how to take advantage of the weak points of his opponents. He loves to use oratory and eloquence in expressing himself. He has the capacity to pursue his objectives and knows very well how to plan to achieve his ends. He is deeply interested in occult subjects and has a fancy to master all the intricacies of such abtruse subjects. He possesses a pleasant character and dislikes inactivity. He is sociable and has many acquaintances. He is fond of variety and change and trips. Whatever the situation, he can get out of it.

Born on 14th August

you have all the basic characteristics of those born on the 5th, of the month, so first go through them and then read your own.

This person has an attractive personality and is liked by all. His nature is co-operative and he does not like to provoke others. He usually occupies a good position in life and is successful in his business. He is not talkative but slightly reserved. His is an intelligent and shrewd number. For women, the number indicates good marriage but they should be careful in child--bearing. A number 5 man is inconsistent in love and experiences some romantic and impulsive attachment in early years. He is fortunate in money matters. He is industrious and positive in speech and action. Usually he is fond of gambling and of solving riddles.

Born on 23rd August

you have all the basic characteristics of those born on the 5th of the month, so first go through them and then read your own.

He is usually popular with women. His fortune is near the water. He is successful in life and enjoys honour and wealth. He may get money through inheritance. He keeps himself busy in his own way. He gets help from superiors and gets protection from them. He is a lucky person. He is affectionate and loves freedom. He is averse to formalities. He has a spirit of independence and a desire to dominate.

b) FINANCE

Since number 5 is a business number, the person can expect opulence. With his shrewdness he iscapable of developing his industry and carrying out his plans systematically with the result that he gets good returns for his efforts. He is lucky in his financial position. He is exceptionally clever in originating schemes for others. He is versatile and adaptable but his greatest danger lies in acquiring undesirable acquaintances who may lead him into trouble before he is aware of their influence.

c) VOCATION

He can adapt himself to the role he has to play in the drama of life. With his adaptability he comes in contact with various classes of people and is successful in any business.

Banking is a good line for him. The planet Mercury also shows ability for medicine or surgery. His capacity to argue his points can make him a good lawyer.

d) HEALTH

He will be inclined to live too much on his nerves and to exhaust his system by lack of moderation. He will be liable to suffer from neuralgia in various parts of the body and at times to have acute attacks of indigestion and deranged internal organs. At such times he will be inclined to fly to the quickest means of relief and may become an addict to drugs' or stimulants if he does not keep himself under absolute control. His basic health defects are biliousness and nervousness. However, his biliousness has close relation with his psychological disturbances. Experience shows that his biliousness increases with the increase in tension and is reduced or disappears when his nervous trouble is under control. Number 5 rules over the nerves, neck, arms and respiratory system.

e) MARRIAGE AND FRIENDS :

He has a natural attraction towards persons born in the period from 20th September to 20th October, and 20th January to 20th March. He also has affinity for those who are governed by numbers 1, 7 and 8. It is, therefore, advisable that he should select his marriage partner from one of these periods or numbers.

A Number 5 husband

He is lucky and successful in his married life. His selection is good and usually he selects a person of his own type. He loves his partner. He expects neatness and cleanliness from her and also desires that she should· share in the enjoyment of life. He is proud of his wife and likes to see her well-dressed. He proves to be a good husband. He loves his children and is fond of his home. Even if he travels long, he is very much attracted to his home and is eager to return early to his family. He is liberal in spending on clothes and other wants of the members of his family and furnishes his house with good taste.

A Number 5 wife

She has interest at home as well as outside. She has many activities and manages them well. She likes tidiness. Though she seldom does her own work, she gets it done through her commanding personality. She pays every attention to the welfare of her husband and children. Only she knows what sacrifices she makes for them, others seldom understand her devotion. She is very passionate and needs a virile and masculine husband to satisfy her romantic nature.

Friends

His best friends are those who are governed by numbers 1,3,4,5,7 and 8. He has a natural affinity also towards people born in November, February and May and in his own month i.e. August. He likes those who have originality, activity and brilliance.

f) FORTUNATE DAYS AND NUMBERS : His lucky days are Wednesdays, Fridays and Saturdays and lucky numbers are 3, 5 and 7. He should therefore take all important steps on one of these days and also dates if possible. He should try his luck in lottery by purchasing a ticket where the total of all the digits is 3,5 or 7, or where the last digit is 3, 5 or 7.

g) LUCKY COLOURS : He should use white and all shades of green.

h) LUCKY JEWELS AND STONES : His lucky jewels are Emerald,and Diamond. He may use Sapphire also.

i) IMPORTANT YEARS IN LIFE :   His important years are 5.
                               14, 23, 32, 41, 50, 59, 68,
                               77 etc.

j) HIS GOOD QUALITIES AND DRAWBACKS ARE AS UNDER:

Good Qualities	Drawbacks
Co-operation	Lack of perseverance
Practicality	Scepticism
Shrewedness	Unreliability
Vigilance	

CHAPTER 69

BORN ON
6th, 15th and 24th August

All those born on the 6th, 15th and 24th of August of any year are governed by the number 6 and the planet Venus. August is governed by the Sun. The character reading relating to number 6 given below is equally applicable to the other dates. In addition, special characteristics of those born on 15th and 24th August are given separately.

Born on 6th August

a) CHARACTER

This person is governed by the planet Venus which stands for love, sympathy and adoration. He is a born artist, and art and beauty in life have an attraction for him. He is a pleasant personality. His company is always charming. He is full of enthusiasm, energy and charm. His talk is interesting and lively. We may sometimes be required to put aside our ideas of morality and social conduct to understand and appreciate his feelings and views. Number 6 stands for beauty· health, vitality, warmth, attraction, and, above all, love. A person of this number is fond of music, dancing and poetry. He loves to have a life full of ease and luxuries, money and happiness. He prefers spending to saving. He will have rich clothes, jewellery, perfumes and all sorts of beautiful things·

His mission is to give life, energy and enthusiasm to the world at large. He has many talents but they are of a spontaneous nature. He has a style and a grace which influence others; he attracts people with his natural brilliance and versatility. He is fond of theatres, shows and picnics.

Born on 15th August you have all the basic characteristics of those born on the 6th of the month, so first go through them and then read your own.

This person has high intelligence and a good memory. He is fit for responsible positions such as those of ambassadors consuls, governors etc. He is very ambitious and boastful but hasty and proud by nature. He is interested in the lower type of occultism. He has interest in art and music also. He has a habit of worrying inwardly and leads a melancholy life. His destiny is such that he has to make sacrifices for others.

Born on 24th August you have all the basic characteristics of those born on the 6th of the month, so first go through them and then read your own.

He is fortunate in getting assistance from people of high rank. He benefits through the opposite sex. He marries a rich girl and prospers after marriage. He succeeds in speculation and enjoys good monetary status. He strictly defines the line between personal and social matters. He is methodical in his ideas. He possesses a strong ego and sometimes tries to force his opinions on others.

b) FINANCE

He is not attracted to money. All his interest is in attaining pleasures and gratifying his desires. He, therefore, spends his earnings on whatever attracts him. He also never repents having spent his money on art which may not ultimately give him monetary rewards. He is seldom wealthy but he somehow has the knack of making both ends meet and having the minimum comforts he wants. He may sometimes be lucky in getting windfalls.

c) VOCATION

He will shine as an interior decorator, architect, jeweller, musician, hotel manager or a confectioner. He can be equally successful as a broker, an estate broker or as a commission agent.

d) HEALTH

On the whole he is a healthy person.   However, he is susceptible to epidemic fever and influenza.   Occasionally, he is prone to nervousness but not in a chronic way.   He may also suffer from rheumatic trouble.

e) MARRIAGE AND FRIENDS

He has a natural attraction towards persons born in the period from 20th July to 20th September and 20th November to 20th January. He also has affinity for those who are governed by numbers 2, 4, 6 and 9. It is, therefore, advisable that he should select his wife from one of these periods or numbers.

A Number 6 husband

He expects his partner to be neat and have charm and grace. Though he creates a lively atmosphere in the house, he somehow finds it difficult to provide all the necessities of the members of his family. This may sometimes create unpleasantness and make him unhappy in his domestic life. His opinions are fixed; he has fixed ideas as to what he should get from his wife and children. He may have a romantic affair outside but will not tolerate such behaviour on the part of his wife. In that way he is very suspicious of her.

A Number 6 wife

She never resorts to divorce and endures extreme hardship rather than desert her husband. She is a devoted mother and a loving wife, satisfied with her husband's efforts in her behalf. She loves dometic life and makes a perfect home.

Friends

His best friends are those who are governed by numbers 2, 3, 4, 6, and 9. He also has a natural affinity towards people born in November, February, May and in his own month i.e. August. He likes those who have originality, activity and brilliance.

f) FORTUNATE DAYS
    AND NUMBERS : His lucky days are Mondays, Tuesdays
                  and Thursdays and lucky numbers are
                  2, 3 and 6. He should there-
                  fore take all important steps on one of
                  these days and also dates if possible.
                  He should try his luck in lottery by
                  purchasing a ticket where the total of
                  all the digits is 2, 3 or 6, or where the
                  final digit is 2,3 or 6.

g) LUCKY COLORS : He should use all shades of blue, rose
                   and pink.

h) LUCKY JEWELS & STONES : He can use Turquoise,
                            Emerald, Pearl and Diamond

i) IMPORNANT YEARS IN LIFE : His important years are 6,
                              15, 24, 33, 42, 51, 60, 69,
                              78 etc.

j) HIS GOOD QUALITIES AND DRAWBACKS ARE AS UNDER:

Good qualities	Drawbacks
Harmony	Absence of foresight
Love	Interference
Peace	Moodiness
Strong memory	Timidity

CHAPTER 70

BORN ON
7th, 16th and 25th of August

All those born on the 7th, 16th and 25th of August of any·year are governed by the number 7 and the planet Neptune. August is governed by the Sun. The character reading relating to number 7 given below is equally applicable to the other dates. In addition, special characteristics of those born on 16th and 25th of August are given separately.

Born on 7th August

a) CHARACTER

He is extremely ambitious but not in ordinary ways. His ambition may not be to dominate or rule others, but will be related to his work. He will be ambitious for its success more than from a personal standpoint. He loves all the fine arts, such as music, painting, poetry, the dramatic arts and the opera, and also occult and philosophical subjects. He will be quiet and rather dignified in manner; he is highly emotional, more or less spiritually inclined, and has a warm-hearted and benevolent nature towards his fellow beings. He will have many heartaches and disappointments in matters of the affections without becoming hard or embittered. He will have very decided attractions and aversions to people, many exciting adventures and peculiar, out of the ordinary romances with criticism and trouble.

Being governed by Neptune, he has individuality and is original and independent in thought and action. He is restless by nature and is fond of change. He likes to visit foreign countries

and becomes interested in far off lands. He has peculiar ideas
about religion and dislikes following the beaten track. His
behaviour is a mystery to others. He is often absent-minded.
He thinks out logically and achieves great aims. He is stubborn
and disregards the opinions of others. He is good at earning
money. In general, he is somewhat indifferent to materialistic
desires. He desires the best or none at all. He is sensitive
and hides his real feelings by apparent indifference. He dislikes mingling with common people. He prefers to spend his
hour with his favourite book. When his opinion is solicited. he
speaks with authority. He knows his ground.

Born on 16th August

you have all the basic characteristics of those born on the 7th
of the month, so first go through them and then read your own.

He is rather easy-going and does not like to work hard. He
is good humoured and generous. He is very sensitive and
emotional. He soon gets upset and is soon pleased. He is
frequently indisposed. He is fortunate in getting good and
successful children. However, there is some sort of sorrow in
his married life. He appears to be calm but his mind is always
in turmoil and he is sometimes short-tempered. He will not
disclose his nervousness and is slow in taking decisions. He
does not like interference.

Born on 25th August

you have all the basic characteristics of those born on the 7th
of the month, so first go through them and then read your own.

He is a jack of all trades but master of none. He is interested in several subjects but does not have the ability to go
into details. His knowledge therefore is very shallow. He
likes to travel and has connections with foreign countries. He
is honest, faithful and good-natured. But he is fickle-minded
and inconsistent. His memory is good and he is a good orator
and a good teacher.

b) FINANCE

As regards finance it is difficult to say anything positively.
He does not love money or any routine business life, yet out of
the spirit of self-sacrifice he desires to make money and so is
likely to take up positions which he may not like. Usually,

there are many changes in the life of this person and so it is
difficult for him to amass wealth. However, his being a mystic
number, the person can be well placed in life provided he finds
a job of his choice. In that case he can be a wealthy person
with all amenities and comforts.

c) VOCATION

His love of sea-travel and interest in foreign countries can
make him a successful merchant, exporter or importer. He can
also deal in dairy products, fishery, and other products such
as soap etc, or manage a chemical industry. He can also study
medicine and surgery.

d) HEALTH

He does not look very robust physically but he is able to
endure more than persons who look vigorous. He is peculiar
in all matters relating to diet and is guided by his instinct in
such matters. His main trouble is his nervous constitution ;
all his illness will be due to his nervousness. He is liable to
suffer from faulty blood circulation, stomach disorder and
fever.

e) MARRIAGE AND FRIENDS

He has a natural attraction towards persons born in the
period from 20th Octoder to 20th December and 20th February
to 20th April. He has affinity also for those who are governed
by numbers 3, 5 and 8. It is therefore advisable that he should
select his wife from one of these periods or numbers.

A Number 7 husband

He is generous and desires his wife to shine in society. He
has a kind and loving disposition and a great heart. He is
proud of his family and gives them the best of everything. His
love is deep and romantic. He expects his family members to
dance to his tunes and will not tolerate disrespect. His opinion are fixed; he has fixed ideas as to what he should get

from his wife and children. He may have a romantic affair outside but will not tolerate such behaviour on the part of his wife.
In that way he is very suspicious of her.

He is very emotional and understands the feelings of his
wife   He is very considerate and will never try to impose his
ideas on her.   He is liberal and fond of picnics, travels, the
cinema and theatres.   He is a spendthrift and likes to live
lavishly.   His family is moderate in size and has all comforts.

A Number 7 wife

She pays every attention to the welfare of her husband
and children.   Only she knows what sacrifices she makes for
them, but others hardly understand her devotion.   She is very
passionate and needs a virile and masculine husband to satisfy
her romantic nature.   However, she is very moody and her
behaviour is unpredictable.   She is very uneasy and gets disturbed over small matters.   She is good at entertaining friends
and she likes to invite people to a party or dinner.   She expects
her husband to look after her all the time.

Friends

His best friends are those governed by numbers 1,3,4,5,7,
8 and 9.   He has a natural affinity also towards people born in
November, February, May and in his own month i.e August.
He likes those who have originality, activity and brilliance.

f) FORTUNATE DAYS
    AND NUMBERS : His lucky days are Sundays, Mondays,
                  Wednesdays and Thursdays and his lucky
                  numbers are 2, 4 and 7.   He should
                  therefore take all important steps on
                  one of these days and also dates if
                  possible.   He should try his luck in
                  lottery by purchasing a ticket where the
                  total of all the digits is 2, 4, or 7, or
                  where the last digit is 2,4, or 7.

g) **LUCKY COLOURS :** He should use all shades of green and yellow.

h) **LUCKY JEWELS AND STONES :** His lucky jewels are topaz and emerald, and lucky stones are moonstone and cat's eye.

i) **IMPORTNNT YEARS IN LIFE :** His important years are 7, 16, 25, 34, 43, 52, 61 70, 79 etc.

j) **HIS GOOD QUALITIES AND DRAWBACKS ARE AS UNDER:**

Good qualities	Drawbacks
Austerity	Despondency
Peace	Diffidence
Reflection	Restlessnes
Serenity	Whimsicality
Tolerance	

CHAPTER 71

BORN ON

8th, 17th and 26th of August

All those born on the 8th, 17th and 26th of August of any year are governed by the number 8 and the planet Saturn. August is governed by the Sun. The character reading relating to number 8 given below is equally applicable to the other dates. In addition, the special characteristics of those born on 17th and 26th August are given separately.

Born on 8th August

a) CHARACTER

The peculiarity of number 8 is delay in all things. Whatever may be the career of the person, his work will never be done in time. In spite of his best efforts he will always experience difficulties and obstacles. This is mainly due to the influence of Saturn which governs number 8 and its series. Both the planets i.e. Saturn and the Sun, have powerful characteristics which are practically opposed to one another. The Sun is optimistic whereas Saturn is pessimistic. The Sun indicates activity whereas Saturn indicates stedfastness. In short, the person has a controversial personality. His nature is analysed in detail below.

If we take into consideration the prominence of Saturn, he shows an extreme sense of discipline, steadfastness, constancy and dutifulness. The person is sober and loves solitude. He is a lover of classical music but mostly of a melancholy type. In art he loves landscapes, natural scenery and flowers. Number 8 is considered to be a balance wheel to the character. The man naturally looks at the other side of the coin. He is pessimist. He prefers solitude to company. He shuns society rather than courts it.   He is cautious about his future and he takes decisions very carefully on matters which pertain to mundane affairs. He is a prudent person, his number is a wise and sober one amongst all the numbers. He is never over-enthusiastic and is more or less gloomy and melancholy. He is also ambitious and persevering. He is capable of enormous efforts to attain his object.   He is sceptical and analytical. He is creative, productive and dominating.   He is likely to be misunderstood. He usually feels lonely at heart. He understands the weak and the oppressed and treats them in a warm-hearted manner.   He is a born manager who can keep others busy.   He admires fair play and is willing to pay a fair compensation. He has a good memory for names and faces.

If we now take into consideration the influence of the Sun, we note that the person has originality, dignity, prestige and honour.   He has a majestic personality which commands respect. His assistants   either at home or in business, adore him and work willingly.   He is generous and has a good comprehension of human problems.   He always succeeds in his career and acheives the highest position.   He is fond of theatres, shows and picnics.   He is spontaneous in outlook and responds to nature and has the capacity to enjoy life.   He is usually popular due to his active nature and capacity to mix in any society.   His mission is to give life, energy and enthusiasm to the world at large.   He has a style and a grace which influence others. He attracts people with his natural brilliance and versatility.

Born on 17th August | you have all the basic characteristics of those born on the 8th of the month, so first go through them and then read your own.

He is a good organizer and a good thinker.   He has a creative and constructive mind.   He is a lover of peace and a philanthropist. He is attracted towards occultism and mysticism. He is courageous and proud. He has a strong individuality. He is highly intelligent and clever.   As regards emotions, he is calm. At times he is generous to a fault and at times very stingy. He is interested in research and loves knowledge. He is conservative and dominating.

Born on 26th August | you have all the basic characteristics of those born on the 8th of the month, so first go through them and then read your own.

He wants to enjoy life without doing anything. He is sluggish and lethargic. He revels in wine and women and is fickle-minded. He is careless about the number of children. He is lucky in money matters and gets easy money. He is smart but lacks positiveness. He likes to put up a good appearance but has a worrying nature. He has problems in his love affairs.

b) FINANCE

The peculiarity of number 8 is delay in life in all respects. Naturally in financial matters also there is delay and stability is achieved at a very late age. This person has to work hard. He seldom acquires wealth. He will have to exercise great caution in all money transactions. He finds it difficult to trust others. He is likely to be robbed or defrauded by servants or inferiors. In order to get success, it is better if he keeps his business affairs in his own hands. He may make money by investment in old established concerns and also in dealings connected with land, houses, mines and minerals.

In order to avoid the delaying effect of number 8, the person has to avoid number 8 playing a part in his life. Instead he can choose number 1 or 3 for all important steps. However, if his experience shows that 1 is lucky for him, he can insist on that number only and acquire wealth and prosperity. I 8 is found to be a lucky number in his life he can try his luck in lottery and horse races. But usually this number is connected with delays and hard work, and a person has to be very cautious in his financial affairs.

c) VOCATION

Subjects suitable for him are occult sciences, chemistry,

physics, medicine and also higher mathematics. He can be successful in industries dealing with coal mines, timber etc. and construction companies. He can be a good accountant and also a good administrator. However as stated earlier, he has to strive hard in his career and can get the fruits of his hard work only in the later years of his life.

d) HEALTH

In the matter of health we can expect one of two opposite results. He will either be unusually strong or will have indifferent health. Experience shows that some mysterious psychic influence control his health. Even the hostile thoughts of others can make him ill. His main health defects are nervousness, irritation, trouble with legs, teeth, ears, paralysis and rheumatism. He is a bilious type and often suffers from chronic melancholia. It is very interesting to note that the delay characteristic of his life is also observed in his sickness. The ailments he suffers from also take a long time to cure. Varicose veins and haemorrhoids are a common problem of a strong personality.

e) MARRIAGE AND FRIENDS

He has a natural attraction towards persons born in the period from 20th March to 20th May and 20th July to 20th September. He has affinity for those who are governed by numbers 5 and 7. It is therefore advisable that he should select his marriage partner from one of these periods or numbers.

A Number 8 husband

He is generous and desires his wife to shine in society. He has a kind and loving disposition and a great heart. He is proud of his family and gives them the best of everything. His opinions are fixed. He has fixed ideas as to what he should get from his wife and children. He prefers loneliness. He finds it difficult to choose a wife. He is very orthodox in his views and does not allow his wife to adopt modern ideas in dress at home or in public places. If he desires to have good married life, he should prefer a person who is also interested in deep and serious studies and likes to devote herself to philosophy and occult subjects.

A Number 8 wife

She is capable and systematic. She enjoys her family life and likes to make sacrifices for her children and for the ambition of her husband. Her fault is that she lacks feminine warmth, sentiment and delicacy. Being governed by the Sun, by her grace, dignity and social nature, she attracts many people. She can manage her house very efficiently. She is just the wife for an energetic husband. She is patient and sacrificing. Only she knows what sacrifices she makes for her husband and children. She is very passionate and needs a virile and masculine husband to satisfy her romantic nature.

Friends

His best friends are those who are governed by numbers 3,4,5,7 and 8. He has a natural affinity towards people born in November, February, May and in his own month i.e. August. He likes those who have originality, activity and brilliance.

f) FORTUNATE DAYS AND NUMBERS : His lucky days are Wednesdays, Thursdays and Saturdays. His lucky numbers are 2,7 and 8. He should therefore take all important steps on one of these days and also dates if possible. He should try his luck in lottery by purchasing a ticket where the total of all the digits is 2, 7 or 8 or where the last digit is 2, 7 or 8.

g) LUCKY COLOURS : He should use dark grey, dark blue, purple and black colours.

h) LUCKY JEWELS AND STONES : His lucky jewels are Sapphire, Black Pearl and Black Diamond. His lucky stones are Cat's Eye and Amethyst.

i) IMPORTANT YEARS IN LIFE : His important years are 8, 17, 26, 35, 44, 53, 62, 71, 80 etc.

j) HIS GOOD QUALITIES AND DRAWBACKS ARE AS UNDER:

Good qualities	Drawbacks
Authority	Cynicism
Method	Delay
Practical approach	Vindictiveness
Steadiness	Nervousness
System	Laziness

CHAPTER 72

BORN ON
9th, 18th and 27th of August

All those born on the 9th, 18th and 27th of August of any year are governed by number 9 and the planet Mars. August is governed by the Sun. The character reading relating to number 9 given below is equally applicable to the other dates. In addition, the special characteristics of those born on 10th, 18th and 27th August are given separately.

Born on 9ht August

a) CHARACTER

The combination of Mars and the Sun will make the person very impulsive. He will be energetic in all his actions. He will be inclined to be rather hasty in words, too frank and outspoken, quick in temper and prone to make enemies by his actions. He will be extremely independent in character and will rebel against any form of restraint or dictation. He will have a keen sense of justice, law and order, and as a general rule will take the part of the "under-dog" in all disputes. He will be very conscientious and insist on straight dealing from others; being of an enterprising spirit he tends to take on too many burdens on his shoulders. Unless he practices control and husbands his reserve forces he will wear himself out and not complete the average span of life. He will be most useful in positions of responsibility in business or in the domain of municipal affairs, public offices, politics and government or in connection with military matters. He must expect to meet many ups and downs in whatever his career may be. He is likely at times to fill high positions and at other times to be immobilized by events.

In whatever he does, consciously or unconsciously he tends to arouse much enmity and opposition. He will be likely to create bitter enemies whose hostility will be life long. At heart he will be really magnanimous and generous, but unable to show these qualities while the fighting lasts. When the opponent is down and out, he will be quite likely to help him. He may expect to have to cope with many unusual situations, danger to his life from violence and also from fire, explosions and firearms. He is prone to meet with accidents causing injury to the head and lower parts of the body. He will be likely to have many odd love affairs, secret alliances and romantic episodes, but generally with the wrong people and nearly always with some element of danger attached to them. He loves strenuous sports and adventures full of risk and daring. He also has the ability to handle machines and is good at inventions connected with such things. He cultivates those in high ranks or positions superior to his own. His greatest trouble will come from inferiors and servants.

Number 9 is governed by Mars and shows aggression, resistance, courage, dash and quickness. A Martian is considered as a fighter. He is always aggressive and does not stop till he achieves his end. He has the capacity to fight even against odds. A Martian does not know defeat and if we have an army of Martians, there would not be anything like defeat for them. It would be either victory or death. It is said that Emperor Napoleon Bonaparte was a believer in this science and he had a battalion of soldiers who were pure Martians. A Number 9 person is not very tactful or delicate in his talk but his intention is good and his vigorous manner should not be misunderstood for rough behaviour. He should not criticise others and should use words carefully, otherwise they will boomerang on him.

He is fiery and dashing and does not have sickly sentiments. He is daring and vigorous from start to finish.

He is also fond of games and vigorous exercise. When the date of the month is 9 and the total of all the digits in the date of birth is also 9, he is governed by a strong number 9 and his Mars is very powerful. In such a case he has strong sexual passions and he is attracted towards the opposite sex. He is prepared to go through any ordeal to gratify his desire.

He is a brave person to whom conflict does not bring the thought of danger. He is exceedingly devoted to his friends and will fight for them. He has sympathy and consideration for the weak. He loves children and animals. He takes delight in showing mercy to others. He likes the healing profession. He is backed by self-control, moral courage and the power of forgiveness. His psychological aptitude is remarkable and under all circumstances he proves his strength of will and exhibits courage. He is short-tempered.

Born on 18th August

> you have all the basic characteristics of those born on the 9th of the month, so first go through them and then read your own.

This person has tenacity and will-power which will overcome any difficulty. He is not so dashing as a number 9 person, but he is fearless and courageous. His strong health makes him passionate. He inherits property from his father. He has a disciplined mind and likes to help others. He is painstaking, with good judgement and is wise. He loves to exercise total control over others. He does not like to be cautioned by others.

Born on 27th August

> you have all the basic characteristics of those born on the 9th of the month, so first go through them and then read your own.

On the whole he is a conflicting personality. He is confident and likes to do something for those whose life is miserable or who are handicapped. He can develop a spiritual personality and can practise spiritual healing. On the other side, he is fond of women and may develop illicit contacts and cause a scandal. Sometimes he creates unhappiness in his married life. He is very sensitive and moody and his actions and moves are unpredictable. He is self-assured and strong in resolution. He is a seeker of independence and tends to dominate. He hates to work under others. Usually, he is dogmatic.

b) FINANCE

He is lucky in monetary affairs. He earns far more than an average person. He is also very liberal in spending, especially for his sweetheart. He enjoys all the comforts that mone' can bring.

c) VOCATION

A number 9 person is found in all walks of life but he will be more suitable for the army and to professions where there is full scope for his aggression and courage. In the military he will rise to high positions, in politics he will be eminent and in business he will exhibit his dashing and pushing nature. He can be a good doctor, or a chemist or a businessman dealing in iron and steel or an engineer.

d) HEALTH

His main health defect arises from heat and he is susceptible to troubles such as piles, fevers, etc. He is also likely to suffer from trouble kidney or bladder stone. Throat touble, bronchitis and laryngitis also usually trouble him.

e) MARRIAGE AND FRIENDS

He has a natural attraction towards persons born in the period from 21st July to 20th August and from 21st November to 20th December. It is therefore advisable that he should select his partner from one of these periods. He has affinity also for those who are governed by numbers 3 and 6.

A Number 9 husband

He is vigorous in health and has strong circulation of blood which makes him very passionate and enthusiastic about married life. He is fond of a beautiful wife and likes her to be submissive and passive to his sexual desires. He is fond of his family and children and likes to have a good house. Usually he leads a good married life in spite of his hot-tempered nature and eccentricities. He has a romantic mental picture of what he wants from his wife. This mental picture demands perfection. The most difficult thing in the married life of a number 9 person is to satisfy his romantic conception of physical love. He has a voracious appetite and his wife with her devotion can harmonise with him physically. Usually, we find him suspicious of his wife.

A Number 9 wife

She will make a wonderful wife for an ambitious man. She is a witty and clever conversationalist with a wonderful social presence. She will assist her husband in his business. She may also start her own activity and add to the family income. She will be happy if married to a passionate and possessive man.

Friends

His best friends are those who are governed by numbers 1, 2, 3, 4, 6, 7 and 9. He has a natural affinity also towards people born in November, February, May and in his own month i.e. August.

f) FORTUNATE DAYS
   AND NUMBERS : His lucky days are Mondays, Tuesdays, Thursdays and Fridays and lucky numbers are 3 and 6. He should therefore take all important steps on one of these days and also dates if possible. He should try his luck in lottery by purchasing a ticket where the total of all the digits is 3 or 6, or where the last digit is 3 or 6.

g) LUCKY COLOURS : He should use white and all shades of red and yellow colours.

h) LUCKY JEWELS AND STONES : His lucky jewels are topaz, pearl and ruby and lucky stones are Blood-stone and Garnet.

i) IMPORTANT YEARS IN LIFE : His important years are 9, 18, 27, 36, 45, 54, 63, 72 etc.

j) HIS GOOD QUALITIES AND DRAWBACKS ARE AS UNDER:

Good qualities	Drawbacks
Activity	Destructive tendency
Courage	Erratic
Dash	Hot tempered
Energy	Impatient
Enthusiasm	Quarrelsome.

CHAPTER 73

BORN ON
1st, 10th, 19th, and 28th September

All those born on the 1st,10th, 19th and 28th of September of any year are governed by the number 1 and the Sun· Septmber is governed by the planet Mercury. The character reading relating to number 1 given below is equally applicable to the other dates. In addition, the special characteristics of those born on 10th, 19 and 28th of September are given separately.

Born on 1st September

a) CHARACTER

He possesses a keen intellect with a wonderfully retentive memory. He is cautious and discriminating about those he associates with and as a rule is not easily deceived. He analyzes andreasons things closely· He makes a good critic, generally too much so for his own good or happiness. He notices things out of place quickly and has an excellent taste in things about his home. He is not as a rule an originator, but he carries out with success any plan or work that appeals to him or things which others have failed to complete. But if anything captures his attention, he exercises great concentration and will never rest until he has carried out his object. He has an unusual respect for rank and position and is a supporter of the law and the law's decision. He is an excellent lawyer and debater, but tends more to support precedents than to orginate any new ordinance. He succeeds well in scientific reasearch and business, but more by his steady, industrious peristence, will-power and determination than anything else. He is inclined to become wrapped up in himself and his own ideas and appears to become selfish in the close pursuit of his aims. He has always his wits about him and is generally self-possessed and self-reliant. He is more capable of going to extremes in good and evil than any other type. If he develops a love of money he will stick at nothing to acquire it. He can adapt himself to almost any pursuit in life. In his real attitude towards love he is most difficult to understand, the very best and the very worst of men and women being born in this month. In early years he is intensely virtuous and pure-minded. If he changes, he does so with a vengeance and becomes the exact reverse, but on account of his inborn respect for the law and his natural cleverness, he succeeds in covering up his tendencies better than any other class. He has often a tendency to indulge in drugs or drinks unless he has control over himself.

He is dominated by the Sun which shows originality, activity, energy, enthusiasm, art and brilliance. He is usually successful in life due to his active nature and capacity to mix in any society. He is gifted with intuition and he seldom makes a deep study of any subject. He has a quick grasp of a subject and can participate effortlessly in conversation. He loves invention and has creative talens. A new ideas is a very great thrill and he will always be young by reason of new ideas.

Born on 10th September

you have all the basic characteristics of those born on the 1st of the month, so first go through them and then read your own.

This man has the capacity to judge the ability of his opponents in games and knows very well how to take advantage of the weak point of his opponents. He loves oratory and eloquence in expressing himself. He is energetic, constantly working and is adroit: he is crafty and a constant schemer. He gets financial benefits from relatives such as father, father-in-law, wife, mother etc. This birth date shows honour and self-confidence. The person likes to help people but hardly gets a response from them. This is more true in the case of relatives.

Born on 19th September

you have all the basic characteristics of those born on the 1st of the month, so first go through them and then read your own.

He is very skilful and has intuition. He is quite proficient in games where he uses his hands as well as his brain. He has the capacity to pursue his objectives and knows very well how to plan to achieve his ends. He is deeply interested in occult subjects and wishes to master all the intricacies of such abstruse subjects. He is also interested in reading books, not of romance, but on scientific subjects. He takes quick decisions and always likes to keep himself busy with some concrete project. He is hasty and impetuous in love affairs which end in quarrels.

Born on 28th September

you have all the basic characteristics of those born on the 1st of the month, so first go through them and then read your own.

He is very generous and spends on charitable institutions such as schools, hospitals etc. He is not as lucky as number 1,10 and 19 and has to face difficulties in public and private life. He should select his wife carefully. He has to provide carefully for the future as he is likely to lose through trust in others. He is also likely to make many changes in his career. He rarely reveals his emotions and therefore appears cold. He has an unyielding will power and does not hesitate to carry out his plans.

b) FINANCE

As a rule he enjoys favourable conditions for making money. He inspires confidence easily in others and is pushed by them into positions of trust and responsibility. If he has to earn money by himself, he will be fortunate in investments and in industries or business. Even though he is extravagant due to his overenthusiasm, he also earns sufficient to maintain his ostentatious disposition in life. He may not amass wealth but his personality and behaviour will create the impression that he is a rich person. He has a temptation to gamble, and if not controlled in time, he may lose considerably.

c) VOCATION

The main difficulty with a number 1 person is that he does not stick to any one profession or job for a long time. Usually,

every three years there is a change in his career. He is, however, suitable for advertising concerns, newspaper business
and the cinema industry and can also be successful in theatrical
performances. He can show his artistic skill as an interior
decorator. Being a good salesman, he can choose a vocation
which will be connected with foreign coutries, such as that of
a political ambassador or a trade dealing in foreign commodities. He is a leader and can be the head of a department, a
managing director etc. He can succeed equally well as a
surgeon, jeweller and electrician, and in research projects.

d) HEALTH

September is dominated by Mercury, which shows biliousness and nervousness. This man may also have stammering
or impediments in speech. He is also governed by the Sun
and therefore he has to take precautions not to overexert himself, and should not be overenthusiastic. He has also to take
care of his eyesight and the functioning of the heart.

e) MARRIAGE AND FRIENDS

He has a natural attraction towards persons born in the
period from 20th July to 20th Sepetember, 20th November to
20th January and 20th March to 20th May. He has
an affinity for those who are governed by numbers, 1,2,4,5 and
.7. It is therefore, advisable that he should select his wife
from one of these periods or numbers.

A Number 1 husband

He is a lucky and successful husband. His selection is
good and usually he selects a person of his own type. He
loves his partner. He expects neatness and cleanliness from
her and also desires that she should share with him the enjoy_
ment of life. He wants her to be stylish and full of fire and life.
He loves his children and is fond of home life.

A Number 1 wife

She is aristocratic by temperament and attracts people to
her home and commands great respect. She needs a virile

husband who can provide her with the romantic outlets that her passionate nature requires.

Friends

His best friends are those who are governed by numbers 1,3,4,5,7 and 9. He has a natural affinity also towards people born in December, March and June and in his own month i.e. September. He likes those who have dash, courage, activity and a fighting spirit.

f) FORTUNATE DAYS AND NUMBERS : His lucky days are Sundays, Mondays and Thursdays and lucky numbers are 1, 3 and 5. He should therefore take all important steps on one of these days and also dates if possible. He should try his luck in lottery by purchasing a ticket where the total of all the digits is 1, 3 or 5 or where the final digit is 1, 3 or 5.

g) LUCKY COLOURS : His lucky colours are all shades of gold, yellow, orange and purple.

h) LUCKY JEWELS AND STONES : His lucky jewels are Ruby and Emerald and lucky stones are moonstone and pale green stone.

i) IMPORTANT YEARS IN LIFE : His important years are 1, 10, 19, 28, 37, 46, 55, 64, 73 etc.

25

j) HIS GOOD QUALITIES AND DRAWBACKS ARE AS UNDER:

Good qualities	Drawbacks
Strong will–power	Obstinacy
Aspiration	Aloofness
Assertiveness	Domination
Authority	Impertinence
Confidence	Inflexibility
Determination	Pride
Research	Ostentation
Vigour	Extravagance

CHAPTER 74

BORN ON
2nd, 11th, 20th and 29th of September

All those born on 2nd, 11th, 20th and 29th of September of any year are governed by the number 2 and by the Moon. September is governed by the planet Mercury. The character reading relating to number 2 given below is equally applicable to the other dates. In addition, the special characteristics of those born on 11th, 20th and 29th of September are given separately.

Born on 2nd September

a) CHARACTER

This man has a very fertile imagination and excellent mental ability but he is inclined to seek changes to make the most of his abilities. He has a keen desire for all intellectual studies. He is not ostentatious or pretentious but has a quiet life. He is trustworthy in any work but lacks initiative due to lack of self-confidence. He is reserved and undemonstrative but is capable of holding friends, particularly those of the opposite sex. He is liable to make many changes of place and is likely to travel a great deal. He should be careful in his selection of a wife and should not be hasty. It is better if he marries late in life so that his unsteady nature will be under control after middle age.

He is somewhat nervous but social, and is liked by others. He is warm-hearted and shows little resistance against oppression. He has noble sentiments. He is unassuming but pleasing and has a good taste in clothes. He likes peace and harmony. He has hypnotic power and attracts others.

Born on 11th September

> you have all the basic characteristics of those born on the 2nd of the month, so first go through them and then read your own.

He is usually successful in life and in love, and gets honour, position and authority. He is loyal to his friends and is of a royal disposition He should guard himself from secret enemies. He has interest in mysticism, philosophy and science He can expect travel, favours and honours in life. He is very impulsive and gets excited easily. He worries too much over small matters. He can take quick decisions and so can be a leader. He is a born advisor and an inspiration to others.

Born on 20th September

> you have all the basic characteristics of those born on the 2nd of the month, so first go through them and then read your own.

He has many friends and benefits through wealthy women. He has a flair for writing and can be known as an author or a novelist. His prosperity lies near water, river or the sea. This number has a peculiar significance. It shows new plans and new resolutions for the betterment of people at large.

Born on 29th September

> you have all the basic characteristics of those born on the 2nd of the month, so first go through them and then read your own.

This person is moody and changing and therefore uncertain about his actions. He is courageous; he takes risks in life and does not stick to anything to the end. He is intelligent and also a deep thinker but there is a tendency to carry everything to extremes. He is not very lucky in his married life. His interest is in his business. He is blessed with good fortune. His life is eventful.

b) FINANCE

He is likely to earn money as a result of brain work. If he has an attraction for wealth he should do well as the head of big enterprises. However, he does not have the physical stamina to stand the strain of every day life. He can improve his financial position if he is able to create art out of his imagination. He can be a good author or a painter and earn a good livelihood. However, his unstable mind often drags him away from routine work and this makes his income uncertain. He is, therefore, not quite stable as far finances is concerned.

c) VOCATION

The high imaginative power possessed by this person will help him to be a good composer of music or a writer of fiction, stories or romance. He has a rich vocabulary and linguistic capacities and can be successful as a teacher or a professor of languages. He can also be a good research student or a chemist.

d) HEALTH

His main health weakness is his poor blood circulation. He. is susceptible to anaemia and a weak heart. He is extremely sensitive to food not properly cooked.

e) MARRIAGE AND FRIENDS

He has a natural attraction towards persons born in the period from 20th October to 20th November and 20th February to 20th March. He also has affinity for those who are governed by numbers 2 and 6. It is therefore advisable that he should select his wife from one of these periods or numbers.

A Number 2 husband

He has a greater love and attraction for home than any other type. There are two types of husbands belonging to this number. One is dominating and exacting. He is fault-finding and nothing satisfies him. The other type is passive, lazy and indulgent. He will marry for the sake of money, so that he may ultimately get comforts.

A Number 2 wife

She is sympathetic, affectionate and devoted. She is satisfied with anything her husband provides her with. However, she is moody, changeable and sensitive.

Friends

His best friends are those who are governed by numbers 2, 4, 6 and 9. He also has a natural affinity towards people born in December, March and June and in his own month i.e. September.   He likes those who have energy, dash. courage and a fighting spirit.

f) FORTUNATE DAYS AND NUMBERS : His lucky days are Mondays, Tuesdays and Fridays and his lucky numbers are 2 and 6.   He should therefore take all important steps on one of these days and also dates if possible.   He should try his luck in lottery by purchasing a ticket where the total of all the digits is 2 or 6, or where the last digit is 2 or 6.

g) LUCKY COLOURS : He should use white and all shades of cream or blue as his lucky colours.

h) LUCKY JEWELS AND STONES : His lucky jewels are pearl and diamond and lucky stones are moonstone and agate.

i) IMPORTANT YEARS IN LIFE : His important years are 2, 11, 20, 29, 38, 47, 56, 65, 74 etc

j) HIS GOOD QUALITIES & DRAWBACKS ARE AS UNDER:

Good qualities	Drawbacks
Emotionality	Coldness
Fellowship	Envy
Honesty	Haste
Imagination	Introvert
Simplicity	Shyness
	Whimsicality

CHAPTER 75

BORN ON
3rd, 12th, 21st and 30th of September

All those born on the 3rd, 12th, 21st and 30th of September of any year are governed by number 3 and the planet Jupiter. September is governed by the planet Mercury. The character reading relating to number 3 given below is equally applicable to the other dates also. In addition, the special characterstics of those born on 12th, 21st and 30th September are given separately.

Born on 3rd September

a) CHARACTER

At heart this man will be intensely ambitious, of an aspiring nature, determined to rise above the conditions and circumstances of his birth and early surroundings. He will not be easily satisfied no matter what position he may reach. He will drive himself with a whip of iron and unless he curbs the insatiable desire for success and excessive work he will be likely to suffer at times a very serious breakdown of the nervous system. Dominating those around him comes naturally to him. He will have a strong will, a firm determination to carry out his plans, but at the same time he will hold himself well under check using considerable caution to prevent going too far against the opposition of others. He will be inclined to be materialistic in his desire to accumulate wealth, and yet he will be generous and magnanimous to others provided he is allowed his own way in being generous. He will be discreet and prudent in all his dealings and rather suspicious of people in general. His mind will be of a practical type, quick to analyze any

matter placed before him.   Scientific investigation and research
will appeal to him but will be used by him as one would
employ a servant, to serve his aims and carry out his purpose
If he becomes wealthy he will employ his riches to endow
universities or assist students in their researches.   He will
find his best field in positions of responibility, authority and
trust.   He will he good at organization, making laws for others
to follow, but in his own personal life he will be a law unto
himself, very probably not seeing anything wrong or out-of-
the-way in carrying out his own plans.   He will be highly
intellectual, comprehending with ease the most difficult
problems that may confront him in the various phases of his
career.   He will be extremely critical and careful in his choice
of friends and acquaintances, allowing few to get really.
intimate with him at any time.

A person born on this date is governed by Jupiter which
stands for morality, pure love and justice with mercy and is
known as the greatest benefactor and uplifter   The vibrations
emitted by this number are essentially harmonious and they
lead to sympathy and an untiring effort to do good to all.   The
man is devout and has true dignity.   The abuse of the same
vibrations causes the stimulation of Jupiterian virtues, leading to
hypocrisy, especially in religious matters.   The good nature
is marred by excess in many directions.

He is usually lucky in life.   Vibrations radiating through
him attract all that is good to him and his affairs prosper as a
consequence.   The judge who gives sane decisions and
merciful sentences, the physician and the church dignitary,
the world's teachers and philosopers are all mostly governed
by the number 3.

This is a good number.   The person is confident about his
ability.   He is self-reliant and takes his own decisions.   He
has a habit of talking loudly.   He is fond of show and likes to
observe form, order and the law.   He is jovial in spirit and
cordial in manner.   His passions are healthy, spontaneous and
without inhibitions.   He is free in his expressions.   He is a
good conversationalist.

He takes an active interest in sports and outdoor activities from his earliest youth. He has tremendous enthusiasm and is not self-centred. His intellect is of a very high quality. He has a kind of vision that understands the world and loves it for what it is and not for what it ought to be. He is a broad-minded person, tolerant, humorous and truthful. He is open-hearted with a good understanding and is entirely lacking in malice or petty jealousies. If he is not alert, people take undue advantage of his good nature.

The main characteristics of this 3 person are ambition, leadership, religion, pride, honour, love of nature, enthusiasm, generosity, respect and reverence.

Born on 12th September
you have all the basic characteristics of those born on the 3rd of the month, so first go through them and then read your own.

He loves oratory and eloquence. He is energetic, constantly working and is adroit; he is crafty and a constant schemer. He is not indolent; industry is his basic characteristic. He has interest in occult subjects. Authority and honours are the significant aspects of this person's. He has vanity and is proud, ambitious and aspiring. He is fond of pleasures and is attracted to the opposite sex. However, sometimes he prefers loneliness. He likes to make sacrifices for others but becomes a victim of other people's plans or intrigues. His relations with others are smooth and harmonious. He is quick to notice trifles, He has lofty ideals.

Born on 21st September
you have all the basic characteristics of those born on the 3rd of the month, so first go through them and then read your own.

He is kind and generous and is a loving father. He achieves fame, reputation and honours at a very late age. He is cheerful and fond of travels. He has a strong sense of self-respect. Surprisingly, he has a suspicious nature.

Born on 30th September
you have all the basic characteristics of those born on the 3rd of the month, so first go through them and then read your own.

He is fortunate, generous and optimistic. He has a noble and religious mind. He likes to travel and visit places of pilgrimage. He can be successful as a teacher or an educationist or in administration. He appears gentle and sincere, but has a hidden characteristic. He may be active but is restless. When faced with difficulties, he is strong enough to overcome them.

b) FINANCE

He is a lucky type and somehow manages to earn enough for his livelihood. He also gets opportunities for high positions in life and earns quite a lot. His ambition, leadership and enthusiasm always push him forward and usually he gets all comforts in life. Hewever, he is overanxious about financial matters. He has foresight and judgement and always tries to be one step ahead of his rival in his career.

c) VOCATION

He will gain by invesments in land or house property. He will succeed in trades far away from his birth place. He will have success in public life or in a career which will bring him before the public. He can accept positions such as those of a minister, an ambasaador, a judge or a secretary. He is gifted for public life, statesmanship and high offices in the army or in the church. He is a good teacher as well as a good preacher. Professions such those of doctors, bankers, advertisers and actors are also suitable for him.

d) HEALTH

His principal health problem will be with the upper stomach, liver, spleen, and digestive organs. He is liable to suffer from chest and lung disordes, throat afflictions, gout and sudden fevers.

e) MARRIAGE AND FRIENDS

He has a natural attraction towards persons born in the period from 20th June to 20th July and 20th October to 20th Novembed. He has an affinity for those who are governed by numbers 3,6 and 9. It is therefore advisable that he should select his wife from one of these periods or numbers.

A Number 3 husband

He is a lucky and successful husband. However, being ambitious, he expects too much from his wife and so he gets disappointed. He desires to have a wife of whom he can be be proud. It is always better for him to choose a number 3 person or a number 6 person as his wife. He is most loving, thoughtful and considerate. His passions are adventurous and demand immediate satisfaction.

A Number 3 wife

She is the best companion to her husband. She is not an intruder but takes an active interest in the business of her husband. She has interest at home as well as outside. She likes tidiness, and though she seldom does her own work, she gets it done through her commanding personality.

Friends

This man's best friends are those who are governed by numbers 1, 3 5, 6, 7, 8 and 9. He has a natural affinity also towards people born in December, March June, and in his own month, i.e. September. He likes those who have dash, courage, wisdom and shrewdness.

f) FORTUNATE DAYS
   AND NUMBERS : His lucky days are Tuesdays, Thursaays and Fridays and lucky numbers are 3, 5 and 6. He should therefore take all important steps on one of these days and also dates if possible. He should try his luck in lottery by purchasing a ticket where the total of all the digits is 3, 5 or 6 or where the last digit is 3, 5 or 6.

g) LUCKY COLOURS : He should use all shades of yellow, violet, purple and green as his lucky colours.

h) LUCKY JEWELS AND STONES : His lucky jewel is Topaz and lucky stones are amethyst and cat's eye.

i) IMPORTANT YEARS IN LIFE: His important years are 3, 12, 21, 30, 39, 48, 57, 66, 75 etc.

j) HIS GOOD QUALITIES AND DRAWBACKS ARE AS UNDER:

Good qualities	Drawbacks
Ambition	Cruelty
Dignity	Dictatorship
Individuality	Hypocrisy
Philosophy	Extravagance
Prestige	Vanity

CHAPTER 76

BORN ON

4th, 13th and 22nd of September

All those born on the 4th, 13th and 22nd of September of any year are governed by number 4 and the planet Uranus. September is governed by the planet Mercury. The character reading relating to number 4 given below is equally applicable to the other dates. In addition, the special characteristics of those born on 13th and 22nd of September are given separately.

Born on 4th September

a) CHARACTER

The influence of Uranus has a very interesting significance. It will cause a person to be so original and independent in his thoughts and actions that the majority of persons he meets are likely to consider him odd and perhaps eccentric. If his conditions of life are such that he is forced to mix with his fellows as a rule he will find things very difficult and troublesome. He will not make friends easily and if he has any, they will not be of any assistance to him or to his plans. He will see life from such a different angle that he will find himself at variance with the views of most people and especially of the members of his own family. His will and determination will be exceptionally strong, rather inclining towards obstinacy. He will have many enemies because his motives are not understood. He will have curious experiences of persons who plot and plan his downfall. He will have many false stories circulated about him, anonymous letters and scandals cropping up again and again from hidden quarters. It is better for him to avoid litigation as much as possible as he will find it difficult to get justice. For some occult reason, difficult to explain, he will find other people causing one muddle after another in his affairs. He should not decide any question in the heat of a discussion for the simple reason that his nature will prompt him to see the opposite side of any argument and the original question gets complicated.

Uranus shows revolution and unexpected happenings in life. Usually the changes that take place are for the better. They show activity and intelligence engaged in the reconstruction or the betterment of human life. The peculiar nature of this person is that he constantly aims at changes in life and society and seeks the liberation of the mind from bondage to environment and society. He dislikes hypocrisy and loves art and music. He has an attractive personality. He is methodical in his own way. He has a bad habit of forcing his opinions on others. He has a keen, analytical and logical mind. He feels lonely in life.

Born on 13th September
you have all the basic characteristics of those born on the 4 of the month, so first go through them and then read your ow

He is an intelligent person, of tall stature and good complexion. He is considerate and benevolent. He likes literary and scientific books. He likes to be active though in a quiet way. He occupies positions of high responsibility and gets riches. His success and career start after his 31st year. Though outwardly he looks mild, inwardly, he is obstinate. He is faithful and sympathetic but has difficulty in expressing his love. He has all the qualities of number 4 but in an exaggerated form.

Born on 22nd September
you have all the basic characteristics of those born on the 4t of the month, so first go through them and then read your own.

He is also tall and has good eyes. Usually he occupies good positions but without much responsibility. He is rather easy-going but unsteady by nature. Sometimes his actions are spasmodic. On the whole he is lucky in his affairs and benefits from the opposite sex. He is happy in his family life but is also fond of a companion. He is faithful and dedicated to

others. Sometimes, he feels very lonely. His social field is
limited and he has few friends. He does not care for disputes.
He has too much economy of sentiments.

b) FINANCE

He will have to depend largely on his own efforts to make
money. He is usually successful while working alone. He is
liable to meet with treachery from employees servants and
inferiors. He may not amass wealth but he is usually well
settled in life though he experiences delays and difficulties in
his undertakings. He is a spendthrift and his home is well
decorated. His financial prosperity usually starts after the age
of 40.

c) VOCATION

He will be successful in trades such as transport and those
connected with electricity and all sorts of machinery. He will be
equally successful as an engineer, a building contractor, a
scientist and an industrialist. He is also attracted towards mystic
subjects such as palmistry and astrology and can do well in
these subjects also.

d) HEALTH

His respiratory system is usually weak and he suffers from
breathlessness. His kness, shanks and feet are also affected.
Sometimes he suffers from urinary infection. His health will
be an enigma to medical men. He recovers as rapidly as he
falls ill.

e) MARRIAGE AND FRIENDS

He has a natural attraction towards persons born in the
period from 20th February to 20th March and 20th October to
20th November. He also has affinity for those who are governed by numbers 1, 2, 7 and 8. It is therefore advisable that he
should select his wife from one of these periods or numbers.

A Number 4 husband

He is shrewd and intelligent and expects his wife to share his views. He is dominating and wants all affairs of the house to run accoriding to his wishes. He is generous and has a kind and loving heart. He is a lucky and successful husband. He loves his wife and children and home life.

A Number 4 wife

She is smart and attractive. She has the art of dressing well and has a strong will-power. She aims at several things but seldom succeeds in getting mastery over one. She loves interior decoration but does not have the capacity to work hard and so she will get it done through others. She is often dictatorial and moody and spoils her day due to her own whimsical nature. She loves her home but is not attached to it very much. She is often uneasy. It is good for her to find a friend governed by number one or two.

Friends

This man's best friends are those who are governed by numbers 1, 2, 4, 5, 7, 8 and 9. He also has a natural affinity towards people born in December, March and June and in his own month i. e. September. He likes those who have dash, courage and enthusiasm.

f) FORTUNATE DAYS
   AND   NUMBERS : His lucky days are Sundays, Mondays and Saturdays. His lucky numbers are 1, 4 and 7. He should therefore take all important steps on one of these days and also dates if possible. He should try his luck in lottery by purchasing a ticket where the total of all the digits is 1, 4 or 7, or where the last digit is 1, 4 or 7.

g) LUCKY COLOURS : He should use electric blue, electric grey, marcon and white.

h) LUCKY JEWELS AND STONES : His   lucky   jewels   are
                              Diamond, Coral and   Pearl.

i) IMPORTANT YEARS IN LIFE : His important years are 4,
                                13, 22, 31, 40, 49, 58, 67,
                                76 etc.

j) HIS GOOD QUALITIES AND DRAWBACKS ARE AS UNDER:

Good qualities	Drawbacks
Activity	Changeablity
Endurance	Domination
Energy	Stubbornness
Reliability	Vindictiveness
Method and system	Jealousy

CHAPTER 77

BORN ON
5th, 14th and 23rd of September

All those born on the 5th, 14th and 23rd of September of any year are governed by number 5 and the planet Mercury. September is governed by the planet Mercury. The character reading relating to number 5 given below is equally applicable to the other dates. In addition. the special characteristics of those born on 14th and 23rd September are given separately.

Born on 5th September

a) CHARACTER

This person has a very special quality of adapting himself to the different types of persons he comes into contact with. He has considerable freedom of action and, therefore, is not restricted to any special walk of life but is found in all professions. His drawback is that he is too versatile, has too many irons in the fire and makes too many changes in the course of his life. He detests monotonous work and seeks an occupation in which he can make money quickly. He usually succeeds in his undertaking provided he does not allow himself to be influenced by others. With his adaptable nature he makes friends very easily and adjusts readily to surroundings. He has great tact and diplomacy in handling people. He is a good companion, a clever entertaining host and a social favourite.

He acquires the qualities of Mercury which are shrewdness, quickness scientific pursuits, business ability, industry, intuition and diplomacy. A person governed by this number is active and quick,this applies not only to physical agility but also to mental activity. He is very skilful and has intuition. He loves oratory and eloquence in expressing himsef. He has the capacity to purse his objectives and knows very well how to plan plan to achieve his goals. He is deeply interested in occult subjects and wishes to master all the intricacies of such abstruse subjects. He possesses a pleasant character and dislikes inactivity. He is sociable and has many acqaintances. He is fond of variety and change and trips and travels. However difficult the situation, he can master it. He is a nervous person. He is therefore restless. He has an intuitive perception. He may turn out to be either good or bad. On the good side, he is a shrewd person and not vicious or criminal. He loves family life and children. His pleasures are mainly mental and he evaluates everything in terms of business. He is amiable.

Born on 14th September | you have all the basic characteristics of those born on the 5th of the month, so first go through them and then read your own.

This person has an attractive personality and is liked by all. His nature is co-operative and he does not like to provoke others. He usually occupies a good position in life and is successful in business. He is not talkative but is slightly reserved. This is an intelligent and shrewd number. For women it indicates good marriage but they should take care in child bearing. A number 4 man is inconsistent in love and experiences some romantic and impulsive attachment in early years. He is fortunate in money matters. He is industrious and positive in speech and action. Usually he is fond of gambling and of solving riddles.

Born on 23rd September | you have all the basic characteristics of those born on the 5th of the month, so first go through them and then read your own.

This man is usually popular with women. His fortune is near water. He is successful in life and enjoys honour and wealth. He may get money through inheritance. He keeps himself busy in his own way. He gets help and protection from superiors. He is a lucky person. He is affectionate and loves freedom. He is averse to formalities. He has a spirit of independence and a desire to dominate.

b) FINANCE

Since number 5 is a business number, the person can expect opulence. With his shrewdness he is capable of developing his industry and carrying out his plans systematically with the result that he gets good returns for his efforts. He is lucky as far as his financial position is concerned.

c) VOCATION

He can adapt himself to the role he has to play in the drama of life. With his adaptability he comes in contact with various classes of people and is successful in any business. Banking is a good line for him. Mercury also indicates ability for medicine or surgery. His capacity to argue his points can make him a good lawyer.

d) HEALTH

His basic health defects are biliousness and nervousness. However, his biliousness has close relation with his psychological disturbances. Experience shows that his biliousness increases with the increase in tension and is reduced or disappears when his nervous trouble is under control. Number 5 rules over the nerves, neck, arms and the respiratory system.

e) MARRIAGE AND FRIENDS :

He has a natural attraction towards persons born in the period from 20th September to 20th October, and 20th January to 20th February. He has affinity also for those who are governed by numbers 1 7 and 8. It is therefore advisable that he should select his wife from one of these periods or numbers.

A Number 5 husband

He is lucky and successful in his married life. His selection is good and usually he selects a person of his own type. He loves his partner. He expects neatness and cleanliness from her and also desires that she should share in his enjoyment of life.

He is proud of his wife and likes to see her well-dressed. He proves to be a good husband. He loves his children and is fond of his home. Even if he travels long, he is very much attracted to his home and is eager to return early to his family. He is liberal in spending on clothes and other wants of the members of his family and furnishes his house with good taste.

A Number 5 wife

She has interest at home as well as outside. She has many activities and manages them well. She likes tidiness. Though she seldom does her own work, she gets it done through her commanding personality.

Friends

His best friends are those who are governed by numbers 1,3,4,5,7 and 8. He has a natural affinity also for people born in December, March and June and in his own month i.e. September. He likes those who have initiative, courage and enthusiasm.

f) FORTUNATE DAYS AND NUMBERS : His lucky days are Wednesdays. Fridays and Saturdays and lucky numbers are 1, 5 and 7. He should therefore take all important steps on one of these days and also dates if possible. He should try his luck in lottery by purchasing a ticket where the total of all the digits is 1,5 or 7, or where the last digit is 1, 5 or 7.

g) LUCKY COLOURS : He should use white and all shades of green.

h) LUCKY JEWELS AND STONES : His lucky jewels are Emerald and Diamond. He may use Sapphire also.

i) IMPORTANT YEARS IN LIFE : His important years are 5. 14, 23, 32, 41, 50, 59, 68, 77 etc.

j) HIS GOOD QUALITIES AND DRAWBACKS ARE AS UNDER:

Good Qualities	Drawbacks
Co-operation	Lack of perseverance
Practical approach	Scepticism
Shrewdness	Unreliability
Vigilance	—

CHAPTER 78

BORN ON
6th, 15th and 24th of September

All those born on the 6th, 15th and 24th of September of any year are governed by the number 6 and the planet Venus. September is governed by the planet Mercury. The character reading relating to number 6 given below is equally applicable to the other dates. In addition, the special characteristics of those born on 15th and 24th September are given separately.

Born on 6th September

a) CHARACTER

This man has a most sympathetic nature, one in which love and romance play a very important part. He is likely to have many emotional complications. In his early years he is inclined to be attracted to the wrong person, someone already married or of an inferior position. In later life the situation will be the reverse and he will marry satisfactorily. He will develop maturity early and will have an old head on young shoulders. There will be two courses opening before him at the very beginning. One will be a very strict, pure kind of life with a devotional or deeply religious trend, much influenced by his family and his upbringing. The other will be characterized by a desire for freedom from his home, love of adventure and an active life. He will follow one or the other, according to the circumstances ruling his early years and the attachments he develops. He is fond of outdoor life and good at all kinds of sports and games; he likes dogs, horses and animals in general.

This person is governed by the planet Venus which stands for love, sympathy and adoration. He is a pleasant personality to meet. It is always charming to be with him. His talk is interesting and lively. We may sometimes be required to put aside our ideas of morality and social conduct in understanding and appreciating his feelings and views. Venus stands for beauty, health, vitality, warmth, attraction and above all, love. This man prefers spending to saving. He will have rich clothes, jewellery, perfumes and all sorts of beautiful things. He prefers joy to gloom and has the capacity to make others share in the moments of enjoyment. He is a good converstionalist and enjoys crossing swords intellectually.

Born on 15th September

you have all the basic characteristics of those born on the 6th of the month, so first go through them and then read your own.

This person is very intelligent and has a good memory. He is fit for responsible positions such as those of ambassadors, consuls, governors etc. He is very ambitious and boastful but hasty and proud by nature. He appears to be gentle but has very strong convictions. He has a habit of worrying inwardly and leads a melancholy life. It is his fate to make sacrifices for others.

Born on 24th September

you have all the basic characteristics of those born on the 6th of the month, so first go through them and then read your own.

He is fortunate in getting assistance from people of high rank. He benefits through the opposite sex. He marries a rich girl and prospers. He strictly defines the line between personal and social matters. He is methodical in his ideas. He possesses a strong ego and sometimes tries to force his opinions on others.

b) FINANCE

He is rather fortunate in financial matters. He gets help and assistance from his relatives and friends in times of difficulty. He may profit from legacies and gifts. He makes good investments in houses, land and property in general.

c) VOCATION

He will shine as an interior decorator, architect, jeweller, musician, hotel manager or confectioner. He can be equally successful as a broker, an estate broker or as a commission agent.

d) HEALTH

On the whole he is a healthy person and does not experience many ups and dows in his health. However, he is likely to suffer from problems of the throat, bronchial tubes and lungs. He may also be wounded in his breast, shoulders, arms and feet.

e) MARRIAGE AND FRIENDS

He has a natural attraction towards persons born in the period from 20th August to 20th September and 20th December to 20th January. He has also affinity for those who are governed by the numbers 2,3,4, 6 and 9. It is, therefore, advisable that he should select his marriage partner from one of these periods or numbers.

A Number 6 husband

He loves marriage and usually marries early in life. He expects his partner to be neat and have charm and grace. His is usually a large family with many children. He loves his children and home. He is very kind, generous and devoted. Though he creates a lively atmosphere in the house, he somehow finds it difficult to meet all the needs of the members of his family. This may sometimes create unhappiness and make him unpleasant in his married life. Art is everything to him and he remains impractical, not understanding the material values of a successful life.

A Number 6 wife

She never resorts to divorce and endures extreme hardship

rather than desert her husband. She is a devoted mother and a loving wife, satisfied with her husband's efforts in her behalf. She loves domestic life and makes a perfect house.

Friends

His best friends are those who are governed by numbers 2, 3, 4, 6, and 9. He also has a natural affinity towards people born in December, March, and June and in his own month i.e. September. He likes those who have dash, courage, enthusiasm, activity and a fighting spirit.

f) FORTUNATE DAYS
AND NUMBERS : His lucky days are Mondays, Tuesdays and Thursdays and lucky numbers are 2, 3 and 6. He should therefore take all important steps on one of these days and also dates if possible. He should try his luck in lottery by purchasing a ticket where the total of all the digits is 2, 3 or 6, or where the last digit is 2, 3 or 6.

g) LUCKY COLOURS : He should use all shades of blue, rose and pink.

h) LUCKY JEWELS & STONES: His lucky jewels are Turquoise, Emerald, Pearl and Diamond.

i) IMPORNANT YEARS IN LIFE : His important years are 6, 15, 24, 33, 42, 51, 60, 69, 78 etc.

j) HIS GOOD QUALITIES AND DRAWBACKS ARE AS UNDER:

Good Qualities	Drawbacks
Harmony	Absence of foresight
Love	Interference
Peace	Moodiness
Strong memory	Timidity

CHAPTER 79

BORN ON
7th, 16th, dan 25th of September

All those born on th 7th, 16th and 25th of September of any year are governed by number 7 and the planet Neptune. September is governed by the planet Mercury. The character reading relating to number 7 given below is equally applicable to the other dates. In addition, special characteristics of those born on 16th and 25th September are given separately.

Born on 7th Sepfember

a) CHARACTER

This person is governed by Neptune and has the same. qualities as those of number 2 which is governed by the Moon. He has individuality and is original and independent. He is restless by nature and loves change. He likes to visit foreign countries and becomes interested in far off lands. He has peculiar ideas about religion and dislikes following the beaten track.

This is a spiritual number and Supreme Consciousnesss is developed in this individual. He is like a free bird and likes to break traditional bonds and restrictions. It is possible that the greatest of the prophets and spiritualists may have Neptune dominating them. His behaviour is a mystery to others. He is often absent-minded. He thinks out logically and achieves great aims. He is stubborn and disregards the opinions of others. He is good at making money. In general, he cares little for materialistic goals. He desires the best or none at all. He is sens tive and hides his real feelings by apparent indifference. He dislikes mingling with common people. He prefers to spend his hour with his favourite book. When his opinion is solicited, he speaks with authority. He knows his ground.

Born on 16th September
you have all the basic characteristics of those born on the 7th of the month, so first go through them and then read your own.

He is rather easy-going and does nct like to work hard. He is good humoured and generous. He is very sensitiy and emotional. He soon gets upset but is soon pleased. He is frequently indisposed. He is fortunate in getting good and successful children. However, there is some sort of sorrow in his married life. He appears to be calm but his mind is always in turmoil. He is sometimes short-tempered. He will not disclose his nervousness and is slow in taking decisions. He does not like interference.

Born on 25th September
you have all the basic characteristics of those born on the 7th of the month, so first go through them and then read your own.

He is a jack of all trades but master of none. He is interested in several subjects and cannot go into details. His knowledge therefore is very shallow. He likes to travel and has contact with foreign countries. He is honest, faithful and good-natured. But he is fickle-minded and inconsistent. His memory is good. He is a good orator and teacher.

b) FINANCE

Usually there are many changes in the life of this person. It is therefore difficult for him to amass wealth. In all matters of finance he is inclined to be over-anxious. He is helpful in other people's affairs and may even make money for them, but in matters concerning himself he is too cautious to take full advantage of the opportunities that come his way. However, this date being a mystic one, the person can be well placed in life provided he finds a job of his choice. In that case he can be a wealthy person with all amenities and comforts.

c) VOCATION

This man can be successful as a writer, musician, chemist or organiser of industries. His love of sea travel and interest in foreign counties make him a successful merchant, exporter or importer. He can also successfully deal in dairy products, fishery, soap products etc. He can also study medicine and surgery.

d) HEALTH

This person's main trouble is his nervous constitution; all his illness will be due to his nervousness. He is easily upset. His digestive organs will give him considerable trouble.

e) MARRIAGE AND FRIENDS

He has a natural attraction towards persons born in the period from 20th October to 20th November and 20th February to 20th March. He has affinity for those who are governed by numbers, 3, 5 and 8. It is, therefore, advisable that he should select his wife from one of these periods or numbers.

A Number 7 husband

He is very emotional and understands the feelings of his wife. He is very considerate and will never try to impose his ideas on her. He is liberal and fond of picnics, travels and cinema theatres. He is a spendthrift and likes to live lavishly. His family is moderate in size and has all comforts in life.

A Number 7 wife

She is very moody and her behaviour is unpredictable. She is oversensitive and gets disturbed over small matters. She is good at entertaining friends and likes to invite people to a party or dinner. She expects her husband to look after her all the time

Friends

This man's best friends are those who are governed by numbers 1, 3, 4, 5, 7, 8 and 9. He also has a natural affinity towards people born in December, March and June and in his own month i. e. September. He likes those who have dash, courage, enthusiasm and a fighting spirit.

f) FORTUNATE DAYS
AND NUMBERS : This person's lucky days are Sundays, Mondays, Wednesdays and Thursdays and lucky numbers are 3, 5 and 7. He should therefore take all important steps on one of these days and also dates if possible. He should try his luck in lottery by purchasing a ticket where the total of all the digits is 3, 5 or 7, or where the last digit is 3, 5 or 7.

g) LUCKY COLOURS : He should use all shades of green and yellow.

h) LUCKY JEWELS AND STONES : His lucky jewels are Topaz and Emerald and lucky stones are Moon Stone and Cat's Eye.

i) IMPORTANT YEARS IN LIFE : His important year are 7, 16 25, 34, 43, 52, 61, 70, 79 etc.

j) HIS GOOD QUALITIES AND DRAWBACKS ARE AS UNDER :

Good qualities	Drawbacks
Austerity	Despondency
Peace	Diffidence
Reflective	Restlessness
Serenity	Whimsicality
Tolerance	

CHAPTER 80

BORN ON
8th, 17th and 26th of September

All those born on the 8th, 17th and 26th of September any year are governed by the number 8 and the planet Saturn. September is governed by the planet Mercury. The character reading relating to number 8 given below is equally applicable to the other dates. In addition, the special characteristics of those born on 17th and 26th September are given separately.

Born on 8th September

a) CHARACTER

He will have many restricting influences in his early years, up to about the age of 35, but thereafter he will be able to become independent of adverse surroundings and realize his ambitions. He will ha e a serious turn of mind, inclined to a study of unusual subjects and rather inclined to keep in his own shell. He will have a tendency to be overcritical and sceptical of people in general. He will be persevering and extremely conscientious in whatever he may be engaged in. He will love old books, libraries and museums and will be inclined to write or compile works on such subjects.

Being governed by Saturn he has a rigorous sense of discipline, steadfastness, constancy and dutifulness. The person has a sober and solitary personality. He is a lover of classical music, mostly of a melancholy type. He loves landscapes, natural scenery and flowers. Number 8 is considered to be a balance wheel to the character. He can look at the other side of the coin. He is a pessimist. He prefers solitude to company. He is cautious about the future and he takes decisions very carefully on matters which pertain to mundane affairs. He is a prudent person, wise and sober among all the numbers. He is never overenthusiastic and is more or less gloomy and melancholy. He is also ambitious and persevering. He is capable of enormous efforts for the attainment of his objects. He is sceptical and analytical. He is creative, productive and dominating. He understands the weak and the oppressed and treats them in a 'warm-hearted manner. He is a born manager who can keep others busy. He admires fair play and is willing to pay a fair compensation. He has a good memory for names and faces.

Born on 17th September | you have all the basic characteristics of those born on the 8th of the month, so first go through them and then read your own.

He is a good organizer and a good thinker. He has a creative and constructive mind He is a lover of peace and a philanthropist. He is attracted to occultism and mysticism. He is courageous and proud. He has a strong individuality. He is highly intelligent and clever. By nature he is calm. At times he is generous to a fault and at times very stingy. He is interested in research and loves knowledge. He is conservative and dominating.

Born on 26th september | you have all the basic characteristics of those born on the 8th of the month, so first go through them and then read your own.

He wants to enjoy life without doing anything. He is sluggish and lethargic. He revels in wine and women and is fickle-minded. He is careless about the number of children. He is lucky in money matters and gets easy money. He is smart but lacks positiveness. He likes to put up a good appearance but has a worrying nature. He has problems in his love affairs.

b) FINANCE

The peculiarity of number 8 is the delay in life in all respects. Naturally in financial matters also there is delay and stability is achieved at a very late age. This person has to

work hard and he seldom becomes rich. He has therefore to avoid number 8 playing a part in his life; instead he can
choose number 1 or 3 for all his important actions and
moves in life. However, if experience shows that 8 is a lucky
number for him, he can insist on that number, in which case
wealth and prosperity come to him. If 8 is found to be a lucky
number in one's life, one can try lottery and luck in horse
racing. But usually this number is connected with delays and
hard work, and a person has to be very cautious in
financial matters.

c) VOCATION

Subjects suitable for him are occult sciences, chemistry,
physics, medicine and also higher mathematics. He can be
successful in industries dealing with coal mines, timber, etc.
and in construction companies. He can be a good accountant
and also a good administrator. However, as stated earlier, he
has to strive hard in his career and can get the fruits of his hard
work only in the later years of his life.

d) HEALTH

His main health defects are nervousness, irritation, trouble
with legs. teeth and ears, paralysis and rheumatism. He is a
bilious type and frequently suffers from chronic melancholia. It
is very interesting to note that the delay which characterizes his
life is also take a long time to cure. Varicose veins and haemorrhoids often trouble a strong 8 personality.

e) MARRIAGE AND FRIENDS

This man has a natural attraction towards persons born in
the period from 20th April to 20th May and 20th August to
20th September. He has affinity also for those who are
governed by numbers 5 and 7. It is therefore advisable that he
should select his wife from one of these periods or numbers.

A Number 8 husband

Basically, a number 8 person does not want to get married. He prefers loneliness and likes to be left to himself. He has little attraction for the opposite sex. Usually he tries to postpone his marriage with the result that if at all he marries, it is at a very late age. He also finds it difficult to choose his wife. As he prefers seclusion to company he often makes his married life miserable. He is very orthodox in his views and does not allow his wife to adopt modern ideas in dress at home or in public places. The natural result is disappointment for his wife and hatred for her husband. If, however, he desires a happy married life, he should prefer a person who is also interested in deep and serious studies and likes to devote herself to philosophy and occult subjects.

A Number 8 wife

She has a masculine personality. She is capable and systematic. She enjoys family life and likes to make sacrifices for her children and for the ambition of her husband. Her fault is that she lacks feminine warmth, sentiment and delicacy.

Friends

His best friends are those who are governed by the numbers 3, 4, 5, 7 and 8. He has a natural affinity also towards people born in December, March and June and in his own month i.e. September. He likes those who have dash, courage, enthusiasm and a fighting spirit.

f) FORTUNATE DAYS
   AND NUMBERS : His lucky days are Wednesdays, Thursdays and Saturdays and lucky numbers are 3 and 7. He should therefore take all important steps on one of these days and also dates if possible. He should try his

luck in lottery by purchasing a ticket
where the total of all the digits is 3
or 7 or where the last digit is 3 or 7

g) LUCKY COLOURS : He should use dark grey, dark blue,
purple and black.

h) LUCKY JEWELS AND STONES : His lucky jewels are
Sapphire, Black Pearl
and Black Diamond. His
lucky stones are Cat's
Eye and Amethyst.

i) IMPORTANT YEARS IN LIFE : His important years are
8, 17, 26, 35, 44, 53, 62,
71, etc.

i) HIS GOOD QUALITIES AND DRAWBACKS ARE AS UNDER:

Good qualities	Drawbacks
Authority	Cynicism
Method	Delay
Practicality	Vindictiveness
Steadiness	Nervousness
ystema	Laziness

CHAPTER 81

BORN ON
9th, 18th and 27th of September

All those born on the 9th, 18th and 27th of September of any year are governed by number 9 and the planet Mars. September is governed by the planet Mercury. The character reading relating to number 9 given below is equally applicable to the other dates. In addition, the special characteristics of those born on 18th and 27th of September are given separately.

Born on 9th September

a) CHARACTER

Mars and Mercury are friendly to each other in the sense Mars lends to Mercury much of its fire, energy and determination. The person is mentally very active and has considerable love of risk and adventure. He is rather satirical at times, very observant, critical and easily annoyed over small matters. He is suited to constructive work, enterprises or engineering, or to the development of an industrial factory. He is likely to make use of machinery in all his enterprises.

Mars shows aggression, resistance, courage, dash and quickness. A Martian is considered as a fighter. He is always aggressive and will not stop till he achieves his end. He can fight even against all adverse elements and circumtances. A Martian does not know defeat and if we have an army of Martians, there would not be anything like defeat for them. It would be either victory or death. Such a man is not very tactful or cautious in his speech but his intention is good,

and his vigorous manner should not be misunderstood as
rough behaviour. He should not criticise people but should
choose his words carefully, otherwise they will act as
a boomerang.

He is fiery and dashing and does not have sickly sentiments. He has audacity and vigour from start to finish. He is
also fond of games and vigorous exercise. He has strong
sexual passions and is attracted towards the opposite sex. He
is prepared to go through any ordeal to gratify his desire. He
is a brave person to whom conflict does not bring the thought
of danger. He is exceedingly devoted to his friends and will
fight for them. He has sympathy and consideration for the
weak. He loves children and animals. He takes delight in
showing mercy. He likes the healing profession. He is backed
by self control, moral courage and the power of forgiveness.
His psychological aptitude is remarkable and under all circumstances he proves his strength of will and exhibits courage.
He is short-tempered.

Born on 18th September

you have all the basic characteristics of those born on the 9th of the month, so first go through them and then read your own.

This person has tenacity and will-power which will overcome any difficulty. He is not as dashing as a number 9, but
he is fearless and courageous. His strong health makes him
passionate. He inherits property from his father. He has a
disciplined mind and likes to help others. He is painstaking
with good judgement and is wise. He loves to exercise total
control over others. He does not like to be cautioned.

Born on 27th September

you have all the basic characteristics of those born on the 9th of the month, so first go through them and then read your own.

On the whole he is a conflicting personality. He is confident and likes to do sometimes for those whose life is miserable or who are handicapped. He can develop a spiritual
personality and can practise spiritual healing. On the other
side he is fond of women and may develop illicit contacts and
cause a scandal. Sometimes he creates unhappiness in his
married life. He is very sensitive and moody, and his actions

and moves are unpredictable. He is self-assured and strong in resolution. He hates to work under others. He is dogmatic in his thoughts.

b) FINANCE

He is lucky in his monetary affairs and earns more than an average person. He is also very liberal in spending, especially for his sweetheart. He enjoys all the comforts that money can bring.

c) VOCATION

A Number 9 person is found in all walks of life but he will be more suitable for the army and professions where there is full scope for his aggression and courage. In the army he will rise to high positions, in politics he will be eminent and in business he will exhibit his dashing and pushing nature. He can be a good doctor, or a chemist or a businessman dealing in iron and steel.

d) HEALTH

His main health defect arises from heat; he is susceptible to troubles such as piles and fevers. He is also likely to suffer kidney trouble or bladder stone. Throat trouble, bronchitis and laryngitis generally afflict persons in this group.

e) MARRIAGE AND FRIENDS

This man has a natural attraction towards persons born in the period from 20th July to 20th September and 20th November to 20th January. He has affinity also for those who are governed by numbers 3 and 6. It is therefore advisable that he should select his wife from one of these periods or numbers.

A Number 9 husband

He is vigorous in health and has strong circulation of blood which makes him very passionate and enthusiastic about married life. He is fond of a beautiful wife and likes her to be submissive and passive to his sexual desires. He is fond of family and children and likes to have a good house. He usually leads a good married life inspite of his hot-tempered nature and eccentricities. He has a romantic mental picture of what he wants in his wife. This mental picture demands perfecction. The most difficult thing in the married life of a number 9 person is to satisfy his conception of physical love. He has a voracious appetite and his wife with her devotion can harmonise with him physically. Usually, we find him suspicious of his wife.

A Number 9 wife

She makes a wonderful wife for an ambitious nan. She is witty and a clever conversationalist, with a wonderful social presence. She will assist her husband in his business. She may also start her own activity and add to the family income. She will be happy if married to a passionate and possessive man.

Friends

His best friends are those who are governed by numbers 1,2,3,4,6,7 and 9. He has a natural affinity towards people born in December, March and June and in his own month i. e. September. He likes those who have shrewdness, intelli gence and business ability.

f) FORTUNATE DAYS

AND NUMBERS : His lucky days are Mondays. Tuesdays, and Fridays. His lucky numbers are 3,6 and 9. He should there- fore take all important steps on one of these days and also dates if possible. He should try his luck in lottery by purchasing a ticket where the total of all the digits is 3, 6 or 9 or where the final digit is 3, 6 or 9.

g) LUCKY COLOURS : He should use white and all shades
of red, yellow and green.

h) LUCKY JEWELS AND STONES : His lucky jewels are
Topaz, Pearl and Ruby
and his lucky stones
are Blood-stone and
Garnet.

i) IMPORTANT YEARS IN LIFE : His important years are
9, 18, 27, 36, 45, 54, 63,
72 etc.

j) HIS GOOD QUALITIES AND DRAWBACKS ARE AS UNDER:

Good qualities	Drawbacks
Activity	Destructiveness
Courage	Erratic nature
Dash	Hot temper
Energy	Impatience
Enthusiasm	Qiarrelsomeness

CHAPTER 82

BORN ON
1st, 10th, 19th and 28th of october

All those born on the 1st, 10th, 19th and 28th of October of any year are governed by the number 1 and the Sun. October is governed by the planet Venus. The character reading relating to number 1 given below is equally applicable to the other dates. In addition, the special characteristics of those born on 10th, 19th and 28th October are given separately.

Born on 1st October

a) CHARACTER

The combination of the Sun and Venus is usually a favourable one for gaining prominence in the world and opportunities for developing individual talents. The person has a sincere love of justice and a desire to create peace and harmony in the surroundings. He abhors bloodshed and war in all its forms unless forced into it by his strong sense of justice. He craves for love and affection and will make sacrifices for them but yet gets very little satisfaction. He has a great ambition but is restricted in realizing it.

He has originality, activity, energy, enthusiasm, art and brilliance. He is spontaneous and responds to nature and has the capacity to enjoy life. He is usually successful in life because of his active nature and the capacity to mix in any society. He has good taste and chooses always the beautiful. He has a quick grasp of any subject and can participate in conversation. He has interest in occult subjects and does wonders with his natural gift of intuition. He has a strong will power and is independant in thought and action. Sometimes he is obstinate and selfish. He is born to lead, not to follow. To him a new idea is a greater thrill than money in the bank. He will always be young by reason of fresh ideas.

Born on 10th October | you have all the basic characteristics of those born on the 1st of the month, so first go through them and then read your own.

This man is very impressive with a magnetic personality and is respected for his knowledge and intelligence. He gets financial benefits from relativessuch as his father, father-in-law, wife, mother etc. He gets success after his 46th year. He gets a good position in service and succeeds in business also. He has broad shoulders and a manly figure. He loves truthfulness. This number shows honour and self-confidence. The person gets fame or notoriety depending upon his will-power and character. He usually enjoys good health and quickly recovers from sickness. He likes to help others, but hardly gets any response from them. This is more true in the case of relatives.

Born on 19th October | you have all the basic characteristics of those born on the 1st of the month, so first go through them and then read your own.

This man has a pleasant personality. He is always enthusiastic, energetic and charming. We may sometimes be required to keep aside our ideas of morality and social conduct in understanding and appreciating his feelings and arguments. He is gifted with health, vitality and warmth. He always likes to understand the grievances and difficulties of others with a considerate approach. He has research aptitude and likes to handle a subject in a systematic and methodical way. He takes quick decisions and always likes to keep busy with some concrete project. He is hasty and impetuous in love affairs which end in quarrels. He can keep secrets and others can confide in him.

Born on 28th October | you have all the basic characteristics of those born on the 1st of the month, so first go through them and then read your own.

This person is very generous and spends on charitable institutions like schools and hospitals. He is not as lucky as those born on 1st, 10th and 19th of the month, and has to undergo difficulties in public and private life. He should select his wife carefully. He has to provide carerully for the future as he is likely to make many changes in his career. He hardly reveals his emotions and therefore appears cold. He has an unyielding will power and does not hesitate to carry out his plans.

b) FINANCE

He is likely to gain money by mental occupations and by carrying out his own individual ambitions. He is not attracted towards money and accumulation of wealth is not his aim in life. All his interest is directed towards attaining pleasures and gratifying his desires. He therefore spends his earnings on whatever attracts him. He also never repents having spent his money on his art which may not ultimately give him monetary rewards. Opulence therefore seldom comes to him but he has the knack of somehow making both ends meet and having the minimum comforts he wants. He may sometimes have windfalls.

c) VOCATION

The main difficulty with this person is his inability to stick to any one profession or job for a long time. Usually, every three years there is a change in his career. He is, however, suitable for advertising concerns, newspaper business and the cinema industry and can also be successful in theatrical performances. He can show his artistic skill as an interior decorator. Being a good salesman, he can choose a vocation which requires relations with foreign countries, such as that of a political ambassador or a trade dealing in foreign commodities. He is a leader and can be the head of a department, a managing director etc. He can succeed equally well as a surgeon, jeweller or electrician and in research projects.

d) HEALTH

On the whole he has good health but is sometimes susceptible to impurities of blood and peculiar maladies of the skin. It is better he takes care of his sight and avoids over-exertion.

e) MARRIAGE AND FRIENDS

He has a natural attraction towards persons born in the period from 20th July to 20th September, 20th November to 20th January, and 20th March to 20th May. He has affinity also for those who are governed by numbers 1,2,4,5 and 7. It is therefore advisable that he should select his wife from one of these periods or numbers.

A Number 1 husband

He likes marriage immensely and usually marries early in life. He expects his partner to be neat and have charm and grace. His is usually a large family. He is very kind,generous and devoted and loves his children and home. Though he creates a lively atmosphere in the house, he somehow finds it difficult to provide all the needs of the members of his family. This may sometimes create unpleasantness in the family and make him a little unhappy.

A Number 1 wife

She is a devoted mother and a loving wife, satisfied with her husband's efforts in her behalf. She loves domestic life and is a perfect house-maker and will never resort to divorce; she endures extreme hardship rather than desert her husband. She has the tact to get along with people and attracts an interesting social circle. At the same time she never neglects her domestic duties. Though she is attractive and has a group of admirers seeking her favour, she is well balanced and will never encourage indiscriminate flirtation.

Friends

This man's best friends are those who are governed by numbers 1,3,4,5,7 and 9. He has a natural affinity also towards

people born in January, April and July and in his ownmonth **i.e.**
October. He likes those who have grace, attraction, art and
brilliance.

f) FORTUNATE DAYS
   AND NUMBERS : His lucky days are Sundays,
Mondays and Thursdays and lucky
numbers are 1, 4 and 5. He should
therefore take all important steps on
one of these days and also dates if
possible. He should try his luck
in lottery by purchasing a ticket
where the total of all the digits is 1,
4 or 5 or where the final digit is 1,
4 or 5.

g) LUCKY COLOURS : He should use all shades of gold,
yellow, orange and purple as his
lucky colours.

h) LUCKY JEWELS AND STONES : His lucky jewels are
Ruby and Emerald and
lucky stones are Moon-
Stone and Pale Green
Stone.

i) IMPORTANT YEARS IN LIFE : His important years are 1,
10, 19, 28, 37, 46, 55, 64,
73 etc.

j) HIS GOOD QUALITIES AND DRAWBACKS ARE AS UNDER:

Good qualities	Drawbacks
Strong will–power	Obstinacy
Aspiration	Aloofness
Aggression	Domination
Authority	Impertinence
Confidence	Inflexibility
Determination	Pride
Research	Ostentation
Vigour	Extravagance
Talents	

CHAPTER 83

BORN ON
2nd, 11th, 20th and 29th of October

All those born on 2nd, 11th, 20th and 29th of October of any year are governed by number 2 and the Moon. October is governed by the planet Venus. The character reading relating to number 2 given below is equally applicable to the other dates In addition, the special characteristics of those born on 11th 20th and 29th of October are given separately.

Born on 2nd October
a) CHARACTER

He has a strong gift of inspiration in whatever career he may follow, with a keen sense of intuition in any great emergency. He is able to visualize the outcome of his plans and having done so, he can carry them out in spite of opposition. In ordinary matters of life he is inclined to be too sensitive and feel criticism keenly, but an emergency will bring the strong side of his nature into action. He should, therefore, be careful to decide on important issues when he is alone and free from the influence of others Sometimes he may be moody and suffer severe fits of depression and be doubtful about his power of execution. At heart he is very affectionate and feels the need of love deeply. He loves to travel and lives in Countries far from his own place.

Since he is governed by the Moon, he has high imagination, idealism and a dreamy nature. He has fantasies and lacks a practical approach in life. He is warm-hearted and shows little resistance to oppression. He has noble sentiments

He is very unsteady, fickleminded and a lover of change. He is unassuming and likes peace and harmony. He has hypnotic power and attracts others.

Born on 11th October
you have all the basic characteristics of those born on the 2nd of the month, so first go through them and then read your own.

He is usually successful in life and in love, and gets honour, position and authority. He is loyal to his friends and is of a royal disposition. He should guard himself from secret enemies. He has interest in mysticism, philosophy and science. He can expect travels, favours and honours in life. He is very impulsive and gets excited easily. He worries too much over small matters. He has the ability to take quick decisions and this makes him a leader. He is a born advisor and an inspiration to others.

Born on 20th October
you have all the basic characteristics of those born on the 2nd of the month, so first go through them and then read your own.

He has many friends and benefits through wealthy women. He has a flair for writing and can be known as an author or a novelist. His prosperity lies near the water, the river or the sea- This number has a peculiar significance. It shows new plans and new resolutions for the betterment of people.

Born on 29th October
you have all the basic characteristics of those born on the 2nd of the month, so first go through them and then read your own.

This person is moody and changing, and therefore uncertain about his actions. He is courageous but takes risks in life and does not stick to anything to the end. He is intelligent and also a deep thinker but there is a tendency to carry everything to extremes. He is not very lucky in his married life. His interest is in his business. He is blessed with good fortune. His life is eventful.

b) FINANCE

This person is not very successful in money matters. This is because other people take advantage of his goodness. He can make money from his gifts of imagination and inspiration in times of emergency. He may be a good author or a painter and earn a handsome livelihood. However, his unstable nature often drags him away from routine work and this makes his income uncertain.

c) VOCATION

The high imaginative power possessed by the number 2 person will help him to be a good composer of music or a writer of fiction or romance. He can also be a good artist and can create works of lasting value. Immortal paintings, dramas and great poems will be the creation of a prominent and influential number 2. He has a large vocabulary and linguistic capacities, and can be successful as a teacher or a professor of languages. He can also be a good translator or an editor.

d) HEALTH

His main health weakness is his poor blood circulation. He is susceptible to all sicknesses arising out of poor blood circulation such as anaemia and a weak heart.

Since the Moon is the ruling planet of this person, the uneasiness which is a prominent characteristic, creates mental worries and sleeplessness. He is also suscestible to diabetes and asthmatic trouble.

e) MARRIAGE AND FRIENDS

This man has a natural attraction towards persons born in the period from 20th September to 20th November and 20th January to 20th March. He has affinity also for those who are governed by numbers 2 and 6. It is therefore advisable that he should select his wife from one of these periods or numbers.

A Number 2 husband

He likes marriage immensely and usually marries early in life. He expects his partner to be neat and have charm and grace. His usually has a large family. He is very kind, generous and devoted and loves his children and home. Though he

creates a lively atmosphere at home, he somehow finds it difficult to satisfy all the needs of the members of his family. This
may sometimes create unpleasantness in the family and make
him a little unhappy.

He has a stronger love and attraction for home than any
other type. There are two types of husbands belonging to this
number. One is dominating and exacting. He is fault-finding
and nothing satisfies him. The other type is passive, lazy and
indulgent. He will marry for the sake of money so that he may
ultimately get comforts.

A Number 2 wife

She is a devoted mother and a loving wife, satisfied with
her husband's efforts in her behalf. She loves domestic life
and is a perfect home-maker, she will never resort to divorce
but endures extreme hardship rather that desert her mate. She
has the tact to get along with people and attracts an interesting
social circle. At the same time she never neglects her domestic duties. Though she is attractive and has a group of admirers seeking her favour, she is well balanced and will never
encourage indiscriminate flirtation.

Friends

This man's best friends are those who are governed by
numbers 2, 4, 6 and 9. He also has a natural affinity towards
people born in January, April and July and in his own
month i.e. September. He likes those who have originality,
an attractive personality and grace.

f) FORTUNATE DAYS
   AND NUMBERS : His lucky days are Mondays, Tuesdays
   and Fridays and his lucky numbers are
   2, 4 and 6. He should therefore take
   all important steps on one of these days
   and also dates if possible. He should
   try his luck in lottery by purchasing a
   ticket where the total of all the digits is

2, 4 or 6, or where the last digit is 2, 4 or 6.

g) **LUCKY COLOURS :** He should use white and all shades of cream or blue.

h) **LUCKY JEWELS AND STONES :** His lucky jewels are Pearls and Diamond and lucky stones are Moonstone and Agate.

i) **IMPORTANT YEARS IN LIFE :** His important years are 2, 11, 20, 29, 38, 47, 56, 65, 74 etc.

j) **HIS GOOD QUALITIES & DRAWBACKS ARE AS UNDER:**

Good qualities	Drawbacks
Emotionality	Coldness
Fellowship	Envy
Honesty	Haste
Imagination	Introvert
Simplicity	Shyness
	Whimsicality

CHAPTER 84

BORN ON
3rd, 12th, 21st and 30th of October

All those born on the 3rd, 12th, 21st and 30th of October of any year are governed by number 3 and the planet Jupiter. October is governed by the planet Venus. The character reading relating to number 3 given below is equally applicable to the other dates. In addition, the special characterstics of those born on 12th, 21st and 30th October are given separately.

Born on 3rd October

a) CHARACTER

This number is governed by Jupiter. It stands for morality, pure love and justice with mercy and is known as the greatest benefactor and uplifter. The good nature is marred by excess in many directions.

This man is usually lucky in life. Vibrations radiating through him attract all that is good to him and his affairs prosper as a consequenc . The judge who gives sane decisions and merciful sen nces, the good physician and the church dignitary, the world's achers and philosopers are mostly governed by the number 3.

3 is a good number. The person is confident about his ability. He is self-reliant and takes his own decisions. He has a habit of talking loudly. He is fond of show and likes to observe form, order and the law. He is jovial in spirit and cordial in manner. His passions are healthy, spontaneous and

without inhibitions. He is free in his expressions. He is a good conversationalist.

He takes an active interest in sports and outdoor activities from his earliest youth. He has tremendous enthusiasm and is not self-centred. His intellect is of a very high quality. He has a kind of vision that understands the world and loves it for what it is and not for what it ought to be. He is a broad-minded person, tolerant, humorous and truthful. He is open-hearted with a good understanding and is entirely lacking in malice or petty jealousies. If he is not alert, people take undue advantage of his good nature.

The main characteristics of this person are ambition, leadership, religion, pride, honour, love of nature, enthusiasm, generosity, respect and reverence.

Born on 12th October
you have all the basic characteristics of those born on the 3rd of the month, so first go through them and then read your own.

Authority and honours are the significant aspects of this person. He has vanity and is proud, ambitious and aspiring. He is fond of pleasure and is attracted to the opposite sex. However, sometimes he prefers loneliness. He likes to make sacrifices for others, but becomes the victim of other people's plans or intrigues. His relations with others are smooth and harmonious. He is quick to notice trifles. He has lofty ideals.

Born on 21st October
you have all the basic characteristics of those born on the 3rd of the month, so first go through them and then read your own.

He is kind, generous and is a loving father. He achieves fame, reputation and honours at a very late age. He is cheerful and fond of travel. He has a strong sense of self-respect. Surprisingly, he has a suspicious nature.

Born on 30th October
you have all the basic characteristics of those born on the 3rd of the month, so first go through them and then read your own.

He is fortunate, generous and optimistic. He has a noble and religious mind. He likes to travel and visit places of pilgrimage. He can be successful as a teacher or an educationist or in administration. He appears gentle and sincere, but has a hidden characteristic. He may be active but is rest-less. When faced with difficulties, he is strong enough to overcome them.

b) FINANCE

As a general rule he is very fortunate in business, finance and industry. He will gain from good friends, from the opposite sex or from marriage. He also gets opportunities for higher positions in life and earns quite a lot. His ambition, leadership and enthusiasm always push him forward and usually he gets all comforts in life.

c) VOCATION

His love for position and command makes him occupy high posts such as those of ministers, ambassadors, judges and secretaries. He is gifted for public life, statesmanship, high offices etc., it may be in the army in the church. He is a good teacher as well as a preacher. Professions such as those of doctors, bankers, advertisers and actors are also suitable for him.

d) HEALTH

It is difficult to name an illness he can have. But he is liable to meet with injuries from accidents especially those caused by motor cars and transport. The chief influence of Jupiter is on blood circulation and the arterial system. It also governs the sense of smell. This person is liable to suffer from chest and lung disordes, throat afflictions, gout and sudden fevers. He may also suffer from sore throat, diptheria, adenoids, pneumonia, pleurisy and tuberculosis of thelungs.

e) MARRIAGE AND FRIENDS

He has a natural attraction towards persons born in the period from 20th May to 20th July, 20th September to 20th November, 20th January 20th February. He has an affinity for those who are governed by numbers 3,6 and 9. It is there-

advisable that he should select his wife from one of these periods or numbers.

A Number 3 husband

As a general rule, he attains puberty at an early age and marries early. However, he is ambitious and his ambitions make him expect too many things from his wife but he is disappointed. He desires to have a wife of whom he can be proud. She should have an attractive personality, a commanding presence, charming manners and intelligence. It is always better for him to choose a number 3 person or a number 6 person for his wife. He is most loving, thoughtful and considerate. His passions are adventurous and demand immediate satisfaction.

A Number 3 wife

She is the best companion to her husband. She is not an intruder but takes an active interest in the business of her husband. She is efficient in house-keeping and has a sympathetic and balanced attitude towards her children. Her passions are healthy and joyous and her approach to physical love is highly refined and inspiring.

Friends

His best friends are those who are governed by numbers 1, 3, 5, 6, 7, 8 and 9. He has a natural affinity also towards people born in January, April, July and in his own month i.e. October. He likes those who have originality, intelligence, an attractive personality and grace.

f) FORTUNATE DAYS

AND NUMBERS : His lucky days are Tuesdays, Thursdays and Fridays and lucky numbers are 3, 6 and 9. He should therefore take all important decisions on one of these days and also dates if possible. He

should try his luck in lottery by purchasing a ticket where the total of all
the digits is 3, 6 or 9 or where the last
digit is 3, 6 or 9.

g) LUCKY COLOURS : He should use all shades of yellow,
violet purple and green as his lucky
colours.

h) LUCKY JEWELS AND STONES : His lucky jewel is
Topaz and lucky stones
are amethyst and cat's
eye.

i) IMPORTANT YEARS IN LIFE: His important years are 3, 12,
21, 30, 39, 48, 57, 66, 75
etc.

j) HIS GOOD QUALITIES AND DRAWBACKS ARE AS UNDER:

Good qualities	Drawbacks
Ambition	Cruelty
Dignity	Dictatorship
Individuality	Hypocrisy
Philosophy	Extravagance
Prestige	Vanity

CHAPTER 85

BORN ON

4th, 13th, 22nd and 31st of October

All those born on the 4th, 13th, 22nd and 31st of October of any year are governed by the number 4 and the planet Uranus. October is governed by the planet Venus. The character reading relating to number 4 given below is equally applicable to the other dates. In addition, the special characteristics of those born on 13th, 22nd and 31st of October are given separately.

Born on 4th October

a) CHARACTER

His life is an unusual one bringing many changes and strange experiences which are beyond his control. He has out of the way experiences relating to love and marriage. He is attracted to odd and more or less eccentric people who will not be of any help from a worldly point of view. He is rather headstrong in such matters and likely to meet with opposition from the members of his family. He is liable to be drawn into tragic or sensational experiences on account of the people around him and is the victim of scandal even if he is innocent. He has unconventional views, rather eccentric, with considerable gifts of expression in literary and artistic work. Partnerships, unions or marriages are not likely to turn out well except under unusual circumstances entailing much self-sacrifice on his side. He is attracted to occult studies of an unusual nature such as hypnotism and mesmerism.

He has activity and intelligence directed to the reconstruction or the betterment of human life. The peculiar nature of this person is that he constantly aims at changes in life and society and is after the liberation of the mind from bondage to environment and society. He dislikes hypocrisy and loves art and music. He has an attractive personality. He is methodical in his own way. He has a bad habit of forcing his opinions on others. He has a keen, analytical and logical mind. He feels lonely in life.

Born on 13th October | you have all the basic characteristics of those born on the 4th of the month, so first go through them and then read your own.

He is an intelligent person, of tall stature and good complexion. He is considerate and benevolent. He likes literary and scientific books. He likes to keep active though in a quiet way. He occupies positions of high responsibility and gets riches. His success and career start after his 31st year. Though outwardly he looks mild, inwardly, he is obstinate. He is faithful and sympathetic but has difficulty in expressing his love. He has all the qualities of number 4 but in an exaggerated form.

Born on 22nd October | you have all the basic characteristics of those born on the 4th of the month, so first go through them and then read your own.

He is also tall and has good eyes. Usually he occupies good positions but without much responsibility. He is rather easy-going but unsteady by nature. Sometimes his actions are spasmodic. On the whole he is lucky in his affairs and benefits from the opposite sex. He is happy in his family life but is also fond of a companion. He is faithful and dedicated to others. Sometimes, he feels very lonely. His social field is limited and he has few friends. He does not care for disputes. He has too much economy of sentiments.

Born on 31st October | you have all the basic characteristics of those born on the 4th of the month, so first go through them and then read your own.

This date shows ambition, pride and austerity. This man is interested in honourable occupations such as working with charitable institutions, institutions for the deaf and dumb, and the physically handicapped etc. He gets success after his 40th year but he expects quick results and an early reputation. He is lucky in financial matters. He is realistic and of strong will power, He has a strong attraction for the opposite sex. He loves travelling.

b) FINANCE

As regards finace and monetary stutus he is usually well settled in life though he experiences delays and difficulties in his undertakings. He may not amass wealth but can maintain the show of riches. He is a spendthrift and his home is well decorated. His financial prosperity usually starts after the age of 40.

c) VOCATION

He will be successful in trade connected with transport, electricity and all sorts of machinery. He will be equally successful as an engineer, a building contractor, a scientist and an industrialist. He is also attracted towards mystic subjects such as palmistry and astrology and can do well in these subjects also.

d) HEALTH

Persons born on the 4th or 13th October may expect sudden illnesses of a more cr less unusual kind: they are also likely to have operations of the throat, nose, face and internal organs. Those born on 22nd or 31st October are generally delicate in childhood, but from their thirty-first year they usually develop great resistance to disease.

A person born on one of these dates suffers from breathlessness. His kness, shanks and feet are also affected. Sometimes he suffers from urinary infection.

e) MARRIAGE AND FRIENDS

He has a natural attraction towards persons born in the period from 20th January to 20th March and 20th September to 20th November. He also has an affinity for those who are governed by numbers 1 2, 7 and 8. It is therefore advisable that he should select his wife from one of these periods or numbers.

A Number 4 husband

He is shrewd and intelligent and expects his wife to share his views. He is dominating and wants all affairs of the house to run according to his views. He expects his partner to be neat and have charm and grace. Though he creates a lively atmosphere at home he somehow finds it difficult to fulfil all the necessites of the members of his family. This may sometimes create unpleasantness in the family and make him a little unhappy.

A Number 4 wife

She is smart and attractive. She has the art of dressing and has a strong will-power. She aims at several things but seldom succeeds in getting mastery over one. She loves interior decoration but does not have the capacity to work hard and she will get it done through others. She is often dictatorial and moody and spoils her day due to her own whimsical nature. She loves her home but is not attached to it very much. She is often uneasy. It is better for her to find a friend governed by number one or two.

Friends

His best friends are those who are governed by numbers 1, 2, 4, 5, 7, 8 and 9. He has a natural affinity also towards people born in January, April, July and in his own month i. e. October. He likes those who have originality, intelligence, art and grace.

f) FORTUNATE DAYS AND NUMBERS :

His lucky days are Sundays, Mondays and Saturdays. His lucky numbers are 2, 4 and 6. He should therefore take all important steps on one of these days and also dates if possible. He should try his luck in lottery by purchasing a ticket where the total of all the digits is 2, 4 or 6, or where the last digit is 2, 4 or 6.

g) LUCKY COLOURS : HIs lucky colours are electric blue, electric grey, white and maroon.

h) LUCKY JEWELS AND STONES : His lucky jewels are Diamond, Coral and Pearl.

i) IMPORTANT YEARS IN LIFE : His important years are 4, 13, 22, 31, 40, 49, 58, 67, 76 etc.

j) HIS GOOD QUALITIES AND DRAWBACKS ARE AS UNDER:

Good qualities	Drawbacks
Activity	Changeablity
Endurance	Domination
Energy	Stubbornness
Reliability	Vindictiveness
Method and system	Jealousy

CHAPTER 86

BORN ON
5th, 14th and 23rd of October

All those born on the 5th, 14th and 23rd of October of any year are governed by number 5 and the planet Mercury. October is governed by the planet Venus. The character reading relating to number 5 given below is equally applicable to the other dates. In addition, the special characteristics of those born on 14th and 23rd October are given separately.

Born on 5th October
a) CHARACTER

The combination of the planets Mercury and Venus is very important in giving the person strength of character. He may expect many unusual trials in all matters of affection. For the greater part in his life he will sacrifice himself to his strong sense of duty and for the sake of a parent or relative he will give up his plans and ambitions. He will feel unhappy because of this sacrifice as he is endowed with an intelligence beyond the average and can prosper if he has the freedom to go out into the world and make full use of his opportunities. He has a very refined nature ; anything coarse or vulgar clashes with his sensibilities. He is kind, sympathetic and compassionate to any form of suffering, yet practical and level-headed. He is strong in his principles but quiet and unassuming. His greatest desire is to bring harmony and peace to those around him. He is not a fighter willing to shed blood. He will detest scenes or quarrels but will remain loyal to his principles and a defender to the death against injustice.

The person is governed by Mercury which confers shrewd-nesss, quickness, scientific pursuits, business ability, industry, intuition and diplomacy. A person governed by this number is active and quick; this applies not only to physical agility but also to mental pursuits. He is very skilful and has an intuitive faculty. He loves oratory and is eloquent in expressing himself. He can purse his objectives and knows very well how to plan to achieve his ends. He is deeply interested in occult subjects and wishes to master all the intricacies of such abstruse subjects. He has a pleasant character and dislikes inactivity. He is sociable and has many acquaintances. He is fond of variety and change and trips and travels. However difficult be the situation, he has the power to get out of it. He is a nervous person and is therefore restless. He has an intuitive perception and has the capacity to be either good or bad. On the good side, he is a shrewd person and not vicious or criminal. He is fond of family life and children. His pleasures are mainly mental and he evaluates everything in terms of business. He is amiable and adaptable.

Born on 14th October | you have all the basic characteristics of those born on the 5th of the month, so first go through them and then read your own.

This person has an attractive personality and is liked by all. His nature is co-operative and he does not like to provoke others. He usually occupies a good position in life and is successful in his business. He is not talkative but slightly reserved. This is an intelligent and shrewd number. In women, it indicates good marriage but they should be careful in child bearing. A number 14 man is inconstant in love and experiences some romantic and impulsive attachment in the early years. He is fortunate in money matters. He is industrious and positive in speech and action. Usually he is fond of gambling and of solving riddles.

Born on 23rd October

you have all the basic characteristics of those born on the 5th of the month, so first go through them and then read your own.

He is usually popular with women. He is successful in life and enjoys honour and wealth. He may get money through inheritance. He keeps himself busy in his own way. He gets help and protection from superiors. He is a lucky person. He is affectionate and loves freedom. He is averse to formalities. He has a spirit of independence and a desire to dominate.

b) FINANCE

In matters of money, persons born on the 5th 14th or 23rd of October give good advice to others, although they seldom can act on it themselves. From their twenty-third year to their fiftieth, they often make a good income from some professional career or by their mental ability. They are good at speculation and investment, but no matter what money they make, there are so many demands on their generosity they seldom if ever put much aside for their old age.

Since number 5 is a business number, the person can expect to be wealthy. With his shrewd characteristics, he is capable of developing his industry and can carry out his plans systematically with the result that he gets good returns for his efforts. He is lucky in financial matters.

c) VOCATION

He is adaptable to the role he has to play in the drama of life. With his adaptability he comes in contact with various classes of people and becomes successful in any business. Banking is a good line for him. Mercury also shows ability for medicine or surgery. His capacity to argue his points can make him a good lawyer.

d) HEALTH

His basic health defect is biliousness and nervousness. However, his biliousness has close relation with his psychological disturbance. It increases with the increase in tension and is reduced or disappears when his nervous trouble is under control.

Number 5 rules over the nerves, neck, arms, ears and the respiratory system.

Persons born on the 5th, 14th or 23rd of October suffer from high-strung nerves; they seldom have a vigorous or strong constitution, but are wiry and have great resistance to disease. As a rule they have to put up all their life with some peculiar weaknes of the stomach and especially the digestive organs. They cannot eat like other people and have to be particularly careful in matters of diet.

e) MARRIAGE AND FRIENDS :

This man has a natural attraction towards persons born in the period from 20th September to 20th October, and 20th January to 20th February. He has affinity also for those who are governed by numbers 1, 7 and 8. It is therefore advisable that he should select his wife from one of these periods or numbers.

A Number 5 husband

He is lucky and successful in his married life. His selection is good and he usually selects a person of his own type. He usually marries early. He is proud of his wife and likes to see her well-dressed. In return, he proves a good husband Even if he travels long, he is very much attracted to his home and is eager to return soon and be with his family. He is liberal in spending on clothing and other wants of the members of his family and furnishes his house with good taste.

A Number 5 wife

She is a devoted mother and a loving wife, satisfied with her husband's efforts in her behalf. She has the tact to get on with people and attracts an interesting social circle. Though she is attractive and has a group of admirers seeking her

favour, she is sensitive and will never encourage indiscriminate
flirtation. She likes tidiness; though she seldom does her
own work, she gets it done through her commanding
personality.

Friends

His best friends are those who are governed by
numbers 1,3,4,5,7 and 8. He has a natural affinity towards
people born in January, April and July and in his own
month i.e. October. He likes those who have intelligence.
shrewdness, business aptitude and love of art.

f) FORTUNATE DAYS
AND NUMBERS : His lucky days are Wednesdays
Fridays and Saturdays and lucky
numbers are 1, 3 and 5. He should
therefore take all important steps on
one of these days and also dates if
possible. He should try his luck in
lottery by purchasing a ticket where
the total of all the digits is 1, 3
or 5, or where the last digit is 1, 3
or 5

g) LUCKY COLOURS : He should use white and green as his
lucky colours.

h) LUCKY JEWELS AND STONES : His lucky jewels are
Emerald and Diamond. He
may use Sapphire also.

i) IMPORTANT YEARS IN LIFE : His important years are 5·
14, 23, 32 41, 50, 59, 68,
77 etc.

j) HIS GOOD QUALITIES AND DRAWBACKS ARE AS UNDER:

Good qualities	Drawbacks
Co-operation	Lack of perseverance
Practical approach	Scepticism
Shrewdness	Unreliability
Vigilance	

CHAPTER 87

BORN ON
6th, 15h and 24th of October

All those born on the 6th, 15th and 24th of October of any year are governed by the number 6 and the planet Venus. October is governed by Venus. Therefore the characteristics of the persons born in this period will be dominated by twice the power of the Venus. The character reading relating to number 6 given below is equally applicable to the other dates. In addition, the special characteristics of those born on 15th and 24th October are given separately.

Born on 6th October

a) CHARACTER

This number is governed by Venus which stands for love, sympathy and adoration. A person governed by this number is a born artist and love of art and beauty in life have an attraction for him. He is a pleasant personality to meet. It is always charming to be with him. He is full of enthusiasm, energy and charm. His talk is interesting and lively. We may sometimes be required to put aside our ideas of morality and social conduct in understanding and appreciating his feelings and discussions. Number 6 stands for beauty, health, vitality, warmth, attraction and, above all, love. A person of this number is fond of music, dancing and poetry. He loves to have a life full of ease and luxuries, money and happiness. He prefers spending to saving. He will have rich clothes, jewellery, perfumes and all sorts of beautiful things.

He is necessarily a loving type and he has a feeling of kinship and humanity. He will therefore not desert his friends, he always likes to understand the grievances and difficulties of others, with a considerate approach. He prefers joy to gloom and has the capacity to make others share his moments of enjoyment. His outlook is bright and vivacious. He is emotional but keeps his emotions to himself. His anger is hard to subside. He is very responsible and loves his children, but receives very little happiness from them. He is a born advisor and needs some audience to whom he can express his views on matters of importance. He is a good converstionalist and enjoys crossing swords intellectually.

Born on 15th October — you have all the basic characteristics of those born on the 6th of the month, so first go through them and then read your own.

This person has good intelligence and a good memory. He is fit for responsible positions such as those of ambassadors, consuls, governors etc. ` He is very ambitious and boastful but hasty and proud by nature. He is interested in the lower type of occultism. He also has interest in art and music. He appears to be gentle but has very strong convictions. He has a habit of worrying inwardly and leading a melancholy life. His destiny is, such that he has to make sacrifices for others.

Born on 24th October — you have all the basic characteristics of those born on the 6th of the month, so first go through them and then read your own.

He is fortunate in getting assistance from people of high rank. He benefits through the opposite sex. He marries a rich girl and prospers. He succeeds in speculation and enjoys a good monetary status. He strictly defines the line between personal and social matters. He is methodical in his ideas. He possesses a strong ego and sometimes tries to force his opinions on others.

b) FINANCE

He is not attracted towards money and accumulation of wealth is not his aim in life. All his interest is directed towards attaining pleasures and gratifying his desires. He, therefore, spends his earnings on whatever attracts him. He also never repents having spent his money on his art which may not ultimately bring him monetary rewards. Therefores he is seldom rich but he somehow has the knack of making both ends meet and having the minimum comforts he wants. He sometimes has windfalls.

c) VOCATION

He will shine as an interior decorator, architect, jeweller, musician, hotel manager or confectioner. He can be equally successful as a broker, estate broker or a commission agent.

d) HEALTH

On the whole he is a healthy person. However, he is susceptible to epidemic fever and influenza Occasionally, he is prone to nervousness but not in a chronic way.

e) MARRIAGE AND FRIENDS

He has a natural attraction towards persons born in the period from 20th August to 20th September and 20th December and 20th January. He has also affinity for those who are governed by numbers 2, 3 ,4, 6 and 9. It is, therefore, advisable that he should select his wife from one of these periods or numbers.

A Number 6 husband

He is attracted to marriage and usually marries early. He expects his partner to be neat and have charm and grace. His is usually a large family with many children. He loves his children and home. He is very kind, generous and devoted. Though he creates a lively atmosphere at home, he somehow finds it difficult to satisfy all the necessities of the members of his family. This may sometimes create unhappiness and make him unhappy in his married life. Art is everything to him and he remains impractical, not understanding the material values of a successful life.

A **Number 6 wife**

She never resorts to divorce and endures extreme hardship rather than desert her husband. She is a devoted mother and a loving wife, satisfied with her husband's efforts in her behalf. She loves domestic life and creates a perfect home.

Friends

His best friends are those who are governed by numbers 2, 3, 4, 6 and 9. He has a natural affinity also towards people born in January, April, and July and in his own month i. e. October. He likes those who have intelligence, shrewdness, business ability and love of art.

f) FORTUNATE DAYS
   AND   NUMBERS : His lucky days are Mondays, Tuesdays, Thursdays and Fridays and lucky numbers are 2,3, and 6. He should there fore take all important steps on one of these days and also dates if possible. He should try his luck in lottery by purchasing a ticket where the total of all the digits is 2, 3 or 6, or where the last digit is 2,3 or 6.

g) LUCKY COLOURS : He should use all shades of blue, rose and pink.

h) LUCKY JEWELS & STONES: He can use turquoise, emerald pearl and diamond.

i) IMPORTANT YEARS IN LIFE : His important years are 6 15, 24, 33, 42, 51, 60, 69 78 etc.

j) HIS GOOD QUALITIES AND DRAWBACKS ARE AS UNDER:

Good Qualities	Drawbacks
Harmony	Absence of foresight
Love	Interference
Peace	Moodiness
Strong memory	Timidity.

CHAPTER 88

BORN ON
7th, 16th, and 25th of October

All those born on the 7th, 16th and 25th of October or any year are governed by number 7 and the planet Neptune. October is governed by the planet Venus. The character-reading relating to number 7 given below is equally applicable to the other dates. In addition, special characteristics of those born on 16th and 25th October are given separately.

Born on 7th October

a) CHARACTER

A person born on one of the above dates is mentally highly gifted and if he can keep his balance of mind, he can do remarkable work in any career, especially in any field of imagination such as poetry, literature, painting, music or the fine arts in general. The person is so over-sensitive that he often seems to hold himself back in any work. He has a strong leaning towards the unconventional in all his actions. On account of this peculiarity, he attracts hostile criticism and in many cases open scandal.

This number is governed by Neptune and has the same qualities as those of number 2 which is governed by the Moon. This man is original and independent. He is restless by nature and is fond of change. He likes to visit foreign countries and becomes interested in far off lands. He has peculiar ideas about religion and dislikes following the beaten track. His behaviour is a mystery to others. He is often absent-minded. He thinks out logically and achieves great aims. He is stubborn and disregards the opinions of others. He has good talent for earning money. In general, he is somewhat indifferent to materialistic desires. He desires the best or none at all. He is sensitive and hides his real feelings by apparent indifference. He dislikes mingling with common people He prefers to spend his hour with his favourite book. When is opinion is solicited, he speaks with authority. He knows his ground.

Born on 16th October
you have all the basic characteristics of those born on the 7th of the month, so first go through them and then read your own.

He is rather easy going and does not like to work hard. He is good humoured and generous. He is very sensitive and emotional. He soon gets upset but is soon pleased. He is frequently indisposed. He is fortunate in getting good and successful children. However, there is some sort of sorrow in his married life. He appears to be calm but his mind is always in turmoil. He is sometimes short-tempered. He will not disclose his nervousness and is slow in taking decisions. He does not like interference.

Born on 25th October
you have all the basic characteristics of those born on the 7th of the month, so first go through them and then read your own.

He is a jack of all trades bnut a master of none. He is interested in several subjects but does not have the ability to go into details. His knowledge therefore is very shallow. He likes to travel and has contact with foreign countries. He is honest, faithful and good-natured. But he is fickle-minded and inconsistent. His memory is good. He is a good orator and teacher.

b) FINANCE

There will be considereable fluctuation in money matters. At times he may be quite rich, at other times the very reverse. As a rule he is not lucky in speculation, as his money will be easily taken from him by unscrupulous persons. It is always good for him to invest in government securities and be happy with a steady interest to protect his advanced years. However, seven is a mystic number and the person can be well placed in life provided he finds a job of his choice. In that case he can be a wealthy person with all amenities and comforts.

c) VOCATION

His love of sea travel and interest in foreign countries make him a successful merchant, exporter or importer. He may also deal in dairy products, fishery, and other products such as soap etc. He can also study medicine and surgery.

d) HEALTH

He may experience peculiar ailments. He is liable to run the risk of poison through food or carelessness. The kidneys, liver, spleen and appendix are likely to give trouble.

e) MARRIAGE AND FRIENDS

He has a natural attraction towards persons born in the period from 20th September to 20th November and 20th January to 20th March. He has affinity for those who are governed by numbers, 3, 5 and 8. It is, therefore, advisable that he should select his wife from one of these periods or numbers.

A Number 7 husband

He is very emotional and understands the feelings of his wife. He is very considerate and will never try to impose his ideas on her. He is liberal and fond of picnics, travels and the cinema theatres. He is a spendthrift and likes to live lavishly. His family is moderate in size and has all comforts.

A Number 7 wife

She is very moody and her behaviour is unpredictable. She gets disturbed over small matters. She is good at entertaining friends and likes to invite people to parties. She expects her husband to look after her all the time.

Friends

This man's best friends are those who are governed by numbers 1, 3, 4, 5, 7, 8 and 9. He also has a natural affinity towards people born in January, April and July and in his own month i. e. October. He likes those who love art.

f) FORTUNATE DAYS
   AND NUMBERS : His lucky days are Sundays, Mondays, Wednesdays and Thursdays and lucky numbers are 1, 5 and 7. He should therefore take all important steps on one of these days and also dates if possible. He should try his luck in lottery by purchasing a ticket where the total of all the digits is 3, 5 or 7, or where the last digit is 1, 5 or 7.

g) LUCKY COLOURS : He should use all shades of green and yellow.

h) LUCKY JEWELS AND STONES : His lucky jewels are Topaz and Emerald and lucky stones are Moon Stone and Cat's Eye.

i) IMPORTANT YEARS IN LIFE · His important years are 7, 16, 25, 34, 43, 52, 61, 70, 79, etc.

j) HIS GOOD QUALITIES AND DRAWBACKS ARE AS UNDER:

Good qualities	Drawbacks
Austerity	Despondency
Peace	Diffidence
Reflection	Restlessness
Serenity	Whimsicality
Tolerance	

CHAPTER 89

BORN ON
8th, 17th and 26th of October

All those born on the 8th, 17th and 26th of October of any year are governed by the number 8 and the planet Saturn. October is governed by the planet Venus. The character-reading relating to number 8 given below is equally applicable to the other dates. In addition, the special characteristics of those born on 17th and 26th October are given separately.

Born on 8th October

a) CHARACTER

He does not have an easy time unless he inherits money and does not have to work hard to make his way. He is highly intellectual, more inclined to devote himself to some serious study than to enjoy social life. From the worldly point of view he is often rich. He spends his money on institutions and hospitals for the furtherance of scientific research or for political reform. He usually suffers sorrows and afflictions, the loss of some loved one, the illness and death of a parent or close relative or an estrangement in family circles. The peculiar influence of Saturn takes him to high positions but in advanced years every thing is swept away and the name is sorrounded by scandal. He is usually misunderstood by others and being of a reserved and quiet disposition he is not good at defending himself. As an employee he often suffers because of broken contracts and harsh treatment from superiors.

He shows an extreme sense of discipline, steadfastness,

constancy and dutifulness. He has a sober personality and prefers solitude. He has an aptitude to look at the ot her side of the coin. He is a pessimist and prefers solitude to company. He is never enthusiastic and is more or less gloomy and melancholy. He is sceptical and analytical. He is creative, productive and dominating. He admires fair play and is willing to pay a fair compensation. He has a good memory for faces and names.

Born on 17th October   you have all the basic characteristics of those born on the 8th of the month, so first go through them and then read your own.

He is a good organizer and a good thinker. He has a creative and constructive mind. He is a lover of peace and a philanthropist. He is attracted to occultism and mysticism. He is courageous and proud. He has a strong individuality. He is highly intelligent and clever. He is calm. At times he is generous to a fault and at times very stingy. He is interested in research and loves knowledge. He is conservative and dominating.

Born on 26th October   you have all the basic characteristics of those born on the 8th of the month, so first go through them and then read your own.

He wants to enjoy life without doing anything. He is sluggish and lethargic. He revels in wine and women and is fickle-minded. He is careless about the number of children He is lucky in money matters and gets easy money. He is smar. but lacks positiveness. He likes to put up a good appearance but has a worrying nature. He has problems in his love affairs.

b) FINANCE

In financial matters he is not very lucky unless he inherits property ; if he does, there are are so many demands on it that it melts away fast. He is usually over anxious about his future and if alone in life he likes to hoard money in peculiar places and often it is lost or stolen. He should avoid all forms of speculation or gambling. The peculiarity of number 8 is the delay in life in all respects. Naturally in financial matters also there is delay and stability is achieved at a very late age. This person has to work hard and he rarely succeeds in getting rich.

c) VOCATION

He can be an excellent doctor or scientist or lawyer. A woman born on this date is a deep reader, often a writer on social reforms and becomes interested in far-reaching political questions that affect the masses or throws herself heart and soul into some cause which she believes is for the good of humanity.

This man usually chooses some difficult career in which he encounters great opposition to his views.

He can be successful in industries dealing with coal mines, timber, etc. and in construction companies. He can be a good accountant and also a good administrator. However, as stated earlier, he has to strive hard in his career and can get the fruits of his hard work only in later years.

d) HEALTH

Persons born on the 8th, 17th or 26th of October, bring on many illnesses by mental despondency and by turning over and over in their minds some injustice they have suffered. In many cases they foster the idea that they are martyrs and brood over their wrongs—real or very often imaginary. Their greatest danger is that they give way to melancholia which only makes matters worse for them, both physically and mentally.

Their health, as a rule, is peculiar, they have a slow digestion, constipation, a sluggish liver and severe headaches. If possible they should live an outdoor life, get plenty of exercise, live on simple diet and use fruits and vegetables liberally.

It is very interesting to note that the delaying characteristic applies to their sickness. The ailments they suffer from also take a long time to cure. Varicose veins and haemorrhoids are a common tendency of a strong 8 personality.

e) MARRIAGE AND FRIENDS

He has a natural attraction towards persons born in the period from 20th April to 20th June and 20th August to 20th October. He also has affinity for those who are governed by numbers 5 and 7. It is therefore advisable that he should select his wife from one of these periods or numbers.

A Number 8 husband

A person born on one of the above dates usually prefers loneliness and likes to be left to himself. He does not have much attraction for the opposite sex. Usually he tries to postpone his marriage with the result that if at all he marries it is at a very late age. He also finds it difficult to choose a wife. As he prefers seclusion to gatherings he often makes his married life miserable. He is very orthodox in his views and does not allow his wife to adopt modern ideas in dress at home or in public places. The natural result is disappointment for his wife and she hates her husband. If, however, he wants to be successful in married life, he should prefer a person who is also interested in deep and serious studies and likes to devote herself to philosophy and occult subjects.

A Number 8 wife

She is of a masculine personality. She is capable and systematic. She enjoys family life and likes to make sacrifices for her children and for the ambition of her husband. Her fault is that she lacks feminine warmth, sentiment and delicacy.

Friends

This man's best friends are those who are governed by numbers 3, 4, 5, 7 and 8. He has a natural affinity also towards people born in January, April, July and in his own month i.e. October. He likes those who have originality, activity, and brilliance.

f) FORTUNATE DAYS AND NUMBERS : His lucky days are Wednesdays, Thursdays and Saturdays and lucky numbers are 2, 7 and 8. He should therefore take all important steps on one of these days and also dates if possible. He should try his luck in lottery by purchasing a ticket where the total of all the digits is 2, 7 or 8 or where the last digit is 2, 7 or 8.

g) LUCKY COLOURS : He should use dark grey, dark blue purple and black.

h) LUCKY JEWELS AND STONES : His lucky jewels are Sapphire, Black Pearl and Black Diamond. His lucky stones are Cat's Eye and Amethyst.

i) IMPORTANT YEARS IN LIFE : His important years are 8, 17, 26, 35, 44, 53, 62, 71, etc.

j) HIS GOOD QUALITIES AND DRAWBACKS ARE AS UNDER:

Good qualities	Drawbacks
Authority	Cynicism
	Delay
Practical Approach	Vindictiveness
Steadiness	Nervousness
System	Laziness

CHAPTER 90

BORN ON
9th, 18th and 27th of October

All those born on the 9th, 18th and 27th of October of any year are governed by number 9 and the planet Mars. October is governed by the planet Venus. The character reading relating to number 9 given below is equally applicable to the other dates. In addition, the special characteristics of those born on 18th and 27th of October are given separately.

Born on 9th October

a) CHARACTER

He is too rash and impulsive for his good. He causes opposition and creates many enemies by his love of argument, and a mental desire to fight hard in defence of his ideas, principles and what he considers right. It would be better if he controls his disposition in such matters and develops a more diplomatic way.

Mars shows aggression, resistance, courage, dash and quickness. A Martian is considered as a fighter. He is always aggressive and will not stop till he achieves his end. He has the capacity to fight even against adverse elements and circumtances. A Martian does not know defeat and if we have an army of Martians, there would not be anything like defeat for them. It would be either victory or death. This man is not very tactful or delicate in his talk but his intention is good, and his vigorous manner should not be mistaken for rough behaviour. He should not criticise others and should use his words carefully, otherwise they will boomerang.

When the date of the month is 9 and the total of all the digits in the birth date is also 9, the man is governed by a strong number 9 and his Mars is very powerlul. He has strong sexual passions and is attracted towards the opposite sex. He is prepared to go through any ordeal to gratify his desire. He is a brave person to whom conflict does not bring the thought of danger. He is exceedingly devoted to his friends and will fight for them. He has sympathy and consideration for the weak. He loves children and animals. He takes delight in showing mercy to others. He likes the healing profession. He is backed by self-control, moral courage and the power of forgiveness. His psychological aptiude is remarkable and under all circumstances he proves his strength of will and exhibits courage. He is short-tempered.

Born on 18th October | you have all the basic characteristics of those born on the 9th of the month, so first go through them and then read your own.

This person has tenacity and will-power which will overcome any difficulty. He is not as enterprisng as a number 9 person but is fearless and courageous. His strong health makes him passionate. He inherits property from his father. He has a disciplined mind and likes to help others. He is painstaking with good judgement and is wise. He loves to exercise total control over others. He does not like to be cautioned by others.

Born on 27th October | you have all the basic characteristics of those born on the 9th of the month, so first go through them and then read your own.

On the whole he is a personality of conflicts. He is confident and likes to do sometimes for those whose life is miserable or who are handicapped. He can develop a spiritual personality and can practise spiritual healing. On the other side he is fond of women and may develop illicit contacts and create a scandal. Sometimes he creates unhappiness in his married life. He is very sensitive and moody and his actions and moves are unpredictable. He is self-assured and strong in resolution. He is a seeker of independence and domination. He hates to work under others. Usually he is dogmatic in his thoughts.

b) FINANCE

He is lucky in his monetary affairs and earns more than an average person. He is also very liberal in spending, especially for his sweetheart. He enjoys all the comforts that money can bring.

c) VOCATION

A number 9 person is found in all walks of life but he will be more suitable for the army and professions where there is full scope for his aggression and courage. In the army he will rise to high positions, in politics he will be eminent and in business he will exhibit his dashing and pushing nature. He can be a good doctor, or a chemist or a businessman dealing in iron and steel.

d) HEALTH

His main health defect arises from heat. He is susceptible to troubles such as piles, fevers etc. He is also likely to suffer from kidney trouble or bladder stone. Throat trouble, bronchitis and laryngitis also trouble him often.

e) MARRIAGE AND FRIENDS

He has a natural attraction towards persons born in the period from 20th July to 20th August and 20th November to 20th December. He has affinity also for those who are governed by numbers 3 and 6. It is therefore advisable that he should select his wife from one of these periods or numbers.

A Number 9 husband

He has robust health and strong circulation of blood which makes him very passionate and enthusiastic about married life. He is fond of a beautiful wife and likes her to be submissive and passive to his sexual desires. He is fond of his family and children and likes to have a good house. He usually leads a good married life in spite of his hot-tempered nature and eccentricities. He has a romantic mental picture of what he wants in his wife. This mental picture demands perfection. The most difficult thing in the married life of this person is to satisfy his romantic conception of physical love. He has a voracious appetite and his wife with her devotion can harmonise with him physically. Usually, we find him suspicious of his wife.

A Number 9 wife

She makes a wonderful wife for an ambitious man. She is witty and a clever conversationalist, with a wonderful social presence. She will assist her husband in his business. She may also start her own activity and add to the family income. She will be happy if married to a passionate and possessive man.

Friends

His best friends are those who are governed by numbers 1,2,3,4,6,7 and 9. He has a natural affinity towards people born in January, April, July and in his own month i. e. October. He likes those who have beauty art, decency and energy.

f) FORTUNATE DAYS
AND NUMBERS : His lucky days are Mondays. Tuesdays, and Fridays and lucky numbers are 3,6 and 9. He should therefore take all important steps on one of these days and also dates if possible. He should try his luck in lottery by purchasing a ticket where the total of all the digits is 3, 6 or 9 or where the last digit is 3, 6 or 9.

g) LUCKY COLOURS : He should use white and all shades of red and yellow colours.

h) LUCKY JEWELS AND STONES : His lucky jewels are Topaz, Pearl and Ruby and lucky stones are Blood-stone and Garnet.

i) IMPORTANT YEARS IN LIFE : His important years are 9, 18, 27, 36, 45, 54, 63, 72 etc.

j) HIS GOOD QUALITIES AND DRAWBACKS ARE AS UNDER:

Good qualities	Drawbacks
Activity	Destructiveness
Courage	Erratic nature
Dash	Hot temper
Energy	Impatience
Enthusiasm	Quarrelsomeness

CHAPTER 91

BORN ON

1st, 10th, 19th and 28th of November

All those born on the 1st, 10th, 19th and 28th of November of any year are governed by the number 1 and the Sun. November is governed by the planet Mars. The character reading relating to number 1 given below is equally applicable to the other dates. In addition, the special characteristics of those born on 10th, 19th and 28th November are given separately.

Born on 1st November

a) CHARACTER

This person radiates enormous energy and has great influence over others. He is creative in every sense of the word, forceful and dominant. He has good ideas for the management of others and is often a great success in political life. He is observant and critical, rather aggressive and determined in his plans, yet courteous and helpful to those under him. He has a keen wit and sense of humour but is apt to reduce the most serious questions to ridicule by his love of the sarcastic which can sting like a scorpion's tail. He is sensitive and easily hurt by neglect but never nurses angry thoughts for long. He is very large-hearted and forgiving.

This person is governed by the Sun and shows originality, activity, energy, enthusiasm, art and brilliance A person governed by this number is spontaneous and responds to nature and has the capacity to enjoy life. He is usually successful in life due to his active nature and his capacity to mix in any society. He is an artist and has many talents but they are all spontaneous in nature. He has good taste in everything and always chooses the beautiful. He is giffted with intuition and he rarely goes deep into a subject. Even then he can influence others with his knowledge and flash. These characteristics make him a hero of the drawing room. He is changeable and is not constant in friendship. He is honest and acknowledges his faults. He has a quick grasp of a subjects and can participate spontaneously in conversation. He has a religious attitude but not in a fanatical or super- stitious way. He has a strong will power and is independent in thought and action. On the one hand he is pracitcal, but on the other hand, he is idealistic. Sometimes he is obstinate and selfish. He loves inventions and has creative talents. He is a better judge of human nature than the average individual. He is born to lead, not to follow. A new idea is a but greater thrill to him than money in the bank. New ideas always keep him young.

Born on 10th November

you have all the basic characteristics of those born on the 1st of the month, so first go through them and then read your own.

He is very impressive with a magnetic personality and is respected for his knowledge and intelligence. He gets financial benefits from relatives such as his father, father-in-law, wife, mother etc. He gets success after his 46th year. He gets a good position in service and succeeds in business also. He has broad shoulders and a manly figure. He loves truth- fulness. This number shows honour and self-confidence. The person can get fame or notoriety depending upon his will-power and character. He usually has good health and quickly recovers from sickness. He likes to help others, but they rarely respond. This is more true in the case of relatives.

Born on 19th November

you have all the basic characteristics of those born on the 1st of the month, so first go through them and then read your own.

He is very active, energetic and enthusiastic. He has research aptitude and likes to handle a subject in a systematic way. He takes quick decisions and always likes to keep busy with some concrete project. Sports is his hobby and he is interested in several sports such as horse-riding and shooting, and in athletic games. He is hasty and impetuous in love affairs which end in quarrels. He is courageous and has force of character. He likes to help others by going out of the way. He can keep others' secrets and people can trust him. This number promises success, honour and happiness. It is very difficult for others to understand him. He is always in company but at heart feels lonely. He is obstinate and finds it difficult to extend co-operation. He is prudent and notices even trifles. He is not an excellent speaker but can explain himself best in writing. He can be a good writer.

Born on 28th November

> you have all the basic characteristics of those born on the 1st of the month, so first go through them and then read your own.

At heart he is extremely ambitious. He generally makes a name for himself and gains prominence in any career, but he is seldom as lucky in money matters as the other number one persons. He should select his wife carefully. He has to provide carefully for the future as he is likety to lose through trusting others too much. He is also likely to make many changes in his carear. He seldom reveals his emotions and therefore appears cold. He has an unyielding will power and does not hesitate to carry out his plans.

b) FINANCE

This person is lucky as far as financial status is concerned. Even though he is extravagant because of his overenthusiastic personality, he also earns enough to support his ostentatious disposition in life. He may not amass wealth but his personality and behaviour will make others believe that he is a rich person. He has the temptation to gamble and if not controlled in time, he may lose heavily.

c) VOCATION

He likes large bold enterprises, he can succeed well as a contractor, architect, engineer on big schemes, or builder of daring original designs The main difficulty with this person is his inability to stick to any one profession or job for a long time. Usually, every three years there is a change in his career. He is however suitable for advertising concerns, newspaper business, and the cinema industry and can also be successful in theatrical performances. He can show his art as an interior decorator. Being a good salesman, he can choose a vocation which will have contacts with foreign countries, such as that of a political ambassador, or a trade dealing in foreign commodities. He is a leader and can be the head of a department, a managing director etc. He succeeds equally will as a surgeon, jeweller or electrician and in research projects.

d) HEALTH

He is liable to suffer from trouble of the throat, the lungs and the bronchial tubes. He should never live in cold, damp climates but should get as much of the beneficial rays of the sun as possible. He is also susceptible to trouble of the eyes and the heart. The most common trouble for this person is overexertion and he should always be on his guard not to exert himself too much. Excessive strain is likely to make him susceptible to fevers.

e) MARRIAGE AND FRIENDS

He has a natural attraction towards persons born in the period from 20th July to 20th August, 20th October to 20th December and 20th February to 20th April. He has affinity also for those who are governed by numbers 1,2,4,5 and 7. It is therefore advisable that he should select his wife from one of these periods or numbers.

A Number 1 husband

He has vigour and strength and is very passionate and enthusiastic about married life. He is fond of a beautiful wife and likes her to be submissive to his sexual desires. He is fond of his family and children and likes to have a good house. He usually leads a good married life inspite of his hot temper and eccentricities. He has a romantic mental picture of what he wentsin his wife. This mental picture demands prefection. He desires a clever and very good wife· The most difficult thing for his wife is to satisy his romantic conception of physical love.

A Number 1 wife

She makes a wonderful wife for an ambitious man. She is a witty and clever conversationalist with a wonderful social presence. She will assist her husband in his business. She may also start her own activity and add to the family income. She will be happy if married to a passionate and possessive man. Though she likes her children she is not very much attached to them and likes them to grow on their own. She must always keep herself busy, otherwise her moodiness will disturb her family life. It is advisable that she should have a friend in whom she can confide.

Friends

This man's best friends are those who are governed by numbers 1,3,4,5,7 and 9. He has a natural affinity also towards people born in February, May and August and in his own month i.e. November. He likes those who have dash, courage, activity and enthusiasm.

f) FORTUNATE DAYS AND NUMBERS : His lucky days are Sundays, Mondays and Thursdays and lucky numbers are 1, 4 and 9. He should therefore take all important steps on one of these days and also dates if possible. He should try his luck in lottery by purchasing a ticket where the total of all the digits is 1, 4 or 9 or where the last digit is 1, 4 or 9.

g) LUCKY COLOURS : He should use all shades of gold, yellow, orange and purple as his lucky colours.

h) LUCKY JEWELS AND STONES : His lucky jewels are Ruby and Emerald and lucky stones are Moon-Stone and Pale Green Stone.

i) IMPORTANT YEARS IN LIFE : His important years are 1, 10, 19, 28, 37, 46, 55, 64, 73 etc.

j) HIS GOOD QUALITIES AND DRAWBACKS ARE AS UNDER:

Good qualities	Drawbacks
Strong willpower	Obstinacy
Aspiration	Aloofness
Dynamism	Domination
Authority	Impertinence
Confidence	Inflexibility
Determination	Pride
Research	Showmanship
Vigour	Extravagance
Talents	

CHAPTER 92

BORN ON
2nd, 11th, 2Oth and 29th of November

All those born on 2nd, 11th, 20th of November of any year are governed by the number 2 and the Moon. November is governed by the planet Mars. The character-reading relating to number 2 given below is equally applicable to the other dates. In addition, the special characteristics of those born on 11th. 20th and 29th of November are given separately.

Born on 2nd November

a) CHARACTER

This man should carefully examine his tendencies in order to make the best of his life. He should make every effort to be decisive and self-reliant. One of his marked peculiarities is that he finds it almost impossible in his early years to choose a career. He has plenty of talent for artistic or imaginative work but he is too much inclined to live in a dreamland all his own and not make practical use of his talent. He has to get help from others and consequently has many bitter disappointments and finds life a very hard battlefield for which he is totally unprepared. Women born on these dates suffer more than men. He is so highly emotional and sentimental that he generally marries the wrong person. He is likely te get involved in romance, and pay too high a price for so-called love. His ties of affection rarely last long.

He is somewhat nervous but is social and is liked by others. He is warm-hearted and shows little resistance against oppression. He is very unsteady, fickle-minded and a lover of change. He, therefore, has a fancy for travel, especially long travels which would satisfy his natural urge for imaginary things. Such travels keep his imagination engaged and he will go on building castles in the air. He is unassuming but pleasing and has a good taste in clothes. He likes peace and harmony. He has a hypnotic power.

Born on 11th November

you have all the basic characteristics of those born on the 2nd of the month, so first go through them and then read your own.

This man is usually successful in life and in love and gets honour, position and authority. He is loyal to his friends and is of a royal disposition. He should guard himself from secret enemies. He has interest in mysticims, philosophy and science. He can expect travel, favours and honours in life. He is very impulsive and gets excited easily. He worries too much over small matters. He has the ability to take quick decisions and this makes him a leader. He is a born advisor and inspiration to others.

Born on 20th November

you have all the basic characteristics of those born on the 2nd of the month, so first go through them and then read your own.

He has many friends and benefits through women. He has a flair for writing and can be known as an author or a novelist. His prosperity lies near the water, the river or the sea. This number has a peculiar significance. It shows new resolution for the betterment of people at large.

Born on 29th November

you have all the basic characteristics of those born on the 2nd of the month, so first go through them and then read your own.

This person is moody and changing and, therefore, uncertain in his action. He is courageous but takes risks in life and does not stick up to anything to the end. He is intelligent and also a deep thinker but there is a tendency to carry everything to extremes. He is not very lucky in his married life. His interest is in his business. He is blessed with good fortune. His life is eventful.

31

b) FINANCE

Unless he is extremely prudent and careful this man will have much anxiety over money matters. He may get wealth and property by his own efforts or by marriage, but such good fortune is not likely to last long. He can make money by developing his own talents and not by relying on the promises of others. He can improve his financial condition, provided he is able to create art out of his imagination. He may be a good author or a painter who can create novels and weird paintings, and earn a good livelihood. However his mind often drags him away from routine work and this makes his income uncertain. This person therefore is not stable as far as finance is concerned.

c) VOCATION

The high imaginative power possessed by this person will help him to be a good composer of music or a writer of fiction or romance. He can also be a good artist and can create works of enduring value. Immortal paintings and dramas and great poems are the creation of a prominent and influential number 2 person. He has a large vocabulary and linguistic capacities, and can be successful as a teacher or a professor of languages. He can also be a good translator or an editor.

d) HEALTH

It is better he does not overstrain his nervous system. He is likely to suffer from internal debility and weakness or inflammation of the sex organs. The nose, throat and ears are likely to cause trouble, restlessness at night and insomnia. He is so oversensitive that unhappy surroundings will have a bad effect on his health.

e) MARRIAGE AND FRIENDS

He has a natural attraction towards persons born in the period from 20th October to 20th November and 20th

February to 20th March. He has affinity also for those who are
governed by numbers 2 and 6. It is therefore advisable that
he should select his wife from one of these periods or
numbers.

A Number 2 husband

He has a stronger love and attraction for home than any
other type. He usually leads a good married life. He has a
romantic mental picture of what he wants in his wife. This mental
picture demands perfection. He usually marries for the sake of
money so that he may ultimately get comforts.

A Number 2 wife

She makes a wonderful wife for an ambitious person. She
is a witty and clever conversationalist with a wonderful social
presence. Though she likes her children she is not very much
attached to them and likes them to grow on their own. She
must always keep herself busy, otherwise her moodiness
will disturb her family life. It is advisable that she should
have a friend in whom she can confide.

Friends

This man's best friends are governed by numbers 2, 4, 6
and 9. He also has a natural affinity towards people born in
February, May and August and in his own month i.e
November.

f) FORTUNATE DAYS
    AND NUMBERS : His lucky days are Mondays, Tuesdays
                  and Fridays and his lucky numbers are
                  2, 4 and 9. He should therefore take
                  all important steps on one of these days
                  and also dates if possible. He should
                  try his luck in lottery by purchasing a
                  ticket where the total of all the digits is
                  2, 4 or 9, or where the last digit is 2,
                  4 or 9.

g) **LUCKY COLOURS :** He should use white and all shades of cream or blue as his lucky colours.

h) **LUCKY JEWELS AND STONES :** His lucky jewels are Pearls and Diamonds   and lucky stones are Moonstone and Agate.

i) **IMPORTANT YEARS IN LIFE :** His important years are 2, 11, 20, 29, 38, 47, 56, 65, 74 etc.

j) **HIS GOOD QUALITIES & DRAWBACKS ARE AS UNDER:**

Good qualities	Drawbacks
Emotionality	Coldness
Fellowship	Envy
Honesty	Haste
Imagination	Introvert
Simplicity	Shyness
	Whimsicality

CHAPTER 93

BORN ON
3rd, 12th, 21st and 30th of November

All those born on the 3rd, 12th, 21st and 30th of November of any year are governed by number 3 and the planet Jupiter. November is governed by the planet Mars. The character reading relating to number 3 given below is equally applicable to the other dates. In addition, the special characterstics of those born on 12th, 21st and 30th November are given separately.

Born on 3rd November

a) CHARACTER

He has self confidence. His qualities help him to shoulder responsibilities that fall on him sooner or later. During the early years of his life he has to face many obstacles and difficulties. The loss of a parent and consequent loss of protection and perhaps money may be one of these handicaps. However, the difficulties will be blessings in disguise. They will train him to shoulder responsibility early. If he looks back to his earlier years he will, find that for one reason or another, his little shoulder had to take the burden of looking after others. As life goes on, responsibilities become heavier and he has to become the head of the family. He always has a feeling that he has the ability to do big things and if he gets a chance, he will do them successfully. This is why, he never shirks responsibility when it comes to him.

He is self reliant and takes his own decisions. He has the habit of talking loudly. He is fond of show and likes to

observe form, order and law. He is jovial in spirit and cordial
in manner. His passions are healthy, spontaneous and without inhibitions. He is free in his expression. He is a good
conversationalist. He has tremendous enthusiasm and is
not self-centred. His intellect is of a very high quality. He
has a kind of vision that understands the world and loves
it for what it is and not for what it ought to be. He is a
broad-minded person, tolerant, humorous and truthful. He is
open-hearted with a good understanding and is entirely lacking
in malice or petty jealousies. If he is not alert, people take
undue advantage of his good nature. The main characteristics
of this person are ambition, leadership, religion, pride, honour,
love of nature, enthusiasm, generosity, respect and reverence.

Born on 12th November | you have all the basic characteristics of those born on the 3rd of the month, so first go through them and then read your own.

Authority and honours are the significant aspects
of this person's life. He has vanity and is proud, ambitious
and aspiring. He is fond of pleasure and is attracted to
the opposite sex. However, sometimes he prefers loneliness.
He likes to make sacrifices for others but becomes a victim of
other people's plans or intrigues. His relations with others
are smooth and harmonious. He is quick to notice trifles. He
has lofty ideals.

Born on 21st November | you have all the basic characteristics of those born on the 3rd of the month, so first go through them and then read your own.

He is kind, generous and is a loving father. He
achieves fame and honours at a very late age. He is cheerful
and fond of travel. He has a strong feeling of self-respect
Surprisingly, he has a suspicious nature.

Born on 30th November | you have all the basic characteristics of those born on the 3rd of the month, so first go through them and then read your own.

He is fortunate, generous and optimistic. He has a noble
and religious mind. He likes to travel and visit pleaces of
pilgrimage. He can be successful as a teacher or educationist
or in administration. He appears gentle and sincere, but has
a hidden characteristic. He may be active but is restless. When

faced with difficulties, he is strong enough to overcome them.

b) FINANCE

He is a lucky type and somehow manages to earn enough for his livelihood. He also gets opportunities for higher positions in life and thereby earns quite a lot. His ambition, leadership and enthusiasm always push him forward and usually he gets all comforts in life.

c) VOCATION

His love of position and command makes him occupy high posts such as those of ministers, ambassadors, judges and secretaries. He is gifted for public life, statesmanship, high offices etc, it may be in the army or in the church. He is a good teacher and preacher. Professions such as those of doctors, bankers, advertisers and actors are also suitable for him.

d) HEALTH

Jupiter has the chief influence on the blood and the arterial system. It also governs the sense of smell. This person is liable to suffer from chest and lung disorders, throat afflictions, gout and apoplexy and sudden fevers. He may also suffer from sore throat, diptheria, adenoids, pneumonia, pleurisy and tuberculosis of the lungs.

e) MARRIAGE AND FRIENDS

He has a natural attraction towards persons born in the period from 20 February to 20th March, 20th June to 20th July and 20th October to 20th November. He also has affinity for those who are governed by numbers 3, 6 and 9. It is therefore advisable that he should select his wife from one of these periods or numbers.

A Number 3 husband

His ambitions also make him expect too many things from his wife. He desires to have a wife of whom he can be proud. She should have an attractive personality, a commanding presence, charming manners and intelligence. He has vigour and strength and is quite passionate and enthusiastic about married life. He is fond of his family and children and likes to have a good house. He usually leads a good married life inspite of his hot temper and eccentricities. it is always better for him to choose a number 3 person or a number 6 person as his wife.

A Number 3 wife

She is the best companion to her husband. She is not an intruder but takes an active interest in the business of her husband. She is a clever conversationalist. She has a wonderful social presence. She must always keep herself busy, otherwise her moodiness will disturb her family.

Friends

This man's best friends are those who are governed by numbers 1, 3, 5, 6, 7, 8 and 9. He also has a natural affinity towards people born in February, May and August and in his own month i. e. November. He likes those who have ambition, energy and dash.

f) FORTUNATE DAYS

AND NUMBERS : His lucky days are Tuesdays, Thursdays and Fridays and lucky numbers are 3, 6, and 9.He should therefore take all important steps on one of these days and also dates if possible. He should try his luck in lottery by purchasing a ticket where the total of all the digits is 3, 6 or 9 or where the last digit is 3, 6 or 9.

g) LUCKY COLOURS : He should use all shades of yellow, violet, purple and green as his lucky colours.

h) LUCKY JEWELS AND STONES : His lucky jewels aro Topaz and lucky stones are Amethyst an. Cat's Eye.

i) IMPORTANT YEARS IN LIFE: His important years are 3, 12, 21, 30, 39, 48, 57, 66, 75 etc.

j) HIS GOOD QUALITIES AND DRAWBACKS ARE AS UNDER:

Good qualities	Drawbacks
Ambition	Cruelty
Dignity	Dictatorship
Individuality	Hypocrisy
Philosophy	Extravagance
Prestige	Vanity

CHAPTER 94

BORN ON
4th, 13th and 22nd November

All those born on the 4th, 13th and 22nd of November of any year are governed by the number 4 and the planet Uranus. November is governed by the planet Mars. The character reading relating to number 4 given below is equally applicable to the other dates. In addition, the special characteristics of those born on 13th and 22nd November are given separately.

Born on 4th November

a) CHARACTER

This number is governed by Uranus and shows energy, force and advancement. It shows revolution and unexpected happenings in life. Usually the changes that take place are for the better. This number represents the higher faculties of the mind. It shows activity and intelligence engaged in the reconstruction or the betterment of human life. The peculiar nature of this person is that he constantly aims at changes in life and society and is after the liberation of the mind from bondage to environment and society. He dislikes hypocrisy and loves art and music. He has an attractive personality.

There is a natural and strong affinity between the planets Uranus and Mars, which produces three different results. The person has a spirit of scientific investigation which is an important element of Mars. Secondly the person may experience treachery and the subtle wit of Uranus. Thirdly he may have strong sensuality and passion. It is necessary that the person should exercise absolute self-control. If he concentrates on any task, he can achieve great prominence in life and make good use of his splendid gifts of inventiveness, originality and even his eccentricity. It is better he develops the spiritual side of the mind, otherwise he is likely to become embittered by the way people treat him. His thoughts and actions are likely to be terribly misunderstood. His originality and eccentricities are likely to be ridiculed and great injustice may be done to him.

It is advisable that all those born on 4th, 13th and 22nd of November should endeavour to curb the eccentric side of their disposition, or else they will be in danger. The good qualities of those born under the combination of Uranus and Mars are their devotion to whatever they believe is their duty and their desire for reform, either of the laws of their country or of social life. These persons should aim at producing harmony and love in their surroundings and when they have found peace in themselves, they should develop the finer and more spiritual side of their nature.

Born on 13th November
you have all the basic characteristics of those born on the 4th of the month, so first go through them and then read your own.

He is an intelligent person, of tall stature and good complexion. He is considerate and benevolent. He likes literary and scientific books. He likes to remain active though in a quiet way He occupies positions of high responsibilities and gets wealth. His success and career start after his 31st year. Though outwardly he looks mild, inwardly, he is obstinate. He is faithful and sympathetic but has difficulty in expressing his love. He has all the qualities of a number 4 person but in an exaggerated form.

Bnrn on 22nd November
you have all the basic characteristics of those born on the 4th of the month, so first go through them and then read your own.

He is also tall and has good eyes. Usually he occupies good positions but without much resposibility. He is rather easy-going but unsteady in nature. Sometimes his actions are spasmodic. On the whole he is lucky in his affairs and benefits from the opposite sex. He is happy in his family life but is also fond of a companion. He is faithful and dedicated to others. Sometimes, he feels very lonely. His social field is limited and he has few friends. He does not care for disputes. He has too much economy of sentiments.

b) FINANCE

He should be cautious and prudent in money matters and depend as little as possible on the help or promises of others. He can succeed by his own unconventional and original ideas. He may not amass wealth but can maintain the show of wealth. He is a spendthrift. His home is well decorated. His financial prosperity usually starts after the age of 40.

c) VOCATION

He can succeed in inventions of an advanced type or can get success in the electrical and electronic fields. He will be equally successful as an engineer, a building contractor, scientist and an industrialist. He is also attracted towards mystic subjects.

d) HEALTH

His respiratory system is usually weak and he suffers from breathlessness. His kness, shanks and feet are also affected. Sometimes he suffers from urinary infection.

His health has a close relation to his outlook on life. He should try to keep a bright outlook and to fit into the surroundings. Mental worry is likely to affect his nervous system which may affect blood circulation.

e) MARRIAGE AND FRIENDS

He has a natural attraction towards persons born in the period from 20th February to 20th March and 20th October to 20th November. He has also affinity for those who are governed by the numbers 1, 2, 7 and 8. It is therefore advisable that he should select his wife from one of these periods or numbers.

A Number 4 husband

He has vigour and strength and is very passionate and enthusiastic about married life. He is fond of a beautiful wife and likes her to be submissive and passive to his sexual desires. He is fond of his family and children, and likes to have a good house. He usually leads a good married life in spite of his hot temper and eccentricities. He has a romantic mental picture of what he wants in his wife. This mental picture demands perfection. He desires a clever and very good wife. The most difficult thing for his wife is to satisfy his romantic conception of physical love.

A Number 4 wife

She is smart and attractive. She has the art of dressing and has a strong will-power. She aims at several things but hardly succeeds in getting mastery over one. She loves interior decoration but does not have the capacity to work hard and she will get it done through others. She is often dictatorial and moody and spoils her day due to her own whimsical nature. She loves her home but is not attached to it very much. She is often uneasy. It is better for her to find a friend governed by number one or two.

She will assist her husband in his business. She may start her own activity and add to the family income. She will be happy if married to a passionate and possessive man. She must always keep herself busy, otherwise her moodiness will disturb her family life.

Friends

This man's best friends are those who are governed by numbers 1, 2, 4, 5, 7, 8 and 9. He has a natural affinity also towards people born in February, May and August and in his own month i. e. November. He likes those who have dash, courage, enthusiasm and oratory.

f) FORTUNATE DAYS AND NUMBERS : His lucky days are Sundays, Mondays and Saturdays and lucky numbers are 1, 4 and 5. He should therefore take all important steps on one of these days and also dates if possible. He should try his luck in lottery by purchasing a ticket where the total of all the digits is 1, 4 or 5, or where the last digit is 1, 4 or 5.

g) LUCKY COLOURS : He should use electric blue, electric grey, white and maroon.

h) LUCKY JEWELS AND STONES : His lucky jewels are Diamond, Coral and Pearl.

i) IMPORTANT YEARS IN LIFE : His important years are 4, 13, 22, 31, 40, 49, 58, 67, 76 etc.

j) HIS GOOD QUALITIES AND DRAWBACKS ARE AS UNDER:

Good qualities	Drawbacks
Activity	Changeablity
Endurance	Domination
Energy	Stubborness
Reliability	Vindictiveness
Method and system	Jealous

CHAPTER 95

BORN ON
5th, 14th and 23rd of November

All those born on the 5th, 14th and 23rd of November of any year are governed by number 5 and the planet Mercury. November is governed by the planet Mars. The character reading relating to number 5 given below is applicable to the other dates also. In addition, the special characteristics of those born on 14th and 23rd November are given separately.

Born on 5th November
a) CHARACTER

The person is quick-witted, with considerable mental ability, great capacity for organisation and good judgement regarding his fellow beings. He is keen, shrewd and inclined to be suspicious of others. He is likely to make money by unusual methods or by a profession or career out of the ordinary run. He has a deep love of art and beauty and is highly gifted for imaginative work. He is very much attracted to the opposite sex and has many love affairs but is changeable and inconsistent in his affections. He is restless, likes to travel as much as possible and has many changes of residence. The domination of Mercury shows shrewdness, quickness, scientific pursuits, business ability, industry, intutition and diplomacy. The person loves oratory and eloquence in expressing himself. He has the capacity to pursue his objectives and knows very well how to plan to achieve his ends. His pleasures are mainly mental. He evaluates everything in terms of business.

Born on 14th November you have all the basic characteristics of those born on the 5th of the month, so first go through them and then read your own.

This person has an attractive personality. His nature is co-operative. He does not like to provoke others. He usually occupies good positions in life and is successful in business. He is not talkative but slightly reserved. This is an intelligent and shrewd number. In women, it indicates good marriage but they should be careful in child bearing. A number 14 man is inconsistent in love and experiences some romantic and impulsive attachment in early years. He is fortunate in money matters. He is industrious and positive in speech and action. Usually he is fond of gambling and of solving riddles.

Born on 23rd November you have all the basic characteristics of those born on the 5th of the month, so first go through them and then read your own.

He is usually popular with women. He is successful in life and enjoys honour and wealth. He may get money through inheritance. He keeps himself busy in his own way. He gets help and protection from superiors. He is a lucky person. He is affecionate and loves freedom. He is averse to formalities. He has a spirit of independence and a desire to dominate.

b) FINANCE

Since he has business ability, he can expect opulence. With his shrewdness he is capable of developing his industry, carrying out his plans systematically with the result that he gets good returns for his efforts. He is lucky in his financial position.

c) VOCATION

He is adaptable to the role he has to play in the drama of life. With his adaptability he comes in contact with various classes of people and is successful in any business. Banking is a good line for him. Mercury also shows an aptitude for medicine or surgery. His capacity to argue his points can make him a good lawyer.

d) HEALTH

His basic health defect is biliousness and nervousness. However, his biliousness has close relation with psychological disturbance. Experience shows that his biliousness increases with the increase in tension and is reduced or disappears when his nervous trouble is under control. Mercury rules over the nerves, the neck, the arms, the ears and the respiratory system.

e) MARRIAGE AND FRIENDS :

He has a natural attraction towards persons born in the period from 20th September to 20th November, and 20th January to 20th March. He has affinity also for those who are governed by numbers 1, 7 and 8. It is therefore advisable that he should select his wife from one of these periods or numbers.

A Number 5 husband

He is lucky and successful in his married life. His selection is good and usually he selects a person of his own type. He loves his partner. He expects neatness and cleanliness from her and also desires that she should share his enjoyment of life. He is proud of his wife and likes to see her-well dressed. He proves to be a good husband. He loves his children and is fond of his home. Even if he travels long, he is eager to return early and be with his family. He is liberal in spending on clothes and other wants of the members of his family and furnishes his house with good taste.

A Number 5 wife

She has interest at home as well as outside. She has many activities and manages them well. She likes tidiness though she seldom does her own work, she gets it done through her commanding personality.

32

Friends

This man's best friends are those who are governed by
numbers 1,3,4,5,7 and 8. He has a natural affinity towards
people born in February, May and August and in his own
month i.e. November. He likes those who have intelligence,
shrewdness and dash.

**f) FORTUNATE DAYS
   AND NUMBERS :** His lucky days are Wednesdays,
Fridays and Saturdays and lucky
numbers are 1, 3 and 5. He should
therefore take all important steps on
one of these days and also dates if
possible. He should try his luck in
lottery by purchasing a ticket where
the total of all the digits is 1, 3
or 5, or where the last digit is 1, 3
or 5.

g) LUCKY COLOURS : He should use white and shades of
green.

h) LUCKY JEWELS AND STONES : His lucky jewels are
Emerald and Diamond.
He may use Sapphire
also.

i) IMPORTANT YEARS IN LIFE : His important years are 5,
14, 23, 32, 41, 50, 59, 68,
77 etc.

j) HIS GOOD QUALITIES AND DRAWBACKS ARE AS UNDER:

Good qualities	Drawbacks
Co-operation	Lack of perseverance
Practical approach	Scepticism
Shrewdness	Unreliability
Vigilance	

November 6-15-23

j) HIS GOOD QUALITIES AND DRAWBACKS ARE AS UNDER

Good qualities   Drawbacks
Co-operation   Lack of perseverance
Practical approach   Scepticism
Shrewdness   Unreliability
Vigilance

CHAPTER 96

BORN ON
6th, 15th and 24th of November

All those born on the 6th, 15th and 24th of November of
any year are governed by the number 6 and the planet Venus.
November is governed by the planet Mars. The character reading
relating to number 6 given below is equally applicable
to the other dates. In addition, the special characteristics of
those born on 15th and 24th November are given separately.

Born on 6th November

a) CHARACTER

He has an extremely loveable nature, most self-sacrificing
for the sake of relatives or parents. He has always some one
.to support or care for. He may meet with many difficulties
and hardships in his early years such as the death of a parent,
which throw responsibilities on his shoulders. Even if he is
born in a rich family, he will find life difficult as he is likely to
spend lavishly on his hobby and to follow the wishes of others.
He has a magnetic attraction for the opposite sex but as a rule
does not make a good choice. Terrible tragedies caused by
love often come into his life. His talents are suited to an
artist's life. He will do well in music and in painting. He is
often forced into positions of great responsibilities and comes
into the lime-light of publicity.

He is a pleasant personality to meet. He prefers spending
to saving. He will have rich clothes, jewellery, perfumes and
all sorts of beautiful things. His company is full of energy
and charm. His talk is interesting and lively. We may some-

times have to put aside our ideas of morality and social conduct to understand and appreciate his feelings and views. He prefers joy to gloom and has the capacity to take others along with him to share his pleasant hours. His outlook is bright and vivacious. He is emotional but keeps his emotions to himself. His anger does not easily subside. He is responsible and loves his children, but receives very little happiness from them.

Born on 15th November

you have all the basic characteristics of those born on the 6th of the month, so first go through them and then read your own.

This person is intelligent and has a good memory. He is fit for responsible positions such as those of ambassadors, consuls, governors etc. He is very ambitious and boastful but hasty and proud by nature. He is interested in the lower type of occultism. He has interest in art and music. He appears to be gentle but has very strong convictions. He has a habit of worrying inwardly and leads a melancholy life. His destiny is such that he has to make sacrifices for others.

Born on 24th November

you have all the basic characteristics of those born on the 6th of the month, so first go through them and then read your own.

This man is fortunate in getting assistance from people of high rank. He benefits through the opposite sex. He marries a rich girl and prospers. He succeeds in speculation and enjoys a good monetary status. He strictly defines the line between personal and social matters. He is methodical in his ideas. He possesses a strong ego and sometimes tries to force his opinions on others.

b) FINANCE

He is not attracted to money. All his interest is in attaining pleasures and gratifying his desires He therefore, spends his earnings on whatever attracts him. He is usually fortunate in money matters if he follows his intuition. He can make money and also keep it, in spite of having expensive tastes especially as regards clothes and keeping up a good appearance.

c) VOCATION

He will shine as an interior decorator, architect, jeweller, musician, hotel manager or confectioner. He can be equally successful as a broker, an estate broker or a commission agent.

d) HEALTH

On the whole he is a healthy person. However, he is also likely to suffer from inflammation of the lungs, throat, nasal passage and the ear.

e) MARRIAGE AND FRIENDS

He has a natural attraction towards persons born in the period from 20th August to 20th September and 20th December to 20th January. He has also an affinity for those who are governed by numbers 2, 3 ,4, 6 and 9. It is, therefore, advisable that he should select his wife from one of these periods or numbers.

A **Number 6 husband**

He likes marriage and usually marries early in life. He expects his partner to be neat and have charm and grace. His is usually a large family with many children. He loves his children and home. He is very kind, generous and devoted. Though he creates a lively atmosphere at home, he somehow finds it difficult to fulfil all the necessities of the members of his family. This may sometimes create unhappiness and make him unhappy in his married life. Art is everything to him and he remains impractical in not understanding the material values of a successful life.

A **Number 6 wife**

She never resorts to divorce and endures extreme hardship rather than desert her husband. She is a devoted mother and a loving wife, satisfied with her husband's efforts in her behalf. She loves domestic life and makes a perfect house.

Friends

His best friends are those who are governed by numbers 2, 3, 4, 6 and 9. He has a natural affinity also towards people born in February, May and August and in his own month i. e. November. He likes those who have grace, beauty and attraction.

f) FORTUNATE DAYS
AND NUMBERS : His lucky days are Mondays, Tuesdays, Thursdays and Fridays and lucky number are 2,4 and 6. He should therefore take all important steps on one of these days and also dates if possible. He should try his luck in lottery by purchasing a ticket where the total of all the digits is 2, 4 or 6, or where the last digit is 2,4 or 6.

g) LUCKY COLOURS : He should use all shades of blue, rose and pink.

h) LUCKY JEWELS & STONES: His lucky jewels are Turquoise, Emerald, Pearl and Diamond.

i) IMPORNANT YEARS IN LIFE : His important years are 6, 15, 24, 33, 42, 51, 60, 69, 78 etc.

j) HIS GOOD QUALITIES AND DRAWBACKS ARE AS UNDER:

Good Qualities	Drawbacks
Harmony	Absence of foresight
Love	Interference
Peace	Moodiness
Strong memory	Timidity

CHAPTER 97

BORN ON

7th, 16th, and 25th of November

All those born on the 7th, 16th and 25th of November of any year are governed by number 7 and the planet Neptune. November is governed by the planet Mars. The characteristics relating to number 7 given below are equally applicable to the other dates. In addition, the special characteristics of those born on 16th and 25th November are given separately.

Born on 7th November

a) CHARACTER

Neptune governs the mental qualities more than the physical qualities. It rules the hidden parts of the mind such as the sub-conscious, producing weird dreams, visions, hallucinations and the higher inventive abilities. This man is over-sensitive to people and surroundings. He is inclined to be too introspective for his own good and finds it difficult to mix with other people. He has deep love for chemistry and advanced science. He is good at scientific research; as a psychologist he can study the inner workings of the human mind. He can rise to great prominence by following his own ideas. He has unusual persistence in any thing he undertakes. He is also exteremly secretive and reserved. The combination of Neptune and Mars also inclines him to the study of occultism, mysticism, hypnotism, and such fields, but it is always the mental that attracts him more than the material. He is much misunderstood; although oversensitive to the actions of others. he is more or less indifferent to their opinions.

He has individuality and is original and independent. He is restless by nature and is fond of change. He likes to visit foreign countries and becomes interested in far off lands. He has peculiar ideas about religion and dislikes following the beaten track.

He thinks out logically and achieves great aims. He is stubborn and disregards the opinions of others.. He has good talent for earning money. In general, he is somewhat indifferent to materialistic desires. He desires the best or none at all. He is sensitive and hides his real feelings by apparent indifference. He dislikes mingling with common people. He prefers to spend his hour with his favourite book. When his opinion is solicited he speaks with authority. He knows his ground.

Born on 16th November | you have all the basic characteristics of those born on the 7th of the month, so first go through them and then read your own.

He is rather easy-going and does not like to work hard. He is good-humoured and generous. He is very sensitive and emotional. He soon gets upset but is soon pleased. He is frequently indisposed. He is fortunate in getting good and successful children. However, there is some sort of sorrow in his married life. He appears to be calm but his mind is always in turmoil and he is sometimes short-tempered. He will not disclose his nervousness and is slow in taking decisions. He does not like interference.

Born on 25th November | you have all the basic characteristics of those born on the 7th of the month, so first go through them and then read your own.

He is a jack of all trades but master of none. He is interested in several subjects but does not have the capacity to go into details. His knowledge therefore is very shallow. He likes to travel and has contact with foreign countries. He is honest, faithful and good-natured. But he is fickle-minded and inconsistent. His memory is good. He is a good orator and a good teacher.

b) FINANCE

Usually, there are many changes in the life of this person.

So it is difficult for him to amass wealth. However, his being a mystic number, the person can be well placed in life provided he finds a job of his choice. In that case he can be a wealthy person with all amenities and comforts. He may receive financial benefits through his discoveries in science or inventions or through his intuitive understanding of what should be done at any moment.

c) VOCATION

His love of sea travel and interest in foreign countries make him a successful merchant, exporter or importer. He can also deal in dairy products, fishery, and products such as soap etc, or run a chemical industry. He can also study medicine and surgery.

d) HEALTH

He is not likely to be physically very strong. He is likely to overtax the mental side of his nature, but at the same time he is likely to develop some philosophy with regard to his diet. He is also likely to suffer from faulty blood circulation, stomach disorder and fever.

e) MARRIAGE AND FRIENDS

He has a natural attraction towards persons born in the period from 20th October to 20th November and 20th February to 20th March. He has affinity for those who are governed by numbers, 3, 5 and 8. It is, therefore, advisable that he should select his wife from one of these periods or numbers.

A Number 7 husband

He is very emotional and understands the feelings of his wife. He is very considerate and will never try to impose his ideas on her. He is liberal and fond of picnics, travel and the cinema theatres. He is a spendthrift. His family is moderate in size and has all comforts in life.

A Number 7 wife

She is very moody and her behaviour is unpredictable. She is very uneasy and gets disturbed over small matters. She is good at entertaining friends and likes to invite people to a party or dinner. She expects her husband to look after her all the time.

Friends

This man's best friends are those who are governed by numbers 1, 3,4, 5, 7, 8 and 9. He has a natural affinity also towards people born in February, May and August and in his own month i. e. November. He likes those who have good imagination, perseverence and inventive abiliiy.

f) FORTUNATE DAYS
   AND NUMBERS : His lucky days are Sundays, Mondays, Wednesdays and Thursdays and his lucky numbers are 5, 7 and 9. He should therefore take all important steps on one of these days and also dates if possible. He should try his luck in lottery by purchasing a ticket where the total of all the digits is 5, 7 or 9 or where the last digit is 5, 7 or 9.

g) LUCKY COLOURS : He should use all shades of green and yellow.

h) LUCKY JEWELS AND STONES : His lucky jewels are Topaz and Emorald and lucky stones are Moon Stone and Cat's Eye.

i) IMPORTANT YEARS IN LIFE : His important years are 7, 16, 25, 34, 43, 52, 61, 70, 79, etc.

j) HIS GOOD QUALITIES AND DRAWBACKS ARE AS UNDER:

Good qualities	Drawbacks
Austerity	Despondency
Reflection	Diffidence
Serenity	Restlessness
Tolerance	Whimsicality

CHAPTER 98

BORN ON
8th, 17th and 26th of November

All those born on the 8th, 17th and 26th of November of any year are governed by the number 8 and the planet Saturn. November is governed by the planet Mars. The character-reading relating to number 8 given below is equally applicable to the other dates. In addition, the special characteristics of those born on 17th and 26th November are given separately.

Born on 8th November

a) CHARACTER

He may expect to have a very steep hill to climb during his early years. He is self-willed and difficult to get on with. He is obstinate in his views whether right or wrong. He tends to look at only one side of a question and is suspicious of other people's actions even when they are for his good. He usually feels that others are against him and if he does not overcome this feeling, he is likely to suffer. He may bring great sorrow into his life through unfavourable love affairs and secret alliances. He is egoistical in such matters and finds it difficult to accept advice. In spite of all this, he is extremely clever. His persistence can be put to good use in striving for his object. His temperament, if under proper control, can be the lever to remove all obstacles from his path and win over people. Usually the first 40 years are the hardest for him.

The peculiarity of number 8 is delay in all respects. Whatever may be the career of the person, his work will never be done in time. In spite of his efforts to go through life smoothly, he will always experience difficulties and obstacles. This is mainly due to the influence of Saturn which governs number 8 and its series. Both the planets i. e. Saturn and Mars, have powerful characteristics which are practically opposed to each other. Mars is optimistic whereas Saturn is pessimistic. Mars indicates activity whereas Saturn indicates steadfastness. In short the person has a controversial personality.

If we take into consideration the prominence of Saturn, he shows extreme sense of discipline, steadfastness, constancy and dutifulness. The person has a sober and solitary personality. He is a lover of classical music but mostly of the melancholy type. In art he loves landscapes, natural scenery and flowers. Number 8 is considered to be a balance wheel to the character. This man has a tendency to look at the other side of the coin. He is a pessimist. He prefers solitude to company. He shuns society rather than courts it. He is cautious about his future and he takes decisions very carefully on matters which pertain to mundane affairs. He is a prudent person, wise and sober amongst all the numbers. He is also ambitious and persevering. He is capable of enormous efforts for the attainment of his objects. He is sceptical and analytical. He is creative, productive and dominating. He is likely to be misunderstood. He usually feels lonely. He understands the weak and the oppressed and treats them in a warm-hearted manner. He is a born manager who can keep others busy. He admires fair play and is willing to pay a fair compensation. He has a good memory for names and faces.

Born on 17th November | you have all the basic characteristics of those born on the 8th of the month, so first go through them and then read your own.

He is a good organizer and a good thinker. He has a creative and constructive mind He is a lover of peace and a philanthropist. He is attracted to occultism and mysticism. He is courageous and proud. He has a strong individuality. He is highly intelligent and clever. As regards emotions, he is calm. At times he is generous to a fault and at times very stingy. He is interested in research and loves knowledge. He is conservative and dominating.

Born on 26th November | you have all the basic characteristics of those born on the 8th of the month, so first go through them and then read your own.

He wants to enjoy life without doing anything. He is sluggish and lethargic. He revels in wine and women and is fickle-minded. He is careless about the number of children. He is lucky in money matters and gets easy money. He is smart but lacks positiveness. He likes to put up a good appearance but has a worrying nature. He has problems in his love affairs.

b) FINANCE

It will be great success or failure, there is no middle path for this man. It is one extreme or the other. The peculiarity of this person is the delay in life in all respects. Naturally in financial matters also there is delay and stability is achieved at a very late age. This person has to work hard and he seldom becomes opulent. He has therefore to avoid number 8 playing a part in his life and instead he can choose number 1 or 3 for all important actions. However, if experience shows that 8 is a lucky number for him, he can insist on that number only in which case wealth and prosperity come to him. If 8 is found to be a lucky number in one's life, one can try lottery and luck in horse racing. But usually this number is connected with delays and hard work and a person has to be very cautious in financial matters.

c) VOCATION

Subjects suitable for him are occult sciences, chemistry, physics, medicine and higher mathematics. He can be successful in industries dealing with coal mines, timber, etc. and in construction companies. He can be a good accountant and also a good administrator. However,as stated earlier, he has to strive hard for his career and can get the fruits of his hard work only in the later years of his life.

d) HEALTH

He is either extremely robust or the reverse. He is liable to suffer from carbuncles, boils and severe abscesses. He should avoid the use of drugs or stimulating liquors which in his case would undermine the brain. At times he is under severe stress or excitement which will unbalance his mind. His main health problems are nervousness, irritation, trouble with legs, teeth, ears, paralysis and rheumatism. The ailments he suffers from also take a long time to cure. Varicose veins and haemorrhoids also often afflict him.

e) MARRIAGE AND FRIENDS

He has a natural attraction towards persons born in the period from 20th April to 20th May and 20th August to 20th November. He also has affinity for those who are governed by numbers 5 and 7. It is therefore advisable that he should select his wife from one of these periods or numbers.

A Number 8 husband

Usually he tries to postpone his marriage with the result that if at all he marries, it is at a very late age. He also finds it difficult to choose his wife. As he prefers seclusion to gathering, he often makes his married life miserable. He is very orthodox in his views and does not allow his wife to adopt modern ideas in dress at home or in public places. The natural result is disappointment on the part of his wife and hatred for her husband. If however he has a desire to be successful in married life, he should prefer a person who is also interested in deep and sreious studies and likes to devote herself to philosophy and occult subjects.

A Number 8 wife

She would make a wonderful wife for an ambitious man. She is a witty and clever conversationalist with a wonderful social presence. She will assist her husband in his business. She may also start her own activity and add to the family income. She will be happy if married to a passionate and possessive man. Though she likes her children she is not very much attached to them but likes them to develop on their own. She must always keep herself busy, otherwise her moodiness will disturb her family life. It is advisable that she should have a friend in whom she can confide.

Friends

His best friends are those who are governed by numbers 3, 4, 5, 7 and 8. He has a natural affinity also towards people born in February, May, August and in his own month i. e. November. He likes those who have thoughtfulness and a sense of duty.

f) FORTUNATE DAYS
    AND NUMBERS : His lucky days are Wednesdays, Thursdays and Saturdays and lucky numbers are 3, 4 and 8. He should therefore take all important steps on one of these days and also dates if possible. He should try his luck in lottery by purchasing a ticket where the total of all the digits is 3, 4 or 8 or where the last digit is 3, 4 or 8.

g) LUCKY COLOURS : He should use dark grey, dark blue, purple and black.

h) LUCKY JEWELS AND STONES : His lucky jewels are Sapphire, Black Pearl and Black Diamond. His lucky stones are Cat's Eye and Amethyst.

33

l) IMPORTANT YEARS IN LIFE : His important years are 8, 17, 26, 35, 44, 53, 62, 71, etc.

j) HIS GOOD QUALITIES AND DRAWBACKS ARE AS UNDER:

Good qualities	Drawbacks
Authority	Cynicism
Methoditcal approach	Delay
Practicality	Vindictiveness
Steadiness	Nervousness
	Laziness

CHAPTER 99

BORN ON
9th, 18th and 27th of November

All those born on the 9th, 18th and 27th of November of any year are governed by number 9 and the planet Mars. November is also governed by Mars. The character reading relating to number 9 given below is equally applicable to the other dates. In addition, the special characteristics of those born on 18th and 27th of November are given separately.

Born on 9th November

a) CHARACTER

This number is governed by Mars and shows aggression, resistance, courage, dash and quickness. A Martian is considered as a fighter. He is always aggressive and will not stop till he achieves his end. He has the capacity to fight even against adverse elements and circumtances. A Martian does not know defeat and if we have an army of Martians, there would not be anything like defeat for them. It would be either victory or death. It is said that the great Emperor Napoleon Bonaparte was a believer in this science and he had a battalion of soldiers who were pure Martians. This person is not very tactful or delicate in his talk but his intention is good, and his vigorous manner should not be mistaken for rough behaviour. He should use his words carefully, otherwise they will boomerang.

516

Dial Your Birth Number

This man is fiery and dashing and does not have sickly sentiments. He has audacity and vigour from start to finish. He also loves games and vigorous exercise. When the date of the month is 9 and the total of all the digits in the date of birth is also 9, he is governed by a strong number 9 and his Mars is very powerful. In such a case, he has strong sexual passions and he is attracted towards tha opposite sex. He is prepared to go through any ordeal to gratify his desire.

He is a brave person to whom conflict does not bring the thought of danger. He is exceedingly devoted to his friends and will fight for them. He has sympathy and consideration for the weak. He loves children and animals. He takes delight in showing mercy to others. He likes the healing profession. He is backed by self-control, moral courage and the power of forgiveness. His psychological aptitude is remarkable and under all circumstances he proves his strength of will and exhibits courage. He is short-tempered.

Born on 18th November
you have all the basic characteristics of those born on the 9th of the month, so first go through them and then read your own.

This person has tenacity and will-power which will overcome any difficulty. •He is not as dashing as a number 9 person but he is fearless and courageous. His good health makes him passionate. He inherits property from his father. He has a disciplined mind and likes to help others. He is painstaking with good judgement and is wise. He loves to exercise total control over others. He does not like to be cautioned by others.

Born on 27th November
you have all the basic characteristics of those born on the 9th of the month, so first go through them and then read your own.

On the whole he is a conflicting personality. He is confident and likes to do something for those whose life is miserable or who are handicapped. He can develop a spiritual personality and can practise spiritual healing. On the other side he is fond of women and may develop illicit contacts and cause a scandal. Sometimes he creates unhappiness in his married life. He is very sensitive and moody and his actions and moves are unpredictable. He is self-assured and strong in resolution. He is a seeker of independence and loves to dominate. He hates to work under others. Usually he is dogmatic in his thoughts.

b) FINANCE

He is lucky in his monetary affairs and earns more than an average person. He is also very liberal in spending, especially for his sweetheart. He enjoys all the comforts that money can bring.

c) VOCATION

He is found in all walks of life but he will be more suitable for the army and professions where there is full scope for his aggression and courage. In the army he will rise to high positions, in politics he will be eminent and in business he will exhibit his dashing and pushing nature. He can be a good doctor, or a chemist or a businessman dealing in iron and steel.

d) HEALTH

His main health defect arises from heat. He is susceptible to troubles such as piles, fevers, small pox etc. He is also likely to suffer from trouble of the kidney or bladder stone. Throat trouble, bronchitis and laryngitis also often trouble him.

e) MARRIAGE AND FRIENDS

He has a natural attraction towards persons born in the period from 20th July to 20th August and 20th November to 20th December. He has an affinity also for those who are governed by numbers 3 and 6. He should select his wife from one of these numbers or periods.

A Number 9 husband

He has robust health and strong circulation of blood which makes him very passionate and enthusiastic about

. married life. He is fond of a beautiful wife and likes her to be submissive and passive to his sexual desires. He is fond of his family and children and likes to have a good house. He usually leads a good married life in spite of his hot temper and eccentricities. He has a romantic mental picture of what he wants in his wife. This mental picture demands perfection. The most difficult thing in the married life of this person is to satisfy his romantic conception of physical love. He has a voracious appetite and his wife with her devotion can harmonise with him physically. Usually, we find him suspicious of his wife.

A Number 9 wife

She will make a wonderful wife for an ambitious man. She is witty and a clever conversationalist, with a wonderful social presence. She will assist her husband in his business. She may also start her own activity and add to the family income. She will be happy if married to a passionate and possessive man.

Friends

His best friends are those who are governed by numbers 1,2,3,4,6,7 and 9. He also has a natural affinity towards people born in February, May and August and in his own month i. e. November.

f) FORTUNATE DAYS
AND NUMBERS : His lucky days are Mondays, Tuesdays, Thursday and Fridays and his lucky numbers are 3,6 and 9. He should therefore take all important steps on one of these days and also dates if possible. He should try his luck in lottery by purchasing a ticket where the total of all the digits is 3, 6 or 9 or where the last digit is 3, 6 or 9.

g) LUCKY COLOURS : He should use white and all shades of red and yellow colours.

h) LUCKY JEWELS AND STONES : His lucky jewels are Topaz, Pearl and Ruby and lucky stones are Blood-stone and Garnet.

i) IMPORTANT YEARS IN LIFE : His important years are 9, 18, 27, 36, 45, 54, 63, 72 etc.

j) HIS GOOD QUALITIES AND DRAWBACKS ARE AS UNDER:

Good qualities	Drawbacks
Activity	Destructive nature
Courage	Erratic nature
Dash	Hot temper
Energy	Impatience
Enthusiasm	Quarrelsomeness

CHAPTER 100

BORN ON

1st, 1Oth, 19th and 28th of December

All those born on the 1st, 10th, 19th and 28th of December of any year are governed by the number 1 and the Sun. December is governed by the planet Jupiter. The character reading relating to number 1 given below is equally applicable to the other dates. In addition, the special characteristics of those born on 10th, 19th and 28th December are given separately.

Born on 1st December

a) CHARACTER

Persons born on the above dates are classed as "Number One" people. They are endowed with sunny, happy, hopeful dispositions; no difficulties seem to dampen their ardour, they are optimists in the highest sense of the word. They are generous even in their thoughts about others, allthough out-spoken and frank in their expression. They are extremely enterprising and courageous. If thwarted in one direction they will try another and again another, until they finally succeed. They give willingly of whatever they have and are inclined to impoverish themselves in their desire to help those less fortunate. At the same time they are rarely deceived, they seem to know intuitively the people who want to cheat them, never show malice and are likely to stretch out a helping hand even to persons who have tried to trick them. They have enormous energy for any work they are engaged in and do not spare themselves in any way. They dislike being under a master and for that very reason they are generally on their own. They have great ambition, but keep it well under control. They

never ask for the impossible. They are extremely honourable
and make no debts they cannot pay. At heart they have a
deep respect for law and order and in any community of which
they are a part they may be relied on to assist constituted
authority in the discharge of its duty. They love outdoor sports
and generally excel in such things. They have deep respect for
science, philosophy and religion, often making excellent preachers or ministers but free from cant and hypocrisy. They love to
listen to good speakers have a great desire to express their
thoughts, but as they are extremely sensitive they can be
eloquent only when they feel they have a message to deliver.
But anything they do or say goes direct, like an arrow to its
They are spontaneous, respond to nature and have the
capacity to enjoy life. They are usually successful in life due
to their active nature and capacity to mix in any society. They
have a quick grasp of any subject and can participate spontaneously in conversation. They have a religious attitude but
not in a fanatic or superstitious way. They also learn occult
sciences and do wonders with their gift of intuition. By nature,
they are cheerful, happy and bright and their outlook on life is
very optimistic. They love inventions and have creative talents.
They are born to lead, not to follow. A new idea is a greater
thrill to them than money in the bank. They will always be
young by reason of fresh ideas.

Born on 10th December you have all the basic characteristics of those born on the 1st of the month, so first go through them and then read your own.

He is very impressive with a magnetic personality
and is respected for his knowledge and intelligence. He gets
financial benefits from relatives such as his father, father-in-law,
wife, mother etc. He gets success after his 46th year. He
gets a good position in service and succeeds in business also.
He has broad shoulders and a manly figure. He loves truthfulness. This date shows honour and self-confidence. The
person gets fame or notoriety depending upon his will-power
and character. He usually has good health and quickly
recovers from sickness. He likes to help others, but they
rarely respond. This is particulary true in the case of relatives.

Born on 19th December you have all the basic characteristics of those born on the 1st of the month, so first go through them and then read your own.

He is very active, energetic and enthusiastic. He has research aptitude and likes to handle a subject in a systematic way. He takes quick decisions and always likes to keep himself busy with some concrete project. Sports is his hobby; he is interested in several sports such as horse-riding, and shooting and other athletic games. He is hasty and impetuous in love affairs which end in quarrels. He is coura-geous and has force of character. He likes to help others even by going out of the way. He can maintain the secrets of others and others can confide in him. This number promises success, honour and happiness. It is very difficult for others to under-stand him. He is always in company but at heart feels lonely. He is obstinate and finds it difficult to extend co-operation. He is prudent and notices even a trivial thing. He is not an excellent speaker but can explain himself best in writing. He can be a good writer.

Born on 28th December you have all the basic characteristics of those born on the 1st of the month, so first go through them and then read your own.

He is very generous and spends on charitable institutions such as schools and hospitals. He is not as lucky as those born on 1st, 10th and 19th of this month and has to undergo diffi-culties in public and private life. He should select his wife carefully. He has to provide carefully for the future as he is likely to lose through trust in others. He is also likely to make many changes in his career. He hardly reveals his emotions and therefore appears cold. He has an unyielding will power and does not hesitate to carry out his plans.

b) FINANCE

This person is lucky as far as financial status is concerned. Even though he is extravagant due to his over-enthusiastic personality, he also earns enough to satisfy his ostentatious disposition in life. He may not amass wealth but his personality and behaviour will convey to others the impression that he is a rich person. He has a temptation for gambling and if not contro-lled in time, he may lose to a great extent.

He is inclined to taks risks and at times loses heavily in speculation. If he loses, he is never downhearted and never blames others for his losses; he just falls back on his work or profession and builds up his bank balance again.

c) VOCATION

There are usually changes in his career. He is however suitable for advertising concerns, newspapers, theatrical performances and interior decoration. He can be equally successful as a surgeon or the head of a department or as a managing director. His love of position and command makes him occupy high posts such as those of ministers, ambassadors, judges and secretaries.

d) HEALTH

On the whole this person enjoys good health but he is also susceptible to chest and lung disorders, throat afflictions and sudden fevers. He should also take care of his eye and adhere to diet which will not affect his heart.

e) MARRIAGE AND FRIENDS

He has a natural attraction towards persons born in the period from 20th March to 20th Apirl, 20th July to August, and 20th November to 20 December. He has affinity also for those who are governed by numbers 1, 2, 4, 5 and 7. It is therefore advisable that he should select his wife from one of these periods or numbers.

A Number 1 husband

His ambitions make him expect too many things from his wife. He desires to have a wife of whom he can be proud. She should have an attractive personality, charming manners and intelligence. He has a kind and loving disposition and a noble heart. He is generous and desires his wife to shine in society.

A Number 1 wife

She is the best companion to her husband. She is not an intruder but takes an active interest in the business of her husband. She is efficient in house-keeping and has a sympathetic and balanced attitude towards her children. Her passions are healthy and joyous and her approach to physical love is highly refined and inspiring.

Friends

This man s best friends are those who are governed by numbers 1,3,4,5,7 and 9. He has a natural affinity also towards people born in March, June, September and in his own month i.e. December. He likes those who have ambition, dignity, honour and prestige.

f) FORTUNATE DAYS AND NUMBERS : His lucky days are Sundays, Mondays and Thursdays and lucky numbers are 1, 4 and 7. He should therefore take all important steps on one of these days and also dates if possible. He should try his luck in lottery by purchasing a ticket where the total of all the digits is 1, 4 and 7 or where the final digit is 1, 4 or 7.

g) LUCKY COLOURS : He should use all shades of gold, and yellow, also orange and purple as his lucky colours.

h) LUCKY JEWELS AND STONES : His lucky jewels are Topaz, Ruby and Emerald and lucky stones are Moon-Stone and Pale Green Stone.

i) IMPORTANT YEARS IN LIFE :   His important years are 1,
                                10, 19, 28, 37, 46, 55, 64,
                                73 etc.

j) HIS GOOD QUALITIES AND DRAWBACKS ARE AS UNDER:

Good qualities	Drawbacks
Strong will power	Obstinacy
Aspiration	Aloofness
Dynamism	Domination
Authority	Impertinence
Confidence	Inflexibility
Determination	Pride
Aptitude for Research	Love of show
Vigour	Extravagance
Talents	

CHAPTER 101

BORN ON
2nd, 11th, 20th and 29th of December

All those born on 2nd, 11th, 20th and 29th of December of any year are governed by the number 2 and the Moon. December is governed by the planet Jupiter. The character-reading relating to number 2 given below is equally applicable to the other dates. In addition, the special characteristics of those born on 11th, 20th and 29th of December are given separately.

Born on 2nd December

a) CHARACTER

He lives more on the spiritual plane of thought than the material. He is endowed with mental gifts of a very high order. He leans to the study of philosophy, religion, mysticism and occultism. He has vivid dreams and visions together with a gift of prophecy or at least an intuitive sense of how things are likely to turn out. As a rule he is too sensitive to make use of his talents unless he meets people who are sympathetic to his point of view. He is a born teacher. He is a great lover of nature and loves to travel and see the wonders of different countries. He is refined in taste and a faddist in regard to food. He cares very little whether he is rich or poor and is contented with his own lot.

He is somewhat nervous but is social, and is liked by others. He is warm-hearted and shows little resistance to oppression. He has noble sentiments. He likes peace and harmony and has a hypnotic power.

Born on 11th December

you have all the basic characteristics of those born on the 2nd of the month, so first go through them and then read your own.

He is usually successful in life and in love and gets honour, position and authority. He is honest with his friends and is of a royal disposition. He should guard himself from secret enemies. He has interest in mysticism, philosophy and science. He can expect travels, favours and honours in life. He is very impulsive and gets excited easily. He worries too much over small matters. He has an ability to take quick decisions and this endows him with the capacity for leadership. He is a born advisor and an inspiration to others.

Born on 20th December

you have all the basic characteristics of those born on the 2nd of the month, so first go through them and then read your own.

He has many friends and benefits through women. He has a flair for writing and can be known as an author or a novelist. His prosperity lies near the water, the river or the sea. This number has a peculiar significance. It shows new plans and new resolutions for the betterment of people at large.

Born on 29th December

you have all the basic characteristics of those born on the 2nd of the month, so first go through them and then read your own.

This person is moody and changing and therefore uncertain about his action. He is courageous and takes risks in life but does not stick to anything to the end. He is intelligent and also a deep thinker but there is a tendency to carry everything to extremes. He is not very lucky in his married life. His interest is in his business. He is blessed with good fortune. His life is eventful.

b) FINANCE

He is more or less indifferent to money. He can however occupy high positions. He may force himself to work for money for some purpose, but he rarely does it for his personal advantage. He can improve his financial position provided he is able to create art out of his imagination. He can be a good author or a painter who can create novels and weird paintings, and earn a good livelihood. However, his unstable mind often drags him away from routine work and this makes his income uncertain. This person therefore is not stable in finance.

b) VOCATION

The high imaginative power possessed by this person will help him to be a good composer of music or a writer of stories or romance. He can also be a good artist and can create works of enduring value. Immortal paintings, great dramas and poems come from a prominent and influential number 2. He has a large vocabulary and linguistic capacities among all the numbers and can be successful as a teacher or a professor of languages. He can also be a good translator or an editor.

d) HEALTH

He is not a healthy person in the true sense. Although his figure is large, he is seldom robust and strong. The food he eats does not appear to give him the nourishment he requires and unless he lives in a dry climate, he is susceptible to lung trouble and delicacy of the bronchial tubes, and trouble with the throat and rheumatism in the joints. His worrying nature also creates sleeplessness and faulty blood circulation.

e) MARRIAGE AND FRIENDS

He has a natural attraction towards persons born in the period from 20th October to 20th December and 20th February to 20th April. He has affinity also for those who are governed by numbers 2 and 6. It is therefore advisable that he should select his wife from one of these periods or numbers.

A Number 2 husband

As a general rule he attains puberty at an early age and marries early. However, his ambition also makes him expect too many things from his wife and so he is disappointed. He desires her to have an attractive personality, commanding presence, charming manners and intelligence. He is most loving, thoughtful and considerate. His passions are adventurous and demand immediate satisfaction.

A Number 2 wife

She is sympathetic, affectionate and devoted. She is satistisfied with anything her husband provides her with. Her passions are healthy and joyous and her approach to physical love is highly refined and inspiring. She is effective in house-keeping. However, she is moody, changeable and sensitive.

Friends

His best friends are governed by numbers 2, 4, 6 and 9. He also has a natural affinity towards people born in March, June and September and in his own month i. e. December. He likes those who have a good imagination and religious bent.

f) FORTUNATE DAYS
   AND NUMBERS : His lucky days are Mondays, Tuesdays and Fridays and his lucky numbers are 2, 6 and 9. He should therefore take all important steps on one of these days and also dates if possible. He should try his luck in lottery by purchasing a ticket where the total of all the digits is 2, 6 or 9, or where the last digit is 2, 6 or 9.

g) LUCKY COLOURS : He should use white and all shades of yellow and purple.

h) LUCKY JEWELS AND STONES : His lucky jewels are Topaz, Pearl sand Diamond and lucky stones are Moonstone and Agate.

34

i) IMPORTANT YEARS IN LIFE : His important years are 2, 11, 20, 29, 38, 47, 56, 65, 74 etc.

j) HIS GOOD QUALITIES & DRAWBACKS ARE AS UNDER:

Good qualities	Drawbacks
Emotionality	Coldness
Fellowship	Envy
Honesty	Haste
Imagination	Introvert
Simplicity	Shyness
	Whimsicality

CHAPTER 102

BORN ON
3rd, 12th, 21st and 30th of December

All those born on the 3rd, 12th, 21st and 30th of December of any year are governed by the planet Jupiter and number 3. December also is governed by Jupiter. The character reading relating to number 3 given below is equally applicable to the other dates. In addition, the special characteristics of those born on 12th, 21st and 30th December are given separately.

Born on 3rd December

a) CHARACTER

This number is governed by Jupiter. It stands for morality, pure love and justice with mercy and is known as the greatest benefactor and uplifter. This man's good nature is marred by excess in many directions. He is usually lucky in life. Vibrations radiating through him attract all that is good to him and his affairs prosper. The judge who gives sane decisions and merciful sentences, the physician and the church dignitary, the world's teachers and philosopers are all mostly governed by the number 3.

This is a good number- The person is confident of his ability. He is self—reliant and takes his own decisions. He has the habit of talking loudly. He is, fond of show and likes to observe form, order and law. He is jovial in spirit and cordial in manner. His passions are healthy, spontaneous and without inhibitions. He is free in his expression. He is a good conversationalist.

He takes an active interest in sports and outdoor activities from his earliest youth. He has tremendous enthusiasm and is not self-centred. His intellect is of a very high order. He has a kind of vision that understands the world and loves it for what it is and not for what it ought to be. He is a broad minded person, tolerant, humorous and truthful. He is open-hearted with good undrstanding and entirely lacking in malice or petty jealousies. If he is not alert, people take unfair advantage of his good nature.

The main characteristics of this person are ambition, leadership, religion, pride, honour, love of nature, enthusiasm, generosity, respect and reverence.

Born on 12th December you have all the basic characteristics of those born on the 3rd of the month, so first go through them and then read your own.

Authority and honours are the significant aspects of this person. He has vanity and is proud, ambitious and aspiring. He is fond of pleasure and is attracted to the opposite sex. However, sometimes he prefers loneliness. He likes to make sacrifices for others but becomes a victim of other people's plans or intrigues. His relations with others are smooth and harmonious. He is quick to notice trifles. He has lofty ideals.

Born on 21st December you have all the basic characteristics of those born on the 3rd of the month, so first go through them and then read your own.

He is kind, generous and a loving father. He achieves fame, reputation and honours at a very late age. He is cheerful and fond of travel. He has a strong sense of self-respect. Surprisingly, he has a suspicious nature.

Born on 30th December you have all the basic characteristics of those born on the 3rd of the month, so first go through them and then read your own.

He is fortunate, generous and optimistic. He has a noble and relig'ous mind. He likes to travel and visit places of pilgrimage. He can be successful as a teacher or an educationist or in administration. He appears gentle and sincere, but has a hidden nature. He may be active but is restless. When faced with difficulties, he is strong enough to overcome them.

b) FINANCE

He is a lucky type and somehow manages to earn enough for his livelihood. He also gets opportunities for higher positions and earns quite a lot. His ambition, leadership and enthusiasm push him forward and usually he gets all comforts. He is early out of puberty and poverty.

c) VOCATION

His love of position and command makes him occupy high posts such as those of ministers, ambassadors, judges and secretaries. He is gifted for public life, statesmanship, high offices etc, may be in the army or in the church. He is a good teacher and preacher. Professions such as those of doctors, bankers, advertisers, actors, contractors, builders and designers of railways, transport and shipping or as heads of industrial concerns are also suitable for him. He believes in the power of the pen and often establishes newspapers and high class periodicals or issues some form of printed publications to advocate his views.

d) HEALTH

This person's number has chief influence on the blood and the arterial system. It also governs the sense of smell. This person is liable to suffer from chest and lung disorders, throat afflictions, gout and apoplexy and sudden fevers. He may also suffer from sore throat, diphtheria, adenoids, pneumonia, pleurisy and tuberculosis of the lungs.

e) MARRIAGE AND FRIENDS

He has a natural attraction towards persons born in the period from 20th June to 20th July and 20th October to 20th November. He also has affinity for those who are governed by numbers 3, 6 and 9. It is therefore advisable that he should select his wife from one of these periods or numbers.

A Number 3 husband

As a general rule, he attains puberty at an early age and marries early. However, his ambitions also make him expect too many things from his wife and so he becomes disappointed. He desires to have a wife of whom he can be proud. She should have an attractive personality, a commanding presence, charming manners and intelligence. It is always better for him to choose a number 3 person or a number 6 person as his wife. He is most loving, thoughtful and considerate. His passions are adventurous and demand immediate satisfaction.

A Number 3 wife

She is the best companion to her husband. She is not an intruder but takes an active interest in the business of her husband. She is efficient in house-keeping and has a sympathetic and balanced attitude towards children. Her passions are healthy and joyous and her approach to physical love is highly refined and inspiring.

Friends

This man's best friends are those who are governed by numbers 1, 3, 5, 6, 7, 8 and 9. He has a natural affinity also towards people born in March, June and September and in his own month i. e. December.

f) FORTUNATE DAYS
AND NUMBERS : His lucky days are Tuesdays, Thursdays and Fridays and lucky numbers are 3, 6, and 9. He should therefore take all important steps on one of these days and also dates if possible. He should try his luck in lottery by purchasing a ticket where the total of all the digits is 3, 6 or 9 or where the last digit is 3, 6 or 9.

g) LUCKY COLOURS : He should use all shades of yellow, violet, purple and green as his lucky colours.

h) LUCKY JEWELS AND STONES : His lucky jewels are Topaz and Pearl and lucky stones are Amethyst and Cat'sEye.

i) IMPORTANT YEARS IN LIFE: His important years are 3, 12 21, 30, 39, 48, 57, 66, 75 etc.

j) HIS GOOD QUALITIES AND DRAWBACKS ARE AS UNDER:

Good qualities	Drawbacks
Ambition	Cruelty
Dignity	Dictatorship
Individuality	Hypocrisy
Philosophy	Extravagance
Prestige	Vanity

CHAPTER 103

BORN ON
4th, 13th, 22nd and 31st December

All those born on the 4th, 13th, 22nd and 31st of December of any year are governed by the number 4 and the planet Uranus. December is governed by the planet Jupiter. The character reading relating to number 4 given below is equally applicable to the other dates. In addition, the special characteristics of those born on 13th, 22nd and 31st December are given separately.

Born on 4th December

a) CHARACTER

Persons born on the 4th, 13th, 22nd and 31st of December will experience the most unexpected twists and turns of Fate. Uranus, which has a strong subtle influence on them, is called the twin brother of Saturn; like those born under Saturn, they also appear to be very much the Children of Destiny. They are clever, highly intellectual and with remarkable mental gifts along peculiar lines of their own. They are endowed with wonderful imagination and, often, with great inventiveness. They seem to live a life apart from others and are greatly misunderstood by the common herd of humanity. As a rule they are subject to the cruellest forms of calumny and appear helpless to defend themselves. Their minds lean to visions, strange dreams, intuition and premonition, and sooner or later they develop a love of occult studies and read deeply on such subjects. Persons born on the above dates are extremely independent in character and crave liberty of thought and action. They live more or less unconventional lives, and cannot put up with any form of restraint or censure. Perhaps for this reason they are seldom successful in married life and generally have disagreements with their partners.

They are seldom free from risk and dangers and have many accidents from fires, motor cars, runaway horses etc. They should never travel by air. They appear to attract opposition and trouble from religious communities or secret societies and would do well never to become affiliated with such bodies. From a material standpoint, they often make money by their brains or literary work of some unusual kind, also in music and painting, but they can seldom keep money or accumulate it. Although extemely broad minded and generous, they have strong likes and dislikes, which they are seldom able to control.

These persons are governed by Uranus which indicates energy, force and advancement. It shows revolution and un-expected happenings in life. Usually the changes that take place are for the better. This number represents the higher faculties of the mind. The activity and intelligence of these persons are engaged in the reconstruction or the betterment of human life. The peculiar nature of these persons is that they constantly aim at changes in life and society and seek the liberation of the mind from bondage to environment and society. They dislike hypocrisy and love art and music. They have an attrac-tive personality. They are methodical. But they have a bad habit of forcing their opinions on others. They have a keen, analytical and logical mind. Because of their peculiar tendency to oppose the views of others or to start arguments, they are often misunderstood and make a great number of secret enemies who constantly work against them. They feel lonely in life.

Born on 13th December

you have all the basic characteristics of those born on the 4th of the month, so first go through them and then read your own.

He is an intelligent person, of tall stature and good com-plexion. He is considerate and benevolent. He likes litera-ry and scientific books. He likes to be active though in a quiet way. He occupies positions of high responsibilities and gets riches. His success and career start after his 31st year. Though outwardly he looks mild, inwardly he is obstinate. He is faithful and sympathetic but has difficulty in expressing his love. He has all the qualities of number 4 but in an exaggerated form.

Born on 22nd December you have all the basic characteristics of those born on the 4th of the month, so first go through them and then read your own.

He is also tall and has good eyes. Usually he occupies good positions but without much responsibility. He is rather easygoing but unsteady by nature. Sometimes his actions are spasmodic. On the whole he is lucky in his affairs and benefits from the opposite sex. He is happy in his family life but is also fond of a companion. He is faithful and dedicated to others. Sometimes, he feels very lonely. His social field is limited and he has few friends. He does not care for disputes. He has too much economy of sentiments.

Born on 31st December you have all the basic characteristics of those born on the 4th of the month, so first go through them and then read your own.

This date shows ambition, pride and austerity. He is interested in honourable occupations such as working for institutions for the deaf and dumb and the physically handicapped etc. He gets success after his 40th year but he expects quick results and early reputation. He is lucky in financial matters. He is realistic and has a strong will power. He has a strong attraction for the opposite sex. He loves travelling.

b) FINANCE

As regards finance he is usually well settled in life though he experiences delays and difficulties in his ventures. He may not amass wealth but can maintain the show of riches. He is a spendthrift. His home is well decorated. His financial prosperity usually starts after the age of 40.

c) VOCATION

He will be successful in trades such as transport, electrical goods and all sorts of machinery. He will be equally successful as an engineer, a building contractor, a scientist and an industrialist. He is also attracted towards mystic subjects such as palmistry and astrology and can do well in these subjects also.

d) HEALTH

There are two classes of people belonging to this period. One is subject to all kinds of peculiar or mysterious illnesses that come on without the least warning. These men often have sudden cramps in the stomach, chills with rapid rise of temperature and delicacy of the lungs, throat and nasal passage, and also sinus trouble. The other class, although never really robust, get through life without any serious illness except those caused by accidents.

The respiratory system of these persons is usually weak and they suffer from breathlessness. Their knees, shanks and feet are also affected. Sometimes they suffer from urinary infection.

e) MARRIAGE AND FRIENDS

This man has a natural attraction towards persons born in the period from 20th February to 20th April and 20th October to 20th December. He has an affinity also for those who are governed by the numbers 1, 2, 7 and 8. It is therefore advisable that he should select his wife from one of these periods or numbers.

A Number 4 husband

He is shrewd and intelligent and expects his wife to share his views. He is dominating and wants all affairs of the house to run according to his desire. He is generous and has a kind and loving heart.

A Number 4 wife

She is smart and attractive. She has the art of dressing and has a strong will-power. She aims at several things but hardly succeeds in getting mastery over one. She loves interior decoration but does not have the capacity to work hard and she will get it done through others. She is often dictatorial and moody and spoils her day due to her own whimsical nature. She loves her home but is not attached to it very much. She is often uneasy and it is better for her to find a friend governed by number one or two.

Friends

His best friends are those who are governed by numbers 1, 2, 4, 5, 7, 8 and 9. He has a natural affinity also towards people born in March, June and September and in his own month i. e. December. He likes those who have authority, dignity and prestige.

f) FORTUNATE DAYS
AND NUMBERS : His lucky days are Sundays, Mondays and Saturdays and lucky numbers are 1, 4 and 7. He should therefore take all important steps on one of these days and also dates if possible. He should try his luck in lottery by purchasing a ticket where the total of all the digits is 1, 4 or 7, or where the last digit is 1, 4 or 7.

g) LUCKY COLOURS : He should use white, electric blue, electric grey and maroon.

h) LUCKY JEWELS AND STONES : His lucky jewels are Diamond, Coral and Pearl.

i) IMPORTANT YEARS IN LIFE : His important years are 4 13, 22, 31, 40, 49, 58, 67, 76 etc.

j) HIS GOOD QUALITIES AND DRAWBACKS ARE AS UNDER:

Good qualities	Drawbacks
Activity	Changeablity
Endurance	Domination
Energy	Stubbornness
Reliability	Vindictiveness
Method and system	Jealousy

HIS GOOD QUALITIES AND DRAWBACKS ARE AS UNDER

CHAPTER 104

BORN ON
5th, 14th and 23rd of December

All those born on the 5th, 14th and 23rd of December of any year are governed by number 5 and the planet Mercury. December is governed by the planet Jupiter. The character reading relating to number 5 given below is applicable to the other dates also. In addition, the special characteristics of those born on 14th and 23rd December are given separately.

Born on 5th December

a) CHARACTER

He will find the mercury influence strong in his life. He will have unusual mental activity, will be clever and quick-witted, but rather restless mentally and physically. He must always be engaged doing something either with his brain or his hands. He is ambitious in his ideas, extremely independent and inclined to be positive in his views. He is also quick and impulsive in his likes and dislikes. At the same time, he has a splendid foundation of brain power to build on and if he will only hold his restlessness under check he will do well in whatever he takes up. As a general rule he is very fond of sport, especially horse racing or anything to do with animals. He is inclined to speed mania and will risk life and limb in fast motor cars or in aeroplanes, if circumtances permit him their use. He seldom gets through his career without having a bad smash up and runs the risk of being in some way badly crippled. He is very fond of argument or debate; he can be bitterly sarcastic, but once the battle of words is over, he bears no animosity or grudge against his opponent. He has much attraction for the opposite sex. He generally marries well, but the later he marries the better his chance of happiness.

He has shrewdness, quickness, scientific pursuits, business ability, industry, intuition and diplomacy. He is fond of oratory in expressing himself. He has the capacity to puruse his objectives and knows very well how to plan to achieve his ends. He is deeply interested in occult subjects and has a desire to master all the intricacies of such abtruse subjects. He possesses a pleasant character. He dislikes inactivity. He is sociable and has many acquaintances. He is fond of variety and change and trips and travels. However difficult the situation he can get out of it.

He is a nervous person. He is therefore restless. He has an intuitive perception and may turn out to be either good or bad. On the good side, he is a shrewd person and not vicious or criminal. He likes family life and loves children. His pleasures are mainly mental and he evaluates everything in terms of business. He is amiable and adaptable.

Born on 14th December

you have all the basic characteristics of those born on the 5th of the month, so first go through them and then read your own.

This person has an attractive personality and is liked by all. His nature is co-operative and he does not like to provoke others. He usually occupies good positions in life and is successful in business. He is not talkative but is slightly reserved. This is an intelligent and shrewd number. In women, it indicates good marriage, but they should be careful in child bearing. A number 14 man is inconsistent in love and experiences some romantic and impulsive attachment in early years. He is fortunate in money matters. He is industrious and positive in speech and action. Usually he is fond of gambling and of solving riddles.

Born on 23rd December

you have all the basic characteristics of those born on the 5th of the month, so first go through them and then read your own.

He is usually popular with women. He is successful in life and enjoys honour and wealth. He may get money through inheritance. He keeps busy in his own way. He gets help and protection from superiors. He is a lucky person. He is affectionate and loves freedom. He is averse to formalities. He has a spirit of independence and a desire to dominate.

b) FINANCE

Since number 5 is a business number, the person can expect opulence. With his shrewd characteristics, he is capable of developing his industry; he can carry out his plans systematically with the result that he gets good returns for his efforts. He is lucky in his financial position. However, he seldom has much regard for the value of money.

c) VOCATION

He is adaptable to the role he has to play in the drama of life. With his adaptability he comes in contact with various classes of people and is successful in any business. Banking is a good line for him. Mercury also shows an aptitude for medicine or surgery. His capacity to argue his points can make him a good lawyer. If he can settle down he can be equally successful in literary work.

d) HEALTH

He is more or less prone to a nervous twitching in he eyes and faces, and stammering or a lisp in speech. His basic health defect is biliousness and nervousness. However, his biliousness has close relation with psychological disturbances experience shows that his biliousness increases with the increase in tension and is reduced or disappears when his nervous trouble is under control. Number 5 rules over the nerves, neck, arms, ears and the respiratory system.

e) MARRIAGE AND FRIENDS :

He has a natural attraction towards persons born in the period from 20th September to 20th October, and 20th January to 20th February. He has an affinity also for those who are governed by numbers 1, 7 and 8. It is therefore advisable that he should select his wife from one of these periods or numbers.

A Number 5 husband

He is lucky and successful in married life. His selection is good and usually he selects a person of his own type. He loves his wife. He expects neatness and cleanliness from her and also desires that she should share his pleasures. He is proud of his wife and likes to see her well-dressed. In return, he proves to be a good husband. He loves his children and loves his home. Even if he travels long, he is eager to return early to his family. He is liberal in spending on clothes and other needs of the members of his family and furnishes his house with good taste.

A Number 5 wife

She has interest at home as well as outside. She has many activities and manages them well. She likes tidiness. Though she seldom does her own work, she gets it done through her commanding personality.

Friends

This man's best friends are those who are governed by numbers 1, 3, 4, 5, 7 and 8. He has a natural affinity also towards people born in March, June and September and in his own month i.e. December. He likes those who have ambition, intelligence and prestige.

f) FORTUNATE DAYS

AND NUMBERS : His lucky days are Wednesdays, Fridays and Saturdays and his lucky numbers are 1, 3 and 5. He should therefore take all important steps on one of these days and also dates if

possible. He should try his luck in
lottery by purchasing a ticket where
the total of all the digits is 1, 3
or 5, or where the last digit is 1, 3
or 5.

g) LUCKY COLOURS : He should use white and green.

h) LUCKY JEWELS AND STONES : His lucky jewels are
Emerald and Diamond
He may use Sapphire
also.

i) IMPORTANT YEARS IN LIFE : His important years are 5,
14, 23, 32, 41, 50, 59, 68,
77 etc.

j) HIS GOOD QUALITIES AND DRAWBACKS ARE AS UNDER:

Good qualities	Drawbacks
Co-operation	Lack of perseverance
Practical approach	Scepticism
Shrewdness	Unreliability
Vigilance	

CHAPTER 105

BORN ON
6th, 15th and 24th of December

All those born on the 6th, 15th and 24th of December of any year are governed by the number 6 and the planet Venus. December is governed by the planet Jupiter. The character reading relating to number 6 given below is equally applicable to the other dates. In addition, the special characteristics of those born on 15th and 24th December are given separately.

Born on 6th December

a) CHARACTER

Persons born on the 6th, 15th and 24th of December have light-hearted, happy dispositions. They love the splendours of nature, and beauty in all its forms. There is nothing mean about such people. They delight in entertaining their friends, making excellent hosts or hostesses. They love outdoor sports, and animals of all kinds, but especially dogs and horses. They love horse racing and generally go in for breeding of thorough breds, often meeting with great success and making money in such enterprises. They love harmony and nothing distresses them more than contact with those who go through life with a chip on their shoulder. They usually derive an income from two sources, everything seems to run in twos for them and in their favour. A woman born on one of these dates is nearly certain to have two husbands and two children. Persons born on these dates often marry foreigners cr those born far from their own place of birth. All are keenly attracted to the opposite sex. If they are not lovers, they are at least good comrades, and are honourable and loyal in their relationships. They are rather inclined to be snobbish, attracting those in big social position or with influence, like government officials, those with titles and church dignitaries. They are extremely fond of travelling and are likely to make lifelong friends while on thier voyages. Both sexes have big ideas and generally attract the necessary wealth to carry out their plans. They have great respect for intellectual people. They draw to their homes men and women who have made a name in literature, painting, music and such arts. Even if they do not accomplish any intellectual work themselves, they have considerable taste in such matters and fill their homes with works of art and beautiful things.

They are pleasant to meet. Their company is full of enthusiasm, energy and charm. Their talk is interesting and lively. They are fond of music, dancing and poetry. They prefer spending to saving. They are emotional but keep their emotions to themselves. Their anger is hard to subide. They are good conversationalists and enjoy crossing swords intellectually.

Born on 15th December you have all the basic characteristics of those born on the 6th of the month, so first go through them and then read your own.

This person has good intelligence and good memory. He is fit for responsible positions such as those of ambassadors, consuls, governors etc. He is very ambitious and boastful but hasty and proud by nature. He is interested in the lower type of occultism. He has interest also in art and music. He appears to be gentle but has very strong convictions. He has a habit of worrying inwardly and leads a melancholy life. His destiny is such that he has to make sacrifices for others.

Born on 24th December you have all the basic characteristics of those born on the 6th of the month, so first go through them and then read your own.

He is fortunate in getting assistance from people of high rank. He benefits through the opposite sex. He marries a rich girl and prospers. He succeeds in speculation and enjoys good financial positions. He defines strictly the line between personal and social matters. He is methodical in his ideas.

He possesses a strong ego and sometimes tries to force his opinions on others.

b) FINANCE

He is not attracted to money and accumulation of wealth is not his aim in life. All his interest is in attaining pleasures and gratifying his desires. He, therefore, spends his earnings on whatever attracts him. He also never repents having spent money on his art which may not ultimately give him monetary rewards. Whether he tries to make money or not, he is generally fortunate in his early years. He gains by marriage, by legacies and by gifts. Luck does not remain with him throughout his life and it would be better if he makes provision for the future.

c) VOCATION

He will shine as an interior decorator, architect, jeweller, musician, hotel manager or confectioner. He can be equally successful as a broker, an estate broker or as a commission agent.

d) HEALTH

Usually he has good health except when he indulges too much in good living. Towards the end of his life he has a tendency to develop cancer and tumours in the intestines and chest.

e) MARRIAGE AND FRIENDS

He has a natural attraction towards persons born in the period from 20th August to 20th September and 20th December to 20th January. He has an affinity also for those who are governed by numbers 2, 3 ,4, 6 and 9. It is, therefore, advisable that he should select his wife from one of these periods or numbers.

A Number 6 husband

As a general rule he attains puberty at an early age and marries early. However, his ambition also makes him expect too many things from his wife and he is thus disappointed. He desires to have a wife of whom he can be proud. She should have an attractive personality, commanding presence, charming manners and intelligence. He is most loving, thoughtful and considerate. His passions are adventurous and demand immediate satisfaction.

A Number 6 wife

She is the best companion to her husband. She is not an intruder but takes active interest in the business of her husband. She is efficient in house-keeping and has a sympathetic and balanced attitude to her children. Her passions are healthy and joyous and her approach to physical love is highly refined and inspiring.

Friends

His best friends are those who are governed by numbers 2, 3, 4, 6 and 9. He has a natural affinity also towards people born in March, June and September and in his own month i. e. December. He likes those who have ambition, religion, prestige and honour.

f) FORTUNATE DAYS
   AND NUMBERS : His lucky days are Mondays, Tuesdays, Thursdays and Fridays and lucky numbers are 2,4 and 6. He should therefore take all important steps on one of these days and also dates if possible. He should try his luck in lottery by purchasing a ticket where the total of all the digits is 2, 4 or 6, or where the last digit is 2,4 or 6.

g) LUCKY COLOURS : He should use all shades of blue, rose and pink.

h) LUCKY JEWELS & STONES: His lucky jewels are Turquoise, Emerald, Pearl and Diamond.

i) IMPORTANT YEARS IN LIFE :   His important years are 6, 15, 24, 33, 42, 51, 60, 69, 78 etc.

j) HIS GOOD QUALITIES AND DRAWBACKS ARE AS UNDER:

Good Qualities	Drawbacks
Harmony	Absence of foresight
Love	Interference
Peace	Moodiness
Strong memory	Timidity

CHAPTER 106

BORN ON
7th, 16th, and 25th of December

All those born on the 7th, 16th and 25th of December of any year are governed by number 7 and the planet Neptune. December is governed by the planet Jupiter. The character reading relating to number 7 given below is equally applicable to the other dates. In addition, the special characteristics of those born on 16th and 25th November are given separately.

Born on 7th December

a) CHARACTER

Neptune has influence over the mind more than on the body. It affects people with strange dreams, visions, inspirations and experiences of a psychic nature. It acts on the subconscious mind in its awakened state. The dreamers under Neptune are forced into action almost in spite of themselves.

They hear the call to make the world realize the power of the mind over matter. It would be all right if they would stop at this point, but there is a class of individuals born under the above combination who so allow their ambition for power to override all other considerations, that sooner or later they bring about their own undoing. The other class, those who allow the psychic and spiritual to dominate the material, have splendid inspirations and leave a name behind them for their worth and mental ability. A person born on this date is stubborn and ignores the opinions of others. He has good talent for earning money. In general, he is somewhat indifferent and cares little for materialistic pursuits. He desires the best or none at all.   He **is** sensitive and hides his real feelings by apparent indifference.   He dislikes mingling with common people.   He prefers to spend his hour with his favourite book. When his opinion is solicited, he speaks with authority.   He knows his ground.

Born on 16th December
> you have all the basic characteristics of those born on the 7th of the month, so first go through them and then read your own.

He is rather easy-going and does not like to work hard. He is good-humoured and generous.   He is very sensitive and emotional.   He soon gets upset and is soon pleased.   He is frequently indisposed.   He is fortunate in getting good and successful children.   However,   there is some sort of sorrow in his married life.   He appears to be calm but his mind is always in turmoil and he is sometimes short-tempered.   He will not disclose his nervousness and is slow in taking decisions. He does not like interference.

Born on 25th December
> you have all the basic characteristics of those born on the 7th of the month, so first go through them and then read your own.

He is a jack of all trades but master of none.   He is interested in several subjects but does not have the ability to go into details.   His knowledge therefore is very shallow.   He likes to travel and has contact with foreign countries.   He is honest, faithful and good-natured.   But he is fickle-minded and inconsistent.   His memory is good and he is good as an orator and as a teacher.

b) FINANCE

As a general rule, financial matters are peculiar for a person born on one of the above dates.   If he makes money, it is seldom from any usual commercial activity.   He is likely to lose heavily in his investments in advanced years.   He becomes a victim of unscrupulous company.   The person can be well placed in life provided he finds a job of his choice.   In that case he can be a wealthy person with all amenities and comforts.

c) VOCATION

His love of sea travel and interest in foreign countries make him a successful merchant, exporter or importer. He can also deal in dairy products, fishery, and products such as soap etc, or choose a chemical industry. He can also study medicine and surgery.

d) HEALTH

He is too highly strung to feel really well. He exhausts himself too much and rarely gets good sleep and rest. His digestion is therefore not very good and his meals are irregular. His main trouble is his nervous constitution and all his illness will be due his nervousness. He is liable to suffer from faulty blood circulation, stomach disorder and fever.

e) MARRIAGE AND FRIENDS

He has a natural attraction towards persons born in the period from 20th February to 20th March and 20th October to 20th November. He has affinity also for those who are governed by numbers, 3, 5 and 8. It is, therefore, advisable that he should select his wife from one of these periods or numbers.

A Number 7 husband

He is very emotional and understands the feelings of his wife. He is very considerate and will never try to impose his ideas on his wife. He is liberal and fond of picnics, travel and cinema theatres. He is a spendthrift and likes to live lavishly. His family is moderate in size and has all comforts.

A Number 7 wife

She is very moody and her behaviour is unpredictable. She is very uneasy and gets disturbed over small matters. She is good at entertaining friends and likes to invite people to a party or dinner. She expects her husband to look after her all the time.

Friends

This man's best friends are those who are governed by numbers 1, 3,4, 5, 7, 8 and 9. He has a natural affinity also towards people born in March, June and September and in his own month i. e. December.

e) FORTUNATE DAYS
AND NUMBERS : His lucky days are Sundays, Mondays, Wednesdays and Thursdays. His lucky numbers are 2, 4 and 7. He should therefore take all important steps on one of these days and also dates if possible. He should try his luck in lottery by purchasing a ticket where the total of all the digits is 2, 4 or 7 or where the last digit is 2, 4 or 7.

g) LUCKY COLOURS : He should use all shades of green and yellow.

h) LUCKY JEWELS AND STONES : His lucky jewels are Topaz and Emerald and lucky stones are Moon Stone and Cat's Eye.

i) IMPORTANT YEARS IN LIFE : His important years are 7, 16, 25, 34. 43. 52. 61, 70, 79 etc.

j) HIS GOOD QUALITIES AND DRAWBACKS ARE AS UNDER:

Good qualities	Drawbacks
Austerity	Despondency
Reflection	Diffidence
Serenity	Restlessness
Tolerance	Whimsicality

CHAPTER 107

BORN ON
8th, 17th and 26th of December

All those born on the 8th, 17th and 26th of December of any year are governed by the number 8 and the planet Saturn. December is governed by the planet Jupiter. The character reading relating to number 8 given below is equally applicable to the other dates. In addition, the special characteristics of those born on 17th and 26th December are given separately.

Born on 8th December

a) CHARACTER

The combination of Saturn and Jupiter gives great strength and force of determination. Usually the man has a hard life and great obstacles at the commencement of his career. He is endowed with enormous endurance. Nothing comes to him easily but with his patient, plodding, persevering disposition, he slowly and steadily builds up a solid position for himself. He is extremely conscientious in whatever he does but if he can develop more dash and self-confidence he will do better for himself from the material stand-point. He is reserved and secretive and too easily hurt or wounded by criticism. When he is aroused by injustice, he is fearless in denoucing it and makes many bitter enemies by his unequivocal attitude. He rises to very high positions and receives honours but he is likely to lose his position by some carelessness.

He shows an extreme sense of discipline, steadfastness, constancy and dutifulness. The person has a sober and solitary personality. He is a lover of classical music but mostly of a melancholy type. In art he loves landscapes, natural scenery and flowers. Number 8 is considered to be a balance wheel to the character. He has the ability to look at the other side of the coin. He is a pessimist. He prefers solitude to company. He is a prudent person, wise and sober among all the numbers. He is never overenthusiastic and is more or less gloomy and melancholy. He is also ambitious and persevering. He is capable of enormous efforts towards the attainment of his objects. He is sceptical and analytical. He is creative, productive and dominating. He understands the weak and the oppressed and treats them in a warm-hearted manner. He is a born manager who can keep others busy. He admires fair play and is willing to pay a fair compensation. He has a good memory for names and faces.

Born on 17th December

you have all the basic characteristics of those born on the 8th of the month, so first go through them and then read your own.

He is a good organizer and a good thinker. He has a creative and constructive mind. He is a lover of peace and a philanthropist. He is attracted towards occultism and mysticism. He is courageous and proud. He has strong individuality. He is highly intelligent and clever. As regards emotions, he is calm. At times he is generous to a fault and at times very stingy. He is interested in research and loves knowledge. He is conservative and dominating.

Born on 26th December

you have all the basic characteristics of those born on the 8th of the month, so first go through them and then read your own.

He wants to enjoy life without doing anything. He is sluggish and lethargic. He revels in wine and women and is fickle-minded, He is careless about the number of children. He is lucky in money matters and gets easy money. He is smart but lacks positiveness. He likes to put up a good appearance but has a worrying nature. He has problems in his love affairs.

b) FINANCE

The peculiarity of number 8 is delay in life in all respects.

Naturally in financial matters also there is delay and stability is achieved at a very late age. This person has to work hard and he seldom becomes opulent. He has, therefore, to avoid number 8 playing a part in his life; instead he can choose number 1 or 3 for all important actions and moves. However, if his experience shows that 8 is a lucky number for him, he can insist on that number only, in which case wealth and prosperity come to him. If 8 is found to be a lucky number in one's life, one can try lottery and luck in horse-racing. But usually this number is connected with delays and hard work, and a person has to be very cautious about his financial matters. He usually has a drain on his resources by less successful relatives or by family ties. He accumulates money slowly but steadily. In spite of his caution he often loses heavily before he comes to the end of his life.

c) VOCATION

Subjects suitable for him are occult sciences, chemistry, physics, medicine and also higher mathematfics. He can be successful in industries connected with coal mines, timber, etc. and in construction companies. He can be a good accountant and also a good administrator. However, as stated earlier, he has to strive hard in his career and can get the fruits of his hard work only in the later years of his life.

d) HEALTH

His main health problems are nervousness, irritation, trouble with legs, teeth and ears, paralysis and rheumatism. He is a bilious type and often suffers from chronic melancholia. It is very interesting to note that the delaying characteristic in life applies to sickness also. The ailments he suffers from also take a long time to cure. Varicose veins and haemorrhoids are a common complaint of a strong 8 personality.

e) MARRIAGE AND FRIENDS

He has a natural attraction towards persons born in

the period from 20th April to 20th May and 20th August to 20th September. He has an affinity also for those who are governed by numbers 5 and 7. It is therefore advisable that he should select his wife from one of these periods or numbers.

A number 8 husband

As a general rule he attains puberty at an early age and marries early. However, his ambition makes him expect too many things from his wife and therefore, he is disappointed. He desires to have a wife of whom he can be proud. She should have an attractive personality, a commanding presence, charming manners and intelligence. He is most loving, thoughtful and considerate. His passions are adventurous and demand immediate satisfaction.

A Number 8 wife

She is a very good companion to her husband. She is not an intruder but takes an active interest in the business of her husband. She is efficient in house-keeping and has a sympathetic and balanced attitude towards her children. Her passions are healthy and her approach to physical love is highly refined and inspiring.

Friends

His best friends are those who are governed by numbers 3, 4, 5, 7 and 8. He has a natural affinity also towards people born in March, June, September and in his own month i. e. December.

f) FORTUNATE DAYS

AND NUMBERS : His lucky days are Wednesdays, Thursdays and Saturdays and lucky numbers are 3, 4 and 8. He should therefore take all important steps on one of these days and also dates if possible. He should try his luck in lottery by purchasing a ticket

where the total of all the digits is 3,
4 or 8 or where the last digit is 3, 4
or 8.

g) LUCKY COLOURS :   He should use dark grey, dark blue,
purple and black.

h) LUCKY JEWELS AND STONES :   His lucky jewels are
sapphire, black pearl
and black diamond. His
lucky stones are cat's
eye and amethyst.

i) HIS GOOD QUALITIES AND DRAWBACKS ARE AS UNDER:

Good qualities	Drawbacks
Authority	Cynicism
	Delay
Practical approach	Vindictiveness
Steadiness	Nervousness
Systematic	Laziness.

CHAPTER 108

BORN ON
9th, 18th and 27th of December

All those born on the 9th, 18th and 27th of December of any year are governed by the number 9 and the planet Mars. December is governed by the planet Jupiter. The character readn g relating to number 9 given below is equally applicable to the other dates. In addition, the special characteristics of those born on 18th and 27th of December are given separately.

Born on 9th December

a) CHARACTER

He is very positive in his views and rather dictatorial. He is especially good in a sudden call or emergency. He is endowed with moral and physical courage, seldom knowing what the word "fear" means. He loves a strenuous outdoor life if he can take the time off from his efforts, and has great command over horses and animals in general. He is greatly attracted to the opposite sex. As a rule he is lucky in marriage, but more than one union may be expected. He has an unusual love of adventure of all kinds and makes an excellent explorer and pioneer. He is restless and has a keen desire to travel, especially in far off or unknown parts of the world. He is ready to take any risk at any moment and often faces great dangers in carrying out his purpose. He is in a sense indifferent to money, very generous to those in trouble, giving large sums to institutions or charities, if he has the money; if not, he gives

his time or the work of his brain. He is endowed with considerable mechanical ability and ingenuity, especially in dealing
with machines made for speed.

He has aggression, resistance, courage, dash and quickness. A Martian is considered as a fighter. He is always aggressive and does not stop till he achieves his end. He has the
capacity to fight even against all adverse elements and
circumstances. A Martian does not know defeat; if we have an
army of Martians, there would not be anything like defeat
for them. It would be either victory or death. This man is
not very tactful or diplomatic in his talk but his intention
is good and his vigorous manne should not be mistaken for
rude behaviour. He should not criticise people and should
use his words carefully, otherwise they will boomerang.

He is fiery and dashing and does not have sickly sentiments. He has audacity and vigour from start to finish. He is
also fond of games and vigorous exercise. He has strong sexual
passions and he is attracted towards the opposite sex. He is
prepared to go through any ordeal to gratify his desire.

He is a brave person to whom conflict does not bring the
thought of danger. He is exceedingly devoted to his friends and
will fight for them. He has sympathy and consideration for the
weak. He loves children and animals. He takes delight in
showing mercy to others. He likes the healing profession. He is
backed by self-control, moral courage and the power of forgiveness. His psychological aptitude is remarkable and under all
circumstances he proves his strength of will and exhibits
courage. He is short-tempered.

Born on 18th December you have all the basic characteristics of those born on the 9th of the month, so first go through them and then read your own.

This person has tenacity and will-power which will overcome any difficulty. He is not as dashing as a number 9
person but he is fearless and courageous. His good health makes
him passionate. He inherits property from his father. He has a
disciplined mind and likes to help others. He is painstaking
with good judgement and is wise. He loves to exercise total

control over others. He does not like to be cautioned by others.

Born on 27th December

you have all the basic characteristics of those born on the 9th of the month, so first go through them and then read your own.

On the whole his is a conflicting personality. He is confident and likes to do something for those whose life is miserable or who are handicapped. He can develop a spiritual personality and can practise spiritual healing. On the other side he is fond of women and may develop illicit contacts and create scandals. Sometimes he creates unhappiness in his married life. He is very sensitive and moody and his actions and moves are unpredictable. He is self-assured and strong in resolution. He is a seeker of independence and domination. He hates to work under others. Usually, he is dogmatic.

b) FINANCE

He is generally lucky in money matters, gaining by unexpected legacies, marriage or speculation. In some cases he succeeds by his daring in enterprises, or in the creation of some business from which he makes a quick profit and sells out quickly. As a rule he does better in some individual work than in commercial pursuits. He is also very liberal while spending, especially for his sweetheart. He enjoys all the comforts that money can bring.

c) VOCATION

He is found in all walks of life but he will be more suitable for the army and professions where there is full scope for his aggression and courage. In the army he will rise to high positions, in politics he will be eminent and in business he will exhibit his dashing and pushing nature. He can be a good doctor, or a chemist or a businessman dealing in iron and steel.

d) HEALTH

His main health defect arises from heat. He is susceptible to troubles such as piles, fevers, small pox etc. He is also likely to suffer from trouble of the kidney or bladder stone. Throat trouble, bronchitis and laryngitis also commonly afflict him. He is also likely to meet with serious accidents in life, generally caused by fires, explosions or accidents of motor cars and aeroplanes or from animals.

e) MARRIAGE AND FRIENDS

He has a natural attraction towards persons born in the period from 20th July to 20th August and 20th November to 20th December. He has affinity also for those who are governed by numbers 3 and 6. It is therefore advisable that he selects his wife from one of these numbers or periods.

A Number 9 husband

He has robust health and has strong circulation of blood which makes him very passionate and enthusiastic about married life. He loves a beautiful wife and likes her to be submissive and passive to his sexual desires. He is fond of his family and children and likes to have a good house. He usually leads a good married life in spite of his hot temper and eccentricities. He has a romantic mental picture of what he wants in his wife. This mental picture demands perfection. The most difficult thing in the married life of this person is to satisfy his romantic conception of physical love. He has a voracious appetite and his wife with her devotion can harmonise with him physically. Usually, we find him suspicious of his wife.

A Number 9 wife

She will make a wonderful wife for an ambitious man. She is witty and a clever conversationalist, with a wonderful social presence. She will assist her husband in his business. She may also start her own activity and add to the family income. She will be happy if married to a passionate and possessive man.

Friends

This man's best friends are those who are governed by numbers 1,2,3,4,6,7 and 9. He has a natural affinity also towards people born in March, June and September, and in his own month i. e. December. He likes those who have ambition, dignity, prestige and honour.

f) FORTUNATE DAYS
   AND NUMBERS : His lucky days are Mondays, Tuesdays, Thursdays and Fridays and his lucky numbers are 3,6 and 9. He should therefore take all important steps on one of these days and also dates if possible. He should try his luck in lottery by purchasing a ticket where the total of all the digits is 3, 6 or 9 or where the last digit is 3, 6 or 9.

g) LUCKY COLOURS : He should use white and all shades of red and yellow .

h) LUCKY JEWELS AND STONES : His lucky jewels are Topaz, Pearl and Ruby and lucky stones are Blood-Stone and Garnet.

i) IMPORTANT YEARS IN LIFE : His important years are 9, 18, 27, 36, 45, 54, 63, 72 etc.

j) HIS GOOD QUALITIES AND DRAWBACKS ARE AS UNDER:

Good qualities	Drawbacks
Activity	Destructiveness
Courage	Erratic nature
Dash	Hot temper
Energy	Impatience
Enthusiasm	Quarrelsome

Books on Astrology and Palmistry

568